AMERICAN RELIGIOUS LIBERALISM

RELIGION IN NORTH AMERICA

Catherine L. Albanese and Stephen J. Stein, editors

AMERICAN RELIGIOUS LIBERALISM

EDITED BY
LEIGH E. SCHMIDT AND SALLY M. PROMEY

INDIANA UNIVERSITY PRESS
Bloomington & Indianapolis

This book is a publication of

Indiana University Press
601 North Morton Street
Bloomington, Indiana 47404-3797 USA

iupress.indiana.edu

Telephone orders 800-842-6796
Fax orders 812-855-7931

∞ The paper used in this publication meets the minimum requirements of the American National Standard for Information Sciences—Permanence of Paper for Printed Library Materials, ANSI Z39.48-1992.

Manufactured in the United States of America

Library of Congress Cataloging-in-Publication Data

American religious liberalism / edited by Leigh E. Schmidt and Sally M. Promey.
p. cm. — (Religion in North America)
Includes bibliographical references and index.
ISBN 978-0-253-00216-7 (cl : alk. paper) — ISBN 978-0-253-00209-9 (pb : alk. paper) — ISBN 978-0-253-00218-1 (ebook)
1. United States—Religion. 2. Liberalism (Religion)—United States. I. Schmidt, Leigh Eric [date]. II. Promey, Sally M., [date]
BL2525.A5443 2012
200.973—dc23
2011050761

1 2 3 4 5 17 16 15 14 13 12

CONTENTS

FOREWORD

In this new book on American religious liberalism, Leigh Schmidt, Sally Promey, and their coauthors have set themselves a daunting task. To define, dictionaries tell us, is to delimit—to draw a line around what is being defined so that we know clearly what it is and what it is not. Definitions are boundary guards to keep out objects that are not under scrutiny and to mark unmistakably the objects that are. Given this police work, what do scholars do when they need to define an important phenomenon that they and others know is real but that evades easy—and even rigorous—attempts to mark it? How do they find the precision on which definitions depend when their "object" spreads amoeba-like outside its holders and blends into a middle ground that is complex and thick with related and unrelated forms?

To say this another way, religious liberalism, in its American context (and probably elsewhere, too) is *messy*. Scholars who seek meticulous nomenclature and characterization will, perforce, go home defeated in their encounter with liberalism. To complicate matters further, editors and authors are grappling here not simply with definition in a steady-state world but instead with the fluid and developmental character of a historically contingent category. Add to this the fact that the story of religious history in America is no longer narrowly confined to what might be called classic or traditional theological, spiritual, and devotional categories.

What is therefore so impressive in this new book is the progress Schmidt, Promey, and their coauthors have made in surveying and untangling strands of the liberal phenomenon in religion as it has appeared from the late nineteenth century on. The essays in this volume document the expanding breadth of the American religious narrative and the exploding variety of issues that fall within its purview. They offer rich and nuanced descriptions of the many cases they document, and Schmidt and Promey's categorizations are both descriptive and persuasive. Furthermore, whereas fifty years ago American religious history was being written primarily by scholars in Protestant seminaries and twenty years ago with the noticeable addition of those in religious studies departments, the assortment of professional locations of the contributors to this volume is striking. In our judgment, their varied and multidisciplinary backgrounds are strongly positive measures of the expansion of the subject area and of the expertise of those engaged with it.

As Leigh Schmidt explains in his reflective introduction, the volume is divided into three large sections. Their titles and contents help to pin down the elusive liberal category. Part 1, "The Spiritual in Art," juxtaposes essays drawing on Walt Whitman and his poetry as foci for religious seekers, Harriet Beecher Stowe and a nice (and banal) Jesus, and liberal visual culture ranging from Horace Bushnell to Paul Tillich. Further contributions look to Juliet Thompson's artistry and her pilgrimage into the Bahá'í religion, and to the paintings of Agnes Pelton, with their American Indian and Theosophical themes. What is especially noteworthy in this section are the ways that American religious liberalism seems to merge with forms of metaphysical religiosity, a phenomenon of which Leigh Schmidt is well aware and with which he deals fruitfully as he argues for the integrity of the liberal category.

Part 2, entitled "The Piety and Politics of Liberal Ecumenism," leaves aesthetic concerns to explore the action orientation of liberalism and liberals in sacred and secular venues. Here the succession of essays moves from an account of the religious and, especially, the ritual position of the liberal Bell Street Chapel in Providence, Rhode Island, to a study of American suffragist Clara Colby, who combined New Thought ideas and the metaphysicalizing views of Bengali poet Rabindranath Tagore in her feminist synthesis. Here, too, we find discussions of the racial and religious views held by writers involved in the Harlem Renaissance, especially George Schuyler and Langston Hughes, and the impact of liberal book culture in the middle twentieth century evident in Rabbi Joshua Loth Liebman's bestseller *Peace of Mind* (1946). Part 2 also includes an essay that focuses on the strange obsession of Charles Fort, whose search for the unexplained led him to pore endlessly over newspapers and other printed material to unearth oddities that nudge the reader strongly toward metaphysical explanations. At the other end of the liberal spectrum, this section includes an essay that analyzes the methods and views of the early twentieth-century Semitic philologist and scholar of religion Morris Jastrow, and another that compares Reform Judaism's liberalism and that of its Christian counterparts. Although the metaphysical overlap does not go away (witness Charles Fort and Clara Colby), a new form of overlap becomes the agenda in this section. Ecumenism clearly spills outside of Christian containers into other forms of religion as well as into a murky in-between place best described as "spirituality." All of these developments are not simply proliferating forms of piety, but instances of human action to persuade, convince, and subtly strong-arm others.

Part 3 explores still another dynamic range of issues under the titular banner "Pragmatism, Secularism, and Internationalism." Introducing this section comes an essay featuring the "pragmatic approach to religion" articulated in William James's *Varieties of Religious Experience,* followed by another that, with strikingly different concerns, follows the pragmatic thread through John Dewey. Still another essay focuses on the post–World War II period and the Roman Catholic liberals who engaged the discourse concerning secularism. A final essay stakes out a liberal position on the geopolitics of religion and raises serious critical questions about the category of liberalism itself. Together these essays address the ideational substructure of liberalism—the emphasis on discourse and action in a plural and multivalent set of communities and cultures. Liberal religion becomes one major response of those who notice contrast, difference, and change. It becomes an important way to negotiate a complex world in which religion, for many, can no longer be safely enclosed in discrete and separate traditions.

David Hollinger's "Religious Liberalism and Ecumenical Self-Interrogation" closes out the volume, using one major historical category with which religious liberalism began—ecumenism—and tracking it through the series of twists and turns that the volume represents. Old-fashioned Protestant ecumenists may have provided nomenclature, but their projects and performances are no longer center stage in this new liberal religious world.

In sum, "revisiting" American religious liberalism with the editors and authors of this volume takes us to destinations far more challenging than scholarly forays into religious liberalism have done before. We believe those destinations—

however much they are still under construction—are well worth the journeys to reach them. This book is a welcome addition, indeed, to the all-too-short list of scholarly studies on religious liberalism in America.

Catherine L. Albanese
Stephen J. Stein
Series Editors

ACKNOWLEDGMENTS

Pulling together a sizeable group of contributors for a collaborative project and then keeping everyone on board and on schedule—these are notorious challenges in the academy. Happily we had an unusually reliable and generous cohort, and fortunately too we had strong institutional support undergirding our enterprise. The Center for the Study of Religion at Princeton University got the endeavor off the ground in 2008, providing the seed money for us to revisit American religious liberalism, its history, and continuing consequence. We thank Robert Wuthnow, Jenny Legath, Anita Kline, Lorraine Fuhrmann, and Barbara Bermel for facilitating our initial collaboration. Among our colleagues, Emily R. Mace, in particular, took the lead in organizing our first meeting at Princeton.

At Yale University, support from the Edward J. and Dorothy Clarke Kempf Memorial Fund and the Yale Institute of Sacred Music (ISM) shaped our second gathering. Deputy Provost Emily Bakemeier and ISM director Martin Jean deserve special mention for their generosity. The Department of Religious Studies; the American Studies Program; and the Women's, Gender, and Sexuality Studies Program also contributed to this collaboration. David Walker capably organized the Yale conference in 2009.

We have benefited greatly from critical commentary and reflection on the project from several colleagues along the way: Wallace Best, Gary Dorrien, R. Marie Griffith, Gordon Lynch, Arie Molendijk, Hélène Quanquin, Paul Raushenbush, Amy Sullivan, Randi Warne, Judith Weisenfeld, and John F. Wilson. We have also been fortunate in having Dee Mortensen as our editor at

Indiana University Press; she has been ever supportive and patient as the project has unfolded over the last four years. Likewise, we feel honored to have the work included in the long-standing series "Religion in North America," which Catherine L. Albanese and Stephen J. Stein so well superintend.

AMERICAN RELIGIOUS LIBERALISM

INTRODUCTION

The Parameters and Problematics of American Religious Liberalism

LEIGH E. SCHMIDT

Historian William R. Hutchison explained at the beginning of *The Modernist Impulse in American Protestantism* (1976), still a scholarly benchmark in the field of American religious history, that he had not attempted to trace "the entire history of Protestant liberalism but rather the development and demise of a cluster of liberal ideas."[1] The crux, for Hutchison, was the conscientious adaptation of Christian thought to modern cultural developments, particularly as evinced in the sciences and social sciences. Hutchison stressed the optimistic attitude—a humanistic progressivism with a distinct Christian inflection (the gradual instantiation of the Kingdom of God)—that propelled the liberal Protestant embrace of change, whether in education, biblical scholarship, missions, or social reform. That hopefulness stood out with especial clarity in contrast with the neo-orthodox rebellion that ensued after 1930 within liberal Protestant ranks. Realism, tragedy, and irony became the dominant lenses through which everything from American history to human nature to foreign policy was viewed. Hutchison patiently reconstructed a history of Protestant modernism beyond the drumbeat of neo-orthodox critique—one in which liberal faith had often been reduced to little more than a religion of gush, cheerfulness, and sentimentality.

As with Hutchison's volume, so with this one: the authors and editors have hardly had the entire history of Protestant liberalism in view, but instead a cluster of interrelated questions. These interrogatives center not so much on liberal ideas about Christian doctrine, human nature, or industrial relations, but instead on the fluid, self-critical, and often wildly creative qualities of American religious liberalism. The intention has been to broaden the conversation beyond the familiar interpretive tropes of the modernist impulse and the Social Gospel—indeed, in many instances, beyond Protestantism itself. The project is a collaborative endeavor, shaped through a threefold engagement with religious liberalism's manifold cultural imbrications: 1) the spiritualization of the arts, 2) the piety and politics of interreligious ecumenism and cosmopolitanism, and 3) the dense and ambivalent exchange between liberal religion and liberal secularism. That thematic trio provides the larger scaffolding for the essays that follow.

The first area of focus (Part 1) centers on the relationship between religious liberalism and the arts: Did religious liberals, in effect, put the arts in the place of churches and synagogues, the poet's inspiration in the place of the priest's liturgy, the novelist's imagination in the place of the biblical expositor's exegesis? It was a common form of romantic displacement—to look for the spiritual in art, not in ecclesial institutions, or to conflate "art and worship" as "one and the same thing."[2] American Transcendentalists and their sundry successors most intensely courted those spiritual aesthetics, but art's singular elevation was evident across a broad swath of religious liberalism. This collaborative endeavor draws attention at several points to the poetics of liberal religion and probes the cultural consequences of that modernist creativity—again in ecumenical Protestant as well as post-Christian terms. That imaginative license came necessarily with its own coercions and compulsions, its own hierarchies of taste and culture, as the essays in the first part of this volume make evident: What counted as banal, trivial, or saccharine? What cultural productions ascended to the level of the spiritual and the beautiful? Why, for example, was high-end abstraction privileged over popular religious kitsch? Stressing the spiritual in art often enhanced liberal appreciation of South Asian, Native American, and other religious traditions, but it also authorized careless, decontextualized absorptions of indigenous symbols and rites in a boundless quest for primeval enchantment and spiritual authenticity. Making an art of religion was an extraordinarily attractive proposition, and yet, on closer inspection, it was also an endlessly problematic dimension of religious liberalism's preoccupations.

The second cluster of concerns (Part 2) revolves around the piety and politics of liberal cosmopolitanism and ecumenism: How were the ideals of religious diversity, pluralism, and universality imagined? From one side, religious liberals look like rank Orientalists, exploiters and exoticizers of whatever sacred book or religious practice struck their fancy; from another angle, they look like self-critical ecumenists, ready to subject their own religious inheritances to an open fluidity of identity and relativistic reappraisal. Time and again, the contributors to this volume ponder whether religious liberals were serious pluralists: How capable were they of critically examining their own exclusions and hierarchies, including those based on race, gender, class, and creed? How often and under what circumstances did religious progressives become anti-imperial agitators and advocates of home rule? How often and under what circumstances did they become frontline agents or bureaucratic managers of America's varied empires—colonial, commercial, educational, and missionary? It is now commonplace to assume that the forces of liberal colonization were far more prevalent than those of cosmopolitan solidarity, but such questions warrant more empirical research and fewer foregone conclusions.[3] Several of the essays in the second part of this volume attempt to provide just that kind of detailed scrutiny, even as they remain fully aware of liberal defenses of empire as well as the brutal exclusions such apologia justified.[4] The complex sentiments and practices of liberal ecumenism, cosmopolitanism, and internationalism are given serious, yet critical reconsideration in these pages; such liberal dispositions are viewed, to use David Hollinger's formulation in the afterword, as characteristically productive of "self-interrogation"—an often withering reappraisal of the privileges accorded white, middle-class Protestantism and its allied institutions.

The third constellation of concerns (Part 3) involves the charged relationship between religious and secular versions of nineteenth- and twentieth-century liberalism. The varieties of religious liberalism do not stand apart from or in the shadows of their multiple political, economic, and freethinking cousins. Instead, the relationship between religious and secular versions of liberalism is taken to be dynamic and mutually constitutive. Agnostic orator Robert Ingersoll, in other words, becomes part of the same narrative as romantic preacher Henry Ward Beecher; likewise, the secular despair of Joseph Wood Krutch's *Modern Temper* is part of the same story as the Protestant hopefulness of Shailer Mathews's *Faith of Modernism;* and the freethinking socialism of Hubert Henry Harrison shares ground in the Harlem Renaissance with the religious connections of Alain Locke (including Ethical Culture and the Bahá'í Faith). Or, to put this interpretive proposition in more contemporaneous terms, the young John Rawls's considerable engagement with mid-century Protestant theology, evident in his senior thesis at Princeton, forms part of the intellectual and cultural backdrop of the mature John Rawls's theorizing of political liberalism at Harvard.[5] Secular liberals, indeed, went to great lengths to narrow religion's public purview through strict constructions of church-state separation, but that hardly eliminated the continual interplay between religious and secular versions of liberalism. Any linear narrative that imagines a once regnant religious liberalism inexorably giving way to its secular rivals is, indeed, doubly misleading. On the one end, it underestimates the secular ambitions of early freethinking liberals in the 1870s and 1880s who congregated in groups like the National Liberal League and under banners like the Religion of Humanity. On the other end, it casts over later religious liberals a pall of ever waning significance, as compared to the ever waxing secularism of state policy makers, liberal political philosophers, humanist educators, and leftist organizers. The essayists in this volume, particularly in the third part of the collection, emphasize the ways in which religious and secular versions of liberalism have routinely been reciprocating impulses.[6]

Spanning these three areas of inquiry is a recurring tension or friction; namely, how to break out of the all too prevalent equation of American religious liberalism with American liberal Protestantism without slighting the latter's cultural force. Heretofore the primary interpretive configurations have presumed very specific Protestant parameters, with orthodox starting points and liberal end points: the Social Gospel arises as a critical response to the preoccupation of evangelical revivalism with personal salvation, and the modernist impulse arises as a critique of Protestant creedalism, a desire to adapt theological doctrines—from original sin to Christology—to the progressive spirit of the age. These familiar Protestant stories remain important, but they have also become an impediment to seeing the broader impact of religious liberalism since the mid-nineteenth century. They represent a taming of the post-Protestant ferment through the maintenance of a clear Protestant groundwork; they establish a Protestant center and then sharply delimit the periphery accordingly. Indeed, the very tenacity of such constructs has given credence to the notion that any talk of religious liberalism is a way of perpetuating, in covert terms, a mainline Protestant narrative about all of American religious history.[7]

No doubt the discourses of religious liberalism offered some convenient disguises through which the Protestant establishment could mask itself in non-sectarian universality. In the long run, though, the liberal ferment did not render Protestant privilege more potent by giving it cover; instead, it fractured the old Protestant notion of a Christian America beyond recognition; it liquefied Christian particularity and dispersed the Protestant mainstream into hard-to-channel rivulets. If the discourses of pluralistic toleration and nonsectarian broadmindedness, so central to religious liberalism, acted as a kind of masquerade—a cloak for hiding the operation of Protestant power and its exclusions—then the revelry soon got out of hand as carnivalesque inversion. A concrete illustration of that topsy-turviness can be garnered from the pages of the *Chicago Tribune* between 1874 and 1899. It serves as a good example of the force of the orthodox Protestant template as well as its vulnerability to the solvents of liberal religious innovations.

In the 1870s the "Religious Announcements" column in the *Tribune* had consisted of little more than a catalog of church services, a structure that closely followed the mainstream Protestant denominational map: Episcopal, Baptist, Presbyterian, Methodist, and Congregational. The newspaper, the city's premier daily, did allow room at the tag end of the announcements for a miniscule "Miscellaneous" category of alternative assemblies, including Spiritualists and freethinkers. Liberal-minded dissidents, though, were more than balanced in the miscellaneous category by other Protestant announcements about, say, a new congregation of English-speaking Lutherans or a tabernacle meeting led by a revival preacher from Kansas. As the *Tribune* presented the religious news in the 1870s, the dozens of Protestant church services had little competition from the small handful of miscellaneous upstarts. The paper's religious announcements offered the very picture of a de facto Protestant establishment.

A quarter of a century later, the *Tribune* was struggling to maintain the old order in its listing of the city's religious meetings. All hell was now breaking loose in the "Miscellaneous" category. Beyond the usual run of alternatives—Unitarians, Quakers, and Spiritualists—there was now the Society of Ethical Culture offering a new rationalistic gospel for what it called "an Age of Doubt"; there were various chapters of the Theosophical Society staging lectures on "Reincarnation" and the "Secret Realization of Truth," among other esoteric subjects; there were any number of New Thought ministries, boasting names such as the Truth Center and the Spiritual Temple of Advanced Thought, that offered advice on techniques of concentration, mental healing, and self-composure; and there was the Chicago Society of Anthropology, devoted to open discussion of religious and philosophical topics, an ecumenical fellowship that emerged in the wake of the World's Parliament of Religions in

1893. The Victorian Protestant order that the *Tribune* had projected twenty-five years earlier seemed to be rapidly fraying as the miscellaneous category split open the tightly stitched seams of the old denominational order.

Take as one concrete example the *Tribune*'s religious announcements for December 17, 1899. At first glance everything looked in good Protestant order as Christmas approached: seventeen listings for Episcopal services, eleven for Methodist, ten for Congregational, nine for Baptist, and nine for Presbyterian. Still placed at the bottom, where it had always been, was the "Miscellaneous" category, but it was now the largest by far, with forty offerings. Even as it had spun off whole new groupings, including "Christian Scientist," it had become, along with its new companion catchall of "Independent," a bewildering hodgepodge. At the Second Eclectic Society of Spiritual Culture, for example, a local judge was lecturing on "Infidelity, Belief, Consciousness of Truth," while the famed reformer Jane Addams was speaking on "Democracy and Social Ethics" at the Society of Ethical Culture. The First Society of Rosicrucians was hearing a meditation on "Thought Intuition," while the Church of the Soul was attending to the medium Cora L. V. Richmond, whose discourse was on "Robert G. Ingersoll in Spirit Life" (the latter title was certainly a fine indication of the religious-secular exchange). At the People's Church, meeting at McVicker's Theater, the Reform rabbi Emil Hirsch and the latter-day Transcendentalist minister Jenkin Lloyd Jones were teaming up for joint services. Swami Abhayananda, an associate of Swami Vivekananda, was speaking at a Vedanta congregation; a freethinking Unitarian dissident was holding meetings for a body she called the Church of Yoga; and the Independent Church for Students of Nature was hearing from its pastor, aptly named Mrs. Summers. In all, the number of assemblies for various liberals, eclectics, and seekers roughly equaled the combined number of services for the top five Protestant denominations. Even if that count suggests little about the numbers of actual members, it certainly reveals the extent of ferment on the more pluralist, cosmopolitan, and metaphysical side of the religious spectrum.

The *Tribune*'s catalog of services had come to point, in spite of itself, to the advance of religious miscellany against Protestant consensus, liberal eclecticism against Christian coherence. In Chicago in 1874, the Presbyterian David Swing had been tried by the church, to sensational effect, for his suspect views on such doctrines as eternal damnation, the Trinity, and justification by faith alone; a quarter century later, the sort of challenge that Swing had represented looked restrained, if not antiquated. In *The Modernist Impulse* and elsewhere,

William Hutchison lifted up the Swing trial of 1874 as a classic salvo of religious modernism in American culture. And yet Swing's trial deserves to be taken as an archetype of liberal unrest only if an evangelical baseline is assumed: Swing was a liberal among orthodox Presbyterians, hardly the best gauge of the full force of modernist currents. Hutchison well knew this, of course, given all the time he had already spent working on Unitarians and Transcendentalists. Yet presenting the Swing trial as an epitome of the liberal, proto-modernist challenge secured the story within the Protestant establishment rather than in creative tension with it. As even a summary look at the pages of the *Tribune* suggests, that focus severely limits the historian's peripheral vision.[8]

By the time Swing died in 1894, the Calvinist/anti-Calvinist wrangling that had long dominated American Protestant thought no longer came close to being an adequate measure of liberal, post-Christian dissent in American culture. In that more diffuse light, Swing's challenge to Protestant orthodoxy (and its Princeton tiger Francis Patton) had come to look exceedingly tame. The turbulent energies of religious liberalism had moved elsewhere. The few heresy trials roiling the Protestant denominational world constituted rearguard scholasticism compared to the miscellany that prevailed among that loosely knit and often unruly parliament of religious liberals: the Society of Ethical Culture, Unitarians, Universalists, Reform Jews, freethinkers, mystic-minded Quakers, Whitmanites, Theosophists, Spiritualists, New Thought progressives, Vedantists, Bahá'ís, Free Religionists, Open-Court monists, convert Buddhists, and the like. Born especially of romantic restlessness and overt Unitarian dissent, American religious liberalism long remained propulsive in its effects, a centrifugal force as much as a centering mechanism. That it was somehow integral to maintaining the Protestant establishment—let alone identical with it—was anything but self-evident. When, for example, the Philadelphia freethinker Voltairine de Cleyre summarized a lecture series on religious modernism that the Ladies' Liberal League hosted in the mid-1890s, she pointed to three great avatars of that impulse: Unitarianism, Theosophy, and Whitmanism. There was not a Presbyterian or Methodist in sight.[9]

It took considerable cultural work to make religious liberalism a dependable stalwart of the Protestant mainstream, and historians certainly played their part in that process. One of the first histories of American religious liberalism, John Wright Buckham's *Progressive Religious Thought in America,* published in 1919, had seven leading figures, all Protestant divines, running from

Congregationalist Horace Bushnell to Congregationalist Newman Smyth, paragons of what Buckham called the progressive wing of the Pilgrim heritage. These men, Buckham assured his readers, were America's intellectual "liberators," and, yet, as revolutions go, this one looked pretty domesticated. Buckham's story line—the gradual deliverance of New England theology from the Westminster Confession—made humanity's progress toward the universal religion both comfortably Protestant and geographically familiar. It also contained American religious liberalism within a small handful of leading Protestant divinity schools and appointed select expositors of the "new theology" as the guardians of its outer limits. One hardly had to fear that Henry Steel Olcott's Buddhist catechism (a distinctly liberal Protestant document in all kinds of ways) was somehow going to get in the narrative's back door.[10]

If Buckham's account now sounds parochial and predictable, more surprising is how often and how long the history of American religious liberalism has remained ensconced within those bounds. Kenneth Cauthen made the same equation, taking the Protestant divinity school as the locus of the movement, in his 1962 history *The Impact of American Religious Liberalism.* Concentrating on eight figures, Cauthen moved from Union Seminary's William Adams Brown to Chicago's Henry Nelson Wieman. Currently, the definitive example of this measuring rod is Gary Dorrien's three-volume history of American liberal theology in which the Protestant canon of figures, texts, and institutions undergirds every chapter. Dorrien clearly has far more than seven or eight men guiding the new theology, but the defining parameters of the narrative are nonetheless much the same as they were for Buckham and Cauthen.[11] Religious liberalism, an expansive and often subversive cultural movement, has been routinely narrowed in such a way that including even a popular devotional writer, let alone a humanistic freethinker or a Whitman-reciting Free Lover, alongside the leading Protestant theologians looks like a distraction, a digression, or perchance a heresy.

It is time to set the centrifuge in motion, but it is important to recognize that this scattering is in itself problematic: When the Protestant center does not hold this story together, are there meaningful limits by which to define a periphery? Once it is recognized, for example, how much of New Thought metaphysics and Theosophical occultism are entwined with these wider liberal religious currents, the Protestant theological bounds are shown to be merely one more protective artifice, and dissolve. Perhaps, as Jeffrey Kripal suggests in this volume and elsewhere through his broad-ranging attention to countervailing spiritual currents, histories of American religious liberalism still need to get "way, way weirder."[12] Yet at what point do our nets catch too many anomalies and oddities and thus cease to be useful screens at all?

Here is the predicament: Once we reconsider American religious liberalism on terms that go far beyond the Buckham and Cauthen wing of American church history, what kind of catchment remains? Certainly, one possibility is to view liberal religion as a significant strand within (and alongside) what Catherine L. Albanese has called metaphysical religion, a category that draws attention to the hybridizing power of the American religious imagination, the ways in which conventional Protestant demarcations have consistently obscured the spiritual porosity of occultism, New Thought, Spiritualism, Unitarianism, and the like. While there is clearly no one-to-one correspondence between these metaphysical and liberal predilections, there are, as Albanese suggests, innumerable meeting points and overlaps.[13] The cosmopolitanism of religious liberalism, for example, was as much a metaphysical preoccupation as it was an ecumenical Protestant realization (if not more so). The same could be said of the bohemian spiritualization of the arts as well as the ambivalent relationship to secularism. Spiritualists and occultists liked to speak of the contact points between this world and the other world as borderlands, and that trope could also be usefully applied to the varied spaces that religious liberals and metaphysical speculators wound up inhabiting together.

To be sure, the starting points for metaphysicians and religious liberals were often different: the former commonly looked to Hermetic inheritances; the latter usually constituted themselves through a more explicit dialectic with the West's prevailing religious orthodoxies, Christian and Jewish. Religious liberals more often remained critical admirers of the traditions they could no longer wholeheartedly embrace, but nonetheless, like the metaphysical innovators, they too had their outright mutineers and tramping wayfarers. Emerson, say, could be counted a saint among esoteric metaphysicians, religious liberals, and secular agnostics alike, and so could Whitman: the lines blur, and that is precisely the point. It is important for historians of religious liberalism to hold off the impulse to tack back to a familiar port, whether Jewish, Christian, or humanist, and thus to remain aloof from these broader currents and connections. It is simply misguided to draw a clear line between the likes of Horace Bushnell and Ralph Waldo Trine, Isaac Mayer Wise and Horace Traubel, Julia Ward Howe and Clara Colby, with the first in each pair inside the "religious liberal" box and the second somehow outside that box. Indeed, Kripal's favored metaphysician, Charles Fort, offered an apt warning: "All would be well. All would be heavenly—If the damned would only stay damned," Fort observed. "By the damned, I mean the excluded."[14]

The precise balancing point—between (to put the tension glibly) a hot-tub harmonialism and a bone-dry Protestant establishment—is elusive, but one suggestive alternative is to be found in the work of the populist journalist Benjamin Orange Flower, a contemporary of John Buckham. The son of a Disciples of Christ minister, Flower migrated into social reform and editorial leadership of the *Arena* via Unitarianism, Spiritualism, psychical research, and New Thought. His *Progressive Men, Women, and Movements of the Past Twenty-five Years,* published in 1914, displayed a much fuller sense of the cultural consequence and scope of American religious liberalism than did Buckham's highly selective theological pantheon. Flower gave liberal Protestant deviators from evangelical orthodoxy due attention, but he turned even more to novelists and poets as religious innovators—from Ralph Waldo Emerson and Harriet Beecher Stowe to Edwin Markham and Katrina Trask. He included the Christian populism and democratic progressivism of William Jennings Bryan, while also attending to staunch labor reformers from Henry Demarest Lloyd to Eugene Debs. He had as well a section on the temperance advocate Frances Willard (he marveled, for one thing, at her surprising fondness for Walt Whitman) and offered another chapter on the leaders of the women's suffrage movement, Elizabeth Cady Stanton, Mary Livermore, and company.

The whole of this ferment Flower called "the Liberal Religious Awakening." He located its American roots among Unitarians—Channing, Emerson, and Theodore Parker—but he quickly moved on to Reform rabbis Solomon Schindler and Charles Fleischer, Spiritualist and Universalist J. M. Peebles, psychical researcher and questing psychologist William James, New Thought progressives Ralph Waldo Trine and James Edgerton, cosmopolitan journalist and occultist William T. Stead, and freethinker Robert Ingersoll. In other words, Flower effectively bridged the religious-secular divide within liberalism and saw the movement in cultural and political as much as theological terms. Not that Flower was without his own limitations of vision: he had, for example, a keener ear for poetry than an eye for the visual arts, and, like so many American liberals, he was a decided anti-papist with almost no awareness of Catholic modernism. Still, his firsthand feel for the tumult of the liberal religious awakening—for its breadth and multiple cultural expressions—offers a better starting point for the reconsideration of that disparate movement than the ecclesial "mainstream" that comes down to us through Buckham's theological genealogy.[15]

A future commentator, channeling anew the historian Jon Butler's ventriloquizing of anti-revivalist Charles Chauncy, may well determine that resurrecting Flower's notion of a liberal religious awakening is an enthusiasm to be decried and cautioned against, but for the moment it suggests a way out of a certain historiographical compartment. Here is a broader cultural, intellectual, and religious movement—one of spiritual-secular ambivalence; one multiply implicated in shifting constructions of gender, race, empire, class, and sexuality; one of expansive engagement with the arts; one enthralled with intuition and experiential authenticity at the expense of creed and tradition; one ever riddled by simultaneous dreams of creative individuality and adhesive community; one possessed by the problematic relationship between universalism and cosmopolitanism, ecumenical unity and unbridgeable plurality, solidarity and difference. To be sure, religious liberalism included a prophetic vernacular of Social Gospel reform, a Protestant dialect of theological modernism, and a non-sectarian disguise for an attenuating Protestant establishment, but it was also a set of cultural exchanges—with art, with cosmopolitanism, and with secularism. Liberal religion, as Richard Wightman Fox has argued, represented not only an intellectual program, but also a profound shift in "cultural sensibility" that reshaped "the broad patterns of living, feeling, and thinking" among those immersed in its modernist currents.[16] The deeper and often more enduring effects appeared in unforeseen places—say, in how one loved or parented, worked or played, read or meditated, as much as in how one thought about eternal damnation or industrial relations. Seen in such capacious terms, with the edges of its own dissent brought into full view, this progressive religious awakening may well start to matter anew to historians and contemporary cultural observers alike.

Perhaps, at the end of the day, Flower's "Liberal Religious Awakening" is ultimately too much of a rhetorical concession to an evangelical Protestant way of imagining the nation's history in revival-laden terms: that said, it yet retains an effective hortatory cadence. The rise of the Religious Right and the flourishing of twentieth-century conservatism have for understandable reasons gripped historians in recent years, so much so that there has not been a lot of oxygen left over for beleaguered religious liberals and ecumenical Protestants. Evangelicals have stolen the show not only among journalists chronicling the current political landscape, but also among historians trying to make sense of conservatism's resurgence in the aftermath of the New Deal and during the religious revival that the Cold War helped incite. The essayists in this volume revisit—and reintroduce—the countervailing tradition of American religious liberalism, convinced of its historical robustness and keen on heightening scholarly attention to it. No revivalist tract, this collection serves as a reminder of just how varied, vigorous, and consequential such modernist currents have been over the last century and more. That recognition is unlikely to spark an awakening, but it just might nurture a renewed awareness of the multiple engagements and instigations of religious progressives in the nation's past and present.

NOTES

1. William R. Hutchison, *The Modernist Impulse in American Protestantism* (New York: Oxford University Press, 1976), 2.

2. For a full-blown statement of this version of the art of liberal religion, see Kenneth L. Patton, *A Religion for One World: Art and Symbols for a Universal Religion* (Boston: Beacon, 1964), with quotation on p. 138.

3. Compare, for example, how the broader history of the field looks when the scholar takes a careful, empirical, contextual approach versus when the scholar assumes a particular postcolonial critique of the whole enterprise. For the former, see Bruce Kuklick, *Puritans in Babylon: The Ancient Near East and American Intellectual Life, 1880–1930* (Princeton: Princeton University Press, 1996); and Suzanne L. Marchand, *German Orientalism in the Age of Empire: Religion, Race, and Scholarship* (Cambridge: Cambridge University Press, 2009). For the latter, see Tomoko Masuzawa, *The Invention of World Religions, or, How European Universalism Was Preserved in the Language of Pluralism* (Chicago: University of Chicago Press, 2005); and Timothy Fitzgerald, *Discourse on Civility and Barbarity: A Critical History of Religion and Related Categories* (New York: Oxford University Press, 2007).

4. This critique is made with particular force and effectiveness in Uday Singh Mehta, *Liberalism and Empire: A Study in Nineteenth-Century British Liberal Thought* (Chicago: University of Chicago Press, 1999); and Uday S. Mehta, "Liberal Strategies of Exclusion," *Politics and Society* 18, no. 4 (December 1990): 427–54. For liberal Protestant exclusions in the American context, particularly on matters of race, see Andrew C. Reiser, *The Chautauqua Moment: Protestants, Progressives, and the Culture of Modern Liberalism* (New York: Columbia University Press, 2003), esp. 10–11, 128–60. There are clearly important counterpoints on racial politics and civil rights questions in liberal religious circles, and these only strengthen with time. See, for example, Barbara Dianne Savage, *Your Spirits Walk beside Us: The Politics of Black Religion* (Cambridge, Mass.: Harvard University Press, 2008), esp. 16, 205–37. For rereadings of Victorian liberalism itself in more sympathetic terms, see, for example, Leslie Butler, *Critical Americans: Victorian Intellectuals and Transatlantic Liberal Reform* (Chapel Hill: University of North Carolina Press, 2007); Carrie Tirado Bramen, *The Uses of Variety: Modern Americanism and the Quest for National Distinctiveness* (Cambridge, Mass.: Harvard University Press, 2000); Leigh Eric Schmidt, *Restless Souls: The Making of American Spiritu-*

ality, 2nd ed. (Berkeley: University of California Press, forthcoming); and Amy Kittelstrom, "The International Social Turn: Unity and Brotherhood at the World's Parliament of Religions, Chicago, 1893," *Religion and American Culture* 19, no. 2 (summer 2009): 243–74.

5. Eric Gregory recently discovered the thesis in Princeton's Mudd Library; it was then edited and elaborated upon by Thomas Nagel and Joshua Cohen. See Eric Gregory, "Before the Original Position: The Neo-orthodox Theology of the Young John Rawls," *Journal of Religious Ethics* 35, no. 2 (June 2007): 179–206; and John Rawls, *A Brief Inquiry into the Meaning of Sin and Faith, with "On My Religion,"* ed. Thomas Nagel (Cambridge, Mass.: Harvard University Press, 2009).

6. The emphasis placed here on the religious-secular exchange within liberal circles is in no way intended to minimize the importance of other formative rivalries, notably Fundamentalist-modernist controversies and Roman Catholic–liberal Protestant battles. See especially George M. Marsden, *Fundamentalism and American Culture,* 2nd ed. (New York: Oxford University Press, 2006); and John McGreevy, *Catholicism and American Freedom: A History* (New York: W. W. Norton, 2003).

7. On the conservative politics of yoking the Protestant establishment to the liberal establishment, see William R. Hutchison, "Protestantism as Establishment," in Hutchison, ed., *Between the Times: The Travail of the Protestant Establishment in America, 1900–1960* (Cambridge: Cambridge University Press, 1989), esp. 13–16. For one account of how liberal Protestants used non-sectarian language to perpetuate their own "establishmentarian outlook" (3), even as they ostensibly went into secular eclipse, see George M. Marsden, *The Soul of the American University: From Protestant Establishment to Established Nonbelief* (New York: Oxford University Press, 1994). For an acute analysis of "the consolidation of a Protestant ideology" under the cloak of the "allegedly universal secular," see Tracy Fessenden, *Culture and Redemption: Religion, the Secular, and American Literature* (Princeton: Princeton University Press, 2007), 5, 12.

8. See William R. Hutchison, "Disapproval of Chicago: The Symbolic Trial of David Swing," *Journal of American History* 59, no. 1 (June 1972): 30–47; and Hutchison, *Modernist Impulse,* 48–68. The *Tribune* examples are an adaptation from Leigh Eric Schmidt, *Heaven's Bride: The Unprintable Life of Ida C. Craddock, American Mystic, Scholar, Sexologist, Martyr, and Madwoman* (New York: Basic Books, 2010), 89–91.

9. Voltairine de Cleyre, "The Past and Future of the Ladies' Liberal League," *Rebel,* November 20, 1895, 32.

10. John Wright Buckham, *Progressive Religious Thought in America: A Survey of the Enlarging Pilgrim Faith* (Boston: Houghton Mifflin, 1919), 3. On the liberal Protestant qualities of Olcott's catechism, see Stephen Prothero, *The White Buddhist: The Asian Odyssey of Henry Steel Olcott* (Bloomington: Indiana University Press, 1996), esp. 103–105.

11. See Gary Dorrien, *The Making of American Liberal Theology,* 3 vols. (Louisville, Ky.: Westminster John Knox, 2001–2006); and Kenneth Cauthen, *The Impact of American Religious Liberalism* (New York: Harper & Row, 1962; Washington, D.C.: University Press of America, 1983). Cauthen defines the tradition through entirely in-house Protestant terms as divided between evangelical liberals and modernistic liberals. Dorrien, while refining that distinction, works within the same Protestant boundaries (2:10–20) and essentially dispenses with the Unitarian/Transcendentalist/post-Christian/humanistic wing after the first volume.

12. See Kripal's chapter on Charles Fort in this volume, but also his *Esalen: America and the Religion of No Religion* (Chicago: University of Chicago Press, 2007).

13. Catherine L. Albanese, *A Republic of Mind and Spirit: A Cultural History of American Metaphysical Religion* (New Haven: Yale University Press, 2007), esp. 17–18, 230–33, 289–91. See as well her ongoing work on these connections, including Catherine L. Albanese, "Horace Bushnell among the Metaphysicians," *Church History* 79, no. 3 (2010): 614–53.

14. Charles Fort, *The Complete Books of Charles Fort* (New York: Dover, 1974), 4, 15.

15. Benjamin Orange Flower, *Progressive Men, Women, and Movements of the Past Twenty-five Years* (Boston: New Arena, 1914), 160. Buckham's inclusion of William Jennings Bryan, a figure so easily consigned to the Fundamentalist camp because of the Scopes trial, nicely augurs Michael Kazin's repositioning of Bryan as a Christian liberal. See Kazin, *A Godly Hero: The Life of William Jennings Bryan* (New York: Knopf, 2006).

16. Richard Wightman Fox, "The Culture of Liberal Protestant Progressivism, 1875–1925," *Journal of Interdisciplinary History* 23, no. 3 (winter 1993): 646. Fox's cultural approach is superbly limned in this piece, but liberal religion is still equated with "mainstream liberal Protestantism," and not with a movement much more protean than that (639). It is defined by David Swing and Henry Ward Beecher, not Henry Olcott, Felix Adler, and Sarah Farmer.

PART ONE

The Spiritual in Art

ONE

Reading Poetry Religiously

The Walt Whitman Fellowship and Seeker Spirituality

MICHAEL ROBERTSON

In his introduction to this volume, Leigh Schmidt notes that when the free-thinking feminist Voltairine de Cleyre wrote about progressive currents in American religion of the 1890s, she highlighted three exemplary movements: Unitarianism, Theosophy, and Whitmanism. There is no shortage of scholarly examinations of the first two of these, but Whitmanism, remarkably, has gone largely unstudied. In *The Varieties of Religious Experience* (1902), William James remarked with thinly disguised dismay on the religious appreciation of the recently deceased Walt Whitman. "Societies are actually formed for his cult," James wrote; "a periodical organ exists for its propagation, in which the lines of orthodoxy and heterodoxy are already beginning to be drawn; . . . and he is even explicitly compared with the founder of the Christian religion, not altogether to the advantage of the latter."[1] In the century since de Cleyre and James noted the existence of Whitmanism, a number of critics have published literary and phenomenological analyses of the religious dimensions of *Leaves of Grass;* however, we lack studies of Whitmanism as a lived religion, of the ways in which spiritual seekers at the turn into the twentieth century used Whitman's poetry in constructing a liberal spirituality.[2]

Whitmanism was, even at its height, a loosely organized religious movement, known largely through the writings of a small group of fervent adherents who had known the poet personally and were highly attuned to the prophetic dimensions of his poetry. Moreover, many of the members of this core group were actively hostile to any attempt to gather like-minded Whitmanites into an organization. As Catherine Albanese observes of the many metaphysical religious doctrines promulgated in the United States over the years, "Metaphysicians do not institutionalize well."[3] Whitmanites belong among the adherents of what Lawrence Buell has wittily called "wildcat freelance post-Protestantism."[4]

Yet even among wildcat freelancers there are many who share the common human urge to seek out like-minded believers. As William James noted, societies were formed for the cult of Whitman, along with a periodical organ for its propagation. The societies were branches of the Walt Whitman Fellowship; the organ was the *Conservator* (1890–1919). In what follows, I want briefly to explore the spiritual messages of Whitman's poetry before sketching an institutional history of the precariously organized Whitman Fellowship. Despite its weaknesses, during the late nineteenth and early twentieth centuries the Whitman Fellowship offered a significant number of North American cultural radicals and spiritual seekers a means of integrating diverse realms of experience—including poetry, socialism, feminism, and sexuality—with an individualistic, cosmopolitan, and mystical spirituality.

LEAVES OF GRASS, THE ROMANTIC POET-PROPHET, AND LIBERAL SPIRITUALITY

Preparing an expanded edition of *Leaves of Grass* in 1857, Walt Whitman confided to his notebook his plans for the volume: "*The Great Construction* of the *New Bible.* Not to be diverted from the principal object—the main life work—the Three Hundred & Sixty Five—(it ought to be read[y] in 1859." In another notebook entry he wrote, "'Leaves of Grass'—Bible of the New Religion."[5] However grandiose Whitman's ambition now seems, in the context of the antebellum United States his plans were not uncommon. This was the era of what Lawrence Buell has dubbed "literary scripturism," when numerous writers believed that their work could serve as scripture for a new religion appropriate to American democracy.[6]

A variety of factors prepared the way for literary scripturism during the early nineteenth century. One of the most important was the rise of the Romantic poet-prophet. William Blake was only the first in a series of major English-language writers who offered a belief system to supplement—or replace—a conventional Christianity that was coming to be seen among artists and intellectuals as outmoded and inappropriate for the modern age. T. E. Hulme's famous dismissal of Romanticism as nothing more than "spilt religion" gets at an important truth that can be stated in more positive terms: the Romantic movement initiated a century-long cultural receptiveness to the religious functions of literature.[7] In Great Britain, Blake's highly personalized mythology, which valorized human creativity as the divine force, was succeeded by other forms of prophetic poetry: Shelley's fervent, humanistic atheism challenged all forms of political and religious authority; Wordsworth's early verse offered an ecstatic nature mysticism. By 1840 Thomas Carlyle could assert confidently that the poet and the prophet are "fundamentally . . . the same; in this most important respect especially, that they have penetrated both of them into the sacred mystery of the universe."[8]

In the United States, Emerson served as the fountainhead of literary scripturism. "Make your own Bible," Emerson admonished himself in an 1836 journal entry.[9] The same year he published "Nature," the first of a series of poetic and prophetic essays that many readers regarded as an American scripture. By the time that Walt Whitman wrote in 1871 that "the priest departs, the divine literatus comes," he was announcing a cultural commonplace; Alfred Kazin has identified the replacement of priest by poet as a central Romantic trope.[10]

Whitman was touchy about his debts to Emerson—originality was as crucial as prophecy to his self-conception—but his poetry reveals the pervasive influence of Emersonian Transcendentalism. Large swaths of "Song of Myself," his longest and greatest poem, read like poetic restatements of Emerson, as in this passage that vividly enunciates the Transcendentalist belief in the divinity of nature and the material world:

> Why should I wish to see God better than this day?
> I see something of God each hour of the twenty-four, and each moment then,
> In the faces of men and women I see God, and in my own face in the glass,
> I find letters from God dropt in the street, and every one is sign'd by God's name,
> And I leave them where they are, for I know that wheresoe'er I go,
> Others will punctually come for ever and ever.[11]

Leigh Schmidt has argued that the origins of American seeker spirituality are to be found in the sort of Emersonian-Whitmanesque mysticism exemplified in this passage; Jeffrey Kripal suggests that Whitman's poetry, along with the work of Emerson and Thoreau, can be read as an "American Mystical Constitution," establishing a more perfect union based on a democratic mysticism.[12]

If Emerson laid the foundation of the mystical, democratic spirituality to be found in *Leaves of Grass,* Whitman's poetry was also profoundly influenced by his family heritage, which connected him to two major strands of nineteenth-century religious liberalism. Whitman's father was a freethinker, an admirer of Thomas Paine who passed on to his children an anti-clerical wariness of religious institutions. His maternal grandmother was a Quaker and an acquaintance of Elias Hicks, the radical Quaker preacher who rejected biblical orthodoxy and emphasized individual experience of the divine—what Whitman called "the religion inside of man's very own nature."[13]

During the early 1850s, in the years leading up to the initial publication of *Leaves of Grass* (1855), Whitman worked out a new poetic aesthetic based on long unrhymed lines; shaped a personal religious philosophy that drew from Transcendentalism, deism, and Quakerism; and created the poetic persona of "Walt Whitman," a larger-than-life figure with grandiose ambitions to unite the American nation and to promulgate a new democratic spirituality. Within ten years after the publication of the first edition, he had gained his first disciples, readers who seized on his religious message and regarded him as a prophet equivalent to Jesus. By the end of his life, spiritually charged Whitmanite circles had formed in both England and the United States. The largest circle was centered in Camden, New Jersey, where Whitman lived after 1873. Following Whitman's death in 1892, his volunteer secretary, a thirty-three-year-old bank clerk named Horace Traubel, assumed leadership of the Camden circle; two years later he established the Walt Whitman Fellowship. By 1894, Whitmanism had moved from an assemblage of disciples united only by their devotion to the living poet to a fledgling religious organization.

HORACE TRAUBEL AND THE WALT WHITMAN FELLOWSHIP

Horace Traubel, the prime mover of the Whitman Fellowship, was an ambitious and almost maniacally energetic spiritual seeker. In addition to his job as a bank clerk and his position as one of Whitman's literary executors, he was a founding member of the Philadelphia Ethical Society as well as editor and publisher of the monthly *Conservator,* which served in its early years as the unofficial organ of the national Ethical Culture movement. However, following a quarrel with Ethical Culture leaders in 1894, Traubel broke his ties to the movement and allied the *Conservator* with the newly formed Whitman Fellowship.

Initially, the organization flourished. Within its first year, the Fellowship held several meetings, gained more than one hundred twenty members, and established branches in Boston, Chicago, Knoxville, and New York. The mid-

1890s were spiritually heady times for Traubel and the Whitman Fellowship. A poem by Laurens Maynard titled "The Walt Whitman Fellowship" and published in the December 1894 *Conservator* gives some sense of the atmosphere within the organization soon after its founding:

Not with desire to found or sect or school—
Too long the world hath fettered been by creeds;
Too long the standard hath been faith, not deeds,
And dogma ruined what it could not rule.
. . .
Therefore, O master, is our flag unfurled
To stand for Truth and Freedom's cause for aye,
While we together banded in thy name
In sacred comradeship, proclaim
Thy life of love, which in our latter day
Hath mirrored Christ to an apostate world.[14]

Maynard's poem champions Whitman as an apostle of "Truth and Freedom" and, if not a new messiah, at least a "mirror" of Christ. As William James noted, comparisons of Whitman and Jesus were common among Fellowship members. British writer Richard LeGallienne, speaking to the New York branch of the Whitman Fellowship, began his address, "You have welcomed me to you in the name of one of the greatest men that ever lived, you have found me worthy to participate with you in an immediate discipleship—or, at all events, an apostolic succession—to the man to whom we owe the most vital, the most comprehensive, and certainly the most original message that has been sent from God to man in nineteen hundred years."[15]

LeGallienne's address reveals the transatlantic dimensions of Whitmanism. Many of Whitman's most prominent early defenders were British, and a good number of these regarded him as a religious figure. In Bolton, England, a small group of disciples, who playfully called themselves the "Eagle Street College," regularly linked Whitman and Jesus. In an 1893 address to the college, their leader, J. W. Wallace, said that the poet had come to earth "that we might have life and have it more abundantly, he too has given us a gospel of glad tidings and comfort and hope and joy, he too has given us a message which is specially precious to the outcast and lowest classes, he too is a Prince of Peace."[16]

Wallace was in close touch with Horace Traubel, whom he met in 1891, shortly before Whitman's death, when the Englishman made a pilgrimage to Camden. Following Whitman's death, Traubel wrote to Wallace daily, keeping him abreast of American Whitmanite activities. In early 1894, as his plans for a new Whitmanite organization took shape, Traubel imagined that the

British disciples would be eager to join; his ambitions are evident in the institution's full name, the Walt Whitman Fellowship: International. "I look to see it become a big thing—extending the globe across," he burbled in a letter to Wallace.[17]

Traubel, the indefatigable organizer, had played a founding role in Philadelphia's Ethical Society and was poised to become a national leader in the movement when he remade the *Conservator* as the voice of Ethical Culture. But he saw his influence in the Ethical movement evaporate entirely following his clashes with the institution's hierarchy. Now, within weeks of his resignation from the Ethical Society, he had emerged as the head of a liberal religious movement that was congruent with Ethical humanism; that was linked to a figure far greater, in the eyes of many, than Ethical Culture founder Felix Adler; and that already had an international following. "We shall look to you to work up the English branches," he breezily instructed Wallace in January 1894. A month later, absorbed in his plans for the global Whitman Fellowship, he wrote Wallace a curt note explaining that the organization's headquarters would be in Camden: "This must be held the center from which the spokes diverge."[18]

To Traubel's surprise, the English branches refused to meekly accept their assigned place on the periphery of the Whitman Fellowship. A breach opened between Traubel and Wallace that would never be fully closed, and the "International" in the Whitman Fellowship's title was never significantly realized. Traubel's original vision for the Fellowship was grandiose and hierarchical; it was as if he imagined that his modest Camden home might become the Vatican of a vast liberal religious movement. However, within months of the organization's founding, it was clear that the Fellowship would not expand beyond the United States. The Traubel-Wallace clash exemplified a tension that lies at the heart of any new religious movement but that is particularly acute among liberal groups: the balance between individual freedom and organizational cohesion.[19] Traubel initially imagined a role as leader of an international organization, but he quickly ran up against the powerful individualist tendencies of Whitman's admirers. He was well aware of this tension; he knew by heart the words of Whitman's poem "Myself and Mine":

> I call to the world to distrust the accounts of my friends,
>   but listen to my enemies, as I myself do,
> I charge you forever reject those who would expound me,
>   for I cannot expound myself,

I charge that there be no theory or school founded out of me,
I charge you to leave all free, as I have left all free.[20]

Writing to Wallace immediately after Whitman's death, Traubel quoted from this passage. "We must always adopt Walt, *leaving all free as he left all free,*" Traubel wrote, "but we must *cohere* and make the world see our brotherhood."[21] Traubel's insistent underlinings emphasize the tension he felt between Whitmanesque individualism and organizational cohesion.

At the Whitman Fellowship's founding, Traubel imagined that he could honor both individualism and cohesion, but the clash with Wallace shattered his global organizational ambitions and caused him to rethink the Fellowship's nature and purpose. In 1896 he amended the Fellowship's constitution, eliminating the dues and establishing a membership card that read, in full, "I announce myself to be a member of the Walt Whitman Fellowship: International." He also began printing the above passage from "Myself and Mine" at the top of the Fellowship's stationery—a clear announcement that the Fellowship prized individual freedom over institutional strength. In years to come, he would rewrite the Fellowship's early history and claim that he had never intended it to be anything more than a loosely affiliated network of Whitman admirers. Within a few years of its founding, the Fellowship's multiple American branches fell away, and the organization's sole activity reverted to annual Whitman birthday dinners in New York and Chicago. However, if the Whitman Fellowship fell short of Traubel's early ambitions, during its twenty-five-year history its annual meetings, along with the monthly appearances of the *Conservator,* provided a forum for interpretations of Whitman that combined liberal religion and left-wing politics in a culturally influential synthesis.

WHITMANITE SPIRITUALITY AND SOCIALISM

Like most Americans of his generation, Walt Whitman was deeply suspicious of socialism, which he regarded as a foreign ideology at odds with American traditions of democratic equality. Yet after his death, the Walt Whitman Fellowship became a major nexus of liberal spirituality and socialist politics. Many of America's most prominent political radicals—including Clarence Darrow, Emma Goldman, Helen Keller, and Jack London—subscribed to the *Conservator* and either attended Whitman Fellowship gatherings or sent greetings to be read aloud. How was Walt Whitman, a Jacksonian democrat, transformed into the apostle of a spiritualized socialism?

A good part of the answer lies in the ties between the Whitman Fellowship and Eugene V. Debs. Debs, who gained a national reputation in the 1890s as a militant labor union leader, announced his conversion to socialism in 1897 and in 1901 founded the Socialist Party of America, the most successful left-wing party in American history. Debs's success came in large part because of his advocacy of a uniquely American socialism that drew deeply on the nation's democratic and religious traditions. Debs, a famously lyrical orator, repeatedly cited as his inspirations Thomas Jefferson, Abraham Lincoln, Walt Whitman, and Jesus. The notion of a dictatorship of the proletariat was anathema to Debs; his ideal was a rose-colored version of the antebellum Terre Haute, Indiana, of his childhood, a classless, democratic small town. Debs was never a churchgoer, but he absorbed the evangelical Protestant fervor of his Midwestern youth, and Debsian socialism had the flavor of a religious crusade, though one appealing equally to Midwestern evangelicals and northeastern religious liberals. One of the keys to Debs's success was that he enabled Americans disenchanted with traditional religion to transfer their millennial aspirations from individual salvation to the transformation of society. European socialism may have been linked to atheism, but Debs cited Jesus so often that his audiences might well have assumed that Christ had been a member of the Nazareth branch of the Socialist Party.[22]

After the turn of the century, the Whitman Fellowship and the *Conservator* shaped an image of Whitman as a working-class poet sympathetic to Debsian socialism. Gene Debs's punishing speaking schedule prevented him from attending the Whitman Fellowship's annual New York City dinners, but he faithfully sent a greeting each year. His 1905 message is typical: "When the . . . Whitman Fellowship assembles, though far away, I shall be there in heart and soul, and share with you in all the delights of the joyous occasion. 'The dear love of comrades' will pervade the gathering and make it holy, and the hands of dear old Walt will be raised above it in benediction."[23] Debs's brief greeting reveals the close connections of spirituality, socialism, and Walt Whitman among early twentieth-century radicals.

Not everyone within the Fellowship was happy with the organization's embrace of socialist politics. Traubel's coexecutor Thomas Harned, who regarded Whitman as "a mighty spiritual force" and *Leaves of Grass* as a "new gospel," complained that the Fellowship had become dominated by "socialists, anarchists, [and] cranks" and that "Traubel has worked the socialistic racket, much to my exclusion and disgust."[24] However, despite Harned's complaints, Traubel never turned the Whitman Fellowship's meetings into purely political gatherings. Throughout the early twentieth century, the Fellowship mixed political and religious perspectives on Whitman. Its eclecticism is nicely illustrated in the program for the 1911 Whitman birthday gathering; among the speeches were both "What Walt Whitman Means to a Revolutionist" and "The Spiritual and Religious Significance of Whitman." Articles in the *Conservator* frequently combined religion and politics, as in Mildred Bain's "The Liberated Human Spirit," a rambling tribute to Walt Whitman, Horace Traubel, and socialism. In her ecstatic peroration, Bain wrote,

> Socialism is something infinitely bigger and better than a scientific philosophy. It is destined to roll away the stone from the tomb in which humanity is imprisoned. It will literally resurrect the spirit of man. It will let us greet each other with: "How are you, brother?" It will make this present existence seem like the hideous nightmare of some monstrous disordered brain. In fact, we can have no idea how wonderful we'll discover ourselves to be. Nothing less than cosmic creatures, relating ourselves to the whole in beauty and usefulness and joy.[25]

Bain and others in her Whitmanite circle viewed socialism as a millennial religious movement that would usher in a utopia of comradeship. Their rhetoric drew from both Christianity—as in the reference to Jesus' resurrection—and the syncretic religious philosophy of R. M. Bucke, the Whitman disciple and author of *Cosmic Consciousness* (1901), a well-known study of mysticism.

Traubel's own rhetoric united Debsian socialism, liberal spirituality, and Walt Whitman. Until Whitman's death he had written standard prose and conventional rhymed poetry, but afterward he developed a highly distinctive style, producing a staccato but poetic prose and prose-like, Whitmanesque free verse. His poetry is almost exclusively concerned with socialism, but it is a socialism indistinguishable from a sentimental spirituality that romanticizes a strategically undefined "people." "The People Are the Masters of Life" is typical of his work:

> The people are the masters of life: the people, the people!
> So I go about in the streets of cities singing with glad assurance,
> the people, the people!—
> Needing no reasons for my great joy beyond the reasons in my own heart,
> Not asserting myself in dubious words, not being afraid,
> Letting the dissenters and scorners have their unhindered way
> with themselves,
> I for my part figuring life out into magnificent totals of love.[26]

The poem continues in this vein for another fifty-four lines. H. L. Mencken dismissed Traubel's poetry as "dishwatery imitations of Walt Whitman," but

Eugene Debs claimed that Traubel "goes far beyond" Whitman. "He not only brings the old Prophet of Democracy up to date," Debs wrote, "but he traverses untrodden fields and explores new realms in quest of the truth that is to light up the heavens of humanity, banish darkness from the face of the earth, and set free the countless captive children of men."[27] Middle-class Debsian socialists hailed Traubel as "the premier socialist of the day" not despite his sentimental verse but because of it. Traubel's poetry avoided the hard-edged analysis of Marxist economics and the violent appeals of revolutionary politics in favor of the spiritual "niceness" that Carrie Bramen discusses elsewhere in this volume as central to nineteenth-century American culture. Yet if Traubel avoided strident political discourse, the pages of the *Conservator* were open to those interested in combining Whitmanesque spirituality with a wide variety of progressive causes, including civil rights and women's suffrage.

WHITMANISM, RACE, AND GENDER

From its beginning, the Whitman Fellowship advocated for racial equality. One of the rare racially integrated institutions of its era, the Fellowship invited Kelly Miller, a dean at Howard University and a prominent black intellectual, to address an early meeting and then named him a Fellowship officer, a position he held for over two decades. Like other members of the Whitman Fellowship, Miller interpreted Whitman from the perspective of a cosmopolitan religious liberalism. In his 1895 address to the Fellowship, "What Walt Whitman Means to the Negro," he began by describing Whitman as a "universal" poet, akin to the Buddha, the apostle Peter, Paul the evangelist, and other great souls who have dwelt upon "the radiant summit" from which one looks "with equal eye on all below." Miller argued that although other white American writers portrayed the Negro in a servile, contemptible, or ridiculous role, Whitman treated blacks as spiritual equals. "Whitman sounds the key-note of the higher emancipation," Miller wrote. "A great poet is necessarily a great prophet. He sees farthest because he has the most faith."[28]

Miller was uninterested in the Walt Whitman of Camden. He asked rhetorically, "What did [Whitman] do practically in his lifetime for the negro? Beyond the fact that he imbibed the anti-slavery sentiment of his environment, and that this sentiment distills throughout 'Leaves of Grass,' I do not know. Nor does it matter in the least." Miller ignored Whitman the man in favor of the prophetic poet who included both blacks and whites in his spiritual democracy. Miller shared the Whitman Fellowship's liberal religious agenda, its effort to place Whitman in a spiritual succession running from the Buddha through Jesus and the apostles to the present day. He ended his speech, "On this first meeting of the Walt Whitman Fellowship all men can equally join in celebrating the merits of their great Comrade, who, in robust integrity of soul, in intellectual comprehension and power, in catholic range of sympathy, and in spiritual illumination, is to be ranked among the choicest of the sons of men."[29] A vast body of scholarship has examined the relationship between black Protestant churches and the civil rights movement of the 1960s; Miller's connection with the Whitman Fellowship reveals an alternative—and as yet virtually unstudied—stream within the black liberation movement of the late nineteenth and early twentieth centuries: a spiritually cosmopolitan approach that drew as heavily on Whitman's poetry as on the Christian gospels.[30]

Miller aside, few black Americans were connected with the Whitman Fellowship, but women made up more than a third of the organization's membership, and several women served on its board of directors. The Whitman Fellowship enabled them to join together and reach an audience of progressive women and men with arguments that united liberal spirituality and the emancipation of women. Ann Braude has powerfully demonstrated how Spiritualism served the same function during the mid-nineteenth century, but no one has yet studied the connections between Whitmanism and the women's movement.[31] Here I can only sketch the outline of such a study.

One might begin with Helena Born, who served as secretary and then president of the Boston Whitman Fellowship. Her essay "Whitman's Ideal Democracy" demonstrates the connections between Whitmanesque spirituality and a wide variety of progressive causes. Born wrote that Whitmanism was part of a procession flying the banners of "Socialism, Individualism, Communism, Anarchism, Egoism, Mysticism, Universal Brotherhood, Idealism, Sex Reform, Evolution, Revolution, etc."[32] She depicted a Whitman whose democratic vision embraced equally both rich and poor, both women and men, and she cited from *Leaves of Grass* Whitman's claim "I am the poet of the woman the same as the man, / And I say it is as great to be a woman as to be a man."[33] Yet Born did not simply praise Whitman's proclamations of gender equality; she shrewdly noted that his notorious, and seemingly very male, egotism could serve as a model for women. She decried the "excessive fostering of the self-abnegating spirit" in women that was promoted by Victorian gender ideology and held up Whitman's celebration of the self as a counter to the cultural idealization of the self-sacrificing woman.[34] Her argument anticipated by decades Alicia Ostriker's celebrated feminist interpretation of Whitman, which argues that

Whitman's value to women readers lies not in his explicit praise of women but in the model he provides of a writer without limits, willing to cross conventional gender categories in his own person and to claim power without relying on hierarchy or violence.[35]

Although Born mentioned "Sex Reform" in her essay on Whitman, she avoided the controversies surrounding the sex reform movement of her era. However, other women associated with the Whitman Fellowship connected Whitmanesque spirituality and progressive sexual politics. For example, Mabel MacCoy Irwin boldly used Whitman to argue for women's control of their own sexuality. She seized on passages from *Leaves of Grass* such as the one in which Whitman writes, "Without shame the man I like knows and avows the deliciousness of his sex, / Without shame the woman I like knows and avows hers."[36] Irwin advanced her argument through a quasi-evangelical spiritual rhetoric. "Verily one must be born again—born into the life of conscious unity with the race—before Whitman can make himself felt, or his words be understood," she begins her book. Later, she makes the parallels between Whitman and Jesus even more explicit. "Whitman so loved the world," she writes, "that he was determined none should escape his love." She continues, "Let those of us to whom vicarious atonement has been a mystery till now, see the greatest of all object lessons, Walt Whitman; for verily he has borne our sins and iniquities, and by his stripes shall we be healed."[37] Irwin's rhetoric here resembles that of R. M. Bucke, who viewed Whitman as a religious messiah. However, her use of religious rhetoric was largely strategic. Her primary interest was in what she called "woman's sex-emancipation," and she used a religiously inflected language in the service of her radical feminist agenda. Whitman's poetry enabled Irwin to advance an argument that, in its defense of women's control of their bodies and their right to sexual pleasure, broke from the more conservative streams of the women's movement dominant at the time.[38]

However, it is important to note that the Whitman Fellowship was not exempt from the pervasive sexism of American society. In Horace Traubel's correspondence at the Library of Congress, one can find a stern letter from Whitman Fellowship member Helen A. Clarke, chastising him for not inviting a single woman to speak at the 1897 Whitman birthday celebration in New York. "Why is it that when women are in charge they always give [men] such a fair representation, but if men are in charge they overlook women if they possibly can?" she asked.[39] And for all her admiration of Whitman, Clarke was aware of the poet's shortcomings as an advocate of gender equality. In an essay co-authored with her life partner Charlotte Porter, Clarke noted that "in all [Whitman's] singing of comradeship and friendship he makes no direct reference to comradeship between women, which is fast becoming one of the most marked characteristics of modern civilization."[40] As women-loving women, Porter and Clarke were highly conscious of Whitman's silence on the subject of female comradeship, despite his frequent celebrations of love between men.

If the *Conservator* ignored comradeship between women, it also avoided the sexual implications of Whitman's poetry of male friendship. However, Traubel's correspondence reveals that he was not unfamiliar with same-sex passion. The experience of Traubel and other Whitmanites illuminates the complex, contradictory reception of Whitman's doctrine of male comradeship among religious liberals in Great Britain and the United States.

WHITMANISM AND SAME-SEX PASSION

Walt Whitman's most celebrated poems of male comradeship were included in a cluster of verses labeled "Calamus," first published in 1860 and included in every subsequent edition of *Leaves of Grass*. It was not until the 1890s that the word *homosexual* was introduced into the English language, and at the time of their publication and for years afterward, the "Calamus" poems were completely uncontroversial. Whitman's own sexuality was assumed to be unexceptional, and the controversy surrounding *Leaves of Grass* centered on poems of male-female sexuality, such as "To a Common Prostitute." In contrast, "Calamus" poems such as "A Glimpse" were read within the presumably asexual tradition of male friendship poetry:

> A glimpse through an interstice caught,
> Of a crowd of workmen and drivers in a bar-room around the stove
> late of a winter night, and I unremark'd seated in a corner,
> Of a youth who loves me, and whom I love, silently approaching,
> and seating himself near, that he may hold me by the hand,
> A long while amid the noises of coming and going, of drinking and
> oath and smutty jest,
> There we two, content, happy in being together, speaking little,
> perhaps not a word.[41]

Within the "Calamus" poems friendship between men is depicted as a morally pure haven from the noise and smut of the larger world.

However, as the nineteenth century progressed, increasing numbers of men, particularly in Great Britain, began to interpret the "Calamus" poems as expressions of a newly emerging homosexual identity—an identity that was being defined almost entirely through criminological and pathological discourses. Whitman's poetry offered a counterdiscourse of same-sex passion, and Englishmen who were familiar with the emerging field of continental sexology used Whitman's poetry as an alternative and more positive means of understanding and expressing their sexual desires.[42] No one was more serious about this enterprise than man of letters John Addington Symonds. Symonds was widely known as a spiritual seeker; in Walt Whitman he found a poet who illuminated both his spiritual and sexual quests.

Symonds's influential study of Whitman, published in 1893, depicts Whitman as the "prophet of a democratic religion," a mystical poet who "dethrones the gods of old pantheons, because he sees God everywhere around him." Symonds coined the term "cosmic enthusiasm" to describe Whitman's religious vision, defining it simply as "a recognition of divinity in all things."[43] However, his study of Whitman made clear that cosmic enthusiasm combined the immanentist belief common among religious liberals with homoeroticism. Symonds quoted approvingly Whitman's line "I hear and behold God in every object," and he also quoted with relish these lines from "I Sing the Body Electric":

> [T]he expression of a well-made man appears not only in his face,
> It is in his limbs and joints also, it is curiously in the joints of his hips and wrists;
> It is in his walk, the carriage of his neck, the flex of his waist and knees—dress
> does not hide him;
> The strong, sweet, supple quality he has, strikes through the cotton and flannel.
> To see him pass conveys as much as the best poem, perhaps more;
> You linger to see his back, and the back of his neck and shoulder-side.[44]

In Whitman's religious vision a well-made man was no less divine than an infant, a saint, the earth itself. Whitman "recognises divinity in all that lives and breathes upon our planet," Symonds wrote with relief.[45] The poet weaved homoeroticism into the divine fabric of a God-permeated universe, implicitly sanctioning the sexual desires that so tormented Symonds.

In Symonds's book on Walt Whitman, published just after the poet's death, he praised Whitman's cosmic enthusiasm in safely general terms, but he also came much closer to identifying the poet with homosexuality than anyone had yet suggested in print. He acknowledged that Whitman "never suggests that comradeship may occasion the development of physical desire." On the other hand, Symonds continued, the poet "does not in set terms condemn desires, or warn his disciples against their perils. There is indeed a distinctly sensuous side to his conception of adhesiveness." Skirting close to an admission of his own proclivities, he wrote that "those unenviable mortals who are the inheritors of sexual anomalies will recognise their own emotion in Whitman's 'superb friendship, exalté, previously unknown.' . . . Had I not the strongest proof in Whitman's private correspondence with myself that he repudiated any such deductions from his 'Calamus,' I admit that I should have regarded them as justified; and I am not certain whether his own feelings upon this delicate topic may not have altered since the time when 'Calamus' was first composed."[46]

Symonds's statements were the closest anyone had yet come to linking Whitman with "sexual anomalies." The Americans in the Walt Whitman Fellowship were outraged, none more than Horace Traubel. He wrote an angry letter to J. W. Wallace protesting Symonds's implications: "Homosexuality is disease—it is muck and rot—it is decay and muck—and Walt uttered the master-cries of health, of salvation, and purity, of growth and beauty."[47] Traubel was determined to insulate Whitman from any association with the newly emerging medical and legal category of the "homosexual," and during the thirty years of the *Conservator*'s existence, no article appeared linking Whitman to same-sex passion.

Yet at the same time as he defended Whitman from any hint of homosexuality, Traubel was engaged in his own highly spiritualized love affair with a male Whitmanite, Gustave Percival Wiksell. Wiksell, like Traubel, was a married man with a family. A Boston dentist, Wiksell joined the local branch of the Whitman Fellowship soon after it was founded, and in 1903 became president of the Walt Whitman Fellowship, a position he held for the rest of the group's existence. He met Traubel in 1894, and within a few years the two men became lovers. The physically passionate nature of their relationship is clear from their correspondence. "I dream of . . . the little bed in your paradise and the two arms of a brother that accept me in their divine partnership," Traubel wrote shortly before a trip to Boston. After his visit he wrote longingly, "I sit here and write you a letter. It is not a pen that is writing. It is the lips that you have kissed. It is the body that you have traversed over and over with your consecrating palm. Do you not feel that body? Do you not feel the return?"[48]

These letters, with their talk of a "divine" partnership and a "consecrating" palm, reveal how the two men mingled the erotic and the religious, interpreting their love affair in spiritual terms. The Christmas season seemed to bring their eroticized spirituality to its height. "Oh darling my brother I hold your hands in mine," Wiksell wrote to Traubel in December 1901. "I kiss you and thank God for you. You are one of God's ties to hold me to the holy things of love." For his part, Traubel wrote to Wiksell on December 25, 1903, "When it is Christmas and I think of Christ I find it natural and easy to think of you. When Christ is present to me you also are present to me. You have done the work of Christ, and that is better than to wear his name. . . . I send you a kiss for this sacred day."[49] Neither Traubel nor Wiksell identified himself as Christian—that is, they did not "wear [Christ's] name"—but they borrowed Christian terminology as a sanction for their affair.

They also borrowed from the language of Theosophy. There was an overlap in membership between the Walt Whitman Fellowship and the Theosophical Society, and although Wiksell and Traubel were no more formally Theosophist than they were Christian, they were influenced by Theosophy's eclectic appropriations from Asian religions. Wiksell wrote Traubel after a visit, "When I left you on the train . . . I had no feeling of loss as we often feel when one we love goes away. I did not have any feeling of separation. Your visit was a bodily one—spiritually we are never separated. 'Kill out all sense of separateness' is one of the laws of yoga. This will be the real heaven when all men have become one and there are no separate persons in the world. My lips to yours dear one."[50] Wiksell's invocation of a vaguely defined but assuredly mystical "yoga" reflects the intersections between Whitmanism and Theosophy in the late nineteenth and early twentieth centuries. During the first year of the Whitman Fellowship's existence, for example, Bucke delivered a speech on cosmic consciousness to the Philadelphia Theosophical Society that was subsequently published in the *Conservator.*[51] Joy Dixon has analyzed in detail the ways in which Theosophical doctrines provided men in the United States and the United Kingdom with an alternative, non-pathological means for understanding same-sex desires;[52] I would argue that Whitmanism offered an even richer discursive field for the spiritualized expression of homosexual passion.

Certainly, Traubel and Wiksell invoked Walt Whitman far more often than the laws of yoga. After 1903 the two men almost always wrote their love letters on official stationery of the Walt Whitman Fellowship, which listed their names below Whitman's: Wiksell as president and Traubel as secretary-treasurer. Whitman's name literally hovered over their correspondence, and they referred constantly to *Leaves of Grass.* Traubel's connection to Whitman was important for Wiksell, who had never met Whitman personally. "In you I find alive so much of our dear friend Walt," he wrote Traubel early in their relationship. When the first volume of Traubel's Whitman biography appeared in 1906, Wiksell's indirect connection to Whitman seemed to intensify enormously: "I feel now as though I know as much about him as you yourself and have kissed his bearded lips. Through you I arrive at kinship with the divine compassionate man."[53] The "divine" Whitman's poetry provided a spiritualized sanction for their love affair. Whitmanism offered Wiksell and Traubel a way to sanctify their love during the opening decades of the twentieth century, when same-sex passion was being turned into the supposedly deviant sexual category of homosexuality. Their identities as members of the Whitman Fellowship enabled them to turn their backs on the emerging psychiatric-legal understanding of male love and locate their passion within a cosmopolitan religious discourse that borrowed terms from Christianity, Theosophy, and, above all, *Leaves of Grass.*

THE DECLINE AND FALL OF WHITMANISM

The Whitman Fellowship's existence in the early part of the twentieth century was precarious; both the Fellowship and the *Conservator* were chronically underfunded, and on numerous occasions Traubel had to beg contributions from subscribers in order to keep the magazine from going under. Neither the Fellowship nor the *Conservator* survived Horace Traubel's death in 1919. Whitmanism had always been a lightly institutionalized movement of independent spiritual seekers, held together largely by Horace Traubel's boundless energy. With the simultaneous disappearance of the movement's high priest and its major organ of communication the religious appreciation of Whitman reverted to a purely individual phenomenon.

Moreover, by the time of Traubel's death, cultural receptiveness to poetry's prophetic dimensions had radically dwindled. In part, this decline is attributable to the institutionalization of literary study within the academy. When Walt Whitman began his career as a poet, departments of English did not exist in higher education. However, by 1919, when Traubel died and the Whitman Fellowship folded, the study of English-language literature was firmly institutionalized, and even so radical a poet as Whitman had been incorporated into the emerging canon of American literature.[54]

The newly created professors of English saw it as part of their mission to rescue writers like Whitman from amateur enthusiasts and to subject them to a dispassionate, professional, and thoroughly secular analysis. Within a remarkably brief period, they succeeded. In his scholarly history of Whitman's

American reception, published in 1950, Charles Willard portrayed the early twentieth century as a period of struggle between crackpot disciples and rational academics. "The last of the band who knew [Whitman] personally, loved him, and believed him the founder of the religion of the future" were gone by mid-century, he noted approvingly, and discussion of the poet was firmly established on the plane of "sane and traditional literary criticism."[55]

The institutionalization of literary studies succeeded in marginalizing amateur enthusiasm for *Leaves of Grass,* but it did not entirely extinguish the interest in Whitman among spiritual seekers. In the course of researching my book on Whitman's nineteenth-century disciples, I encountered numerous individuals in the United States and England who consider Whitman to be an important religious figure. I attended a service at a Unitarian chapel in Bolton, England, where the minister salted his sermon with quotations from *Leaves of Grass;* I participated in a guided-meditation session at a Quaker meetinghouse in Washington, D.C., that used Whitman's words as a guide to higher states of consciousness; and I met with the New Jersey secretary of commerce in his office to talk about how, as a teenager living in Camden, he felt a mystical connection to Whitman as he jogged past the poet's tomb in Harleigh Cemetery. These modern-day Whitmanites have no institutional ambitions for a religion "extending the globe across," as Traubel had originally envisioned. Never having been in Whitman's charismatic presence, they do not imagine that the poet will supersede Jesus, as Bucke thought possible. Instead, *Leaves of Grass* forms one elements of these readers' cosmopolitan, individualistic spirituality. Their ongoing interest in the religious dimensions of *Leaves of Grass* suggests that Whitman's poetry will continue to be important not just to scholars concerned with the history of liberal religion but to anyone interested in tracing the contours of contemporary spirituality.[56]

NOTES

My thanks to Jim Brazell, Ann Marie Nicolosi, and Leigh Schmidt for help with research and to Tim Clydesdale and Amy Kittelstrom for comments on drafts of this essay. Portions of this essay are adapted from my book *Worshipping Walt: The Whitman Disciples* (Princeton: Princeton University Press, 2008).

1. William James, *The Varieties of Religious Experience* (1902; Cambridge, Mass.: Harvard University Press, 1985), 77.

2. The most important recent interpreter of the religious dimensions of *Leaves of Grass* is David Kuebrich; see his *Minor Prophecy: Walt Whitman's New American Religion* (Bloom-

ington: Indiana University Press, 1989) and "Religion and the Poet-Prophet," in *A Companion to Walt Whitman,* ed. Donald D. Kummings (Oxford: Blackwell, 2006), 197–215. M. Jimmie Killingsworth traces the history of religious approaches to Whitman in *The Growth of "Leaves of Grass": The Organic Tradition in Whitman Studies* (Columbia, S.C.: Camden House, 1993), 85–101.

3. Catherine L. Albanese, *American Spiritualities* (Bloomington: Indiana University Press, 2001), 388. Albanese's *A Republic of Mind and Spirit* (New Haven: Yale University Press, 2007), an extensive history of metaphysical religion, does not mention Whitman, but it is clear that Whitmanism fits into the capacious category of metaphysical religion as defined by Albanese.

4. Lawrence Buell, "Religion on the American Mind," *American Literary History* 19, no. 1 (spring 2007): 39.

5. Walt Whitman, *Notebooks and Unpublished Prose Manuscripts,* ed. Edward F. Grier, 6 vols. (New York: New York University Press, 1984), 1:353; and *Notes and Fragments Left by Walt Whitman,* ed. Richard Maurice Bucke (London, Ont.: A. Talbot, 1899), 55.

6. Lawrence Buell, *New England Literary Culture: From Revolution through Renaissance* (New York: Cambridge University Press, 1986), 166–90.

7. T. E. Hulme, "Romanticism and Classicism," in *Speculations: Essays on Humanism and the Philosophy of Art* (London: Routledge & Kegan Paul, 1924), 118. The most important study of literary romanticism and religion is M. H. Abrams, *Natural Supernaturalism: Tradition and Revolution in Romantic Literature* (New York: W. W. Norton, 1971). Hoxie Neale Fairchild, *Religious Trends in English Poetry,* vol. 3 (New York: Columbia University Press, 1949), remains valuable. See also the first chapter of Nancy Easterlin, *Wordsworth and the Question of "Romantic Religion"* (Lewisburg, Penn.: Bucknell University Press, 1996).

8. Thomas Carlyle, *On Heroes, Hero-Worship, and the Heroic in History* (1840; Boston: Houghton Mifflin, 1907), 110.

9. Ralph Waldo Emerson, *The Journals and Miscellaneous Notebooks of Ralph Waldo Emerson,* ed. William H. Gilman et al., vol. 5 (Cambridge, Mass.: Harvard University Press, 1965), 186.

10. Walt Whitman, "Democratic Vistas," in *Complete Poetry and Collected Prose,* ed. Justin Kaplan (New York: Library of America, 1982)—all subsequent quotations from Whitman are taken from this volume, which is cited as *CPCP;* and Alfred Kazin, *God and the American Writer* (New York: Knopf, 1997), 118.

11. Walt Whitman, "Song of Myself," *CPCP,* 244–45.

12. Leigh Eric Schmidt, *Restless Souls: The Making of American Spirituality* (New York: HarperSanFrancisco, 2005), 1–23; and Jeffrey J. Kripal, *Esalen: America and the Religion of No Religion* (Chicago: University of Chicago Press, 2007), 3–24, 463–68.

13. Walt Whitman, "Elias Hicks," *CPCP,* 1221.

14. Laurens Maynard, "The Walt Whitman Fellowship," *Conservator* 5 (December 1894): 147.

15. Richard LeGallienne, "Walt Whitman: An Address," *Conservator* 9 (March 1898): 4.

16. J. W. Wallace, "Walt Whitman's Birthday," May 31, 1893, Walt Whitman Collection, Bolton (England) Central Library.

17. Traubel to Wallace, February 12, 1894, Whitman Collection, Bolton.

18. Traubel to Wallace, January 28, 1894, and March 1, 1894, Whitman Collection, Bolton.

19. The sociological literature on new religious movements is vast; for recent overviews

see Lorne L. Dawson, *Comprehending Cults: The Sociology of New Religious Movements,* 2nd ed. (Don Mills, Ont.: Oxford University Press, 2006); and *Oxford Handbook of New Religious Movements,* ed. James R. Lewis (New York: Oxford University Press, 2004).

20. Walt Whitman, "Myself and Mine," *CPCP,* 380.

21. Traubel to Wallace, June 14, 1892, Sixsmith Collection of Traubel Correspondence, John Rylands University Library, Manchester, England.

22. The best guide to Debs, the socialism of his era, and its religious dimensions remains Nick Salvatore's *Eugene V. Debs: Citizen and Socialist* (Urbana: University of Illinois Press, 1982). See also Harold W. Currie, "The Religious Views of Eugene V. Debs," *Mid-America* 54 (July 1972): 147–56; and Jacob H. Dorn, "'In Spiritual Communion': Eugene V. Debs and the Socialist Christians," *Journal of the Gilded Age and Progressive Era* 2, no. 3 (July 2003): 303–25. Bryan K. Garman analyzes the relationships among Debs, Traubel, Whitman, and socialism in *A Race of Singers: Whitman's Working-Class Hero from Guthrie to Springsteen* (Chapel Hill: University of North Carolina Press, 2000), 1–78.

23. Eugene V. Debs, *Conservator* 16 (June 1905): 56.

24. Thomas B. Harned, "Whitman and the Future," *Conservator* 6 (June 1895): 54, 55; and Harned to Wallace, n.d., Whitman Collection, Bolton.

25. Mildred Bain, "The Liberated Human Spirit," *Conservator* 29 (November 1918): 134.

26. Horace Traubel, *Optimos* (New York: B. W. Huebsch, 1910), 281.

27. H. L. Mencken, "Optimos," *Conservator* 22 (August 1911): 87; Eugene V. Debs, foreword to William English Walling, *Whitman and Traubel* (New York: Albert and Charles Boni, 1916); and Eugene V. Debs, "Whitman and Traubel," *Conservator* 28 (July 1917): 77.

28. Kelly Miller, "What Walt Whitman Means to the Negro," *Conservator* 6 (July 1895): 70. The speech was reprinted in Miller's collection of essays *Race Adjustment* (1908); that volume was reprinted as *Radicals and Conservatives, and Other Essays on the Negro in America* (New York: Schocken, 1968).

29. Miller, "What Walt Whitman Means to the Negro," 73.

30. Miller's speech receives a literary and historical—though not a religious—analysis in George B. Hutchinson, "Whitman and the Black Poet: Kelly Miller's Speech to the Walt Whitman Fellowship," *American Literature* 61, no. 1 (March 1989): 46–58. Barbara Dianne Savage devotes a chapter to black liberal Protestantism in *Your Spirits Walk beside Us: The Politics of Black Religion* (Cambridge, Mass.: Harvard University Press, 2008), but her discussion begins with Benjamin Mays, who was a generation younger than Miller.

31. Ann Braude, *Radical Spirits: Spiritualism and Women's Rights in Nineteenth-Century America,* 2nd ed. (Bloomington: Indiana University Press, 2001).

32. Helena Born, *Whitman's Ideal Democracy* (Boston: Everett, 1902), 18.

33. Walt Whitman, "Song of Myself," *CPCP,* 207.

34. Born, *Whitman's Ideal Democracy,* 19, 60–61.

35. Alicia Ostriker, "Loving Walt Whitman and the Problem of America," in *The Continuing Presence of Walt Whitman,* ed. Robert K. Martin (Iowa City: University of Iowa Press, 1992), 217–31.

36. Walt Whitman, "A Woman Waits for Me," *CPCP,* 259.

37. Mabel MacCoy Irwin, *Whitman: The Poet-Liberator of Woman* (New York: By the author, 1905), 11–12, 52, 56.

38. On the American women's movement at the opening of the twentieth century, see two classic studies: Nancy Cott, *The Grounding of Modern Feminism* (New Haven: Yale University Press, 1987); and Eleanor Flexner and Ellen Fitzpatrick, *Century of Struggle: The Wom-*

an's Rights Movement in the United States, enlarged ed. (Cambridge, Mass.: Harvard University Press, 1996). Beryl Satter's *Each Mind a Kingdom: American Women, Sexual Purity, and the New Thought Movement, 1875–1920* (Berkeley: University of California Press, 1999) shows how the New Thought movement, which was contemporaneous with Whitmanism and which included many women as leaders, embraced the dominant cultural ideology of women's sexual purity.

39. Helen Clarke to Horace Traubel, May 5, 1897, Horace Traubel and Anne Montgomerie Traubel Papers, Library of Congress.

40. Helen Clarke and Charlotte Endymion Porter, "A Short Reading Course in Whitman," *Poet-Lore* 6 (December 1894): 645.

41. Walt Whitman, "A Glimpse," *CPCP* 283. Jonathan Ned Katz, *Love Stories: Sex between Men before Homosexuality* (Chicago: University of Chicago Press, 2001) offers an excellent introduction to both Whitman's "Calamus" poems and nineteenth-century sexuality.

42. On nineteenth-century continental sexology, see Joseph Bristow, *Sexuality* (London: Routledge, 1997), 12–61; Peter Gay, *The Tender Passion* (New York: Oxford University Press, 1986), 219–37; David F. Greenberg, *The Construction of Homosexuality* (Chicago: University of Chicago Press, 1988), 397–433; and Jeffrey Weeks, *Sex, Politics, and Society: The Regulation of Sexuality since 1800*, 2nd ed. (New York: Longman, 1989), 141–59.

43. John Addington Symonds, *Walt Whitman: A Study* (London: John C. Nimmo, 1893), 1, 89, 31, 19.

44. Walt Whitman, "Song of Myself," *CPCP*, 244; and Whitman, "I Sing the Body Electric," quoted in Symonds, *Walt Whitman: A Study*, 91.

45. Symonds, *Walt Whitman: A Study*, 90.

46. Ibid., 157, 72, 75–76.

47. Traubel to Wallace, January 10, 1893, Whitman Collection, Bolton.

48. Traubel to Gustave Percival Wiksell, January 3, 1904, and May 12, 1904, Gustave Percival Wiksell Papers, 1855–1939, Library of Congress.

49. Wiksell to Traubel, December 30, 1901, Traubel Collection, Library of Congress; and Traubel to Wiksell, December 25, 1903, Wiksell Collection, Library of Congress.

50. Wiksell to Traubel, December 28, 1903, Traubel Collection, Library of Congress.

51. R. M. Bucke, "Cosmic Consciousness," *Conservator* 5 (May 1894): 37–39, 51–54.

52. Joy Dixon, "Sexology and the Occult: Sexuality and Subjectivity in Theosophy's New Age," *Journal of the History of Sexuality* 7, no. 3 (January 1997): 409–33; see also Joy Dixon, *Divine Feminine: Theosophy and Feminism in England* (Baltimore: Johns Hopkins University Press, 2001.

53. Wiksell to Traubel, June 27, 1897, and [1906], Traubel Collection, Library of Congress.

54. The standard history of the creation of English as a university subject is Gerald Graff, *Professing Literature: An Institutional History* (Chicago: University of Chicago Press, 1987).

55. Charles B. Willard, *Whitman's American Fame: The Growth of His Reputation in America after 1892* (Providence, R.I.: Brown University, 1950), 32.

56. The individualistic spirituality of contemporary Whitmanites—as well as of their nineteenth-century predecessors—reflects the "new religious consciousness" that Lorne L. Dawson analyzes in *Comprehending Cults*, 183–85; the "New Spirituality" whose origin Linda Woodhead explores in "The World's Parliament of Religions and the Rise of Alternative Spirituality," in *Reinventing Christianity: Nineteenth-Century Contexts*, ed. Linda Woodhead (Aldershot: Ashgate, 2001), 270–91; and the "progressive spirituality" that Gordon Lynch analyzes at length in *The New Spirituality: An Introduction to Progressive Belief in the Twenty-*

first Century (London: I. B. Tauris, 2007). On contemporary spirituality, see also Christopher Partridge, "Alternative Spiritualities, New Religions, and the Reenchantment of the West," *Oxford Handbook of New Religious Movements,* 39–67; Wade Clark Roof, *Spiritual Marketplace: Baby Boomers and the Remaking of American Religion* (Princeton: Princeton University Press, 1999); and Robert Wuthnow, *After Heaven: Spirituality in America since the 1950s* (Berkeley: University of California Press, 1998).

TWO

The Christology of Niceness

Harriet Beecher Stowe, the Jesus Novel, and Sacred Trivialities

CARRIE TIRADO BRAMEN

It is taken for granted today that niceness is one of Jesus' defining traits; but not everyone is happy about this fact. Paul Coughlin recounts in his self-help book, *No More Christian Nice Guy* (2005), how he grew up with the iconic image of "Jesus [as] the Supreme Nice Guy," an image that he blames for creating passive and spineless Christian men. "We choke on a Victorian Jesus, a caricature that has turned men into mice." Instead, he calls for a dissident Jesus, one who loves a "good fight."[1] This dismissal of niceness is not unique to the evangelical Christian press. The literary critic Terry Eagleton, in his introduction to the Verso edition of *The Gospels,* insists that Jesus is "no mild-eyed plaster saint but a relentless, fiercely uncompromising activist," who "is interested in what people do, not in what they feel."[2] Where Eagleton and Coughlin want a more virile Jesus, one more invested in action than feeling, the Pauline turn in recent continental theory finds Jesus a rather pathetic figure, not worthy of serious analysis. Giorgio Agamben, for instance, begins his study of Paul's Letter to the Romans by quoting Jacob Taubes's wry observation that "Hebrew literature on Jesus presents him in benevolent terms—as 'a nice guy.'"[3] Jesus' niceness serves a productive function: it creates Paul's complexity as a messianic thinker within a Jewish tradition. As an iconic figure of niceness, Jesus still sacrifices for the sake of others: in this case, for the sake of Paul's theological depth.

I want to situate the banality of the nice Jesus and its historical origins in the nineteenth century in the context of the rise of liberal Christianity. The story of the change from an understanding of God as a wrathful, authoritarian Calvinist God—full of fire and brimstone—to a perception of the gentle benevolence of a liberal Christian God is a familiar one. Whether it is Ann Douglas bemoaning the decline of Calvinism and the rise of vacuous sentimentalism or religious historians' comprehensive overviews of American Christianity, the claim that the nineteenth century witnessed a significant transformation of religious authority has become something of a historiographic cliché. Not only is the nice Jesus banal, but so is the historical narrative that underwrites him.

My objective is to take banality seriously by describing the formation of this cliché as well as unpacking it. Banality tends to be overlooked as an analytic term precisely because it appears to be so obvious. Working against this tendency, however, several thinkers have attempted to give depth to their explorations of the banal. "Banality?" asks Henri Lefebvre. "Why should the study of the banal itself be banal?"[4] Maurice Blanchot similarly recognizes that "the everyday is platitude, but this banality is also what is most important, if it brings us back to existence in its very spontaneity and as it is lived—in the moment when, lived, it escapes every speculative formulation, perhaps all coherence, all regularity."[5] This romantic understanding of the everyday, where boredom and repetition can yield utopian and political aspirations, justifies the study of banality by showing its capacity for what Lefebvre describes as "the surreal, the extraordinary, the surprising."

But what about the banality of the everyday that remains resolutely ordinary, defined against attempts to redeem it through spectacular variations? This banal form of banality, which lacks the dimension of the magical or the mysterious, is more complex than it appears at first glance, and this complexity emerges more clearly when we study the similarities between banality and two closely related concepts: niceness and triviality. As I will demonstrate shortly, in the nineteenth century, both banality and niceness are seen as ways to infuse everyday encounters and associations with a habitual ease so as to minimize conflict and awkwardness. Moreover, both concepts are deemed to be little more than clichés, hackneyed formations not worthy of serious study. Not surprisingly, there is a close relation between banality and niceness on the one hand and triviality on the other, a concept that is treated in a similarly dismissive fashion.

Significantly, the meaning of "nice," as given in dictionaries, is intimately related to that of "trivial." The synonymic relation between "nice" and "trivial" first appears during the Renaissance, but becomes increasingly insignificant by the nineteenth century; "trivial" is a minor definition of "nice" in Webster's 1828 dictionary. Although the association of niceness with triviality was considered to be obsolete by the postbellum period, I want to argue that the trinity of banality, niceness, and triviality continues to feature prominently in nineteenth-century America, and in a most unexpected form: representations of Jesus. But exactly how do these undervalued concepts of the everyday underwrite such a sacred figure? How, in other words, is the banality of niceness effectively incarnated in the nineteenth-century American Jesus?

The rise of the nice Jesus in the nineteenth century coincides with the proliferation of sects, or what was called the "Great Diversification" of creeds in American religion, when Christians were overwhelmed with consumer options ranging from Methodism and Unitarianism to Millerism and Mormonism. According to Stephen Prothero in *American Jesus: How the Son of God Became a National Icon,* "preachers began to respond to the new Babel of denominations by offering a simpler message. Instead of marketing predestination or free will, the Bible or the Baptists, they began to offer religious shoppers a new relationship with Jesus."[6] This new relationship was based on a personal and intimate bond with Jesus, who became less divine and more human. This personalization of God as friend, epitomized in the popular mid-century hymn "What a Friend We Have in Jesus" (1855), became a religious type as Christianity changed from a religion based on doctrine and theology to one focused on the personality of Jesus. For preachers as well as for writers, the nice Jesus as a Christian type became a way to market Christianity to an increasingly skeptical age, but it can also be seen as a way to inject new vitality into religion.

SACRED TRIVIALITIES

A major writer involved in the formation of the nice Jesus—the Victorian Jesus that Paul Coughlin rejects—is Harriet Beecher Stowe, whose work develops a conceptual understanding of the superficial that has religious, social, and political consequences. By appreciating the significance of the trivial, we can read Stowe as a religious modernist who understands the potential of literature to revitalize Christian platitudes. She makes Christianity "new" again not by shocking the reader into an epiphany, but through a more gentle approach that awakens the reader's religious sensibilities by exploring, through the novel form, seemingly trivial details that highlight characterization and social relationships. Stowe describes this technique in her preface to *Uncle Tom's Cabin:* "The poet, the painter, and the artist, now seek out and embellish the common and gentler humanities of life, and, under the allurements of fiction, breathe a humanizing and subduing influence, favorable to the development of the great principles of Christian brotherhood."[7] Although *Uncle Tom's Cabin,* with its portrayal of the tragic violence of slavery, seems like the antithesis of the trivial, Stowe's understanding of the sacred and the tragic derives, in part, from an appreciation of the power of banality.

For Stowe, banality can be both a redemptive and a destructive force. Her own biography demonstrates the likelihood of the latter: how the details of everyday life can simply overwhelm the individual. By the late 1830s, Stowe, a mother of three young children, experienced bouts of hysteria as she became overwhelmed by the domestic minutiae of family life. "All my days are made up of details," she wrote to a friend in 1838. As Lora Romero observes, Stowe as well as her sister Catharine Beecher "understood hysteria to result from absorption in details."[8] The cure, according to Beecher, is systematization: a method of organizing domestic details so that they do not result in the fragmentation of the woman's psyche, thus rendering her nervous and excitable. Although Stowe rationally understood the importance of organizing the details of daily life, she was temperamentally unsuited to her sister's regime. As she wrote her husband in 1845, she was "constitutionally careless and too impetuous and impulsive easily to maintain that consistency and order which is necessary in a family."[9]

The aspect of ordinariness that interests Stowe is not the arrangement of things, which is what preoccupies her older sister, but rather how the banality of niceness works to inform the mundane relationships that structure our daily lives. Stowe is the most important nineteenth-century theorist of niceness, and in her work niceness functions as an expression of democratic sociability that gives form to interpersonal encounters. For Stowe, niceness integrates three important aspects of religious modernism. First, niceness is an expression of Christian sociability, or what was described in the nineteenth-century Christian press as a "social democracy," based on the belief that "man reaches fullness of life not alone but in relations."[10] Second, religious liberalism assumes a liberal subject who is generous and open-hearted. For an evangelical writer like Stowe, the liberal subject is the evangelical's fantasy—a subject always open to persuasion. Compared to the rigidity of orthodoxy, the liberal character is largely defined by flexibility and open-mindedness. "The charm of polite society," writes Stowe in a sketch called "Self-Will," "is formed by that sort of freedom and facility in all the members of a circle which makes each one pliable to the influences of the others."[11] The liberal Christian, moreover, is susceptible to influence, a susceptibility that is a sign not of weakness but of a democratic sensibility. Third, to convey niceness in aesthetic terms, Stowe employs the novel, a genre that is designed "primarily to please," to quote *The Methodist Quarterly Review* in 1860.[12]

Stowe brings together Christianity, liberalism, and the novel because of what they have in common; all three depend on pleasing, whether the potential convert or the reader considered as a consumer. The nice Jesus is the literal incarnation of pleasing as a form of persuasion. Like the nineteenth-century French historian Ernest Renan, who describes Jesus' voice in *The Life of Jesus* (1863) as "sweet," Stowe says that Jesus possesses a "sweet voice" and "graceful manner."[13] As Bryan Garsten has argued in *Saving Persuasion* (2006), "the word 'persuade' arises etymologically from the same root as the words 'suave' and 'sweet,' which reminds us that democratic persuasion requires insinuating oneself into the good graces of one's audience."[14]

THE BANALITY OF NICENESS

Stowe develops this social understanding of liberal Christianity through a concept that I call "the banality of niceness," a combination of the social with the sacred, the mundane with the spiritual.[15] For Stowe, and for liberal Christianity more generally, the banality of niceness is a social liturgy, made up of the seemingly insignificant rituals of association, where the sacred and the ordinary meet to give form to the everyday. Stowe illustrates this concept in a short sketch called "Home Religion" (1870), where a husband and wife have an amicable disagreement about niceness. The husband advises his wife that the "outward expression of all good things is apt to degenerate into mere form." He earnestly insists that sincerity should guide outward behavior, otherwise social niceties become merely superficial. The wife counters her husband's argument with a defense of superficial niceness:

> The outward expression of social good feeling becomes a mere form; but for that reason must we meet each other like oxen? Not say, 'Good morning,' or 'Good evening,' or 'I am happy to see you'? Must we never use any of the forms of mutual good will, except in those moments when we are excited by a real, present emotion? What would become of society?[16]

Stowe defends niceness not on the grounds of its "feel[ing] right," the famous phrase that appears at the end of *Uncle Tom's Cabin,* but rather in terms of the calm formalization of manners. Stowe, the sentimentalist, makes a rather unsentimental case for niceness through an argument that validates "the forms of mutual good will," and, later, "forms of religion," as the structures that sustain social cohesion. One does not have to feel genuine "good will" in order to behave in an appropriate manner. Stowe's wife liberates us from the burden of emotional authenticity. To act as the husband recommends, requiring every mundane exchange to derive from a sincere inner feeling, would be emotionally exhausting. Niceness establishes a form of sociality that arranges mundane encounters into a predictable pattern, a pattern that is an example of what the sociologist Pierre Bourdieu calls "codification." "To codify means to formalize," according to Bourdieu, and codification is a type of symbolic ordering that minimizes ambiguity in particular situations, such as traffic at an intersection.[17] By standardizing trivial exchanges, niceness represents a form of codification that makes daily interactions and communications relatively clear.

The banality of niceness is a religious concept for Stowe because both niceness and religion provide social and spiritual comfort by anchoring the vicissitudes of life in the predictable rhythms of the everyday. Here, form takes precedence over feeling, and the positions exemplify two conflicting sides of Stowe's own ideological position, namely that a civic society requires both a formalization of social niceties and genuine fellow-feeling. That Stowe plays with gendered stereotypes in casting this dialogue, with the husband, the male sentimentalist, arguing for authentic emotion, while the wife wants a more impersonal, formalist model of social cohesion, points to the subtlety of her own narrative tactic, which expands the bounds of the conventional through the familiarity of a cozy fireside chat.

Niceness has a far greater degree of versatility than either compassion or sympathy, because it can represent both a form of anti-social sociality, a way of maintaining a distance from others, and a means of initiating a superficial social encounter that may develop into something more meaningful. The term's versatility is a sign of its anti-essentialism, a trait that allows Stowe to liberate niceness from feeling and sincerity. Emerson articulates a similar understanding of the significance of the banal in "Experience": "We live amid surfaces, and the true art of life is to skate well on them," because this ability, according to Emerson, allows us to negotiate the "mixture of power and form" that defines life.[18] Niceness, for Stowe, is precisely this "mixture of power and form," a morphology of power that models democratic authority through everyday interpersonal encounters.

FOOTSTEPS OF THE MASTER AND THE AESTHETICS OF ORDINARINESS

If "Home Religion" is Stowe's manifesto on the banality of niceness, then her narrative of the life of Christ, published seven years later in 1877, is its incarnation. *Footsteps of the Master* is a Victorian rewriting of the Gospels that combines biography with the novel, creating an eclectic collection that also includes poems and hymns from well-known writers of the day such as Alfred Lord Tennyson and Elizabeth Barrett Browning. Although advertised as an ideal Christmas gift in 1877, and indeed widely read, this book was seen by reviewers of the time as not up to the same literary standard as *Uncle Tom's Cabin*. It was, however, a book that Stowe thoroughly enjoyed writing. In a letter to her son Charles in 1876, she wrote, "I would much rather have written another such a book as *Footsteps of the Master,* but all, even the religious papers, are gone mad on serials."[19] In her obituary in *Current Literature* in 1896, *Footsteps* is mentioned, alongside *Uncle Tom's Cabin* and *Dred,* as one of her most memorable works.[20] And yet this book is not mentioned in the many recent studies of the nineteenth-century Jesus novel.[21]

One book that does receive attention in these recent studies is one of the best-selling Jesus novels of the nineteenth century, Joseph Holt Ingraham's *The Prince of the House of David* (1855). Ingraham, an ordained Episcopal priest, describes Jesus as having a calm face with soft and expressive eyes, and possessing a demeanor that combines "intelligence, gentleness, amiability and noble ardor." We are also told that he enjoys "domestic intercourse and friendly companionship." Ingraham's Jesus combines amiability and gentleness with sex appeal, the embodiment of a Byronesque figure whose "hair was long, and wildly free about his neck; he wore a loose sack of camel's hair, and his right arm was naked to the shoulder."[22] Ingraham was a prolific writer of boys' adventure stories in the 1840s (he told Longfellow that he had written twenty books in one year) and known for his excessive descriptions; his distinctive style comes into its own, not surprisingly, with the crucifixion scene. He carefully amplifies the sensationalist gore of the crucifixion, and his text is replete with aural details of "the first blow upon the dreadful nails," "the rattling of the hard cord" that binds Jesus to the cross, and the "ringing of the spikes." "Great drops of sweat, when they nailed his feet to the wood, stood upon his forehead." These details highlight Jesus' heroic fortitude in the midst of violence and pain, juxtaposing his calmness against "these howling Jews," who are depicted as a hysterical mass that the Romans regrettably must appease.[23] Combining religious instruction with anti-Semitic truisms (Jews as Christ-killers), *The Prince of the House of David* was championed by those who considered novel reading a sin. Ingraham's son, Prentiss, irreverently describes this book, together with the two others that his father would write about the New Testament, as "dime novels of the Bible."[24]

Breaking with the popular template of the dime novel, Stowe inscribes Jesus within a tradition of sentimental realism, portraying him not as a miracle-worker but as an ordinary person, as a living presence rather than as an action hero or an iconic figure on the cross. In representing Jesus' ordinariness by portraying him as a social being with friends and family, Stowe weds two seemingly antithetical discourses: the banal and the sacred. The exceptional story of Jesus can be told within the rhythms of the everyday, characterized by such things as dinner engagements, feasts, and a tidy home. Stowe seeks to revitalize Christianity not by turning to the exceptional but by using the excessively familiar as a way to defamiliarize Jesus and make him worthy of notice again.

Stowe and other liberal Protestants of the nineteenth century invoked the term "vitality" as a response to the Victorian ennui toward Christianity that John Stuart Mill anatomizes so effectively in *On Liberty*. Mill argues that Christian doctrines had lost their vitality because they had become a habit of mind with no effect on the believer. Christianity, according to Mill, was "full of meaning and vitality for those who originate [doctrines and creeds]," but now the "doctrines have no hold on ordinary believers—are not a power in their minds." Rather, the "sayings of Christ coexist passively in their minds, producing hardly any effect beyond what is caused by mere listening to words so amiable and bland."[25] This nineteenth-century crisis of belief, according to Mill, is characterized not by drama but by boredom. Even for the believers, Christianity has become merely a series of platitudes that are obediently recited. Stowe responds to the crisis of belief by injecting new meaning into hackneyed traits by personalizing the impersonal, thus turning a distant Christ into a friendly and sociable Jesus.

But Stowe understands that sociability is best appreciated against a more serious background, and so she begins *Footsteps of the Master* by acknowledging the crisis of belief in far more theatrical terms than Mill, in a tone reminiscent of a Calvinist preacher invoking destruction, doom, and fear. "When a city is closely besieged and many of its outworks destroyed, the defenders retreat into the citadel." For Stowe, crisis emerges from the questioning of authority, especially religious authority: "Many things are battered down that used to be thought indispensable to its defense." And the citadel is, for Stowe, not a literal place such as a church, but "CHRIST," understood as a sanctuary of the mind, where believers find safety in faith in the midst of modern-day skepticism and doubt. Although Stowe is an emergent liberal Christian, who emphasizes the love and affection of Jesus, she is simultaneously a residual Calvinist, who believes that life is ultimately tragic. Inculcated in the doctrines of Jonathan Edwards, Stowe opens her liberal Christian tract with the stirring words "We are born to suffer" and "We are born to die." One goes to the citadel to escape a terrifying world—and Stowe understands from her Calvinist training that nothing motivates more effectively than fear. For Stowe, liberal Christianity is not a way to oppose her Calvinist upbringing, but rather a way to cope with its traumatic effects; it is a spiritual salve that comforts the aftershocks of Calvinist terror. Even for non-believers, the nice Jesus is a sympathetic "best Friend," "longing to save them from all that they fear."[26]

CHARACTERIZING THE LOVABLE JESUS

Stowe's most important contribution to liberal Christianity was to translate the doctrine of love into a characterization of a lovable Jesus. According to Francis Greenwood Peabody, a professor at Harvard's Divinity School, the teaching of Jesus was primarily a teaching of character. In *Jesus Christ and the Christian Character* (1905), Peabody points out that the gospels are "an artless and incidental summary of an oral tradition"; in the nineteenth century, he adds, "we need to add dimension to his character."[27] Liberal Christians, beginning with the Unitarian minister William Ellery Channing, attempted to elaborate on the character of Jesus, but they were reluctant at first to replace the language of divine exceptionalism with one of human ordinariness. In 1821 Channing describes Jesus as a "solitary being" who lived as if he were from another world: "His character has in it nothing local or temporary."[28]

Horace Bushnell was similarly uncomfortable with humanizing Jesus. In his *The Character of Jesus* (1860), tellingly subtitled "Forbidding His Possible Classification with Men," Bushnell is, at least to some extent, torn about how to characterize Jesus: Does he insist on his divinity or his humanity? On the one hand, we are told that Jesus had a "superhuman or celestial childhood," while on the other hand he is described in rather banal terms, as someone who stays calm in the midst of "petty vexations." To produce a few more markers delineating Jesus' character, Bushnell awkwardly turns to his sense of humor. It is not reported, Bushnell claims, that Jesus ever laughed. That does not mean, however, that Jesus was unhappy or sad; he was, in fact, filled with "sacred joy."[29] The tensions in Bushnell's account of Jesus reveal that characterization, especially when it involves the divine, requires a degree of humanizing detail that Bushnell can give only reluctantly, because he believes that too many such details detract from Jesus' divinity.

It is only with Stowe's younger brother, Henry Ward Beecher, that we get a sense of a sociable and affable Jesus that comes closest to his sister's depiction.[30] Beecher was a Congregationalist minister in Brooklyn who became the most famous liberal Christian of the period, and his hagiography, *The Life of Jesus, The Christ* (1871) calls for the life of Christ to be "rewritten for each and every age." The personality of Jesus, he warns, cannot be lost in "sublime abstraction," but must be captured in depictions of his "personal tenderness and generous love." Appearing just six years before Stowe's life of Christ, Beecher's work represents Jesus as "genial and cheerful," thoroughly enjoying the company of others: "He loved wayside conversations with all sorts of men and women," and actively took part in "social festivity."[31]

Despite portraying a more sociable and festive Jesus, Henry Ward Beecher still falls short because his characterizations are ultimately too descriptive. We are told, for instance, that Jesus enjoys conversation, but there are no scenes of dialogue. His Jesus remains too wooden and flat. What the philosopher and theologian Albert Schweitzer said about David Friedrich Strauss's *The Life of Jesus* (1864) also applies to Beecher and his predecessors, namely that they do not write "like an imaginative novelist, with a constant eye to effect."[32] Stowe, better than anyone else of her generation, brings to her characterization of Jesus precisely the skills of the "imaginative novelist" who translates the moral notion of character, derived from the ethical value we place on our relations to others, into a palpable and sympathetic figure. In other words, she blends the concept of moral character with the novelistic techniques of characterization.

Just as *Uncle Tom's Cabin* describes the inside of Tom's home as a way to introduce her protagonist to the reader, so *Footsteps of the Master* depicts Jesus' surroundings, whether his home or his tomb, by using techniques associated with characterization. Stowe's Jesus is the *exemplum fidei* of Catharine Beecher's ideal housekeeper: He has "careful domestic habits. He was in all things methodical and frugal. The miraculous power he possessed never was used to surround him with any profusion" (68). Even in death, Jesus remains tidy. In describing Jesus' resurrection, Stowe departs from convention by concentrating not on the transcendence of the soul, but rather on the meticulous state of his tomb: "There is a touch of homelike minuteness in the description of the grave as they found it;—no discovery of haste, no sign of confusion, but all in order: the linen grave-clothes lying in one place; the napkin that was about his head not lying with them, but folded together in a place by itself; indicating the perfect calmness and composure with which their Lord had risen" (288). Jesus' things—his folded clothes and shroud—are metonymic expressions of his steadfast and calm temperament. Jesus, in other words, is the anti-hysteric, one who provides a behavioral map for grappling with the demands of everyday life with a degree of peaceful joy. The mundane prevails in Stowe's religious narrative, structuring even her account of the Ascension.

BIOGRAPHY AND THE ETHICS OF EXEMPLARITY

In 1909, Selden Lincoln Whitcomb wrote in *The Study of a Novel* that the novelistic method is "cumulative," by which he meant that "a discovery of character [occurs] by the gradually increasing momentum of items often trivial enough if taken separately."[33] This cumulative strategy of creating character through trivial details is precisely Stowe's technique, which she adapts from the novel form to what were known in the nineteenth century as "spiritual biographies" or "divine biographies." Biography was a popular and even pervasive genre in the nineteenth century. For Thomas Carlyle, the popularity of biographies attests to the innate sociality of human beings: "Man's sociality of nature evinces itself," writes Carlyle in 1832, in "the unspeakable delight he takes in Biography."[34] Literary historian Scott Casper has explained the popularity of this genre as due to its power to allow readers to "learn about public figures and peer into the lives of strangers." More than satiating curiosity, biographies possess the cultural power to "shape individuals' lives and character and to help define America's national character."[35]

Stowe's biographical account of a domesticated Jesus can be seen as part of a larger generic trend dating back to the eighteenth century, when "biographical exemplarity underwent a revolution that replaced the illustrious by the domestic example."[36] Stowe inherits this model of biographical exemplarity in foregrounding the mundane details of Jesus' character as the source of his exceptionalism. Exemplarity is an ethical notion, one that is fused with the Victorian ideal of good character, which for Stowe is a way to translate divine authority from the sublime to the ethical. This emphasis on the ethics of good character would resonate strongly with her Victorian readers as a pedagogical tool of moral instruction. Exemplarity is inscribed in Stowe's very title: the phrase "footsteps of the master" refers to the importance of imitation as a way to model public action.[37]

It would be a mistake, however, to understand Stowe's characterization of Jesus as a secularizing gesture. She fuses exemplarity with the sacred in order to revitalize Christianity through a counterintuitive strategy, one that resists the spectacular and instead portrays the excessively familiar. The biographical novel is an ideal vehicle for portraying an ordinary Jesus because the genre is wedded to the common life, and the source of its aesthetic vitality is derived from the particular details that create a referential world, a world that authenticates Jesus' corporeality. "Romance is full of marvels," writes Terry Eagleton in *The English Novel,* "whereas the modern novel is mundane. . . . It is wary of the abstract and eternal and believes in what it can touch, taste and handle."[38] But Stowe does not use the mundanity that characterizes the novel to construct a secular reaction against eternal values; rather, she uses it as a way to demonstrate the pervasiveness of the eternal in the material practices that give shape to our daily lives. Realist description renders Jesus fully human, representing a form of aesthetic incarnation whereby the prosaic revitalizes the sacred.

SOCIABILITY AND THE NINETEENTH-CENTURY NOVEL

Stowe uses the novel to depict the transformation of religious authority from the "Christology of the sublime," to borrow David Morgan's phrase to describe a highly masculine God who inspires awe, to what I refer to as a "Christology of niceness," according to which Jesus is fundamentally social, amiable, and kind.[39] This emphasis on a humane Jesus is epitomized in Stowe's distinction between an impersonal Christ who represents the "law" and a personal Jesus who is a "soul-friend" (11). Jesus is a "lovable" teacher who "came to love us, to teach us, to save us . . . in the kindest and gentlest way" (186).

Besides employing seemingly trivial details to portray Jesus' calm and gentle demeanor, in *Footsteps of the Master* Stowe also uses novelistic techniques to demonstrate the web of social relations that characterize her protagonist's "gentleness and affability" (178). In a chapter entitled "The Friendships of Jesus," Stowe points out that Jesus did not leave "one line written by his own hand" (133). There is no autobiographical account in the New Testament, only biographical versions through "personal friendships." "Our Lord," writes Stowe, ". . . is represented to us through the loving hearts and affectionate records of these his chosen ones" (133). Jesus is literally a product of friendship, a figure constructed from personal recollections. The "personal" functions in Stowe's narrative as a way not only to authenticate the Gospels, on which her book is based, but also to recast Christianity as a personal religion, as the product of intimate bonds of friendship rather than as an impersonal institution. Stowe idealizes a primitive Christianity, a pre-Pauline religion where friendship replaces law.

Just as the novel form gives Stowe an appropriate way to emphasize the mundane, the genre is also perfect for underscoring the importance of friendship for Christianity because it is devoted to depicting the complex web of associations that constitutes a community. "Victorian fiction, like fiction in general, has a single pervasive theme," writes J. Hillis Miller: "interpersonal relations."[40] In this sense *Footsteps of the Master* is a typical Victorian novel, not necessarily in a formal sense, with its eclectic combination of poetry, hymns, and narrative, but rather in its thematic emphasis on sociability. After all, Jesus has few opportunities to be nice when alone in the desert. Jesus' niceness is a social practice that can only be made visible through its effect on others: "everywhere warming, melting, cheering; inspiring joy in the sorrowful and hope in the despairing; giving peace to the perplexed" (185). In converting sorrow and despair into joy and hope, niceness transforms through interpersonal contact. This social contact is precisely what makes Stowe one of "the most profound of the sentimental apologists," since, according to Joanne Dobson, she believes that "human connection is the genesis, in this life, of the divine."[41]

Stowe's emphasis on sociability challenges Ian Watt's understanding of the relation between Christianity and the novel. For Watt, Christianity influences the novel primarily through the inward movement or introspection of Puritanism, in the process creating a depth and dimensionality in the character that leads to readerly identification.[42] Stowe, by contrast, believes that Christianity influences the novel most when characters cultivate social bonds of connection and affection, when the characters move outward, not inward, to form relationships of various types. Unlike introspection, which is a trait that exists independently of others, niceness, amiability, and kindness are fundamentally social, in that they are primarily perceptual attributes rather than intrinsic qualities.

By characterizing Jesus as fundamentally social, Stowe dramatizes the subjective aspects of niceness. In contrast to Elizabeth Stuart Phelps's *The Story of Jesus Christ*, published twenty years later in 1897, where Jesus seeks solitude to reflect and rejuvenate, Stowe's Jesus prefers company: "We find that Jesus loved social life and the fellowship of men. Though he spent the first forty days after his mission began in the solitude of the desert, yet he returned from it the same warm-hearted and social being as before" (177). Stowe's Jesus is the embodiment of a liberal Christian ethos, epitomized in Henry James, Sr.'s spiritual ideal of society as the "redeemed form of man." As James told his children repeatedly during their childhood, "we need never fear not to be good enough if we were only social enough."[43] Similarly, Stowe's Jesus is rarely portrayed alone, but primarily in relation to others, the epitome of a social democrat who receives invitations from people of all classes: "Jesus was often invited to feasts in the houses of both rich and poor, and cheerfully accepted these invitations even on the Sabbath-day" (178).

Although Stowe portrays more profound levels of intimacy, such as the "soul-love" he has for his mother, what is remarkable is the frequency of his ordinary social encounters. "They [rich and poor] crowded round him and he welcomed them; they invited him to their houses and he went; he sat with them at the table; he held their little ones in his arms; he *gave himself* to them" (180, emphasis in original).[44] By situating Jesus within the home as a domesticated figure surrounded by children, Stowe replicates through prose one of the most influential visual representations of the nice Jesus icon, epitomized in Bernhard Plockhorst's *Christ Blessing the Children* (1885). This image depicts Jesus seated on a low wall with an infant on his lap, surrounded by animated children vying for his attention, with their doting mothers beside them. Rather than peering upward into the heavens, thus appearing aloof, Jesus gazes downward into the faces of the cherubic children, fully engaged in the social scene before him. The

Victorian Jesus, whether in the form of Stowe's prose or Plockhorst's iconography, is the embodiment of maternal love.

THE SEXUAL POLITICS OF THE NICE JESUS

Although Jesus' niceness seems like a rather inconsequential trait, it has significant implications for questions of power. Niceness is not an awe-inspiring category. It is too banal to be sublime. The niceness of Jesus and the divinity of Jesus have a difficult time coexisting. The authority of Jesus could easily be compromised through his humanization, which is to say through his embodiment in a realist narrative of everyday details and social encounters. Stowe's depiction of the nice Jesus requires a radical rethinking of divine authority that involves the question of gender. In 1852, the Unitarian minister Theodore Parker acknowledged the gendered language of niceness in a sermon on the death of Daniel Webster: "Bulk is bearded and masculine; niceness is of women's gendering."[45] Not only is niceness gendered female, but so are the quotidian spaces where this niceness is performed: primarily within people's homes. Niceness, together with the trivial and the everyday, is a feminized concept that represents an alternative form of authority, one that counters the fiery rhetoric of Calvinist catastrophe.

Susan Bordo reminds us of how the "'definition and shaping' of the [gendered] body is 'the focal point for struggles over the shape of power.'"[46] Religious historians have been reluctant to take on the consequences of liberal Christianity's humanization of Jesus at the level of gender and sexuality. Richard Wightman Fox, in his magisterial cultural history of Jesus, insists that liberal Protestant love, embodied in the character of Jesus, was not reducible to "feminized domestic virtue" but was "androgynous," a love that transported both men and women out of social conventions.[47] Androgyny suggests a symmetrical fusion of male and female to produce a synthesis that combines both.[48] But Stowe's gendering of Jesus was far more contentious and uneven. Rather than blurring the binary of masculine and feminine into a gender-neutral third term, her portrayal of Jesus actually maintains the binary. More specifically, Stowe's Jesus is a decidedly feminized figure, a form of asymmetrical union that favors the feminine in unapologetic and uncompromising ways. Stowe's Jesus does not transcend social conventions, but rather exploits the conventions of feminine niceness, and specifically motherly love, presenting those conventions as an exemplary model of democratic power.

For Stowe, Jesus represents a "new style of manhood," based not on "force" but on love: "His mode was more that of a mother than a father. He strove to infuse Himself into them [his friends and followers] by an embracing, tender, brooding love; ardent, self-forgetful, delicate, refined" (136). Stowe further feminizes Jesus by coupling his domestic and sentimental niceness with a biological explanation that implies a proto-genetic argument. In other words, she buttresses her behavioral account of Jesus' love with an essentialist one: "All that was human in him was her [Mary's] nature; it was the union of the divine nature with the nature of a pure woman. Hence there was in Jesus more of the pure feminine element than in any other man. It was the feminine element exalted and taken in union with Divinity" (70). Jesus' incarnation is not a symmetrical blending of God and Mary, where the divine and human each contribute half; instead Jesus' nature is emphatically asymmetrical, one where the human parent Mary is the determining force. As a result, woman becomes the universal standard by which the human is defined.

By emphasizing Mary's role in the biological making of Jesus, Stowe acknowledges the importance not only of women but also of Jewishness to any understanding of Jesus. She anticipates what Nietzsche would later acknowledge, namely that Jesus and Saul were "the two most Jewish Jews perhaps who ever lived."[49] In *Footsteps of the Master,* Stowe writes, "To study the life of Christ without the Hebrew Scriptures is to study a flower without studying the plant from which it sprung, the root and leaves which nourished it. He continually spoke of himself as a Being destined to fulfill what had gone before" (124). Stowe's Jesus is decidedly Jewish, and Jewish men are "*affectionate men.*"[50] In *Woman in Sacred History* (1873), written four years before *Footsteps of the Master,* Stowe argues that one of the most important lessons of the Old Testament is that Jewish men are highly loyal and domestic: "We find no pictures of love in family life more delicate and tender than are given in these patriarchal stories." Jews attach a "sacredness and respect" to family life, which actually encourages Jewish women to have multiple roles that include wife and mother as well as "leader, inspirer, prophetess."[51] This romantic view of biblical Judaism as a proto-feminist religion is reminiscent of her brother Henry Ward Beecher's *Life of Jesus,* in which he writes that "among the Jews, more perhaps than in any other Oriental nation, woman was permitted to develop naturally, and liberty was accorded her to participate in things which other people reserved with zealous seclusion for men."[52] Both brother and sister idealize biblical Jews to the extent that Jewishness becomes an exemplary model for Christian sociability that combines the sacred with the mundane, affection with respect, and domesticated men with powerful women.

In contrast to the works of Stowe's contemporaries such as Octavius Brooks Frothingham, who sought to revitalize Christianity by imagining a transcendent Jesus of metaphysical Spirit, Stowe's narrative involves a retroactive dynamic, where modern Christian sociability is based on ancient Jewish materiality.[53] As the embodiment of Jewish materialism, the demonstrative parent becomes the evangelizing force that revitalizes Christian belief. As Thomas Loebel has argued in his discussion of Stowe's theology, Stowe is a "good Jewish mother," who strives for a "certain recovery of Jewish materiality as necessary for Christian efficacy in transforming the world."[54] In *Footsteps of the Master,* Mary nearly steals the show from her son, since the most suitable image for representing the Master, according to Stowe, is "one of those loving, saintly mothers, who, in leading along their little flock, follow nearest in the footsteps of Jesus" (137). Jesus' love is made equivalent to motherly love, a strategy that Leslie Fiedler identifies in *Uncle Tom's Cabin* when he describes Tom as "a white mother like his author, despite his blackface and drag," representing "the Blessed Male Mother of a virgin Female Christ."[55] This symbiotic relation between the Virgin and a maternal Christ is at the heart of Stowe's Marianism, which wants to feminize liberal Christianity by adapting Catholicism's adoration of the Madonna.[56] By grafting Marianism onto Christology, Stowe explores what Julia Kristeva in *The Feminine and the Sacred* calls "the feminine of man," whereby the feminine becomes a new universal that operates as an "open invitation to man's femininity."[57]

THE CHRISTOLOGY OF NICENESS AND THE QUESTION OF AUTHORITY

By inviting man to value his femininity, the Christology of niceness recasts authority in terms of love, as a force of attraction that inspires an intense personal affection. In describing the authority of the nice Jesus, Stowe writes, "he governed personally" (212), which is to say that he asked "not only for love, but for intimacy—he asked for the whole heart" (182). Stowe defines love, a key term of the liberal Christian lexicon, as a productive and creative force: "He was not merely lovely, but he was love. He had a warming, creative power as to love. He gave birth to new conceptions of love; to a fervor, a devotion, a tenderness, of which before the human soul scarcely knew its own capacity" (67).

The effectiveness of his authority can be seen in his magnetic power of attraction, which is truly global: "Men, women, and children in every land, with every variety of constitutional habit,—have conceived . . . an ardent, passionate, personal love to Jesus" (66).

In "The Authority of Jesus" (1830), Emerson conceives of Jesus' power in similar terms, as representing a new model of authority based not on the ability to make men "cower" but on the power of exemplarity: to inspire others, through love, to "embark in the same cause by word and by act."[58] Jesus persuades organically through truth, according to Emerson, rather than supernaturally through miracles. As Emerson wrote in 1843, "There is nothing in history to parallel the influence of Jesus Christ."[59] In Stowe's theory of power, influence is absolutely central as an alternative to authority and force, as a way to legitimize love as a potent social force of suasion. In *Little Foxes,* which is aptly subtitled *The Insignificant Little Habits Which Mar Domestic Happiness* (1866), she writes, "*Influence* is a slower acting force than authority. It seems weaker, but in the long run it often effects more. It always does better than mere force and authority without its gentle modifying power."[60] Influence, for Stowe, represents a slow transformation that is ultimately more effective and long-lasting than sudden change.

Understanding Jesus' power in terms of influence is vital for Stowe because she is interested in portraying Jesus' niceness not as an end in itself, but rather as a strategy of conversion. As she writes, "the influence of Jesus was no mere sentimental attraction, but a vital, spiritual force" (182). Stowe, in other words, does not reject power but recasts it in terms of gentle persuasion. "Christianity is a system of persuasion," Catharine Beecher wrote in 1837, "tending, by kind and gentle influences, to make men willing to leave off their sins."[61] Stowe's Jesus is the embodiment of her sister's understanding of the power of "gentle influences," which Stowe colorfully conveys through examples: "The dog is changed by tender treatment and affectionate care. . . . Rude human natures are correspondingly changed, and he who has great power of loving and exciting love may almost create anew whom he will" (137). Evangelical niceness has a teleology. It strives toward converting the uncongenial to the genial, the rude to the kind.

Henry Ward Beecher shared his sister's interest in niceness as a strategic and teleological "force" for Christian conversion, believing that persuasion depends on personal likeability. In a lecture entitled "What Is Preaching?" (1872), he explains the "power of personal Christian vitality" by turning to the success of the early Christians at converting others. They understood the power of niceness: to "be so sweet, so sparkling, so buoyant, so cheerful, hopeful, courageous . . . so perfectly benevolent." You cannot "refashion men," argues Beecher, "unless you have some sort of vigor, vitality, versatility . . . and social power in you."[62] Niceness is a form of "social power" that has transformative effects through the force of one's character.

THE LIKEABLE LINCOLN

The purpose of Stowe's theory of niceness is not just to embody God in a personable and lovable form, but also to present the lineaments of a democratic nation. Stowe was instrumental in making Christianity a Jesus faith, and in making the United States a Jesus nation. She speaks of the country as a "Christian democracy," a concept she defines in her preface to *Men of Our Times, or, Leading Patriots of the Day* (1868): "The American government is the only permanent republic which ever based itself upon the principles laid down by Jesus Christ, of the absolute equal brotherhood of man, and the rights of man on the simple ground of manhood."[63] Stowe was a radically unsecular thinker, and she understood democracy as a distinctly Christian practice. For Stowe, the individual who personified this fusion of Christian ideals and American democracy was Abraham Lincoln, whom she eulogized in biographical sketches both in *Men of Our Times* and in a later collection, *The Lives and Deeds of Our Self-Made Men* (1872).

Lincoln was the nineteenth-century real-world incarnation of the nice Jesus. When Lincoln was shot on Good Friday in 1865, he was quickly sanctified in Easter Sunday sermons nationwide. "Jesus Christ died for the world, Abraham Lincoln died for his country," said one clergyman, and the line became a common refrain in the aftermath of the assassination.[64] Like her rendition of Jesus, Stowe's Lincoln is popular and likeable, someone whose storytelling abilities and good nature make him a beloved neighbor as well as a welcome dinner guest: "Of all these traits, Mr. Lincoln's kindness was unquestionably the rarest, the most wonderful. It may be doubted whether any human being ever lived whose whole nature was so perfectly sweet with the readiness to do kind actions; so perfectly free from even the capacity of revenge. He could not even leave a pig in distress." Whether toward animals or rebels, Lincoln's "sweet kindness of feeling" is inexhaustible.[65] Lincoln's kindness toward the rebels is framed after his death as an act of Christian forgiveness. "He quickly came to symbolize," as John Stauffer writes, "an American Christ who forgave rebels their sins and allowed them to reenter the Union."[66]

Stowe is quick to frame Lincoln's kindness as a source of strength rather than a weakness, an expression of what she refers to as "passive power": "Lincoln was a strong man, but his strength was of a peculiar kind; it was not aggressive so much as passive, and among passive things it was like the strength not so much of a stone buttress as of a wire cable. It was strength swaying to every influence, yielding on this side and on that to popular needs, yet tenaciously and inflexibly bound to carry its great end."[67] As she does influence, Stowe understands passive power like Lincoln's as strength through accommodation. Just as the liberal subject is always open to persuasion, remaining "pliable to the influences of the others," to quote Stowe in "Self-Will," so Lincoln personifies this notion of power by remaining flexible but not too flexible, since complete pliability would undermine his ethical principles.

As Marianne Noble has noted in *The Masochistic Pleasures of Sentimental Literature,* Stowe does not want to eliminate or abandon power but seeks to reformulate it, rendering it an ally instead of an enemy.[68] Whether it is Jesus who governs personally, or Lincoln who governs passively, both personify Stowe's theory of power as "influence," an interpersonal mode of persuasion that becomes generalized as a model of democratic governance. The powerful mother, like the hegemonic state, is not one who has to threaten and strike the misbehaving child, but one who quietly guides through affection. At one level then, Jesus and Lincoln—as the embodiment of kind forms of authority—represent a nineteenth-century theory of hegemony, where authority operates invisibly through the internalization of shared meanings as consensus rather than through physical coercion.

Stowe's model of democratic governance relies on a notion of consensus based on interpersonal niceness, but this model is unique neither to Stowe nor to the nineteenth century. Whether it is Habermas's deliberative democracy, which rests in part on a notion of "considerateness," or Martin Luther King Jr.'s ideal of "civil dialogue," where disagreement is vital to democratic debate, democratic consensus requires a model of well-behaved citizens. For Stowe, writing in the aftermath of the Civil War, consensus-building is a way to reunify the nation by standardizing a personality type that exemplifies democratic sociability. Making niceness a rule of conduct is a way to reimagine structures of community at a national as well as an interpersonal level, where disagreement and dissent can be communicated through "civil dialogue" rather than through war.

But what are the limits of niceness? When does persuasion fail? To put it into historical terms, when does "civil dialogue" collapse and Civil War erupt? Even the phrase "civil war" is paradoxical, emphasizing as it does a strained fusion of civility and violence, as if it were possible to have a polite war, a considerate war. What about a necessary war? Could slavery have been eradicated by nice means through "civil dialogue" and "civil listening"? In contrast to Henry Ward Beecher's brand of liberal Christianity, which preached the nonexistence of Hell and avoided such unpleasant topics as the crucifixion, Stowe grapples with catastrophe in its myriad forms, including the national catastrophe of the Civil War.[69]

In doing so, Stowe both recognizes the necessity of war and argues that some good may come out of the destruction caused by it. In the immediate aftermath of the Civil War, in her preface to *Men of Our Times,* Stowe turns the fiery destruction of the Civil War into a cauldron of national cleansing: "The fierce fire into which our national character has been cast in the hour of trial, has burned out of it the last lingering stain of compromise with anything inconsistent with its primary object, 'to ordain justice and perpetuate liberty.'"[70] Destruction is ultimately regenerative for Stowe; it redeems "our national character" of its sins, allowing it to be born again without the stain of slavery. American exceptionalism acts as a form of Christian redemption that ensures the reproducibility of innocence.

As a messianic figure of national redemption, Stowe's Lincoln shares a number of similarities with the nice Jesus: "Never since the times of Christian martyrs has history recorded a contrast more humiliating to humanity, between his kind words and kind intentions on the one hand, and infamous abusiveness and deliberate bloodthirsty ferocity in those who thus slew the best and kindest friend they had in the world."[71] Like Jesus, Lincoln was not protected by his kindness. How could someone so beloved, asks Stowe in *Footsteps,* "be put to so cruel a death in the very midst of a people whom he loved and for whom he labored?" This question, which for Stowe applies equally to Jesus and Lincoln, is answered in the next paragraph: their kindness, which gave them a power over the hearts of men, "was the cause and reason of the conspiracy" (248).

Jesus and Lincoln had to be killed because they were loved too much; they became powerful to the extent that their kindness inspired both affection and hatred.

I began this essay by discussing Paul Coughlin's rejection of the nice Victorian Jesus. As one of the major architects of this particular incarnation of the amiable Jesus, Stowe understands what Coughlin cannot acknowledge, namely that, whether it is niceness or kindness, there is something potentially dangerous, even revolutionary, in behavior that inspires fellow feeling. Niceness, in other words, can be extremely powerful. As the psychoanalyst Adam Phillips and the historian Barbara Taylor have written in *On Kindness* (2008), "Living according to our sympathies, we imagine, will weaken or overwhelm us; kindness is the saboteur of a successful life." It is, moreover, a "virtue for losers."[72] We find our own capacity for kindness terrifying, they argue, because it brings to light our susceptibility to the feelings of others, our vulnerability to and dependency on others. Rather than viewing niceness and kindness, and the whole constellation of related terms of positive sociality, with either suspicion or indifference, I want to conclude this essay by offering a generous reading, as well as a critique, of Stowe's nice Jesus. On the one hand, Stowe's banality of niceness, epitomized in the figures of Jesus and Lincoln, describes the way in which hegemonic ideology permeates the everyday to the extent that it becomes common sense, a non-analytical category of habit. In the figure of Lincoln, it refers to a form of democratic governance based on management through reward rather than brute force, one that establishes cohesion and perhaps even coercion through *consensus,* that "invisible" display of authority that manipulates without even appearing to do so.

In reading the nice Jesus exclusively through this paradigm of social control, however, as a form of discipline that sustains consensus through the etiquette of well-behaved citizens, we preclude another possible reading of this figure, an equally important reading that acknowledges niceness as dangerous. To understand the religious significance of niceness, one has to return to the language of crisis that begins *Footsteps.* Stowe tells us from the start that we must all suffer and we must all die. We must also witness the suffering and death of loved ones, as our social circle gradually becomes smaller, quieter, and lonelier. Now, this sounds distinctly Calvinist at one level, because it forces us to look at our mortality without any colored glasses or soothing reassurances. Religion is certainly not an opiate here, but a sober reminder of the reality principle. Yet Stowe does not stop at this point. She goes on to ask whether we should respond to our common vulnerability with shame and fear (as the result of original sin), or as the source of our humanity. It is precisely by acknowledging this vulnerability that we can show compassion toward ourselves and toward others. The crisis of mortality, in other words, can also be a gift: it creates the conditions for kindness.

It is this double-edged quality of banal niceness—its ability to promote a democratic cohesion that can heal the nation in the aftermath of the Civil War, as well as a perilous recognition of our common vulnerability—that makes Stowe such a nuanced theorist of religious modernism. By using the banal to rethink the sacred in terms of the trivial rather than the transcendental, Stowe differentiates herself dramatically from another religious modernist, William James, who defines banality as "the unprofitable delineation of the obvious."[73] But Stowe refuses to write off the banal; for her, the banality of niceness is a way to reimagine both religious belief and national mourning through a model of democratic sociality that was urgently needed in the postbellum period.

NOTES

Earlier versions of this essay were presented at Princeton, Yale, and Indiana, and I am grateful to these audiences for their feedback. This chapter also benefited from the comments of my colleague Graham Hammill and of my reading group, Ann Colley, Regina Grol and Carolyn Korsmeyer, as well as from the research assistance of Prentiss Clark. Special thanks to David Schmid for his insightful suggestions at multiple stages of this essay's incarnation.

1. Paul Coughlin, *No More Christian Nice Guy: When Being Nice Instead of Good Hurts Men, Women and Children* (Bloomington, Minn.: Bethany House, 2007), 26.

2. Terry Eagleton, introduction to *The Gospels: Jesus Christ* (London: Verso, 2007), xxiv–xxv.

3. Giorgio Agamben, *The Time That Remains: A Commentary on the Letter to the Romans* (Stanford: Stanford University Press, 2005), 2, quoting Jacob Taubes, *The Political Theology of Paul* (Stanford: Stanford University Press, 2003), 5. In the original French edition, Taubes refers to Jesus as a "nice guy" in English.

4. Henri Lefebvre, "The Everyday and Everydayness," *Yale French Studies,* no. 73 (1987): 9.

5. Maurice Blanchot, "Everyday Speech," *Yale French Studies,* no. 73 (1987): 13.

6. Stephen Prothero, *American Jesus: How the Son of God Became a National Icon* (New York: Farrar, Straus, and Giroux, 2004), 55.

7. Harriet Beecher Stowe, preface to the first edition, *Uncle Tom's Cabin,* Norton Critical Edition, ed. Elizabeth Ammons (New York: Norton, 1994), xiii.

8. Lora Romero, "Bio-political Resistance in Domestic Ideology and *Uncle Tom's Cabin,*" *American Literary History* 1, no. 4 (winter 1989): 718. This notion of hysteria as an obsession with detail also characterizes Freud's understanding of hysteria as a "pathology of the detail," to quote Naomi Schor, "reflecting a society sick with the detail." Naomi Schor, *Reading in Detail: Aesthetics and the Feminine* (New York: Routledge, 1987), 70.

9. Quoted in Romero, "Bio-political Resistance," 718.

10. "The Preacher and the Forces of Democracy," *The Methodist Review*, January 1918, 94.

11. Harriet Beecher Stowe, "Self-Will," in *Little Foxes, or, The Insignificant Little Habits Which Mar Domestic Happiness*, author's revised edition (London: Bell and Daldy, 1866), 113.

12. "The Modern Novel," *The Methodist Quarterly Review*, April 1860, 12.

13. Ernest Renan, *The Life of Jesus* (1863; London: The Temple Company, 1888), 28 ("The voice of the young carpenter acquired all at once an extraordinary sweetness"); and Harriet Beecher Stowe, *Footsteps of the Master* (New York: J. B. Ford, 1877), 128.

14. Bryan Garsten, *Saving Persuasion: A Defense of Rhetoric and Judgment* (Cambridge, Mass.: Harvard University Press, 2006), 2.

15. Stowe's banality of niceness shares an important trait with an unlikely point of comparison: Hannah Arendt's famous concept of the banality of evil, which she delineated in her study of the Israeli trial of the Nazi war criminal Adolph Eichmann in *Eichmann in Jerusalem* (1963). Like Stowe, Arendt believes that power operates most potently through the seemingly facile notion of the mundane rather than through metaphysical categories such as sinfulness and wickedness. Arendt argues that banality describes the exercise of power without hatred, without motive, and without thought, because the sadist does not need to hate his victim. It is not anti-Semitism alone that explains Eichmann's actions but "thoughtlessness." Eichmann was simply following orders; his crime was his obedience.

But despite the important similarities between Stowe and Arendt, the banality of niceness differs in important ways from the banality of evil. Where Arendt lays emphasis on "thoughtlessness," the banality of niceness is concerned with forms of thoughtfulness. Furthermore, Arendt argues that the banality of evil is fundamentally impersonal, operating as it does through the totalitarian structures of the state, whereas the banality of niceness is conveyed through personal contact—through a handshake, a smile, or a friendly salutation. This does not mean that the personal is divorced from structures of power, but that it functions as a way of mediating those structures through a variety of direct appeals.

16. Harriet Beecher Stowe, "Home Religion" (1870), in *Household Papers and Stories*, vol. 8 of *The Writings of Harriet Beecher Stowe* (Boston: Houghton, Mifflin, 1896), 213.

17. Pierre Bourdieu, "Codification" (1986), in *In Other Words: Essays towards a Reflexive Sociology*, trans. Matthew Adamson (Stanford: Stanford University Press, 1994), 78.

18. Ralph Waldo Emerson, "Experience," in *Essays and Lectures*, ed. Joel Porte (New York: Library of America, 1983), 479.

19. Harriet Beecher Stowe, "Introductory Note," in *Religious Studies, Sketches and Poems*, vol. 15 of *The Writings of Harriet Beecher Stowe* (New York: AMS Press, 1967), ix.

20. "Harriet Beecher Stowe," *Current Literature* 20, no. 3 (September 1896): 221, APS online.

21. See, for instance, Paul Gutjahr's *An American Bible: A History of the Good Book in the United States, 1777–1880* (Stanford: Stanford University Press, 1999); Gregory Jackson's *The Word and Its Witness: The Spiritualization of American Realism* (Chicago: University of Chicago Press, 2009); and Jefferson Gatrall's "The Color of His Hair: Nineteenth-Century Literary Portraits of the Historical Jesus," *Novel: A Forum on Fiction* 42, no. 1 (spring 2009): 109–30.

22. Joseph Holt Ingraham, *The Prince of the House of David* (1855; Philadelphia: G. W. Pitcher, 1863), 58, 63.

23. Ibid., 415, 410.

24. Don Russell, foreword to *The Life of Honorable William F. Cody, known as Buffalo Bill*, by Buffalo Bill (Lincoln: University of Nebraska Press, 1978), viii.

25. John Stuart Mill, *"On Liberty" and "The Subjection of Women"* (New York: Penguin, 2007), 47, 49, 50.

26. Stowe, *Footsteps,* 5, 6, 9. Subsequent citations are given in the text.

27. Francis Greenwood Peabody, *Jesus Christ and the Christian Character* (1905; New York: Macmillan, 1910), 42.

28. William Ellery Channing, *Discourse on the Evidences of Revealed Religion* (Liverpool, UK: F. B. Wright, 1830), 22. See Richard Wightman Fox, *Jesus in America: Personal Savior, Cultural Hero, National Obsession* (New York: HarperCollins, 2004), 188.

29. Horace Bushnell, *The Character of Jesus: Forbidding His Possible Classification with Men* (1860; New York: Charles Scribner's Sons, 1898), 10, 29, 20. This work was originally a chapter of Bushnell's earlier book *Nature and the Supernatural* (1858).

30. See also Charles Beecher's *The Incarnation,* with an introduction by Harriet Beecher Stowe (New York: Harper, 1849). This book offers a far more vivid portrait of Mary than it does of Jesus, demonstrating that he shared his sister Harriet's Marianism.

31. Henry Ward Beecher, *The Life of Jesus, the Christ* (New York: J. B. Ford, 1871), 5, 11, 111–12.

32. Albert Schweitzer, *The Quest of the Historical Jesus,* ed. John Bowden (Minneapolis, Minn.: Fortress Press, 2001), 168.

33. Seldon Lincoln Whitcomb, *The Study of a Novel* (Boston: D. C. Heath, 1905), 111.

34. Thomas Carlyle, "Essay on Biography" (1832), in *Little Masterpieces,* ed. Bliss Perry (New York: Doubleday & McClure, 1902), 3.

35. Scott Casper, *Constructing American Lives: Biography and Culture in Nineteenth-Century America* (Chapel Hill: University of North Carolina Press, 1999), 2.

36. Michael McKeon, *Secret History of the Domestic* (Baltimore: Johns Hopkins University Press, 2006), 338. See also Catherine Sanok, *Her Life Historical: Exemplarity and Female Saints' Lives in Late Medieval England* (Philadelphia: University of Pennsylvania Press, 2007).

37. On the Renaissance topos of footsteps and imitation theory, see Timothy Hampton, *Writing from History: The Rhetoric of Exemplarity in Renaissance Literature* (Ithaca, N.Y.: Cornell University Press, 1990), 66.

38. Terry Eagleton, *The English Novel: An Introduction* (Oxford: Blackwell, 2005), 3.

39. David Morgan, "The Masculinity of Jesus in Popular Religious Art," in *Men's Bodies, Men's Gods: Male Identities in a (Post-)Christian Culture,* ed. Bjorn Krondorfer (New York: New York University Press, 1996), 251.

40. J. Hillis Miller, *The Form of Victorian Fiction* (Notre Dame, Ind.: University of Notre Dame Press, 1968), 94.

41. Joanne Dobson, "Reclaiming Sentimental Literature," *American Literature* 69, no. 2 (June 1997): 266.

42. Ian Watt, *The Rise of the Novel* (Berkeley: University of California Press, 2001), 177.

43. F. O. Matthiessen, *Henry James: The Major Phase* (1944; New York: Oxford University Press, 1963), 140. For Henry James, Sr.'s philosophical work on spirituality and society, see his *Society: The Redeemed Form of Man* (Boston: Houghton, Osgood, 1879).

44. In contrast to the British version of *Footsteps,* the original U.S. edition did not capitalize pronouns referring to Jesus, except in a very few cases. The use of lowercase pronouns edition emphasizes, at the level of typography, the ordinariness of Jesus rather than his exceptionalism. The lowercase is, furthermore, the typographical equivalent of niceness as the democratization of authority, which the British edition significantly reverses. I am grateful to my copyeditor, Shoshanna Green, for pointing out this difference between the British and U.S. editions.

45. Theodore Parker, *A Discourse Occasioned on the Death of Daniel Webster* (Boston: B. B. Mussey, 1853), 16. Thanks to Prentiss Clark for this reference.

46. Susan Bordo, *Unbearable Weight: Feminism, Western Culture and the Body,* 10th anniversary edition (Berkeley: University of California Press, 2004), 17, quoting Don Hanlon Johnson, "The Body: Which One? Whose?" *Whole Earth Review,* summer 1989, 408.

47. Fox, *Jesus in America,* 258–59.

48. For a discussion of androgyny as a symmetrical model of sexual equality in legal theory, see D. Kelly Weisberg, *Feminist Legal Theory: Foundations* (Philadelphia: Temple University Press, 1993), 250.

49. Walter Kaufmann, preface to *The Antichrist,* in Friedrich Nietzsche, *The Portable Nietzsche,* ed. Walter Kaufmann (New York: Penguin, 1976), 566.

50. Harriet Beecher Stowe, *Woman in Sacred History* (New York: J. B. Ford, 1873), 20 (emphasis in original).

51. Ibid., 20, 27, 28.

52. Beecher, *Life of Jesus,* 35.

53. Octavius Brooks Frothingham wrote in 1852, "The real Christ is the spiritual, or the Spirit. Without the Spirit, the historical Christ is naught. Without the historical Christ, the Spirit is himself." Quoted in Fox, *Jesus in America,* 276.

54. Thomas Loebel, *The Letter and the Spirit of Nineteenth-Century American Literature: Justice, Politics, and Theology* (Montreal: McGill-Queen's University Press, 2005), 138.

55. Leslie Fiedler, *What Was Literature? Class Culture and Mass Society* (New York: Simon and Schuster, 1982), 172.

56. See John Gatta, *American Madonna: Images of the Divine Woman in Literary Culture* (New York: Oxford University Press, 1997).

57. Catherine Clément and Julia Kristeva, *The Feminine and the Sacred,* trans. Jane Marie Todd (1998; New York: Columbia University Press, 2001), 62.

58. Ralph Waldo Emerson, "The Authority of Jesus" (1830), in *Young Emerson Speaks: Unpublished Discourses on Many Subjects,* ed. Arthur Cushman McGiffert Jr. (Boston: Houghton, Mifflin, 1938), 97.

59. Ralph Waldo Emerson, *The Journals and Miscellaneous Notebooks of Ralph Waldo Emerson,* ed. William H. Gilman et al., vol. 9 (Cambridge, Mass.: Harvard University Press, 1971), 7 (entry for August 25, 1843).

60. Stowe, "Intolerance," in *Little Foxes,* 140.

61. Catharine Beecher, *An Essay on Slavery and Abolitionism* (Philadelphia: Henry Perkins, 1837), 46.

62. Henry Ward Beecher, "What Is Preaching?" in *Yale Lectures on Preaching* (New York: J. B. Ford, 1872), 13, 192.

63. Harriet Beecher Stowe, *Men of Our Times, or, Leading Patriots of the Day* (Hartford, Conn.: Hartford Publishing Co., 1868), vi.

64. John Stauffer, *Giants: The Parallel Lives of Frederick Douglass and Abraham Lincoln* (New York: Hachette, 2008), 298–301. See Fox, *Jesus in America,* 246.

65. Stowe, *Men of Our Times,* 63, 65.

66. Stauffer, *Giants,* 301.

67. Stowe, *Men of Our Times,* 110.

68. Marianne Noble, *The Masochistic Pleasure of Sentimental Literature* (Princeton, N.J.: Princeton University Press, 2000), 9–10. Noble quotes Elizabeth Grosz's valuable discussion of the relation between feminism and power: "power has been seen as the enemy of femi-

nism, something to be abhorred, challenged, dismantled, or at best something to be shared more equally, a thing which can be divided in different ways. Power is not the enemy of feminism but its ally. . . . Power is not something that feminism should disdain or rise above for it is its condition of existence and its medium of effectivity" (quoting Grosz's "Feminism, Women's Studies and the Politics of Theory," a paper delivered at American University, November 6, 1997).

69. This is not to say that Henry Ward Beecher was complaisant during the Civil War. He was a committed abolitionist who used the pulpit in the United States and abroad to argue for emancipation. My point is that Beecher and Stowe offered different versions of liberal Christianity, as Thomas Jenkins explains: "Henry Ward Beecher was the premier nineteenth-century writer in this form of sentimental incarnationalism. Harriet Beecher Stowe, however, represents sentimentalism at its most dramatic. Whereas her brother sought a way around difficult passages in the Gospels, she delved into them. Where her brother's work demonstrates a facile ingenuity, her work shows some dramatic profundity. By contrasting their writing, we can take a measure of the shallows and depths of the character of God in sentimental incarnationalism." Thomas E. Jenkins, *The Character of God: Recovering the Lost Literary Power of American Protestantism* (New York: Oxford University Press 1997), 64.

70. Stowe, *Men of Our Times*, vi–vii.

71. Ibid., 97.

72. Adam Phillips and Barbara Taylor, *On Kindness* (London: Macmillan, 2008), 4–5, 9.

73. Quoted in Bliss Perry, *The American Mind* (Boston: Houghton Mifflin, 1912), 15.

A CHRISTIAN HOUSE. 27

flowers. The stairs turn twice with broad steps, making a recess at the lower landing, where a table is set with a

Fig. 2.

vase of flowers, (Fig. 3.) On one side of the recess is a closet, arched to correspond with the arch over the stairs. A bracket over the first broad stair, with flowers or statuettes, is visible from the entrance, and pictures can be hung as in the illustration.

The large room on the left can be made to serve the purpose of several rooms by means of a *movable screen.* By shifting this rolling screen from one part of the room to another, two apartments are always available, of any desired size within the limits of the large room. One side of the screen fronts what may be used as the parlor or sitting-room; the other side is arranged for bedroom conveniences. Of this, Fig. 4 shows the front side; covered first with strong canvas, stretched and nailed on. Over this is pasted panel-paper, and the upper part is made to resemble an ornamental cornice by fresco-paper. Pictures can be hung in the panels, or be pasted on and varnished with white varnish. To

Fig. 3.

FIGURE 1. Catharine E. Beecher and Harriet Beecher Stowe, *The American Woman's Home* (New York: J. B. Ford, 1869), 27, demonstrating display of pictures in "a Christian home."

LITHOGRAPHS.

	LITHOGRAPHS.	NAMES OF THE		Length.	Height.	PRICE	PRICE
		Painters.	Lithogrph'rs.			plain.	colored.
						$ c.	$ c.
3201	**The Youth of Rousseau** (The Cherries)................	Roqueplan.	Leroux.	13½	19	2 00	4 00
3202	**Christ and his Disciples, St. Peter and St. John**...... *Companion to No. 707 of Catalogue.*	Landelle.	Fanoli.	11¾	19½	2 00	4 00
3203	**Luther burning the Pope's Bull**..................... *Companion to No. 734 of Catalogue.*	Mastersteig.	Thielley.	28½	18½	4 00	8 00
3204	**St. Francis of Assise, dying, blesses his native village**	Bonbuville.	Tessier.	31	12½	2 50	5 00
3205	**The Sleep of Jesus**.................................. *Suite to No. 722 of Catalogue.*	Sasso Ferato.	Lemoine.	14	14	1 75	3 25
3206	**Panorama of San Francisco**...........................	Delessert.	Bousquet.	34½	9½	3 00	6 00
3207	**View of Constantinople**..............................	Raulin.	Clerget.	18½	12¾	1 00	2 50
3208	**The Barrier of the Nile**.............................	Mongel Bey.	Cicerid Ben't.	28	15	2 00	4 00
3209	**View on the Rhine** (Rock of Lurley)..............No. 3,	Sabatier.	Sabatier.	25¼	15	2 00	4 00
3210	— (Caub and Phaltz).............. " 4,	—	—	—	—	—	—
3211	— (Oberwesel).................... " 5,	—	—	—	—	—	—
3212	— (Rolandsbeck).................. " 6, *Suite to No. 852 of Catalogue.*	—	—	—	—	—	—
3213	**Farm Horses** (Cock Robin), No. 1......................	De Dreux.	Lasalle.	23¾	18½	1 00	2 00
3214	— (Alexander), " 2......................	—	—	—	—	—	—
3215	**The Fisherman's Children**............................	Alophe.	Alophe.	10¼	13¾	80	1 75
3216	**The Orphan's Prayer**.................................	—	—	—	—	—	—
3217	**The Mother of the Orphans**...........................	—	—	—	—	—	—
3218	**The Last Hope of the Poor**........................... *Suite to No. 756 of Catalogue.*	—	—	—	—	—	—
3219	**Group of Flowers and Fruits,** No. 3..................	Bouvier.	Bouvier.	18	22		3 00
3220	— " 4.................. *Suite to No. 809 of Catalogue.*	—	—	—	—		—

FIGURE 2. Lithographs advertised in "First Supplement to the Catalogue of Goupil and Co., New York, January 1855." *Courtesy of American Antiquarian Society.*

FIGURE 3. *Above.* Currier & Ives, *The Last Supper. Private collection.*

FIGURE 4. *Left.* Image of Jesus engraved by W. E. Marshall, after Leonardo's *Last Supper.* H. W. Beecher, *Life of Jesus, the Christ* (New York: J. B. Ford, 1871), frontispiece.

FIGURE 5. Print of Raphael's *Sistine Madonna,* from the *London Art Journal,* 1860. *Private collection.*

FIGURE 6. Detail (upper half) of broadside advertising Rosalie Pelby's "Exhibition of Wax Statuary," including her *Last Supper. Courtesy of American Antiquarian Society.*

Perhaps no other form of religious art is more saddening and at times more nauseating than the anemic, weak, sentimentalized "likenesses" of the Christ. Hofmann, Sallman and more recently Christy have portrayed a Christ that is not worthy. Remember, we do not know what Jesus *looked* like. We do know what he *was like*. Christ was not weak. The very fact that Christ is shown as being physically handsome is open to question. Perhaps he was, but he was a Jew living in Palestine some nineteen hundred years ago and he led a hard life. He could be both tender and powerful in this strength and terrible in his attack on the Scribes. He did not always say nice things to people. He died a horrible death of torture. None of these things do I find in these pictures. Instead I find a prettied portrait for the sentimental that has no character. These portraits of Christ do indicate the degree to which we have weakened and sentimentalized our faith. We don't like the sermon that hits us, only those vague ones that hit other people.

Truth in Art

The end of art is not beauty but satisfaction through experience.

BY MARION JUNKIN

WHEN MARTIN LUTHER threw an ink pot at the devil, the decorative splash it made on the wall was the final signature to an era of glorious religious art. For three centuries the artists of Italy, Flanders, Germany and Spain had ministered to the needs of the church for paintings, stained-glass windows, carved pews, sculpture, illuminated books, and anything else that might make the service of the church more beautiful. When the Protestant churches hung up a "no help wanted" sign to the artists, much of the richness and beauty of church worship was lost. For the artists served the church well and made more real those things of the spirit and soul. Today the Episcopal Church alone has retained some of the warmth and feeling of reverence which the Gothic architecture evokes.

As a Protestant, I know the causes of the Reformation and why these reforms were necessary, but I do not think so much that was good should have been surrendered to the Catholic Church. I believe that when the church rejected the artist and no longer needed his work, it lost a spiritual ally. The church needs what the artist can give and certainly the artist needs what the church can give. In its beginning Christianity was a mystical Eastern religion and the Western peoples have very cleverly turned it into a code of ethics that fits well into our materialistic pattern of life. No better illustration of this can be found than in the ethical imperatives of the Sermon on the Mount and in the disregard shown it by both laymen and ministers.

In many churches the Sunday worship service is held in a building devoid of aesthetic satisfaction. At times I have wondered if this was deliberate. In some denominations I am sure it is. This cold atmosphere for worship places on the minister a heavy burden. If the sermon is a flop then the entire service is

22 motive

a failure, but where there is beauty, as in a Gothic chapel, and satisfying music, one is helped to feel a reverence that induces meditation and spiritual contact so that even if the sermon is not inspiring, one feels that something has been received. When I worship in an ugly church, I often feel that my religion is being received as an unpleasant medicine, something I ought to take but that actually tastes nasty.

ANOTHER and perhaps more important respect in which the church should assume a long-neglected responsibility is in helping to form the aesthetic standards of young people so that they will have some appreciation for the finer things of life. Art, music, literature, architecture, drama and poetry are forms of expression. People who love these things have inner resources that make them finer and more interesting people. I think that a Christian should be as interesting as possible in addition to being good. To be good but dull does not attract others to our way of life. By this I do not mean that we should turn our services into art classes and book review clubs. But there are many ways in which we could direct our youth toward a wider understanding of cultural things.

Take, for example, the dreadful colored pictures distributed each Sunday in the church schools. They are made by commercial hacks who have no interest in religion, and are devoid of any expressive sense. These pictures instill into the child's consciousness a feeling that in Bible times people lived in a purple and pink landscape with lovely flowers, where everything was sweet. No wonder then when these tots grow up they like trashy pictures, trashy movies, trashy radio programs. There are several things that could be done to change this situation. First, if pictures must be used why not reproduce the old masters whenever possible. Second, insist that the lithograph companies get a more vigorous group of artists to do their work. Third, have the children draw their own versions of the story (and do not be too critical). Fourth, a few large reproductions of the old masters' works around the walls would certainly add to the attractiveness of the rooms. Fifth, if there are any artists who are members of the church ask them to talk to the children about the paintings and about good art.

The suggestion of having the children draw their own versions of the story is the best because it gives a creative approach. Often there is opposition to this sort of thing both in art and in music. A friend attempted to help with the music in the primary department of a large city church recently. She is a fine musician and has had a lot of experience. She began immediately to teach the children some of the older German, English and French hymns and carols with the idea that it would be well for them to know good music rather than the stupid songs so often indicated in the weekly lesson. She was actively opposed in this, however, by teachers who wished to continue in the set pattern of procedure regardless of how inane it was. There was no question that the children loved the better music, but tradition and habit won and my friend was obliged to give up the work.

We underestimate the importance of early impressions and I am sure that childhood contact with good art and music will go on through life. I am so convinced of this that I destroy the offending art work as soon as my child gets home from Sunday school and substitute something better from my collection of prints or books.

I SERIOUSLY doubt if much can be done about the art and music in the church and church school unless there are in each community a few people who understand and know good art and music. Many of the young people of college age are receiving fine training in the arts today and should be trusted to help in these matters. For the sake of those who would like to have a clearer understanding, I would like to make a few notes that may be of help, and to show in the illustrations for this article a few comparisons of good and bad art. These examples are for adults and are not suggested for children in the church school.

It is necessary to remember that art is, after all, not a representation of what something looks like. This should be self-evident but it is depressing to realize how many people still believe this. Again art is not beauty. Art is not what God made in nature. *Art is man's way of expressing his feelings*, and many mediums are used such as paint, stone, copper, wood, etc. A painting is supposed to be felt rather than looked at. This can be done with a little training and discipline. Lines for instance have many different qualities such as:

In this portrayal of the Christ Rouault is in no way attempting to show us what Christ looked like. He is trying to express what Christ suffered. This torture is a torture expressed in the very lines and colors, not something added to a visual image. The ability to feel form and respond to line and color directly is fundamental to an appreciation of art and in religious art especially the feeling must be a direct contact with these elements. This may take time and training but it is worth the effort in the enrichment of our natures and the increased capacity we have for spiritual experience. The end of art is not beauty but satisfaction through experience. We can look at great art and see nothing just as we can read or hear and not understand. "To him that hath ears to hear. . . ."

October 1949 23

FIGURE 7. Marion Junkin, "Truth in Art," *motive* 10, no. 1 (October 1949). *Courtesy of the General Board of Higher Education and Ministry, The United Methodist Church, Nashville, Tennessee. Used by permission.*

FIGURE 8. Union Theological Seminary Exhibition of Contemporary Religious Art, *motive* 13, no. 6 (March 1953). *Courtesy of the General Board of Higher Education and Ministry, The United Methodist Church, Nashville, Tennessee. Used by permission.*

FIGURE 9. Warner Sallman, *Head of Christ*, 1940. *Copyright 1941 Warner Press, Inc., Anderson, Indiana, all rights reserved. Used by permission.*

"The Sermon on the Mount," by Fred Nagler (American, 1891 -)

Mr. Nagler has painted many pictures based on the life of Christ. His statements concerning Christ in historic settings are contemporary and convincing. In "The Sermon on the Mount" Jesus is shown towering over an amorphous crowd, his disciples behind him. He is speaking with an authority that amazes his hearers. Nagler never gets lost in his subject matter. As one is drawn into the picture he is aware that among the crowds of our own day the Christ is with us, speaking with authority.

Courtesy, Midtown Galleries

Young people like them modern

by Charles H. BOYLES

Executive Staff, National Conference of Methodist Youth, Nashville, Tennessee

"Maze and Chi Rho."

Margaret Rigg, art editor of *motive*, has stated the same theme Nagler treats above—God with us—in a radically different way. Using two symbols, one a contemporary maze and the other the ancient Chi Rho, she has suggested that in the midst of life's conflict Christ speaks his word.

Courtesy, motive

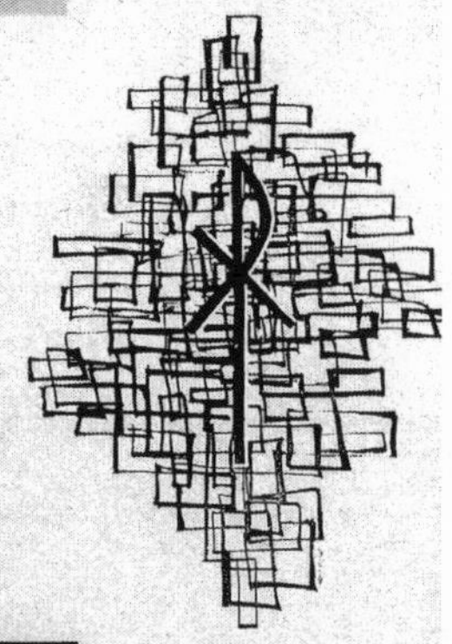

"The Last Supper," by Robe[rt] Hodgell (Contemporary Ame[r]ican)

In "The Last Supper," t[he] "subject matter" is concern[ed] with our Lord's revelation: "O[ne] of you will betray me." T[he] "content," on the other hand, [is] the meaning of Holy Commu[n]ion—namely, that around t[he] Communion table, the Christ [is] in our midst, revealing us gr[o]tesque creatures for what we a[re] and at the same time redeemi[ng] us. The feelings of the discipl[es] involved in the scene are n[ot] different from the estrangeme[nt,] meanness, and despair, felt [by] the youth of this day.

Courtesy, motive

FIGURE 10. "Young People Like Them Modern," in "Art in Christian Education," special issue, *International Journal of Religious Education* 35, no. 6 (February 1959). *Presbyterian Historical Society, Presbyterian Church (U.S.A.), Philadelphia.*

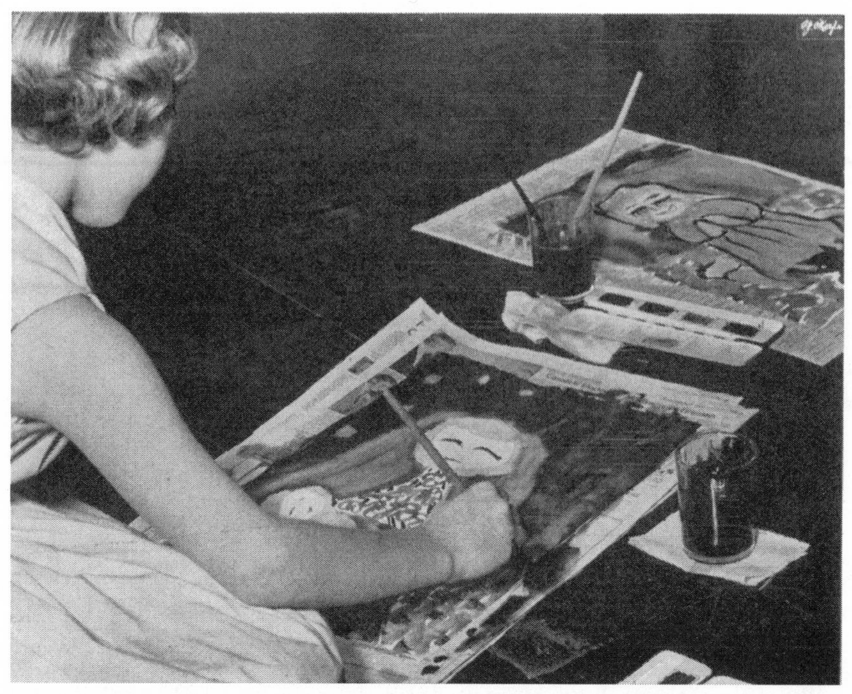

FIGURE 11. Girl in Sunday School painting a picture of Mary with baby Jesus, in "Art in Christian Education," special issue, *International Journal of Religious Education* 35, no. 6 (February 1959): 28. *Presbyterian Historical Society, Presbyterian Church (U.S.A.), Philadelphia.*

THREE

Visible Liberalism

Liberal Protestant Taste Evangelism, 1850 and 1950

SALLY M. PROMEY

It is tempting to posit a special relationship between liberal religion and visual culture—and especially between liberal religion and fine art. Liberalism comports well with certain prospects for art; the overlap between liberal theology and art theory, and between liberal theology and aesthetics, in the nineteenth and twentieth centuries is striking. Liberal religious authors, one after another, assert affinities joining art to spirituality. The particular shape of the partnership, however, is heavily dependent on the specificities of the contexts in which conversations and connections take place.

This chapter's pages consider, first and most extensively, a range of key liberal figures of mid-nineteenth-century Protestantism in terms of their commitments to the visual arts. Having examined the shape of this engagement in the several decades around 1850, my narrative turns, by way of comparison, to the mid-twentieth-century liberal Protestant taste evangelism I have explored in the past.[1] The moments that catch attention here are episodes in the spiritualization of art. In each instance proponents connected, in various ways and degrees, to the institutional church advocated a sort of aesthetic spirituality, which they insisted was even more intensely available outside the church's walls than within them.

Religious liberalism has long had high expectations for art. Romanticism, from which American liberal thought in its Transcendentalist and Bushnell-ian modes drew deeply, assigned both art and religion to the faculty of the imagination and emphasized the familial relationship by referring to the two as "sisters."[2] From the beginning, as it took shape, Protestant liberalism was "visible" in the sense that it explicitly articulated its connections to visual practices, to art, and to taste. In 1847 the Hartford Congregationalist pastor Horace Bushnell described Christian nurture as a process of moral and spiritual refinement, akin, one might justifiably argue (and he did), to the development of taste.[3]

Just a few years prior to the publication of his *Discourses on Christian Nurture* Bushnell wrote an essay defining taste as the capacity that "distinguishes the glorious and fair in all earthly things, and especially in their divinely constituted relation to truth and the life of the mind." He continued, "The highest known example of taste is that of the Almighty, when he invents the forms, colors, and proportions, of this visible creation. . . . The whole fabric of creation is an exertion of taste." The aim of the tasteful Christian, then, he argued, must be to discern the proximity of things to an ideal of beauty and truth designed by God as divine artist. Taste, as exercised, practiced, and ritually performed by humans, was similar to God's taste in creation except that in humans it was "slowly cultivated and matured" and not at once "inherently complete," as in Bushnell's God. Human taste "is a power which goes to school, as we may say, to nature [i.e., to God's creation], and by exercise on the forms of natural beauty, is waked into action." Human taste, once awakened, Bushnell insisted, "is as truly original as the taste of God, and is one of the highest points of resemblance to him in [human] nature. . . . the forms it invents [i.e., the arts] . . . are all original, and are the offspring of the soul's great liberty." "In all the fine arts, in statuary, painting, [poetry,] music, gardening, landscape," and dress, "the beauty created is a vehicle of truth and feeling." The artist "fills your soul at once with the thronging images of truth—truths of the head, truths of the heart—all coming in visible shapes to be a spell upon you and fill you with their power."[4]

Human taste, the ability to discern beauty and to exercise discretion in this respect, was a key constituent of liberal theology for Bushnell and his cohort and, for them, a key factor in humanity's likeness to deity. In Bushnell's rendering, taste was democratic in that anyone could cultivate it: taste was a "universal possibility," open "to all."[5] Bushnell's theology of Christian nurture, dependent on a gradual process of moral and spiritual refinement, with the child imbibing much from familial surroundings and example, upped the ante for religious uses of art, especially in the home, which was, for him, the "church of childhood."[6] Liberal theology, in Bushnell's terms, relied on familiar visual ministries of the domestic environment to participate in shaping Christian individuals, families, and society, and it relied on tastefully decorated homes to help realize the Christian nurture of children.

Prominent Congregationalist Henry Ward Beecher would have agreed with Bushnell on this matter; both men urged parents to "refine" their offspring's "thoughts by early familiarity with art."[7] Like Bushnell, Beecher (and many of his contemporaries) constructed aesthetics and domestic design as liberal Christian practices. Like Bushnell, Beecher operated within a domestic economy that assumed the presence of pictures, and he promoted this pictorial availability within an explicitly liberal Christian frame of expectation. Illustrations in popular periodicals and books articulated the visual association of homes with Christian devotional spaces.[8] Within the Beecher family, Henry Ward's sisters Catherine Beecher and Harriet Beecher Stowe provided explicit instructions for manifesting the domestic-religious link in the multiple editions of their *American Woman's Home* (fig. 1).[9]

The pages of the liberal *Christian Union,* between 1870 and 1878 edited by Henry Ward Beecher, contributed much to the industry in Christian home decoration, what one slightly later anonymous essayist for this journal called "the household art craze."[10] Looking back in 1871, Blandina Conant (professor of English literature at Rutgers College and daughter of the biblical scholar Reverend Thomas Jefferson Conant) celebrated, as a "most hopeful sign," the "growing love of the beautiful among our people, testified to by the multiplication of engravings, chromos, photographs. . . . For the love of beauty lifts the soul above its ordinary tone, above the sordid cares of life; and as the taste becomes refined and ennobled, the whole nature is enriched and elevated."[11] It is not hyperbolic in the least to say (with a nod to Jon Butler)[12] that, in this period of exponential growth in print reproductive techniques and the commercial print market, mid-nineteenth-century liberal Christianity found itself awash in a sea of pictures, available through catalogues (fig. 2) and various retail venues at relatively little expense.

Writing in 1846 in the liberal *Christian Examiner,* an author identified as GFS asserted that the introduction into the Christian home of inexpensive prints, like one derived from Leonardo's *Last Supper* (fig. 3, e.g.) to which GFS pointed, "is of more importance to those that live in it, than all the ornaments of mechanic art." Valued for its beauty as well as "in a religious way," the picture preaches more persuasively than a sermon, it comments on the characters of the Apostles more distinctly and graphically than the annotator, and by fixing permanently that great event in a definite form before the eye, it wins the imagination to linger on it, corrects our narrow ideas by the truer and larger conceptions of genius, and becomes the suggestor and the nucleus of a multitude of sacred affections of our own. . . . a certain moral illumination is spread [in proximity to the picture], and the tempers and occupations of the family are guarded and presided over, as it were by a household angel. By the magic of art and the multiplication of mechanical contrivance, the poor man ornaments his apartment with the image, which in the happier moments of a sacred age visited and adorned the quiet recesses of a great, a pure, and a consummately instructed soul.[13]

From Protestantism's inception material objects (pictures, works of art, ritual artifacts) represented key pressure points.[14] Protestants jettisoned many "Catholic" objects and practices and reframed or repurposed others. They struggled to invent and justify, and to reclaim and reconfigure. They nonetheless continued to occupy a rich and richly visual material universe, all the while understanding their own tradition (vis-à-vis Catholicism) to require a certain suspicion of objects—or at least the assertion of suspicion of objects. In fact, the *stuff* of Protestant devotions acquired a kind of energy from the very ambivalent positions art, artifacts, and decorated objects now held, being fraught (rhetorically at least) with the potential for aiding spiritual growth or for eliciting idolatry. It became a distinctly Protestant practice to claim, in each new moment over time, clear boundaries between Protestant and Catholic devotions, to position Protestant material practice (whatever its specific historical or denominational shape in that moment) as *Protestant.*

Among liberal Protestants in the mid-nineteenth-century decades of our interest here, a great deal of ink was spilled in locating and asserting some middle ground between two posited (negative) extremes: uses (and abuses) of pictures deemed "Puritan" and those deemed "Catholic." Liberal commentators argued that the new world (by which they meant the United States), its natural treasures, its democratic ways, and even its addition of "French vivacity and grace" to "English coldness and gravity" elicited "new and kinder elements" in the "Puritan" that "became essential parts of [a new American] character" and paved the way for renewed flourishing of taste and of the arts.[15] Agreeing with a critic going by the initials GEE that "Christian art and symbolism belong not to the Roman Church alone,"[16] GFS claimed for Protestants the great religious masterworks of Europe. He maintained, for example, the explicitly "Protestant" character of the Catholic Leonardo's *Last Supper:*

> And herein the picture is particularly interesting to us,—that the subject did not belong peculiarly to the Roman Catholic Church, but to the Church in all time, and that it was treated in such a manner as to be equally symbolical to every nation and time as to his own. No gilded halos around the heads, Peter is not burdened with the keys, nor are any saints in monkish garments introduced as assisting; but all is liberal, untechnical, simple, appealing to the Christian heart, nay, to the human heart, to the best and most universal sensibilities in our nature, so that in the various copies of itself, manifold in their degrees of imperfection, which, while it [the original] is fading away, it has called into life, and sent, as it were like messengers from Leonardo's heart, all over Europe and into the residences of other races, it will continue to charm and raise the soul for generations upon generations, wherever tenderness or generosity of heart is found.[17]

For RCW (another liberal religious critic), far from being "mere matters of luxury" or Catholic "idols," the fine arts can speak "the language of heaven." In interpreting and representing not merely outward appearances but the "inward life" of nature and persons and things, art, whether its subject is otherwise religious or not, can be "one of the chief instrumentalities in spiritualizing mankind."[18]

A bit over two decades later, Blandina Conant focused her attention on "art illustrations of the Bible," especially those in Beecher's *Life of Christ* (fig. 4), pictures she lauded for their ability to "set before us the veritable scenes of Christ's earthly ministry," while not relinquishing productive uses of imagination. Like others quoted in this chapter, Conant recuperated Leonardo's *Last Supper* as Protestant art:

> The finest illustration of the whole book is the frontispiece, a splendid steel engraving after Leonardo da Vinci's "Last Supper." The original picture, neglected by the stupid monks to whose care this inestimable treasure was committed, has long been fading, and is now almost obliterated. But it has been restored, painted and engraved by one of our own artists, Mr. W. E. Marshall, expressly for this work. This representation of our Saviour, long acknowledged to be the finest ever conceived, has been made familiar to us by innumerable copies and engravings. . . . But here the artist has sought to reproduce not merely the outward form, but the spirit of the original. Love and sorrow, the human and the superhuman, meet in that wonderful countenance. The sorrowful words, "One of you shall betray me," have just been uttered, and the drooping eyes, the parted lips, the bowed head, testify of wounded affection, human infirmity, mingling with divine compassion.[19]

Art historian Rachael DeLue is the most astute interpreter to date of the visual theory of Henry Ward Beecher. DeLue considers Beecher in her 2004 book *George Inness and the Science of Landscape.* She demonstrates that Beecher, an early collector of the Swedenborgian Inness's paintings, sought a kind of spiritual viewing of nature and of art, a vision that "penetrated beyond the surface of things and toward the divine."[20] Beecher described what he meant in a cluster of essays that first appeared in various newspapers in the 1840s and '50s and were then gathered and published as *Star Papers* (1855) and *Eyes and Ears* (1862). He relied in his notion of taste on Archibald Alison's late eighteenth-century theory of association, to which many of his contemporaries, including Bushnell, also had frequent recourse.[21] Following Alison, Beecher's aesthetic depended on the capacity of art and nature (which he and others of his time read as "God's second book") to elicit memory and imagination and the feelings linked to them. For Beecher, feelings and emotions were as much a part of this experience as rational thought. (One task the arts performed for religious liberalism, in fact, was to chart new space for affective experience in decades when various evangelicalisms claimed religious "passions" for themselves, criticizing liberalism's lack of "zeal.")[22] Furthermore, the viewing of a work of art, God's art in nature or humanity's on canvas, not only brought to mind Beecher's own affective memories but invited him to imagine the memories of anyone who had ever looked at these works of art.

Beecher's viewing of Niagara Falls, for instance, which natural wonder he understood as the creation of the divine artist, evoked "recollections" reaching back to biblical times and connected to the varying emotions of all those Beecher imagined to have set foot at the falls before him. The galleries of the Louvre Museum collected the works of human artistry and genius. Strikingly, Beecher referred to the museum as "this wilderness of beauty."[23] It pays to note here his description of the art museum as a natural paradise, and this assertion's connections to places of natural beauty. The art museum worked on Beecher's imagination, he claimed, in a manner similar to Niagara Falls. In Beecher's terms, each had a similar effect:

> The [gallery's] walls beam upon you as if each was a summer; and, like one strolling at summer's eve, you cannot tell whether it be the clouds, the sky, the light, the shadows, the scenery, or the thousand remembrances which rise over the soul in such an hour, that give the pleasure. I saw all that the painter painted, and more; I imagined in each scene . . . what had gone before, and what has followed. I talked with the beautiful or fearful creatures, and they spake to me. . . . The sense of beauty, beauty of every kind . . . was inexpressible. . . . It was a blessed exhalation of soul, in which I seemed freed from matter and, as a diffused intelligence, to float in the atmosphere. . . . I had a sense of expansion, of etherealization, which gave me some faint sense of a spiritual state.[24]

In the aesthetic vocabulary of romanticism, he might well have called the self-transcendence he experienced "the sublime." Beecher described yielding, before art, to "sympathy and enthusiasm," to an "intuitional moral instruction" provided by this "higher mood of feeling." "The subjects of many of the works," he said (and only some of them represented religion), "seemed a not unfitting accompaniment to my mind, and suggested to me, in a glorious vision, the drawing near of a redeemed soul to the precincts of Heaven!"[25]

Unitarian and Transcendentalist Cyrus Bartol, writing at almost precisely the same moment in time, was even more emphatic than Beecher about the elevated spiritual facility presented by immersion in the fine arts. In a book aptly titled *Pictures of Europe, Framed in Ideas,* Bartol invited other "pilgrims" to the "shrine," the "splendid temple of art." He recommended what he called "picture-language" as superior to text for its (presumed) universal legibility. "Looking at good pictures [of almost any subject] is . . . an informing and elevating study for the soul."[26] A landscape painting, for example, is a

> speaking likeness of Nature herself, made lively by touches of imagination out of the finest recollections of the artist. . . . What a device and discovery of enjoyment and improvement [are these] visions of light, serenity, and verdure, that bring back pleasant spots in your actual pilgrimage, remind you of other days, or transport you . . . to the place where you were born.[27]

"The images of religion" Bartol celebrated as the highest art, "the New Testament turned into colors. . . . Among all the versions so famous of the Bible into different tongues of the nations, is this translation into the one universal language of mankind. Particularly the career of Jesus Christ is thus represented in hues and forms that speak with moving eloquence to every soul." The "sublime speech of the canvas" communicates beyond the Babel of competing languages, and

> Art becomes another, yea, a fifth, evangelist before you, proclaiming with her mute but mighty trumpet, like that she paints in the mouth of angels, the eternal lessons of truth and duty. . . . And here are discourses and conversations and parables, the holiest ever uttered, without words or accents. . . . The prodigal returns to his father's arms, and you almost hear upon the strings—for we listen to pictures as well as look at them—the tune that gives the time to those flying feet.[28]

Art was not only a fifth evangelist but also a "second gospel" into which the artist converted the first:

> Verily, Art is nothing less than a preacher, the most penetrating and convincing in all the company of those that preach,—their welcome sister. . . . So the one figure most

> beautiful and sublime in art, is . . . the figure of Jesus Christ. In every situation,—a babe in his mother's arms, a boy in the temple among the doctors, healing the sick, raising the dead, or himself rising, transfigured, crucified, glorified; his life, his passion, his ascension,—every thing about him is seized by Art for her best endeavors, and often finest success.
>
> So I felt, especially before one delineation of the holy mother and her child Jesus, which makes the pride and glory of the German city of Dresden [fig. 5]. . . . It mixed for me the transport of wonder with the ecstasy of delight; it affected me like the sign of miracle; it was the supernatural put into color and form; for certainly no one, who received the suggestion of those features . . . could doubt any longer . . . of there being a God, a heaven, and, both before and beyond the sepulchre, an immortal life. . . . [In this image] was Christianity itself. . . . The argument for religion . . . which was offered to my mind in the great Madonna of Raphael, cannot fail.[29]

Art itself was justified in its testimony to religion.

Print reproductions of fine paintings did not constitute the only media for bringing the splendors of European arts to American shores, and domestic spaces did not function in a vacuum as venues for engaging pictorial and material arts. Rosalie French Pelby (1793–1857), born in Kinderhook, New York, began her professional career as a chorus singer in Boston in 1813. An entry in *Appleton's Cyclopedia* indicates that she excelled in melodrama and quickly became a popularly acclaimed actress.[30] It is for her work as another kind of performer, however, that she merits attention here. She became a sculptor of wax figures illustrating religious and moral subjects, working in a wide variety of scales; the largest of her works offered viewers the sensation of personally witnessing the scenes she depicted (fig. 6).

For at least two decades, beginning as early as 1834 with her life-size wax rendition of *The Last Supper,* Pelby took her displays on the road, making especially frequent stops in Philadelphia, New York, and Boston. While her aims were certainly also commercial, she presented her work and its subjects as both art and religion and claimed for the artist a vocation that was religious as well as artistic. An exhibition pamphlet for a slightly later Pelby display explicitly articulated her investment in this dual aim: "The Artist, in portraying this memorable event, has entered fully into the spirit of the subject, and produced a work worthy of the attentive study of all lovers of the Arts, and the disciples and followers of the lowly Jesus."[31] In 1843, one Boston critic applauded Pelby's *Sermon on the Mount* for its facility in "prepar[ing] the heart to receive those pure and sublime doctrines" from the mouth of Jesus.[32]

When Pelby sculpted *The Last Supper,* she chose as the model for her three-dimensional display the two-dimensional masterpiece by Leonardo da Vinci.

The booklet designed to orient and inform the ensemble's paying viewers asserted that "the Arrangement of this Exhibition is Entirely Novel in its Character. The Figures of our Saviour and his Apostles. In Wax. The Size of Life, and the Proprietor is confident the whole will be pronounced a Correct, Spirited, and Beautiful Representation, on a Large Scale, of the celebrated Da Vinci's Greatest Production."[33] With no discernible irony, Pelby's recitation reproduced an earlier scholarly description of Leonardo's fresco as an explication of her own sculptural work in wax. She could, moreover, count on fairly widespread public recognition of the work of the Italian Renaissance master, since many variations on his design circulated in popular print media in the United States, and the liberal Protestant press on numerous occasions referred to the famous original as well as its many copies. Despite Leonardo's Catholicism, and like other liberal Protestant descriptions of the time, the exhibition pamphlets that Pelby and her sponsors published articulated from a decidedly liberal Protestant perspective the scriptural event depicted in her life-scale wax production. Pelby emphasized commemoration rather than transubstantiation, and she framed commemoration with a latitude that would have embraced a wide range of Protestant interpretations among her presumed spectators:

> He [Christ] saw, in the broken bread and in the flowing wine, the symbols and mementos of his own body and blood. It was instituted in remembrance of our Lord; therefore it is a means of spiritual improvement, and is kept for Christ's sake, to glorify him amongst men. It is in accordance with human nature, which has ever delighted to commemorate the lives and deaths of the great and good. All who feel their obligations to Jesus Christ as their spiritual benefactor, cherish a living faith in him as the Son of God, resolve to keep his commandments, and profess his name, are entitled to a place at his table. Let this feast of love be kept with the pure aim for which it was instituted—in remembrance of him who died, that we might live.[34]

Often exhibited against a mirror to let viewers see her ensembles "in the round," the creations of this "Celebrated Female Artist," through their facial expressions, gestures, and costumes, and through the "life-like" material qualities of the medium, were "calculated to awaken sensations not only pleasing but [morally and spiritually] profitable."[35] In the descriptive texts, guidebooks, and orientation manuals, the apparatus of aesthetic education and religious formation combined with that of commercial entertainment. A reporter from *Zion's Herald* enthused about one of her other sculptural ensembles, *Trial of Christ,* and its role in moral and religious formation: "When we were there about two hundred children of one of our Sunday Schools were there with their Pastor, who was very happy in his remarks upon the subject. . . . The Rev. Mr. Gray, by aid of the descriptive pamphlet, explained each figure separately, . . . and we venture to say [the children] will never forget it."[36]

Pelby's wax creations, far from being aberrations or oddities, suggest the degree to which Protestant (and other) audiences in the United States were prepared to entertain intimate connections with the visual and plastic arts. While contemporary critics acknowledged a definite hierarchy in the visual arts and entertainments, they appreciated the capacities of many sorts of objects to cultivate taste and emotion; among these objects they included not only fine oil painting and sculpture but also such displays as Pelby's wax ensembles and the panoramic paintings that circulated among audiences in the same decades. One commentator expounded,

> The same increasing and improving taste is seen in the number of excellent engravings, richly illustrated books, busts, and other works of art which abound. . . . Modern science has brought new materials to the aid of art, and if these are used for circulating only good models, it will tend incalculably to foster a more refined taste. The panoramas, which have become centres of attraction to multitudes, manifest the same popular tendency. It is true that many of these are very rudely executed. Yet they are an infinitely more refined means of pleasure than many which have hitherto been offered, and some of them deserve to be spoken of as works of art.
>
> We know there is a great danger of vitiating, instead of improving, the public taste, where quantity rather than quality is considered. A good picture is seldom to be measured by the mile. Still, this is a fair field for talent, and in proportion as such works possess real merit, they open to the multitude a source of innocent gratification, and often of positive improvement. They bring delineations before the eye, which may lead to a closer observation of nature itself; and the portrayal of beauty, even thus given, will awaken in many minds a taste for works of a higher order. It is an interesting fact, that hundreds and thousands, throughout our land, after the toils of the day, seek in such exhibitions a refined pleasure.[37]

Another example of the mid-nineteenth-century liberal religious thinking about art's material capacities with respect to religion inclines attention toward James Jackson Jarves, whose career suggests the fundamental role played by liberal religion in shaping fine art appreciation and art history in the United States. Jarves's books were widely reviewed in liberal religious periodicals. One reviewer in 1855 identified his *Art Hints* as a "noble sermon on Art" that showed beauty to be the "natural ally and handmaid of true religion and civilization." Following Jarves, the anonymous reviewer maintained his own conviction that the United States was "in a far better condition to profit by the wonders of Art than our European brethren who are in possession of them." Liberal religion (i.e., liberal Protestantism), according to this reviewer, was still possible in the United States, where it occupied a broad middle ground between Europe's Catholic and Enlightenment "extremes." In the United States, he continued, "bigotry and despotism, the priest and the tyrant, have not yet drained the lifeblood from our souls. Religion still holds us in her firm grasp or her gentle embrace. Our educated men are not yet atheistic, as is so largely and sadly the case with educated men on the continent of Europe." Calling for a religion of love and sentiment rather than fear and dogma, the reviewer issued what might stand as a liberal Protestant manifesto in praise of Jarves's volume.[38]

Much of what is known about the particulars of Jarves's commitments, scholarship owes to art historian Charles Colbert's expert analysis.[39] Unlike Bushnell, Beecher, and Bartol, Jarves was not a member of the clergy but a newspaper editor, a sometime diplomat, and an early art critic, historian, and American collector of Italian Old Master paintings. The attractions of works of art for Jarves included the associative powers endorsed by Beecher and Bartol. Beyond this, however, Jarves's involvements in Spiritualism, mesmerism, and Swedenborgianism (which signaled for him the welcome demise of religious dogmatism) led him to invest even greater spiritual powers in aesthetic objects: Jarves understood the work of art (through the operation of mesmeric, psychometric "imponderable fluids") to retain the literal and figurative traces not just of its maker but of every person with whom it came in contact over time. Mediums (and art critics and enthusiasts), responding to these traces, could reconnect with long-departed souls through sensitive proximity to the objects.

Art, for Jarves (who became a medium himself), was thus a reservoir of human longing and devotion; art objects gathered up the tides of grief and gratitude residual to human emotion and experience. He meant it when he said of one of his key publications on art, "If I had not had the spiritual communion with generations gone, through the medium of what they have left behind visible to our senses, it would have been impossible to have written this book."[40] To attain the requisite "quality of judgment," the art critic "must have an affinity for the motives and understanding of the artist as sensitive as the wire to electric current"; this refined "quality of judgment" was available to those who studied and meditated diligently and attentively at the altar of art.[41] Reinforcing and elaborating space that had been cleared, by Bushnell, Beecher, and the like, for liberal Protestant household altars to art, Jarves fully expected American "progress" to soon produce a population "ripen[ed] into an aesthetic and worshipping race, with a spiritual God."[42]

> Humanity errs . . . in always fixing on a future period for its realization of its ideal heaven; not seeing that its coveted happiness depends rather on present conditions of mind . . . when those conditions are in harmony with spiritual laws. Material objects then become gracious accessories [and he meant this theologically—*gracious* accessories] instead of being the imperious principles of life.[43]

Jarves's theological aesthetic provided a concrete material rationale for Beecher's associationism: contact with the spiritual world was literally mediated by physical objects that retained traces of all those spirits who had ever touched them—or even enjoyed close proximity.

This chapter has so far established that a number of key nineteenth-century figures had (primarily) personal connections to liberalism and the fine arts. Through these people and others like them, theological liberalism also had a considerable impact on arts institutions and arts education. John Ferguson Weir, first dean of the School of Fine Arts at Yale University, for example, was a liberal Episcopalian and, along with his wife Mary, a believer in Spiritualism. He served Yale's fine art program for forty-four years, during which time he wrote and lectured widely on religion and art.[44] When, in 1879, Weir sought the right candidate for Yale's first professor of art history, he selected Congregationalist clergyman James Mason Hoppin, a veteran Yale professor of homiletics (1861–79) who also held a law degree from Harvard. Hoppin taught in this fine arts capacity for twenty years, bringing (along with Weir) a liberal Protestant believer's perspective to bear on the process of shaping visual arts education at this elite academic institution.

American liberal Protestantism, from its cultural, theological, and institutional advents, then, made of visual art an implement in its drawer of utensils, a tool in its workbox, a fifth evangelist, and a second gospel—and, looking ahead to the next century, a weapon in its arsenal. This chapter now redirects the reader's attention to another moment in time and another liberal Protestant engagement with art. The jump ahead should not be taken to suggest that liberal Protestants relinquished visual culture in the decades between 1880 and 1940. While much changed, the intensity of connection was consistent over time—despite the rhetoric of the 1950s parties, who argued that they sought to reimplement a Christian engagement of art lost to Protestantism since the Reformation. (In precisely this respect, it pays to bear in mind that mid-nineteenth-century liberal Protestants claimed the same innovative recuperation for themselves, as had others before them.) In the 1850s and the 1950s professionals in both religion and art participated in bridging liberal religion and visual culture and, in both cases, the fine arts were seen to play a special elevating role—in both cases discernment and taste were fundamental constituents in the equation.

In the 1950s, however, a sense of crisis hardened the language framing the conversation into a set of rigid dualisms, positing two distinct taste cultures and marking aesthetic, theological, social, and cultural fault lines between them (fig. 7).[45] These 1950s liberal Protestants essentially reacted to their own visual history, rejecting as anti-art the "sentimental" Christian Romanticism of earlier Protestant liberalism (and, not coincidentally, contemporary Protestant evangelicalism) and elevating a "virile," "masculine" Romantic alternative in Expressionism and Abstract Expressionism. The highly gendered nature of this engagement is worth remarking. Its experts' revisions of the aesthetics of the sublime, for example, worked to instantiate a particular ideal of heteronormative masculinity. The vehemence of the attack, moreover, suggests the success of earlier campaigns to put sentimentalizing pictures in Protestant homes and churches.

From 1945 to 1965 liberal Protestant professionals in fields of both art and religion promoted a particular theological aesthetic: The objective was not simply the beautiful but beauty (and other valued terms) distinguished by orientation toward the ultimate value and concern of "ultimate reality," in the words of the existentialist theologian Paul Tillich. Tillich, along with Alfred Barr (founding director of the Museum of Modern Art and an active Presbyterian) and Marvin Halverson (an executive of the National Council of Churches and a Congregationalist clergyman), most publicly, persuasively, and persistently articulated the connections between "authentic" art and "authentic" religion. Tillich's theology of culture contributed substantially to the framing and specific vocabulary of the "new" liberal Protestant aesthetics. And his notion of ultimate reality presented an especially popular contemporary theological variation on the Romantic sublime.

Barr and Tillich joined ranks in arguing that the religious content of a work of art resides most significantly in its style rather than subject matter, in "expression" rather than "depiction." This meant that a painting could be "religious" even when its subject matter was not—and, furthermore, even when its subject matter was not recognizable. Barr's highly influential 1943 book, *What*

Is Modern Painting?, played a significant role in laying out, for a large American audience, the terms that liberal Protestantism would use in its association of expressionist styles, spirituality, and artistic freedom.[46]

Tillich and his liberal allies wished to cultivate aesthetic discernment as Christian practice and to assert normative status for the taste culture they promoted. They recommended this discerning behavior as one that could be learned and applied to a wide variety of activities and situations, including religious decoration, exhibition (fig. 8), and display in the church, in the home, and in various kinds of public spaces. By comparison to the 1850s, this was an illiberal liberalism, manifesting latitude and sympathy for real and imagined modernist allies in Catholicism and Judaism but not for folks in the pews (or elsewhere) who embraced a different aesthetic.

The hyperbole of this 1950s liberal enterprise makes most sense in relation to the stakes of the particular historical moment. Broader contingencies surrounding the Second World War and its political and cultural aftermath intensified and extended the terms of a culture war that, in the United States, had begun several decades earlier. At its foundations, this cultural critique depended on perceived connections between certain stylistic tendencies in artistic production and political totalitarianisms of several sorts. An ideologically diverse and publicly prominent group of intellectuals attacked mass commercial culture in the United States as a proto-fascist phenomenon that debased sensibilities, enslaved individual minds and wills, and eradicated autonomy. The visual equivalent of mass culture was "kitsch." Tillich was a refugee, and for him "kitsch" was not simply a generic name, a synonym, for mass culture (although it was that too). It was, even more importantly, a stylistic designation, a name for a particular sentimental and idealized mode of art-making that characterized the worst, the most dangerous, of mass cultural representation. In direct response to Hitler's derision of modernist abstraction's "degeneracy," Tillich characterized this beautifying naturalism or kitsch, which he conflated with all forms of contemporary realism, as the "really degenerate art" (fig. 9).[47] Barr, for his part, included in *What Is Modern Painting?* a section titled "Expressionism and the Religious Spirit"; he concluded his thoughts on this subject with a statement on Adolf Hitler's aversion to expressionist art. The sentimentalizing styles rejected by Barr and Tillich looked a lot like the art that Bushnell and Beecher and later nineteenth-century liberal Protestants had promoted.

For many involved in this mid-twentieth-century liberal taste culture, direct contact with the right kind of art not only provided a satisfying aesthetic experience but also increased the beholder's "capacity . . . for spiritual experience."[48] In this debate, high cultural abstraction's "liberation" from the task of reproducing the appearance of the visible world rendered it a contemporary equivalent of freedom and asserted its capacity to function as "pure spirit." Released in this manner from subservience to the superficiality of objects as held by the eye (and the camera), abstract artists now painted out of their own inner "depths" of experience, connecting them to "ultimate" realities beneath and beyond the "mere surface" of things.[49] Mid-nineteenth-century naturalisms suited that period's commitments to sentiment and affect and its pursuit of the "historical Jesus," its interest in a particular kind of verification. In the mid-twentieth century, "realism" carried an entirely different set of aesthetic, political, and theological implications.

Liberal Protestantism's embrace of high modern abstraction not only visually distinguished it from dictatorships abroad, but also stocked its domestic arsenals in a heated exchange with evangelical Protestant "mass culture." In modernist abstraction, liberal Protestant social and political currency might be regained through endorsement of a specific sort of high religious art, deemed inhospitable to material, sentimental, commercial, and evangelical interests. Not content with simply reclaiming art for the church by promoting its widespread practice, this cohort and its allies called first and foremost for the critical viewing and valuation of art, and for a "purging" of practices and aesthetic values perceived to be not just outdated but dangerous. In an address to a constituency of liberal Protestant leaders, Alfred Barr delivered his most withering criticism:

> In the arts of painting, sculpture and book illustration our churches and churchmen seem, generally speaking, both ignorant and blind.
>
> Our churches do of course use art—but what art! Consider the vulgarity and banality of the pictures of Christ now in general use. "Gentle Jesus, meek and mild" is translated into art on the level of cosmetic and tonic advertisements. Yet these saccharine and effeminate images are distributed by millions with the tolerance and often the well-intentioned blessing of our churches. They look up at us from bulletins and calendars and Sunday school magazines and down at us from the walls of church houses and parsonages. They corrupt the religious feelings of children and nourish the complacency and sentimentality of their elders. They call for iconoclasm.[50]

Seeking to implement a strategy of opposition, containment, and replacement, the promoters of this new modernist religious aesthetic asked observant liberal Protestants to break and then to re-form visual habits. They sought to substitute one sort of Christian image for another, denouncing the alternatives as idols of conformity and sentimentality.

In 1850, liberal Protestant spiritualization of art made art more accessible in the church and home and as American cultural currency. In 1950, aesthetic spiritualization had a more complicated outcome. While it may well have made art more accessible to some audiences, and certainly improved relations between liberal churches and contemporary arts, it also made many kinds of pictures less accessible in church and home and generally sequestered its own valued "originals" in museums of fine art. Perhaps most troubling, it intensified the fear that an artistic misstep might reveal the viewer's own morally flawed "bad" taste, made many feel that they were inadequate to judge their own visual environments, and discouraged them from embracing much of the (now disapproved) art they had otherwise enjoyed.

Two major and related factors (aside from hot and cold wars and the politics of the mass culture debate) played a substantial role here: first, the larger development and reification of elitist aesthetic and economic cultural hierarchies, which, as the scholarship of Paul DiMaggio, Lawrence Levine, and others demonstrates, was actively underway by the late nineteenth and early twentieth centuries;[51] and second, the related advent of artistic abstraction. By 1950, the highest register in the visual fine arts was occupied by abstraction, a visual language that parses in peculiar ways around cultural hierarchy. Abstraction, its proponents would argue, on the one hand is open and free; it can mean anything, and so it accents the authority of the individual viewer. Abstraction, on the other hand (and this was demonstrably the majority opinion in households and among parishioners of churches across the country), is opaque; it demands an expert interpreter. The outcomes of the 1950s taste culture wars might have been different had Tillich, Halverson, and Barr embraced abstraction as an *additional* mode of visual expression, had they attended more carefully to the many kinds of realisms and the things those styles and modes accomplish in representation. If one assented to the political aesthetic they asserted, the stakes were indeed high, but the target as they imagined it was also much too large, their own visual and cultural discrimination not finely enough tuned. Things looked "alike" to them that were not alike, and the comparison of these things served ulterior purposes and signaled other sorts of investments as well.

In religious education, as Bushnell, Beecher, and Conant recognized, there was a content to be communicated, a story to be told. In this regard, abstract styles, like the ones promoted in the 1950s, had diminished narrative potential. The 1850s, with their commitments to Christian nurture, to growing healthy Christian families in a period of rapid industrialization and urbanization, offered a usually child-centered and virtually always child-friendly aesthetic. The 1950s substituted an elite and decisively adult-centered aesthetic, though Barr and his cohorts claimed intense interest in the Sunday schools and youth (fig. 10) and pointed to the abstractions of children's drawings as one source of their investment (fig. 11).

In the 1940s and '50s, arts professionals allied themselves with liberal Christian intellectuals and denominational executives in a war against bad taste, seeking to eradicate the "terrible taste of Protestantism."[52] This war magnified and rigidified the softer dualisms of Bushnell's time (his "taste," too, after all, posited its own degraded opposite in "fashion" and pushed off against other "disapproved" varieties of Protestant affect).[53] All in all, though, the decades around the 1850s evinced more confidence in every person's capacity to develop high levels of Christian taste and to embody and express that taste—there was an optimism in Beecher, Bartol, and Conant that was almost palpable. Bushnell and Beecher argued that exposing oneself to great works of art cultivated freedom and salvation. A picture might fail to satisfy, might not have the desired effect, but there was always another picture to see. Halverson, Barr, and Tillich, however, claimed that exposure to the wrong pictures (including ones that looked like those promoted by Beecher and Bushnell) paved the way to disaster. While much of the overt argument was similar and while both moments asserted the accessibility of taste to all applicants, liberal Protestants in the mid-nineteenth century promoted art principally for its positive spiritual and theological outcomes; they worried less about the negatives. The 1950s were more cautious, more vigilant, in a word, more suspicious of the powers of images and the ways art might undermine as well as support "authentic" expression of "true" Christianity, "ultimate" realities, and American moral, political, and aesthetic ideals.

The 1850s and 1950s also represented different moments in the shifting cultural capital of religion itself—and of religion vis-à-vis art in this calculation. In 1850, religion had the upper hand, "improving" art's American lot by anchoring aesthetics in pious virtues and devotional domesticities. By the 1950s, art had attained the ascendant role and now religion stood most to gain from the connection, especially in New York and in urban areas (and among wealthy philanthropists) where this episode in art's spiritualization and religion's aestheticization had its greatest strength. To oversimplify a complicated equation, in 1850 religion aided art; in 1950 art aided religion. The conversation, however, was mutual in both moments to the extent that contemporary experts in each period and in both fields of professional activity understood the American destinies of art and religion in relation to each other. Jarves and Pelby and Weir and Barr shared in this work with Bushnell and Beecher and Conant and Tillich. While historians now most frequently encounter the first four in relation to their vocations "in art" and the latter four in relation to their vocations "in religion," each of the eight publicly articulated investments in liberal religion and investments in fine arts. In both the nineteenth and twentieth centuries, liberal religious commitments of various sorts occupied a place at the heart of fine arts appreciation and the growth of fine arts infrastructure; in both the nineteenth and twentieth centuries, fine arts engagement shaped American liberal Protestant practices.

NOTES

I am grateful to David Walker, Yale University doctoral candidate in religious studies, for excellent research assistance and substantive contributions to this essay.

1. See, e.g., Sally M. Promey, "Taste Cultures and the Visual Practice of Liberal Protestantism, 1940–1965," in *Practicing Protestants: Histories of the Christian Life in America,* ed. Laurie Maffly-Kipp, Leigh Schmidt, and Mark Valeri (Baltimore: Johns Hopkins University Press, 2006), 250–93; and Sally M. Promey, "Interchangeable Art: Warner Sallman and the Critics of Mass Culture," in *Icons of American Protestantism: The Art of Warner Sallman,* ed. David Morgan (New Haven: Yale University Press, 1996), 148–80.

2. For an excellent essay on this subject, see David Morgan, "Toward a Modern Historiography of Art and Religion," in *Reluctant Partners: Art and Religion in Dialogue,* ed. Ena Giurescu Heller (New York: Gallery of the American Bible Society, 2004), 16–47.

3. Horace Bushnell, *Discourses on Christian Nurture* (Boston: Massachusetts Sabbath School Society, 1847).

4. Horace Bushnell, "Taste and Fashion," *The New Englander,* no. 2 (April 1843): 156–57, 164–65.

5. Ibid., 168, 167.

6. Bushnell, *Christian Nurture,* 18.

7. Henry Ward Beecher, *Norwood, or Village Life in New England* (New York: Charles Scribner, 1868), 213.

8. See Colleen McDannell, *The Christian Home in Victorian America, 1840–1900* (Bloomington: Indiana University Press, 1994).

9. Catharine E. Beecher and Harriet Beecher Stowe, *The American Woman's Home, or, Principles of Domestic Science* (New York: J. B. Ford, 1869). See also Catharine E. Beecher, *Treatise on Domestic Economy* (1841; Boston: Thomas H. Webb, 1843); and Catharine E. Beecher and Harriet Beecher Stowe, *Principles of Domestic Science* (New York: J. B. Ford, 1873).

10. "Art in America," *Christian Union* 30, no. 18 (October 30, 1884): 428. See also Miss O. M. E. Rowe, "The Home: About Prints," *Christian Union* 36, no. 16 (October 20, 1887): 400.

11. Blandina Conant, "The Latest Triumphs of Photography," *Christian Union* 3, no. 6 (February 8, 1871): 83.

12. Jon Butler, *Awash in a Sea of Faith: Christianizing the American People* (Cambridge, Mass.: Harvard University Press, 1992).

13. GFS, "Art VII—Leonardo da Vinci's Painting of the Last Supper," *Christian Examiner and Religious Miscellany* 40, no. 3 (May 1846): 411–12.

14. Sally M. Promey and Shira Brisman, "Sensory Cultures: Material and Visual Religion Reconsidered," in *Blackwell Companion to Religion in America,* ed. Philip Goff (Malden, Mass.: Wiley Blackwell, 2010), 177–205.

15. DC, "Art II—The Fine Arts in America," *Christian Examiner and Religious Miscellany* 39, no. 3 (November 1845): 324–25.

16. GEE, "Art I—The Artistic and Romantic View of the Church of the Middle Ages," *Christian Examiner and Religious Miscellany* 46, no. 3 (May 1849): 382. See also Blandina Conant, "The Beautiful as a Help to Devotion," *Christian Union* 4, no. 1 (July 5, 1871): 3.

17. GFS, "Art VII—Leonardo da Vinci's Painting of the Last Supper," 418–17.

18. RCW, "Art II—American Art and Art Unions," *Christian Examiner and Religious Miscellany* 48, no. 2 (March 1850): 206.

19. Blandina Conant, "Art Illustrations of the Bible," *Christian Union* 5, no. 8 (February 14, 1872): 158.

20. Rachael Ziady DeLue, *George Inness and the Science of Landscape* (Chicago: University of Chicago Press, 2004), 121; see generally 121–26.

21. Ibid. See also reviews of Alison in the liberal religious press, such as "Article 4," *General Repository and Review* 3, no. 1 (January 1, 1813): 189–219.

22. See, e.g., John Brazer, *The Power of Unitarianism over the Affections,* American Unitarian Association Tracts, first series (Boston: L. C. Bowles, 1829). I am grateful to David Walker for calling these connections to my attention.

23. Henry Ward Beecher, *Star Papers, or, Experiences of Art and Nature* (New York: J. C. Derby, 1855), 57; and see DeLue, *George Inness,* 121–26.

24. Beecher, *Star Papers,* 59–61.

25. Ibid., 59–63.

26. Cyrus A. Bartol, *Pictures of Europe, Framed in Ideas,* 2nd ed. (Boston: Crosby, Nichols, 1856), 193–95.

27. Ibid., 196.

28. Ibid., 198–99.

29. Ibid., 200–201, 204.

30. *Appleton's Cyclopedia of American Biography,* ed. James Grant Wilson and John Fiske (New York: D. Appleton, 1887–89), entry for William Pelby.

31. *Grand Exhibition of Statuary Executed by Mrs. W. Pelby . . .* (Boston: Hooton's Press, 1846), 18.

32. Quoted from a broadside titled "Mrs. Pelby's Exhibition of Wax Statuary, at Lee's Saloon," January 1843, collection of the American Antiquarian Society (hereafter AAS), BDSDS 1843.

33. J. Saunders, *Last Supper* (Boston: Boston Bewick Company, 1834), AAS Pams. S257 Last 1834a, title page.

34. *Grand Exhibition,* 19; see also J. Saunders, *Christ's Last Supper* (Boston: Boston Bewick Company, 1834), AAS Pams. S257 Last 1834. Pelby's twenty-three life-size figures for the later *Trial of Christ* (also called *Trial of Jesus* and *Trial of Our Savior*) make clear the limits of

her religious latitude, however. Not only were her interpretations decidedly Protestant rather than Catholic, but the broadsides and text that accompanied the wax ensemble pandered to contemporary antisemitism in recounting and elaborating the scriptural record; see *The Trial of Jesus, Represented in Twenty-three Wax Figures, the Size of Life, Executed by Mrs. Pelby,* AAS Misc. Pams. Pelb.

35. "Mrs. Pelby's Exhibition."

36. Quoted from a broadside titled "The Trial of Our Saviour!" AAS BDSDS 1846. The Catholic *Boston Pilot,* too, advised its readers to visit Pelby's exhibition, the critic's words relaying the power invested in visual experience: "an hour spent in that silent hall, gazing upon that scene, will give to the reflections of the Christian a higher and firmer tone than hours in listening to the sagest and most eloquent discourse" (ibid.).

37. RCW, "Art II: American Art and Art Unions," 211–12.

38. Review of *Art Hints: Architecture, Sculpture, and Painting,* by James Jackson Jarves (New York: Harper and Brothers, 1855), *Christian Examiner and Religious Miscellany* 59, no. 2 (September 1855): 308–309.

39. Charles Colbert, "A Critical Medium: James Jackson Jarves's Vision of Art History," *American Art* 16, no. 1 (spring 2002): 18–35. See also Charles Colbert, *Haunted Visions: Spiritualism and American Art* (Philadelphia: University of Pennsylvania Press, 2011).

40. James Jackson Jarves, *Art Thoughts* (New York: Hurd and Houghton, 1869), 360, quoted in Colbert, "Critical Medium," 23; see also Jarves, *Art Hints.*

41. James Jackson Jarves, *Art Studies* (New York: Derby and Jackson, 1861), 34–35, quoted in Colbert, "Critical Medium," 27.

42. Jarves, *Art Studies,* 493, quoted in Colbert, "Critical Medium," 32.

43. Jarves, *Art Thoughts,* 52–53, quoted in Colbert, "Critical Medium," 33.

44. Weir based Yale's art program on the model of the French atelier system, largely through the influence of his half-brother, Julian Alden Weir, who studied in Paris at the École des Beaux Arts from 1874 to 1877. At John's request, Julian also ordered plaster casts in Paris for the Yale program. It is worth considering in far more detail the impact of liberal Protestant aesthetic theologies in the shaping of arts institutions in the United States. I am indebted to Marian Wardle, Curator of American Art at Brigham Young University Museum of Art, and Danielle Hurd, M.A. student in history of art at Brigham Young University, for drawing to my attention Weir's commitments in this regard.

45. See Promey, "Taste Cultures"; and Promey, "Interchangeable Art."

46. Alfred H. Barr Jr., *What Is Modern Painting?* (New York: Museum of Modern Art, 1943), 20–21. As early as 1941, Barr proposed a Museum of Modern Art exhibition he called "The Religious Spirit in Contemporary Art"; see "The Religious Spirit in Contemporary Art," summaries of meetings, December through April 1941, preparatory to exhibition, Alfred H. Barr Jr., Papers, MoMA Archives, AAA, reel 3154, frame 1296. While this exhibition never finally materialized, the Protestant Barr invited the Catholic Agnes Mongan, of the Fogg Art Museum at Harvard University, and the Jewish Meyer Schapiro, a prominent art historian on the faculty of Columbia University, to contribute expertise. This inclination toward religious "inclusivity" was characteristic and, while the present chapter focuses on the liberal Protestant situation, Catholic and Jewish intellectuals in the first half of the twentieth century, and on both sides of the Atlantic Ocean, actively (though somewhat differently) promoted a modernist aesthetic of abstraction and decried "sentimental realisms." Important periodicals providing insight into the larger interfaith aspects of religion's conversations with modern art include *Liturgical Arts, Catholic Art Quarterly, L'Art Sacré,* and *Menorah Journal.*

47. See, e.g., Paul Tillich and Theodore Greene, "Authentic Religious Art," in *Masterpieces of Religious Art: Exhibition Held in Connection with the Second Assembly of the World Council of Churches, July 15 through August 31, 1954* (Chicago: Art Institute of Chicago, 1954), 9 (this essay, despite its joint authorship, clearly represents Tillich's thought); and Paul Tillich, "Protestantism and the Contemporary Style in the Visual Arts," *Christian Scholar* 40, no. 4 (December 1957): 311.

48. Marion Junkin, "Truth in Art," *motive* 10, no. 1 (October 1949): 23.

49. Paul Tillich, "Contemporary Visual Arts and the Revelatory Character of Style," in *On Art and Architecture,* ed. John Dillenberger and Jane Dillenberger (New York: Crossroad, 1987), 132–33n3.

50. Typescript dated November 9, 1957, recording comments Barr delivered at an October 1957 meeting of the executive board of the Division of Christian Life and Work on behalf of the Department of Worship and the Arts of the National Council of Churches, Alfred H. Barr Jr., Papers, AAA, reel 2184, frame 1148.

51. See, e.g., Paul DiMaggio, "Cultural Entrepreneurship in Nineteenth-Century Boston, Part I: The Creation of an Organizational Base for High Culture in America," *Media, Culture, and Society* 4, no. 1 (January 1982): 33–50; and Lawrence W. Levine, *Highbrow/Lowbrow: The Emergence of Cultural Hierarchy in America* (Cambridge, Mass.: Harvard University Press, 1990).

52. The phrase belongs to Elwood Ellwood, "Return from Miltown: The Terrible Taste of Protestantism," *motive* 18, no. 1 (October 1957): 14–17.

53. See Bushnell, "Taste and Fashion."

FOUR

Discovering Imageless Truths

The Bahá'í Pilgrimage of Juliet Thompson, Artist

CHRISTOPHER G. WHITE

Though Juliet Thompson (1873–1957) lived in what one reporter of her time called one of the most "materialistic and sordid corners of the world," New York City, she had spiritual dreams, intuitions, and awakenings. She had one of them when she was a young woman, probably in her late twenties, while recovering from diphtheria, an illness that almost killed her. "One evening, while I was lying in bed," she remembered, "I heard the doctor say to mother from the next room, 'Juliet is dying.' When I went to sleep that night I did not expect to wake up again." But as she slept her fortunes changed, for sometime in the night an unexpected visitor appeared in a dream, offering a healing benediction. "I had a dream and in it I saw a most wonderful-looking man. He said to me with complete assurance, 'You will get well.'" She had no idea who this person was, but she did recover, and after her illness she told her brother that something about this experience had made her more thoughtful about spiritual things. She wondered—Were the miracles and wonders spoken of in the Bible true, and were they still happening today? Was the spirit of Christ still in the world, healing and guiding us? Somehow, it was hard to believe.[1]

The next day brought another providential sign. A friend named Laura Barney arrived unannounced at Thompson's door, looking as "though she had found the secret of happiness" and blurting out something to the effect that the Holy Spirit had come back into the world. There was a new divine messenger, and his followers were living in British Palestine, the Holy Land. "I am sailing from New York tomorrow for the Holy Land, and I could not go till I had told you the marvellous thing I know now," Barney exclaimed. "The Great Messenger of God promised in all the Sacred Scriptures, foretold by all the Prophets as the One who would bring peace to the earth, has come. His name is Bahá'u'lláh. He died, a prisoner, in the Holy Land." His son and successor, Abdu'l-Bahá, was still in Akka (Acre), an old fortress city in Palestine, and Barney was sailing to meet him. This was a moment of real excitement for Thompson, but though she listened to her friend attentively, she seems not to have pursued the matter further. And she certainly did not connect Barney's Holy Land prisoner with that wonderful-looking man in her feverish dream. Before she could make that connection, other providential signs would have to appear. She would need to make her own visit to the Holy Land, where she could see for herself that the Holy Spirit did indeed produce signs and wonders in the modern world.[2]

Juliet Thompson was a woman of great spiritual sensitivity, someone who felt deeply the religious dilemmas of her age and searched with determination for solutions. Like many others living at the turn of the twentieth century, she felt challenged and disoriented by dramatic changes that made religious belief difficult. Life in American cities fostered nervousness and an unsettling spiritual coldness. Like others, Thompson wondered if there was a place for spirit, or spiritual longing, in the cold, angular, urban spaces of modern America. And the new American city was not the only reason it was hard to believe. Christian practices and traditions, those religious forms that for so many years clothed the spirit and made it real, now suddenly seemed out of date, superstitious, or irrational. Scientists and intellectuals often labeled them as such, calling into question the veracity of the Bible, the reasonableness of belief, and the usefulness of any kind of worship. For religiously sensitive souls such as Juliet Thompson, and for millions of other Americans who, while uncertain about Christianity, were incapable of doubting the existence of God, trying to sustain a sensitivity to spiritual realities was truly difficult. Was it possible to believe in prophets, miracles, or the Holy Spirit in the modern world? What forms would these spiritual entities take? In this essay I turn to Thompson's life to point to different ways that this era's spiritual seekers both tore down older religious forms and built up new methods of imagining the spirit and how it animated and guided human beings.

DRIFTING

Thompson was born in 1873 in Virginia and raised in Washington, D.C., by a Protestant mother and a lapsed Irish Catholic father. (Her father, Ambrose Thompson, a wealthy land developer and shipping magnate, was by an unfortunate turn of events in the hands of nuns when he died, who hastily administered Catholic final rites. His Protestant wife, Celeste, discomfited by the ritual, sat next to her dying husband wringing her hands. "Never mind, Celeste," he reassured her, "it doesn't amount to a damn.") The social and business circles that Ambrose inhabited were not appealing to his daughter, who even as a young person was freethinking, unconventional, and occasionally brusque. "She did not hesitate to speak well of the Germans during World War I," one friend recalled, pointing to one or two examples, "and to exhibit the Kaiser's picture on her living room table." This was about the equivalent, she estimated, of "setting up a statue of Herod in a cathedral." Thompson spoke her mind. Later in life, when she was an accomplished portrait painter, she spoke freely even to the President and First Lady of the United States. While she was painting the portrait of Grace Coolidge, President Coolidge "came in to watch," Thompson remembered, "chewing on an apple, and I told Mrs. Coolidge that I could not put up with that."[3] Thompson painted likenesses not only of the Coolidges, but also of President Wilson, his cabinet members, and others, though she also did landscapes and abstract art. Like other artists of her time, especially abstract artists, she thought of art as a way of exploring the deeper realities of nature and human nature. She wanted to see the spiritual essences undergirding all things. It was a preoccupation born of nascent religious questions and anxieties.

By her twenties, Thompson was somewhere in between her Protestant mother and lapsed-Catholic father—in other words, she was an Episcopalian. At this time, at approximately the time when her friend and fellow artist Laura Barney informed her about a new Holy Land prophet, she moved to New York and joined New York City's Ascension Church, a well-heeled Episcopal church led by the freethinking rector Percy Grant. Grant shared many passions with Thompson—liberal Christianity, poetry, art—and the two were close friends for many years. Thompson loved the Bible and the Church, but her piety was not confined to what was going on at Ascension. She spoke of art as a spiritual practice. She was interested in other religious trends—Theosophy, New

Thought, Asian religions. She had a magnanimous personal style and organized salons in her studio in Greenwich Village that were attended by a large, incongruous group of seekers, artists, actors, writers, and spiritual inquirers. (These gatherings were so large, in fact, that the actor Romeyne Benjamin, the brother-in-law of Enrico Caruso, worried that the crowd upstairs would crash through the ceiling.) Her brownstone on West 10th had once been owned by P. T. Barnum's midget General Tom Thumb—or so Thompson liked to tell people. It was just that kind of place, a friend remembered, inhabited by eccentric strangers, avant-garde artists, and extraordinary events. One night a roommate "left his bed briefly in the night, and returned to find a sailor in it, complete with live parrot." Thompson was part of a widening circle of religious liberals, ecumenical in outlook, cosmopolitan in intellectual and artistic interests (fig. 12).[4]

Thompson suffered from spiritual strains and anxieties common to Americans in the early decades of the twentieth century. There were several discourses of anxiety and spiritual coldness at the time. One concerned the rise of the city and its problems. America was rapidly urbanizing, and new, urban ways of living challenged older ways of thinking and being in the world. In this period, doctors, teachers, psychologists, and clergy were continually warning the public about pollution, bad air, industrial work, loud noises, overcrowding—all of these things weakened our bodies and minds. The New York neurologist George Beard, alarmed by the rise of nervous disorders, popularized the idea that the harsh, jarring sounds of machines, cramped living and working conditions, electronic communications, new ideas and technologies, and the "friction and unrest" of American capitalism drained our nervous powers. Again and again, he saw the results in his clinical practice: unremitting anxieties, unaccountable fears, mysterious neuralgias, depression. Others, including a platoon of new professionals called "psychologists," worried that Americans were agitated, tense, and breathless. (The great psychologist William James thought Americans were the most fidgety people on earth.) Clergymen, for their part, thought that city living was destroying spiritual and moral sensibilities. In any case, for those Americans who felt a loss of nervous or spiritual force, the question was how to regain that power and confidence, how to overcome the anomie and alienation of living in the American city. Thompson also worried about these issues, joining many others who pondered the problem and its possible solutions. Like many, she wondered if more primitive, mystical cultures or religions in the East might serve as antidotes to Western obsessions with consumption, industry, and efficiency.[5]

There are hints and suggestions in Thompson's art that she wrestled with precisely these modern dilemmas, though much of her work and virtually all of her views on art have been lost. We might view, for example, her *Shop Window* (fig. 13) with these dilemmas in mind. This piece appears to take as its subject a divided self projected into the angular spaces of a storefront window. Here Thompson sees her split reflection in a featureless, divided mannequin illuminated by electricity—a modern wonder if there ever were one—uncovering all the dark spaces of the self, from the front (the light bulb) to the rear (the illuminated triangular panel). Nothing escapes modernity's glare. But instead of solving the puzzles of anomie and anxiety, instead of providing a solution, the light that modernity sheds on her only illuminates the problem: a fragmented self. There are the heart's pulsing desires, and the head's ticking calculations. Are we human beings or machines? And what is the fate of deep, personal needs, desires, and aspirations—aspirations even for transcendence—in an environment that imprisons us in mechanical laws, right angles, and geometric shapes? Is this our fate in an urban landscape—a life that is cold, fragmented, and mechanical?

Of course, people have ways of steadying themselves when they are agitated, uncertain, or nervous; but the tragedy of Thompson's era was that the religious consolations that could anchor or calm them were also being buffeted and in some cases entirely swept away. And so there was a second discourse of spiritual coldness developing in this period, a discourse of critical questions, not easily dismissed, concerning Christianity and whether belief in it could be sustained in the modern world. There were scientific studies of the Bible that called into question miracles and biblical understandings of nature; there were textual studies that called into question the Bible's consistency, morality, and divine authorship; and there were even studies that called into question the very existence of biblical prophets and saviors, including Jesus of Nazareth. In addition, Christian claims to uniqueness and superiority were undermined by increased travel and interreligious contact. Narratives of all of these critical discourses and more generally about what many have called a "critical period" of doubt in American culture have been told before.[6] The doubts were not so pervasive that they contaminated every believer's supplications, but there was a portion of the American populace that felt acutely the strain produced by these challenges, and for some it was enough to set them entirely free of old moorings, out on journeys of spiritual seeking across wide oceans and cultural gaps that had previously been impassable. The religious liberal Octavius Frothingham may have said it best. "Ours is an age of restatements and reconstructions, of conversions and 'new departments' in many directions. There is an uneasy feeling in regard to the foundation of belief. The old foundations have been sorely shaken."[7] It was a time of real uncertainty about Christianity in particular.

Something of the intensity of this critical situation is apparent in this era's urgent efforts to make more vivid images and historical narratives of Jesus—all ways of shoring up a religious figure fading under the critical gaze of modernity. An intense search for the historical Jesus was on, a quest pursued not only by scholarly readers of Strauss and Renan. Run-of-the-mill Americans also worried about how to imagine the personality and disposition of the person they prayed to. The result was a new visual culture of Jesus. All of a sudden, illustrated lives of Jesus, picture cards of Jesus and of the Holy Land, frameable images, and gift books were made and sold. Book-length treatments of Christ were increasingly dominated by imagery; some of it was fine art from Europe, older renderings of Jesus, but much of it was done by contemporary Christians who had journeyed to the Holy Land and reimagined these places and figures for doubting Christians living in the modern West. Lives of Christ were adorned with ethnographic, archeological, and even botanical illustrations of "details and customs of biblical life," one historian has pointed out, in order to "bolster the historical claims made for the life of Christ." (The impulse was pursued with determination by the prominent preacher Thomas De Witt Talmage in his *From Manger to Throne* [1890], which included more than four hundred engravings of details of life in the Holy Land, nearly two hundred well-known paintings of Jesus, and a color panorama of the "crucifixion that folded out to ten feet in length." Like others, Talmage was unsatisfied with all attempts to capture the Messiah in oils or ink. Could any depiction of Christ show him in his true humanity—and in his absolute divinity?)[8]

Juliet Thompson also was interested in using art not only to understand Christ but to think more generally about how spiritual essences were "fixed" or incarnated in material forms. She remembered that as a ten-year-old girl she had prayed that "someday she could paint Christ," finally rendering his image in a more satisfactory way. She said she wanted to correct those mistaken images of him that portrayed him as "sweet and ineffectual." He deserved to be painted more like a "King of Men." She almost certainly argued about this with her pastor and close friend Percy Grant, also an artist, and also concerned with finding more satisfactory images of Jesus. The two disagreed on Jesus' true nature: she thought he should be depicted in a kingly manner; Grant thought he was meek, innocent, and maternal. He had not been raised in a strenuous, industrial society, Grant reasoned; why would he have been strong and sovereign? Today we read about these arguments and wonder why they were so crucial, and so pervasive. I think the answer to this is that there were deeply personal motivations behind them, as there were behind all efforts to reimagine Jesus in more vivid and lifelike narratives. It was a devotional concern: believers were concerned that they did not have a reliable understanding or image to ponder when reflecting and praying. Did Jesus exist? Who was he? How did he embody (incarnate) the spirit?[9]

As Juliet Thompson pondered these questions about soul and matter, spiritual essence and outer form, another providential sign appeared. This one came in 1900 in Paris, where she was studying art, and where she came upon a picture of a holy man originally from Persia but now living in Palestine, a new religious figure who brought a message of peace, religious universalism, and ecumenism. Like many Americans, she knew that the East was a place of wisdom and mysticism. She looked closely at the man's face. Was this, finally, what the spirit looked like in human form? It was an older face with engraved lines and shadows, wrapped in a white beard. When she looked closer she saw something else, something she recognized about the face, and at that moment she made an incredible discovery. Here was the same man who had visited her in her feverish dream years ago, the one who told her she would survive diphtheria. She turned and asked his name. It was Abbas Effendi, or Abdu'l-Bahá.[10]

LIT UP

Soon, on a trip to Palestine in 1909, she got to meet him. A friend and roommate who later redacted Thompson's diaries recalled that Thompson's journey to meet Abdu'l-Bahá was a "breathless, ecstatic, tear-drenched pilgrimage," and the accounts that Thompson left behind certainly bear this out. "We were in the Holy Land. We were in a bygone age. We drove along a wide white beach, so close to the sea that its little waves curled over our carriage wheels. To our right, a long line of palm trees. Before us, its domes and flat roofs dazzling white beneath the deep blue sky: 'Akká, the Holy City, the New Jerusalem.

Camels approached us on the sand, driven by white-cloaked bedouins, their veils bound by circlets; or sheep, led by shepherds in tunics and carrying crooks, striped headcloths framing their faces." She ascended the worn steps of a great stone house, passing a crowd of Persian expatriates with smiling "faces miraculously pure." She too was smiling, then sobbing, then bowing her head, compressing into an hour all the emotions of conversion: contrition, remorse, uncertainty, elation. Finally, she came face to face with Abdu'l-Bahá, who greeted her with a smile. Thompson's companion Alice knelt down and spoke in brief sentences to Abdu'l-Bahá and his translator. But Thompson stood still. Abdu'l-Bahá addressed her, and she did not respond. Alice answered for her. After some time, Thompson said that her heart spoke, and he said he heard her, and she asked him to forgive her failures, and he said she could be sure of God's forgiveness, and she said that being there was like being at home, and he said yes; and that was it. Then those indubitable outer signs of inner spiritual transformation, tears, streaked down her face, and Thompson knelt until Abdu'l-Bahá picked her up and asked her to sit next to him (fig. 14).[11]

She saw him with the eyes of a religious seeker and an artist, examining light and shadow as they fell on his face, sorting elements of his personality into what she thought of as their essences and their outer forms, studying him for signs of the Holy Spirit or other miraculous energies. Writing of her first encounter with him she said that his face had an ineffable quality to it, that it was, she said, full of "Power" (with the capital letter). He had a human body, she said, "charged with a Power I have seen in no *human* being, restless with the Force that so animated it."[12] A body restless with spiritual energies. After returning to New York she tried to explain the experience in a letter to her friend and fellow Bahá'í Agnes Parsons, scratching out sentences with underlines and exclamation points. How could a pen speak of supernatural things? Abdu'l-Bahá revealed the spirit, she said, with "*such* a tenderness . . . such a closeness" that many spiritual things that were once far away, hazy, now seemed clear. He unraveled the mystery of Christ and solved the problem of his remoteness. "As I knelt at His feet . . . *how* I understood the woman who broke her most precious treasure at the feet of the Christ, poured out all her precious ointment at His feet. I understood many things I had read of that Holy One Jesus the Christ." The experience was a wonder "undreamt of by any artist—a strength, a tenderness, a light impossible to conceive . . . a touch from another Kingdom." "Only be sure that he is true," Thompson exclaimed, "*be sure that it is true.*"[13] There are several fascinating things about this letter, none more so than the fact that meeting Abdu'l-Bahá helped her understand who Christ was and what biblical stories meant. Thompson saw signs of the Holy Spirit in Abdu'l-Bahá's face; she saw divinity in Abdu'l-Bahá's manner, his bearing, and his words. She said repeatedly that he helped her see what the Holy Spirit looked like when it came into matter. She said she finally understood how spirit got into material form—she finally "saw divinity incarnate," she said.[14] She said all of these things even though she knew (because Abdu'l-Bahá made it clear) that he was neither God, nor Christ, nor the return of Christ. (Bahá'ís believe that his father, Bahá'u'lláh, was a prophet, but Abdu'l-Bahá himself was not.)

Thompson was not the only one powerfully affected by Abdu'l-Bahá; she was not the only one who saw in his faith the antidote to Western materialism and unbelief; she was not the only one who felt powerful emotions or energies in his presence. She wept when encountering him, but compared to the ecstatic experiences of other inquirers her reaction was tame and sober. Others fell to the floor or shouted spontaneously. Some said they were healed. One woman reported feeling an "electric shock that went from my head to my feet." Another pilgrim, a skeptic from Cleveland, Ohio, spoke of magnetic forces and energies pulsing in Abdu'l-Bahá's room. It was not unusual, either, for Abdu'l-Bahá to appear in visions or dreams. A distant relation to the great evangelist Lyman Beecher, the Bahá'í convert Ellen Beecher, reported seeing a "Benign Face" next to her during her meditations, a presence that took her in his embrace. "I had attained to the Meeting—and Glory be to GOD! my soul was clothed with the 'Wedding Garment' such as mortal could never create or conceive of." Again and again she heard, "The Holy Spirit dominates my limbs."[15]

Being dominated by the Holy Spirit was precisely the point of all of this spiritual seeking and journeying—it was precisely the point of going to the Holy Land, seeking an alternative, vital experience of religious truth. Seekers were looking for this emotional *extra*. The emotional charge that many found here was exactly what was missing in overcivilized American cities and buttoned-up religious communities. "In our day," one psychologist diagnosed the American situation, "the hot life of the feelings is remote and decadent. Culture represses, and intellect saps its root. The very word passion is becoming obsolete."[16] Modern living expanded our intellectual lives but unnaturally repressed our emotions. This combination meant that modern Americans had a harder time practicing religion or feeling religious emotions.

Thompson, then, was taking part in a wider cultural phenomenon—Americans seeking in foreign cultures for alternatives to the artificial, urban, anxious lifestyles they endured at home. Many Americans, for example, would have agreed with Thompson that the meditative quietness of the East was a cure for the incessant noises and unrest of city living. But there was another reason to journey to the Holy Land. Holy Land experience gave Americans a way to fix in their minds the devotional images that had faded under the critical gaze of modernity and science. They could see again markers and evidences of divine inspiration in the physical landscape, in Middle Eastern artifacts, and, in the case of Abdu'l-Bahá, in modern holy men and women. "Every step I advanced on the soil of Palestine offered some new and startling evidence of the truth of the sacred story," wrote William Prime, first professor of art history at Princeton and author of *Tent Life in the Holy Land* (1857). "The Bible was a new book, faith in which seemed now to have passed into actual sight, and every page of its record shone out with new, and a thousand-fold increased lustre." This was precisely Thompson's experience: the Holy Spirit touched her again. Thompson and many other travelers felt strangely at home in the Holy Land. The Methodist Episcopal bishop Henry Warren said Palestine was "the first country where I have felt at home," even though, he continued, "I have been in no country that is so unlike my own."[17] The reasons Thompson and Warren felt this way are clear enough: they *had* lived their whole lives imaginatively in the biblical world. Thompson, for one, knew the Bible well and could quote it from memory.

FIXING THE SPIRIT

When Juliet Thompson visited Akka, Abdu'l-Bahá seemed to know what to say to an artist-seeker yearning for a vivid image of deeper spiritual realities. He spoke to one of Thompson's concerns in particular: how to sustain a clear, vivid image of the divine in mind during worship. First of all, no image of God, he cautioned Thompson and others in Akka in 1909, accurately represented God. "Whatever form is produced in the mind is imagination, that is, one's own conception," he said. There was no connection between it and God's reality—no connection. This was not an unfamiliar theme for Bahá'ís, Muslims, or other believers over the centuries: God was wholly transcendent, unknowable, literally unimaginable. But the interesting part of Abdu'l-Bahá's message here was that even though he insisted God was unknowable, he also recognized that believers needed a way to hold him close in imagination, to see him. So while he pointed out that all images are products of the mind, he also said that “at the time of prayer one must hold in one’s mind some object,” [illegible] image or picture, and “[the believer] must turn his face and direct his mind to this picture.” Such pictures could be provided by artists, and Abdu’l-Bahá even directed Thompson’s attention to a portrait of Bahá’u’lláh that was then on display in Akka. On a number of occasions he told Thompson that good art pointed our attention to the divine, helped us hold on to it, even if it could never contain or exhaust the divine reality.[18]

Even before journeying to Akka in 1909, Thompson was sensitive to this problem and to the ways that art might capture the spirit and bring it close. In a handwritten reflection dated February 13, 1907, she wrote that artists made invisible things visible, transforming deep, immaterial truths into material forms. True art, then, had a religious function—it *was* religion, she said—because it helped human beings unfold spiritual essences in the world, giving them suitable forms, and thus helping human souls realize inner longings for the “Beautiful and the Sublime” (an artist’s definition of God if there ever was one). Achieving this kind of artistic religiousness involved concentration and spiritual receptivity, for true artists lost themselves in their work, letting their hands work by “the dictates of the heaven-kissed genius which dwells in the center of his being.” Thompson’s statement here was essentially a statement of artistic method, something she repeated now and again, including once for a reporter interested in an exhibit of her frescos in Washington, D.C. “I do not know when I put the paper before me what form or colors the picture I am about to do will take,” she said. “I lightly pencil the paper in a smudge and there, before my eyes, as a picture grows in a crystal, my picture develops and I paint it.”[19] True art comes from a transcendent place. This exhibit included a number of allegorical pastels and paintings with religious themes—depictions of death, resurrection, angels, the Madonna, and Jesus’ disciples. In other exhibits she used abstract elements to explore ways of depicting other elusive spiritual things, what she called “deep, imageless Truths,” that took on forms in different times and places.

It is likely that Thompson was influenced by a number of nineteenth-century artists who pondered ways of capturing the spiritual in art. Her close friends, the artist Alice Pike Barney and her daughter Laura Barney, were both influenced by the French Symbolists, who reacted against earlier emphases on objectivity and realism and turned toward subjectivity, mysticism, imagination, and dreams. Thompson also found these congenial themes. Another movement beginning in the late nineteenth century, abstract art, drew on similar

ed an ambitious agenda for art as a spiritual discipline. abstract artists, including Wassily Kandinsky and Pieter o capture spiritual states in iconoclastic art that, by smash- forms, tried to destroy the materialism that these artists be- d the human spirit. Probably the most influential book by a twen ry artist, Kandinsky's manifesto *On the Spiritual in Art* (1911), announced that avant-garde artists, restless and uneasy with older orders and systems, were pushing ahead toward a "spiritual revolution" that would illuminate the "dark picture" of the "soulless life of the present." Kandinsky touched on themes familiar to Thompson and other Americans—materialism, urban ennui. The soulless present had been made so by a ubiquitous materialism that made it impossible to recognize, feel, or express the deep, transcendent parts of the self. And old, incompetent religions were not helping. "The abandoned churchyard quakes and forgotten graves open and from them rise forgotten ghosts"—this was Kandinsky's way of sweeping Christianity into its own grave. Kandinsky believed in new prophesies and new revelations, but he believed they would be fashioned not by a modern Moses but by avant-garde artists who knew best how to capture spirit in forms that spoke to modern sensibilities.[20]

Kandinsky developed his unconventional religious vision by drawing on an influential spiritual movement that other artists borrowed from as well, Theosophy. Founded by a Russian-born mystic named Helena Blavatsky, Theosophy was a new religion that insisted that spiritual states could be perceived in moments of trance, clairvoyance, or "superconciousness." Kandinsky wanted his work to express "spiritual impressions," "internal harmonies," and "soul vibrations," believing that his art would point a way toward new visions of metaphysical things. For Kandinsky and others, the modern artist was in the vanguard of those whose discoveries would usher in a new spiritual renaissance.[21] This is not a bad way to think of Thompson's art, either—as a form of spiritual seeking, as an impulse to find and uncover new spiritual realities. Both Kandinsky and Thompson also were interested in the problem of capturing spiritual entities in material forms—in pastels, oils, and canvases—and using these forms to see or understand spiritual things better. When Abdu'l-Bahá spoke to Thompson about holding an image in mind when she meditated he spoke to a similar concern, namely how to come closer to spiritual realities in life.

But Abdu'l-Bahá's notions did not solve Thompson's problems once and for all; Abdu'l-Bahá himself recognized that spiritual growth was difficult and ongoing, and there is no question that while Thompson's Holy Land experiences infused her with vivid new images and close-up realizations of spiritual things, these experiences quickly faded in memory. "There was more: much more" about being in Palestine, she worried in her diary. The closeness of it all was fading. "How could my memory serve me so cruelly?" she complained late in 1909.[22]

So she did everything she could to remember—she wrote letters about the trip, she sketched it, she painted it, she later fictionalized it in a story about Holy Land prophets and holy men. She wrote about her trip in a regular column entitled "Pen Pictures of Abdu'l-Bahá" in the American Bahá'í news magazine, *The Star of the West.* Then, in 1912, came a crucial moment: Abdu'l-Bahá traveled to Europe and America, and he agreed to let Thompson paint his portrait. She knew the difficulty of this task and its significance: it was another chance to fix the Holy Spirit in material form.

And she knew it would require a miracle. On the day of the event, Abdu'l-Bahá made the task more difficult by asking her to "paint the soul," a request that made Thompson more nervous, not less. She objected—who could paint any soul, let alone the soul of a holy man? "Who can paint the soul of Abdu'l-Bahá?" The best she could do was bring two girlfriends, May and Lua, to pray by her side as she did her work, "perceiving and encouraging while I painted with a breathless and blind speed, lifted up on a wave of inspiration, only feeling!" At some point, Thompson remembered, she let go, "relying on the promise and on the prayers of May and Lua; and then a great wave of inspiration came, lifting me to unimagined heights of confidence, endowing me with clear, sure perception, above all, filling, thrilling me with feeling, so profound and immense that my hand, strangely certain, as direct as though guided by a more powerful one, trembled so it could scarcely execute. In five half-hours the portrait was done." "A portrait this size," Thompson noted, "normally takes forty hours at least."[23] Here was another confirming sign, for an artist anyway, of the closeness of spiritual things. Her art had allowed her to render the spiritual in material form (fig. 15).

People certain that they have made deep spiritual discoveries generally do not keep such things to themselves, and Thompson, who was always magnanimous and sometimes blunt, was not going to keep Abdu'l-Bahá to herself. She told friends and artists that there was something in this great man that revealed the closeness of the spirit, its true nature. One friend she spoke to, a neighbor in Greenwich Village and a writer and artist also keenly concerned with capturing spirit in artistic forms, was the great Lebanese Christian poet and writer Kahlil Gibran, the man who would write *The Prophet* and many other religious books beloved by religious liberals in the twentieth century. Warming him up, Thompson first passed Gibran some of the Arabic writings of Bahá'u'lláh, whose message of unity and religious ecumenism he admired. (Later in his life Gibran called these writings the most "stupendous literature that ever was written." It was a new kind of Arabic, he said, with "new and wonderful words."[24]) Thompson asked Gibran if he wanted to try his hand at seeing and rendering Abdu'l-Bahá's face for himself, and he agreed (fig. 16).

During his sitting in Thompson's New York studio with Abdu'l-Bahá, Gibran had the same remarkable experience that Thompson did. "For the first time," Gibran wrote, "I saw form noble enough to be a receptacle for the Holy Spirit." Here, finally, was an adequate form for that inner essence and spirit in all religions. After his sketch was done, many crowded around and shook his hand, saying he had "seen the soul of [Abdu'l-Bahá]." Abdu'l-Bahá then turned and spoke to Gibran in Arabic, and, quoting Muhammad, produced a phrase that must have pleased both of them: "Prophets and poets see with the light of God." Indeed—prophets and artists see with God's eyes! Gibran thought that in Abdu'l-Bahá's smile he saw "the mystery of Syria and Arabia and Persia," and much later he recalled to Thompson that when he sketched Abdu'l-Bahá he had "seen the Unseen, and been filled."[25] He also told her that his meetings with Abdu'l-Bahá deeply influenced his biography of Jesus, *Jesus, the Son of Man* (1928). Like Thompson, Gibran now had a new way of visualizing, a new way of imagining, how spirit got into matter—and how God's spirit animated Jesus' body in particular. Abdu'l-Bahá had shown it to him.

Gibran could not see his way to embracing the Bahá'í Faith, though Thompson nudged and coaxed him. He faced the same dilemma that she and many other cosmopolitan religious seekers did, searching for the unseen essence underneath all religious forms, hoping to bring that spirit into life again somehow. Gibran was content to continue to do this as an artist, revealing religious truth in inspirational verse and images, insisting he needed no prophetic mediator, no holy man or form other than those literary and artistic ones he created. He would have an unmediated relationship with the divine. Still, while he often said he wanted to smash images and forms, he spent a good deal of time creating new ones that modern people might see and understand better. His poetry, his art, his life of Jesus—they all were the imaginative product of a spiritual art that, like Kandinsky's, probed and discovered spiritual dimensions and tried to embody them.

I, MARY MAGDALEN

Thompson had a different way of reconciling the tensions involved in wanting to destroy images and desperately needing them: she converted to the Bahá'í Faith. Here was a faith that captured the old, eternal religious essence and embodied it in new, more vital ways. She appears to have known two things quite well: one, that she needed some kind of mediator, form, or institution to have a religious life; and two, that the forms that even the most radical iconoclast created would be shaped decisively by the traditions that they were trying to obliterate. The spiritual biographies of liberal seekers in this period usually bear this out: the new religious forms, beliefs, and practices they embraced were deeply influenced by their childhood religions and dilemmas of faith. So in a profound way, there was no way out. Though Juliet Thompson knew the difference between Bahá'í and Christian, between Bahá'u'lláh and Christ, she conflated them in her imaginative art and work.[26]

This is nowhere more apparent than in the life of Christ that she wrote near the end of her life. Reimagining Christ's life was an obsession among unsettled believers in this era when, as I've noted, Christ's reality was fading into a demythologized past. But the novel Thompson wrote was different, for as reviewers in many papers noted (including the *New York Times,* which called it vivid with "emotional rapture"), her book drew on new images and stories, images not from a fading biblical past but from fresh teachings given by a great teacher in the Holy Land. It had been there, in the Holy Land, other reviewers confirmed, where "she interviewed peasant and prophet," including the great saint Abdu'l-Bahá. Her recent visit to the Holy Land had shown her the customs and devotional lives of biblical characters. Thompson's novel *I, Mary Magdalen* (1940) was a retelling of the Christ story, a novel marketed to Christians and read by them, a novel with an obviously Christian theme. And yet there was something different about it as well, for while the novel retells the Christ story through Mary Magdalen's eyes it does so with a crucial difference: it does so by reimagining Christ as Abdu'l-Bahá and Thompson as Mary Magdalen. Thompson draws from her own passions and interests as she creates Mary; and she draws on Abdu'l-Bahá's personality and his teachings as she reimagines Christ. In the illustrations Thompson drew for the book, Mary has Thompson's face and Christ has Abdu'l-Bahá's (fig. 17).[27]

The book's front matter makes it explicit that the Bahá'í revelation both renewed and clarified the older Christian story. The introduction, written by the popular writer and Nietzsche scholar Emily S. Hamblen, points to key Persian influences on world religions and on Christianity in particular. Then the foreword makes the importance of the Bahá'í Faith more explicit. This foreword, which was written by a Bahá'í friend of Thompson's who accompanied her to the Holy Land, calls the book a "vivid and subtle word painting" that uses words and images drawn from Holy Land meetings with Bahá'í leaders. "As pilgrims we journeyed together to the Holy Land," this writer remembered, "first to Carmel, that Mountain of the Lord, to meet Shoghi Effendi; to the shrines of the Bab and of AbdulBaha; to Akka, the scene of the long imprisonment of Baha Ullah [*sic*] and his son; and to Baha'u'llah's shrine and tomb at Bahji." By seeing new Holy Land teachers and saints, Thompson was able to understand how older holy souls in the Christian era believed and acted. Thompson was a particularly sensitive observer; the landscape fired her imagination, drew her into itself, transformed her from a seeker to a disciple. "So sensitive was the artist-author to the vibrations that emanate from the spots which have been frequented by the Holy Messengers and Martyrs, that she was irresistibly drawn to an obscure path that led to a small dome-shaped dwelling, and I recall poignantly her joy when she learned from a peasant that it was the traditional site of the home of Mary of Magdala." Thompson believed she had a connection to the place and its old stories. She was a new Mary.[28]

Was there a better way to overcome a sense that old religious stories were no longer real than by becoming a part of them? Thompson's providential life, her enchanted dreams and experiences, her journey to the land of prophets and seers—all of this was a modern reenactment of the older stories. She was a modern Mary Magdalen, an early witness of a new revelation in a cold and unbelieving world. Like Mary, she would go and tell others that Christ had risen—this time with a new name. So she wrote, and sketched, and painted.

CONCLUSION

There are a couple of important things to say in conclusion about Thompson's Middle Eastern pilgrimage and her religious experiences. First of all, her conversion clearly was shaped by a key dilemma of her age: how to find Jesus again, how to bring him back into a closer relationship to the world, how to find him and know who he was—*how to be certain*. The broader framing of this problem, a more appropriate framing for liberals and metaphysical believers who had left behind Christian symbols altogether, might be stated as how to understand the relationship between spirit and form, how to fix the spirit in a material medium. Holy Land pilgrimages solved these problems for many American believers, Christian and otherwise, by helping them reimagine the Holy Spirit and its closeness and vitality. Thompson was acutely concerned about ways of accomplishing this. What were the procedures for solving spiritual coldness? How could one overcome a sense of uncertainty, loss, nervousness? Abdu'l-Bahá helped Thompson with this problem by encouraging her to hold in mind some image or object while praying. Abdu'l-Bahá himself gave her a renewed set of images of holy events and objects that she then tried to fix in material media and thus hold closer. Thompson's portraits and her novel, *I, Mary Magdalen,* were produced to accomplish these goals, to help her and others hold in their minds something vital and alive about the spirit, a new, living religious form.

At the end of her life, Thompson had a final vision of Abdu'l-Bahá, but this time, instead of telling her she would get healthy and live, he comforted her as she suffered and died. Though by this time the pastel portrait of Abdu'l-Bahá she had painted years ago had faded—pastels are unfortunately an impermanent medium—Abdu'l-Bahá's image had stayed with her, and she must have turned to this image again and again in her mind as she lay dying. A friend was with her. It was December of 1956. "Do you want to come with me, and be with 'Abdu'l-Bahá?" Thompson asked. "No," was the reply, "I am not ready yet." And then, as her friend sat next to her, Thompson died.[29]

NOTES

1. Fabius, "The God Intoxicated People," *Streator (IL) Daily Independent-Times,* October 31, 1914, in the Juliet Thompson Papers, Bahá'í National Archives, Wilmette, Ill. Biographical information on Thompson is from O. Z. Whitehead, *Some Early Bahá'ís of the West* (Oxford: George Ronald, 1977), 76–77; and a typescript autobiographical statement by Juliet Thompson in the Thompson Papers, hereafter cited as "Autobiography."

2. Whitehead, *Some Early Bahá'ís,* 76–77; and Thompson, "Autobiography."

3. Marzieh Gail, "At 48 West Tenth," foreword to *The Diary of Juliet Thompson* (Los Angeles: Kalimat, 1983), xi–xiii, xviii.

4. Ibid., ix–xii.

5. There is a vast literature on the spiritual anxieties and strains of late nineteenth-century American life. Representative works include Walter Houghton, *The Victorian Frame of Mind, 1830–1870* (New Haven: Yale University Press, 1957); Paul Carter, *The Spiritual Crisis of the Gilded Age* (DeKalb: Northern Illinois University Press, 1971); James Moore, *The Post-Darwinian Controversies: A Study of the Protestant Struggle to Come to Terms with Darwin in Great Britain and America, 1870–1900* (Cambridge: Cambridge University Press, 1979); Paul

Croce, *Science and Religion in the Era of William James* (Chapel Hill: University of North Carolina Press, 1995); James Turner, *Without God, Without Creed: The Origins of Unbelief in America* (Baltimore: Johns Hopkins University Press, 1985); T. J. Jackson Lears, *No Place of Grace: Antimodernism and the Transformation of American Culture, 1880–1920* (1981; Chicago: University of Chicago Press, 1994); and E. Brooks Holifield, *A History of Pastoral Care in America: From Salvation to Self-Realization* (Nashville, Tenn.: Abingdon Press, 1983).

6. Gail, "At 48 West Tenth," ix–x.

7. Quoted in Umar F. Abd-Allah, *A Muslim in Victorian America: The Life of Alexander Russell Webb* (Oxford: Oxford University Press, 2006), 69.

8. David Morgan, *Protestants and Pictures: Religion, Visual Culture and the Age of American Mass Production* (Oxford: Oxford University Press, 1999), 293, 296–98.

9. Whitehead, *Some Early Bahá'ís*, 79; and Morgan, *Protestants and Pictures*, 300.

10. Whitehead, *Some Early Bahá'ís*, 75–76.

11. Gail, "At 48 West Tenth," xv; and Thompson, *The Diary of Juliet Thompson*, 15–21. Thompson's accounts of this event are different in mostly unimportant details in her letters and in Thompson, "Autobiography."

12. Thompson, *Diary of Juliet Thompson*, 93–94.

13. Juliet Thompson to Agnes Parsons, October 18, 1909, Agnes Parsons Papers, Bahá'í National Archives, Wilmette, Ill.

14. "At last we saw divinity incarnate," she said once on seeing Abdu'l-Bahá during his 1912 American visit. She used similar phrases at other times. See Thompson, *Diary of Juliet Thompson*, 236.

15. Accounts referred to here are from Allan Ward, *239 Days: Abdu'l-Bahá's Journey in America* (Wilmette, Ill.: Bahá'í Publishing Trust, 1979), 206; Archie Bell, *The Spell of the Holy Land* (Boston: Page, 1915), 306; and Leigh Eric Schmidt, *Restless Souls: The Making of American Spirituality* (San Francisco: HarperSanFrancisco, 2005), 217–18. Juliet had her own ecstatic moments, to be sure. For instance, when she encountered a picture of the prophet founder of the Bahá'í Faith, Bahá'u'lláh, she reported being overwhelmed by the experience. "The instant I saw that photograph I fell with my face to the ground, trembling and sobbing. It was as though the Picture were alive and Something had rushed from it and struck me a blow between the eyes. I cannot explain it. The power and the majesty were terrific. . . . Yet—dare I say it?" she continued, "I love the Face of Abdu'l-Bahá more." Thompson, *Diary of Juliet Thompson*, 88.

16. G. Stanley Hall, quoted in Gail Bederman, *Manliness and Civilization: A Cultural History of Gender and Race in the United States, 1880–1917* (Chicago: University of Chicago Press, 1995), 95. See also Lears, *No Place of Grace*, 142.

17. Hilton Obenzinger, *American Palestine: Melville, Twain and the Holy Land Mania* (Princeton: Princeton University Press, 1999), 41, 43.

18. Juliet's conversation with Abdu'l-Bahá is from Thompson, *The Diary of Juliet Thompson*, 90–91.

19. Juliet Thompson, "As Essay on Art," Thompson Papers; and *Washington Post*, "Inspiration School," April 25, 1934, Thompson Papers.

20. Wassily Kandinsky, *Concerning the Spiritual in Art*, trans. M. T. H. Sandler (1911; Whitefish, MT: Kessinger, 2004), 20–22.

21. For information in this and the previous paragraph I am indebted to Pam Meechem and Julie Sheldon, *Modern Art: A Critical Introduction* (London: Routledge, 2005), 67–70; Maurice Tuchman, ed., *The Spiritual in Art: Abstract Painting, 1890–1985* (New York: Abbe-

ville, 1986), 34–43; and Roger Lipsey, *An Art of Our Own: The Spiritual in Twentieth-Century Art* (Boston: Shambhala, 1988).

22. Thompson, *Diary of Juliet Thompson,* 144.

23. Juliet Thompson, "Pen Pictures of Abdu'l-Bahá in America," *Star of the West,* August 1, 1921, 146–50.

24. This is Juliet's recollection of Gibran's words. See Juliet Thompson to Horace Holley, March 17, 1945, Thompson Papers.

25. Suheil Bushrui and Joe Jenkins, *Kahlil Gibran: Man and Poet* (Oxford: Oneworld, 1999), 126.

26. Leigh Schmidt probes the limits of liberal iconoclasm in this era and in the twentieth century in *Restless Souls.*

27. *New York Times,* "Recent Religious Books," August 17, 1940, 12, Thompson Papers; and John Francis Kelly, "Review of Irish and Catholic Books and Authors," *New York Advocate,* July 13, 1940, Thompson Papers.

28. Marguerite P. Smyth, foreword to *I, Mary Magdalen,* by Juliet Thompson (New York: Delphic Studies, 1940), ix–x.

29. Gail, "At 48 West Tenth," xvi.

FIVE

Where "Deep Streams Flow, Endlessly Renewing"

Metaphysical Religion and "Cultural Evolution" in the Art of Agnes Pelton

NATHAN REES

In 1932, Agnes Pelton (1881–1961), a moderately recognized artist who made a living painting landscapes and portraits, surprised her family and friends by moving across the country, at the age of fifty, to a small town in the inland California desert. There she hoped to find new inspiration for her abstract paintings, images that she referred to as her "especial light message to the world."[1] Pelton conceived of her modernist paintings as more than just experiments in formal composition, seeing them as expressions of her own religious convictions—she maintained that her art had the potential to elevate humanity by directly conveying spiritual knowledge.

Pelton's theory of an ideal aesthetic for religious art, framed by her study of Theosophy and related systems of belief, provides insight into the significance of metaphysical religion in American modernism. Beyond inspiring formal innovation, Theosophy provided artists with specific religious interpretations as they addressed contested contemporary social issues. Theosophists promoted racial and religious equality, worked against the colonialist suppression of Asian religions, and advocated a new, synthetic system that would incorporate beliefs and practices from traditions around the world. In the United States, metaphysical writers lauded Native Americans, asserting that they possessed ancient wisdom with power to liberate Western culture from the bonds of scientific materialism.

Pelton actively participated in this discourse, painting images that interpreted Native American cultural practices in metaphysical terms, synthesizing elements from American Indian and metaphysical religions. Her work also conveys the Theosophical belief that as the religion of the new age developed, the various traditions from which it appropriated would gradually diminish. Theosophists in the early twentieth century were not immune to the pervasive influence of contemporary theories of "cultural evolution," which tied advancement to industrial progress. Metaphysical writers anticipated that "ancient" cultures would disappear by being absorbed into a universal modern society as civilizations evolved. Although Pelton's references to Native Americans in her work seem superficially celebratory, they reflect Theosophy's deep ambivalence toward non-Western religious traditions. Pelton lauded the ancient wisdom she believed American Indians maintained, but her abstractions depict a world evolving toward a new age, relegating actual contemporary Native Americans to the past.

Pelton's abstract paintings reflect the synthetic character of her beliefs. *Future* (1941; fig. 18), for example, portrays a metaphysical narrative unfolding in the Southwest desert. The night sky, pulled back like an open curtain, reveals two stone pillars, energized by bolts of red and blue electricity. Hovering in the far distance, above a mountain peak, four patches of brilliant light open into a realm of intense white. Pelton described the work in her notes as a "kind of 'Pilgrim's Progress' through darkness and oppression, across a stony desert," leading ultimately to "windows of illumination."[2] By invoking John Bunyan's seventeenth-century text, Pelton related her image to an exceptionally familiar trope in American art and literature, but reworked the terms of the narrative to express her metaphysical perspective. For Pelton *Future* is an allegory of the spiritual journey from the darkness of materialist doubt to the revelatory radiance of metaphysical religion.

Pelton's search for illumination began when she was first exposed to metaphysical religious literature as a young art student. Her teacher at the Pratt Institute in New York, Arthur Wesley Dow, interpreted Asian art in terms derived partly from Theosophy, and advocated "synthesis" as the ultimate goal of all artistic endeavor.[3] Pelton began a serious study of Theosophy and related metaphysical belief systems, eventually participating in an association headed by Will Levington Comfort called the "Glass Hive." Introduced by a mutual friend, Pelton traveled to Pasadena, California, in 1928 and spent eight months with the group. Comfort was an ardent advocate of the value of work, and conceived of the hive as an ideal metaphor for a community of shared work with shared rewards. The work that his participants engaged in, however, was mostly literary and artistic, and the reward that he expected was increased spiritual knowledge with the potential to improve the social and physical condition of humanity.[4]

For Pelton, the experience of creating and viewing art was central to its spiritual function. In her view, a work of art was not a physical repository of meaning so much as a nexus through which diverse interpretations brought by the artist and the viewer could converge in a rich polyvalent field. Pelton's theory of reception was indebted to Wassily Kandinsky, a fellow Theosophist and artist whose work she read and admired. Drawing on his assertion that art ideally "appeals less to the eye and more to the soul," Pelton wrote that she intended her paintings to lead the viewer to a mental state similar to the one she had experienced while painting; she described her aim as to "give life and vitality to the visual images which have come to me from time to time as fleeting but meaningful experiences—to sound their harmonies through the painter's hand and express their potencies that others may see and hear."[5]

Pelton meant to do more than simply elicit a particular emotional response through her art—she considered the "inner realm" from which she felt her paintings arose to be a fount of spiritual knowledge more immediate than that derived from any outside source. The inner visions that she sought to portray were intended to be not *descriptive,* but *prescriptive:* instead of illustrating religious concepts or conveying specific meanings through particular symbols, she meant her work to allow others, though the act of viewing, to access their own internal sight, awaken their own spiritual perception. As she wrote, "though art lends itself willingly to illustration of mental concepts . . . [it] can contribute to the apprehension of spiritual life, and the expansion of a deeper vision."[6]

Pelton determined that in order to reach this level of spiritual significance in her art, she needed to seek out a physical locale that would be more conducive to inspiration than the East Coast, where she had lived nearly her entire life.[7] As she described in her journal in an entry dated August 28, 1930, pondering the possibility of relocating, "I need an opportunity [of] remaining always connected to the 'source.'" In the margin, she wrote, "Shambhala."[8] The word "source" had a dual meaning for Pelton, referring at once to her convictions of an inner connection to divinity, a spiritual essence that permeated the universe, and to a physical wellspring from which perceptible glimpses of that essence might emanate. She was searching not only for a location where she could be productive as an artist, but for a place that would be her own Shambhala, her archetypal utopia.

Pelton drew on Comfort's description of Shambhala as the physical residence of the "White Council," advanced beings whom Helena Blavatsky, the founder of Theosophy, claimed led the progress of humanity on Earth, but also as the "Inner Temple," a location accessible only through inward concentration. Once a person, "only a most pure and potent messenger," had learned to access this spiritual place, they could approach those "holding the cup continually for revelation, guiding and guarding humanity's soul," who would grant them wisdom, with the responsibility of sharing it with the world. Reflecting his embrace of contemporary liberal religious writers' emphasis on the "interiority" of spiritual experience, Comfort admonished those seeking to provide humanity with truly uplifting art to connect with the inner Shambhala, the source of profound revelation.[9]

Pelton sought both the internal and external Shambhala. As Comfort and Pelton each maintained, some physical locations were better than others for finding the clarity of mind that could grant access to spiritual realms. The deserts of the Southwest, they felt, provided ample space for meditation far from the presence of any human intervention in the landscape. Pelton believed that by living away from the distractions of civilization, she could better access the Inner Temple of revelation. She wrote in her application for a Guggenheim grant in 1932 that the California desert would reflect the "abstract beauty of the inner vision, which would be kindled by the inspiration of these rare and solitary places."[10] She sought out Cathedral City as her own Shambhala, the place where she could stay "connected to the 'source.'"

To aid in accessing the inner Shambhala, Pelton built a meditation room in her Cathedral City studio. She felt that by meditating, she could transcend the boundaries of physical space and experience a glimpse of higher realms. When she meditated, she wrote, "it seemed as if all the bricks of the wall stretched, or cracked slightly, showing a slight radiance through."[11] It was the combined power of the physical space in which she lived and the spiritual plane she reached through meditative practice that brought her to what she recognized as the Inner Temple. Pelton's letters describing her love for the desert and her sense of belonging in Cathedral City suggest that she felt she succeeded in finding her Shambhala; after arriving in 1930, she never left.[12]

Pelton conveyed her impression of the region in her abstract works, many of which are set in vast, expansive deserts. *Future* evokes Pelton's conception of Shambhala; in the painting, the desert literally provides a portal to the realm of illumination. Pelton may also have intended the image to represent the path to the Inner Temple, as the two pillars resemble Jachin and Boaz, the twin columns of the Temple of Solomon, which are frequently referenced in Theosophical literature. As the columns guarded the sanctuary of the temple at Jerusalem, the pillars in *Future* signify the sacredness of the space beyond, the inner connection to what Blavatsky called the "universal divine principle," the "universal mind" that connected every object and force in the cosmos and served as the ultimate source of truth.[13]

Future further resonates with Blavatsky's assertion that all of the world's religious traditions were originally based on the same underlying universal principle. As Theosophist Paul F. Case wrote, the motif of the twin columns was incorporated in religious art from around the world, tying together Hermetic, early Christian, Judaic, and Egyptian philosophies, finding modern expression in Tarot and Masonic imagery.[14] Recognizing this significance, art historian Michael Zakian asserted that the columns "allude to an ancient culture—a repository of non-western wisdom granting spiritual transcendence."[15] More specifically, though, the pillars refer to the ancient inhabitants of the desert in which Pelton's modernist "Pilgrim's Progress" takes place. Pelton did not depict the columns as part of an ancient temple, but as elements standing alone in the empty California desert. She included the Native Americans of the Southwest in her understanding of the combined wisdom of antiquity, following contemporary Theosophists in recognizing the ancient inhabitants of the Americas as having possessed unsurpassed spiritual knowledge.

In fact, Pelton may have had local ruins in mind when she painted *Future,* as the desert in which she lived is the ancestral home of a still-vital indigenous culture. Cathedral City is located partially within the Agua Caliente reservation of the Cahuilla Indians, and tribal members have long played an important role in the area's economy and government.[16] Pelton was personally familiar with some of the Cahuilla, as she often drove to their reservation to paint landscapes.[17] On the Cahuilla reservation, remnants of structures made from rough desert rock mark faintly discernable geometric forms in the landscape, which Edward Curtis, a contemporary photographer renowned for his depictions of Native Americans, had reproduced in his multivolume work *The North American Indian.*[18] Much like the ruins in the Cahuilla reservation, the structure Pelton depicted in *Future* interrupts the visual monotony of the desert, forming the only clear geometry or evidence of human activity in the painting. Metaphysical writers interpreted ruins across the Southwest as proof that Native Americans' ancestors had developed civilizations far grander than the scientific establishment would concede. Searching for evidence of the common origins of all historical civilizations, Theosophists asserted correspondences between ancient American architecture and ruins in Egypt, Asia, and other parts of the world.[19]

As a Theosophist, Pelton believed that the knowledge of the past was an essential ingredient in the synthesis of the world's religious traditions. In the coming time that Pelton depicted in *Future,* the synthetic project of metaphysical religion would bring together sufficient spiritual knowledge to bring humanity to an enlightened state. Theosophy also provided Pelton with a sense that the future was not up to chance, but followed a predetermined evolutionary trajectory. In Pelton's view, the history of past civilizations not only evidenced the cyclical patterns through which Western society was moving, but provided knowledge essential for the successful continuation of the evolutionary process, furnishing necessary wisdom to help modern civilizations learn from the lessons of the past and avoid repeating mistakes. As one result of her study of metaphysical religion, Pelton understood that the world was moving through a definite chronological progression leading ultimately toward a new era of illumination. *Future* demonstrates Pelton's belief in the cyclical nature of human existence, a concept that had significant influence on Theosophists' interpretations of Native American cultural practices.

Although Blavatsky and the first generation of Theosophists wrote relatively little about Native Americans, when later writers attempted to interpret American Indian religious ideas, they borrowed many of the concepts that their predecessors had originally used to describe cultures of Asia. Pelton, who began studying Theosophy around the turn of the twentieth century, would have been exposed to all of these ideas as they unfolded in the Theosophical literature. Blavatsky and her followers directly confronted late nineteenth-century scientific racism as they argued that Asian cultures were in many ways superior to Western society. In other respects, however, Theosophical writers capitulated to established stereotypes, which, buttressed by alleged scientific evidence, erected formidable obstacles to their society's commitment to "universal brotherhood." In practice, Theosophy maintained conflicting perspectives regarding non-Western cultures. Despite the fact that the Theosophical

Society was one of the most liberal advocates of racial equality among turn-of-the-century religious organizations, Theosophists fashioned their official understanding of racial difference under the influence of a contemporary scientific academy in which, as Helen Carr described, "unselfconscious racism was the norm."[20]

Blavatsky's monumental work, *The Secret Doctrine* (1888), sparked a revolution in metaphysical religion by directly addressing Asian religious beliefs and practices.[21] In 1878, she and Henry Steel Olcott, cofounder and first president of the Theosophical Society, traveled to India and Sri Lanka; they officially moved the headquarters of the Theosophical Society to Adyar, India, the following year. Traveling through South Asia, Blavatsky and Olcott aroused significant ire from the British colonial government by promoting the study of indigenous religions and actively opposing Christian missionary efforts in the region. Olcott achieved lasting fame in Sri Lanka for his *Buddhist Catechism* (1881), which was enormously influential and widely used in Sri Lankan schools. He helped spur a revival of Buddhism on the island, contesting missionaries' claims of Christianity's moral superiority. In India, he and Blavatsky promoted the study of traditional Hindu religion in local schools.[22] Following Olcott, and in contradistinction to contemporary cultural evolutionists, Theosophists encouraged the preservation of local cultures and religions, and argued against the synonymy of Westernization and progress.

In other respects, however, Theosophists were influenced by contemporary notions of Western superiority. This was especially evident in their judgments about precisely which practices and traditions in Asian religions expressed an elevated spirituality, and which were morally questionable; the latter they proscribed as later accretions or degradations. Olcott, in fact, considered contemporary Hinduism and Buddhism "but brutalizations of their primal types."[23] This gave him the leeway to condemn various cultural practices in Asia while insisting that his own understanding of indigenous traditions surpassed that of local leaders and practitioners. "Olcott's uncritical and unconscious appropriation of . . . academic Orientalism," Stephen Prothero observed, "led him to the rather absurd conclusion that Ceylon's Buddhists knew little, if anything, about 'real' Buddhism. . . . Olcott assumed the right to define what Buddhism really was."[24] Theosophists frequently failed to recognize the ways in which their own programs intended to promote local religions actually acted as a form of Westernization. As Prothero has described, for example, Olcott's

Buddhist Catechism interpreted Buddhism through the lens of late nineteenth-century liberal Protestantism, advocating a hybrid, imported belief system, despite Olcott's stated intentions.

While Blavatsky, Olcott, and their associates in the Theosophical Society were instrumental in positively changing Western perceptions of Asian religions, as well as in effecting measurable political progress against Western colonialism, they were nonetheless outside interpreters of indigenous cultures whose conclusions were neither largely accurate nor uniformly laudatory. They privileged the allegedly ancient cultures of South Asia, considering them spiritually superior to the West, but in other respects, they clearly favored their own Western societies. This deep ambivalence was a frequent characteristic of Theosophical approaches to non-Western cultures, and continued in the work of later Theosophists who turned their attention to ancient societies within the United States.

Theosophists had focused on Asiatic cultures during the first decades after the society's organization, but around 1915, they began writing extensively about Native Americans. In the years that followed, Theosophy as an organization underwent a gradual but significant decline, and various offshoots experienced tremendous growth. Nonetheless, Theosophy remained the organizing structure for the majority of these groups, providing core beliefs for diverse metaphysical religions throughout the twentieth century.[25] Thus, as later metaphysical and New Age writers turned their attention to American Indian cultures and religions, they incorporated a number of the key themes that Theosophists had already established in their approach to Asian religions in the late nineteenth century.[26]

Central to these were the twin propositions that indigenous cultures preserved ancient wisdom that was once known worldwide, and that the excavation and study of this wisdom was essential to furthering the evolutionary progression of humanity. The idea that cultures evolved was important in Theosophy and derivative metaphysical traditions; historian of religion Olav Hammer described it as a philosophy of "meliorism," "the concept that history goes forward and that people and cultures progress." This concept allowed Theosophists to explain the progression of societies and religions in successive periods of ascendancy not as an accident of history but as an expression of "universal law." As Hammer asserted, "Such a basic schema does not so much derive from the empirical facts of history, as provide a framework within which historical events can be understood."[27] Thus, Theosophical studies of world cultures seldom emphasized the objective analysis of scientific evidence, but drew selectively from existing amateur as well as scholarly accounts, making liberal interpretative leaps to fit particular cultures' histories to the preexisting patterns to which Theosophists understood all societies to conform.

The Theosophical conception of evolution traces back to Blavatsky's attempt to reconcile late nineteenth-century science with her understanding of liberal, "universal" religion. Blavatsky expounded her evolutionary worldview in *The Secret Doctrine.* She described a vast cosmology in which the world and its inhabitants move through a cyclical progression of states of being; the seven iterations of the world, called "planetary rounds," are each divided into seven "root races," temporal rather than ethnic divisions that succeed each other until the beginning of a new planetary round. As Blavatsky wrote, in any one era, essentially all people belong to a particular root race, which, after completing its progress, would be replaced by another. Most individuals would be reincarnated in every successive root race, allowing them to accumulate knowledge and experience from one lifetime to the next.[28]

In Blavatsky's cosmology, the cycle of seven root races that make up each planetary round begins with the most spiritual and the least physical; as they advance through the seven root races, they become successively more corporeal until they reach a spiritual nadir near the midpoint. From that point on, she claimed, the evolutionary trajectory would reverse itself and the root races would then progress spiritually while becoming increasingly less attached to physicality. Although Blavatsky clearly privileged the spiritual over the physical, she nonetheless considered corporeal existence essential to the evolution of each individual. As she argued, it is only by undergoing the experiences unique to physical existence that a fundamentally spiritual being can reach its maximum potential. In this cosmology, by the time the evolutionary cycle has completed a full circuit from spiritual to physical and back to spiritual, every being in the universe has increased in both knowledge and spiritual capacity, and will then enter yet another planetary round composed of seven new root races.[29]

Blavatsky insisted on the scientific veracity of her propositions, and explicitly posited this series of ascending and descending "arcs" as a religious alternative to Darwinian evolution. While Blavatsky accepted Darwin's general argument that species change and adapt over time, she denied that random mutation drove the process. In her teleological perspective, evolution operated progressively rather than randomly, working toward universal improvement as a result of ineradicable natural law. She disavowed Darwin's presupposition of a procession from the lowest to the highest forms of existence; Blavatsky saw the process of evolution as cyclical, but ultimately upward-moving, and considered humanity to be presently at a relative low point, having devolved from a more spiritually advanced state. As she wrote, "All things had their origin in spirit—evolution having originally begun from above and proceeded downward, instead of the reverse, as taught in the Darwinian theory. In other words, there has been a gradual materialization of forms until a fixed ultimate of debasement is reached."[30] This reverse-Darwinian evolution, as Blavatsky saw it, would change course as a new root race came into being and the arc began to swing back upward.

Blavatsky advocated complete racial equality in her statement of the Theosophical Society's mission to "form the nucleus of a Universal Brotherhood of Humanity without distinction of race, colour, or creed."[31] She emphasized that her use of the term "root race" to distinguish between different evolutionary levels did not imply that certain cultures were less physically evolved than others. But despite her anti-racist agenda, Blavatsky nonetheless wrote that while nearly all of the world's inhabitants were members of the fifth root race, a few ethnicities were actually remnants of previous root races. There were no clear boundaries between the root races, she held, meaning that small populations of one root race might continue to live long after the advent of the next. Specifically, she claimed that the Native Americans and Mongolians were the last remnants of the fourth root race, the "Atlanteans," whose destruction by flood precipitated the rise of the first fifth-race civilizations, the "Aryans" in India and Egypt.[32]

Blavatsky's pseudoscientific cosmology, proffered in direct competition with Darwinism, challenged scientific materialists with an alternate explanation of the process of evolution. Hers was a teleological progress that worked according to a universal plan directed by the divine force permeating all matter. In her acceptance of the general principles of evolution, however, she also acceded to the theories promulgated by contemporary cultural evolutionists, anthropologists, sociologists, and others who applied the principles of Darwinism to the historical development of world cultures. Prior to Boas's promotion of cultural relativism and historical particularism, which did not gain widespread acceptance in anthropology until after the First World War, scholars assumed that Western society was the most technologically advanced, and had therefore reached a higher point on an evolutionary scale.[33]

Drawing from metaphysical religion and contemporary science, writers advocated widely divergent perspectives on the significance of the concept of root races in Theosophical literature over the next several decades, arguing that people belonging to earlier root races were superior to the peoples of the modern West in some respects and inferior in others. Many implied both positions at once, and most, especially when addressing Native American cultures, simply repeated platitudes about authentic and ancient spirituality that were superficially laudatory, but potentially demeaning.

In this respect, Theosophists were not far removed from American culture as a whole, and their ideas about Native Americans generally paralleled those of the wider populace. In the early twentieth century, Annie Besant, Olcott's successor as the president of the Theosophical Society at Adyar, represented the popular contemporary view that American Indians exemplified bravery and nobility, but were morally degenerate and unsanitary, and thus in need of civilizing acculturation.[34]

By around 1915, however, Theosophists began to seriously interrogate the significance of the Native Americans' status as (supposedly) the last remaining members of the fourth root race. Writers diverged dramatically from Besant's racist formulations and reinterpreted this status to suggest that the American Indians maintained ancient religious knowledge with the potential to advance the spiritual state of cultures of the West. This new approach mirrored changing attitudes toward Native Americans in a broader spectrum of American culture; on the scientific front, anthropologists had begun to adopt Boas's cultural relativism as an alternative to earlier formulations of cultural evolution, arguing that history, rather than ineluctable evolutionary forces, determined individual expressions of culture.[35]

Cultural and political attitudes toward Native Americans changed dramatically during this era; Alan Trachtenberg has described the period surrounding the turn of the twentieth century as marking a "turn toward the 'good' Indian."[36] No longer a threat to manifest destiny, American Indians began to exemplify honor, rather than savagery, in the popular imagination. During this time, people dissatisfied with various aspects of modernity began to look to Native Americans, along with other cultures around the world, as exemplifying a more natural, healthful existence. Concomitantly, numerous writers, activists, artists, and cultural critics in the first decades of the twentieth century sought to overturn conventional depictions of American Indians and promote a newly positive, if equally stereotyped, image.

The emerging discourse that celebrated rather than repudiated the "otherness" of Native Americans was, as historian Robert Berkhofer has argued, just as dependent on fictive constructions of "Indian-ness" as were the earlier discourses advocating paternalistic assimilation. This new image was promoted by those who, according to Berkhofer, "portrayed Indian cultures as manifesting the wholeness of man, the humanity of interpersonal relationships, and the integrity of organic unity," but who "had abandoned the liberalism of the mid-nineteenth century for the liberalism of the mid-twentieth as their way of judging the presumably splintered culture of their own industrial society."[37] The resulting image was, if superficially positive, nonetheless artificial, imposed, and, frequently, unwanted. In discussing "Indian wisdom," writers generally ignored the actual beliefs, arts, literatures, and historical accomplishments of the diverse indigenous peoples of North America, and instead created a generalized fictive being who exemplified the opposite of the modern neurasthenic.[38]

During this era, prevailing attitudes toward Native American religions changed dramatically, as well. Tisa Wenger has documented shifting conceptions of Pueblo ceremonialism in the early twentieth century, noting the multiple strategies that the Pueblo employed to frame their cultural practices to their own advantage within competing definitions of religion. Furthermore, as Wenger asserted, representatives of various liberal social and religious organizations, despite their problematic assumptions about the naturalness and antiquity of Pueblo traditions, were instrumental in aiding the Indians' own efforts toward self-determination by establishing that their cultural practices constituted a religion deserving of First Amendment protection.[39]

Numerous contemporary authors were explicit about the need to refashion Western mores after those of idealized and imaginary Indians, suggesting that Indians held religious beliefs equaling or even surpassing Christianity. Ernest Thompson Seton, for example, wrote in *The Gospel of the Red Man,* "The civilization of the White man is a failure; it is visibly crumbling around us," whereas the Indians were "representative of the most heroic race the world has ever seen, the most physically perfect race the world has ever seen, the most spiritual civilization the world has ever seen."[40] Charles Alexander Eastman, an outspoken advocate of Indian rights who was himself part Sioux, argued in

The Soul of the Indian that Christianity in its original state was essentially what the Sioux believed, but that it had subsequently degenerated. He wrote, "I believe that Christianity and modern civilization are opposed and irreconcilable, and that the spirit of Christianity and of our ancient religion is essentially the same."[41]

Theosophical writers also contributed to this discourse, noting apparent similarities between American Indian and metaphysical beliefs. The *Theosophic Messenger* reprinted an entire chapter of *The Soul of the Indian* in its 1911 issue, in which Eastman portrayed the American Indians as espousing ideologies that were markedly similar to points of Theosophical doctrine. First, his assertion of the fundamental unity of all religions in their original state closely corresponded to the Theosophists' belief in a single truth underlying the world's belief systems. Second, he claimed that the Indians did not worship an anthropomorphic god, but rather the "Eternal, the 'Great Mystery' that surrounds and embraces us," in agreement with Blavatsky's description of God not as a being, but as the "Eternal Cause." Furthermore, Eastman stated that many Native Americans believed in reincarnation, noting that "there were some who claimed to have full knowledge of a former incarnation."[42]

Lastly, and perhaps most tellingly, the editors of the *Theosophic Messenger* chose to excerpt the chapter in which Eastman discussed the "occult powers" of the Indians, with "remarkable prophecies and other mystic practices," including powers of premonition, spirit communication, and telepathy, which he suggested were a result of their unrivaled understanding of natural forces. These ideas resonated strongly with Theosophists, as the American Indians, the supposed remnants of the Atlantean root race, were likewise portrayed in metaphysical literature as maintaining psychic powers that were well developed in the fourth root race but subsequently lost to the preponderance of humanity. According to Besant, it was the open teaching of sciences that should have remained occult that led to the destruction of Atlantis, as "men became giants in knowledge but also giants in evil," leading directly to their downfall.[43]

One of the most prominent advocates of synthesizing American Indian religions with Western metaphysics was Mabel Dodge Luhan, a wealthy New York socialite who had moved to Taos, New Mexico, in 1917. Luhan attempted to physically enact the combinative strategy that she suggested was the only hope for the West, adopting what she conceived of as "Indian" philosophy and marrying Antonio Lujan of the Taos Pueblo.[44] She accepted many of the Theosophical tenets regarding the Indians' authentic and surpassing spirituality, interpreting "Indian religion" as the positive antipode of religion in the West; in her view, sectarian Christianity had become oppressive, external, and devoid of substance, whereas she saw the Pueblos' beliefs as natural, integral, and empowering. "Their religion," she wrote, "all of love & joy & the sun & growing things fills them constantly, *daily,* with wonder & worshipful delight."[45]

Agnes Pelton had befriended Luhan before she left New York—Pelton's first trip to the West was an extended visit to Luhan in Taos in 1919. As Pelton later formulated her own interpretations of Native American cultures, she relied on the framework that Luhan and others had constructed to explain their cultural practices in the context of metaphysical religion. She followed Luhan in the belief that the forward progression of humanity was dependent on synthesizing ancient wisdom with modern understanding, creating a new, universal religion. This development, in Pelton's view, was of tremendous import, as it signaled the waning of the fifth root race and the emergence of the sixth. Theosophists argued that the world, following its inalterable evolutionary trajectory, was beginning to enter a new stage of development, marked by the revitalization of occult sciences and philosophies. Blavatsky and her followers asserted that a new, sixth root race was arising, marked by unparalleled spiritual power as well as scientific advancement. As Blavatsky wrote, "even now, under our very eyes, the new Race and Races are preparing to be formed.... It is in America that the transformation will take place, and has already silently commenced."[46]

Pelton frequently alluded to the cyclical cosmology of Theosophy in her abstract work. *Evensong* (1934; fig. 19), for example, symbolizes the process of death and rebirth, both of individuals and of root races. The painting is set on a cosmic scale; the horizon curves to show a vast, planetary perspective, and the sky fades from blue near the horizon to a starry black in the upper distance. A radiant, glowing vessel wafts out incense-like ribbons of smoke or vapor over the world below. Despite its cosmic setting, the painting bears a title referring to a familiar religious practice common to a number of Christian denominations in which congregants gather late in the day, generally for a service of prayer and song. Though such services were not a part of Pelton's personal religious observance, "evensong" was a common metonym in contemporary writing, signifying constant devotion. The immediate emotive impact of Pelton's image corresponds closely with contemporary descriptions of the significance of the evensong service; the starlit, rippling water suggests a tranquil, reflective mood akin to the "service of quiet and thoughtful worship, of meditation, of learning, remembering, and reflection" that Percy Dearmer described as the purpose of evensong in *Everyman's History of the Prayer Book.*[47]

But *Evensong* also encompasses complex layers of intertwined meaning that reflect the diversity of Pelton's religious convictions. The sunset, presaging an eventual sunrise, was a common symbol of immortality, employed frequently across numerous religious groups in Pelton's time. It was a particularly salient metaphor for Theosophists, as the daily rising and setting of the sun aptly symbolized the unending cycle of death and rebirth in which Theosophy situated humanity. As Emmett Small wrote in "Sunset Reflexions" (1926), "The sun had set; and so our lives set; but Death? . . . Death died long ago to all who are awake; it never was born to Theosophists. To them it is a time of serenity and peace and silence and aloofness from things unnecessary to real life."[48]

Small's description of the state an individual experienced after death, which Blavatsky characterized as a period of rest between incarnations, seems appropriate for the exceptionally peaceful mood of *Evensong,* in which soft, warm colors in the center fade gradually to deep, cool blues around the edges, and the rippling water and flowing smoke lull the viewer into a sense of serenity.[49] Pelton's work suggests the idea of death and rebirth through more than just the symbolic sunset; in a poem accompanying the painting, she wrote,

> The evening stars glow softly down
> Above a flowing urn
> Day's overflow that disappears
> Within the sunset's turn
> A tear, a pearl, a flower white
> A memory upon the night
> Within the urn the fires are banked
> Conserved and glowing
> While underground the deep streams flow
> Endlessly renewing.[50]

Pelton's poem evokes funereal imagery, referring to the vessel as an urn and alluding to the flowers and tears common in contemporary grieving practice.[51] Simultaneously, it suggests that death is not a final end, and that the fire of any individual existence still burns safely within the urn, ready to find new expression in a new life, through the "endlessly renewing" stream of eternal progression.

On another level, *Evensong* refers to the cyclical nature of cosmic evolution. The painting reflects Theosophical writers' use of "evening" as a theme representing not just the end of an individual's life but the close of an era of cosmic time. This metaphor was especially common in descriptions of the then-current state of humanity, on the cusp of tremendous change with the anticipated passing of the fifth root race and rising of the sixth. In "Sunset Reflexions," Small went on to compare the gradually fading light of the setting sun with a root race "sinking to rest" after working along its evolutionary path during the day.[52] Likewise, numerous metaphysical writers referred to the coming of the sixth root race as the "dawn" of a new age.

The vapor flowing out of the vessel suggests the radiance of an earlier era spilling out and enlivening the next, a process that operated in several different contexts in Theosophy. The wisdom possessed by ancient peoples, in Blavatsky's assertion, provided the core material that would allow the West to escape the cultural malaise induced by scientific materialism. In reference to this concept, the vase in Pelton's *Evensong* might represent a generalized antiquity emanating lost religious knowledge, which flows out over the world once more after its rediscovery by the practitioners of metaphysical religions.

Perhaps more crucially, though, Theosophists held that a new era or root race could be born only through the death of the previous one. Pelton's close associate Dane Rudhyar, a noted composer, astrologer, and metaphysical writer, compared this process to the lifecycle of an annual plant. At the end of the season, a plant goes to seed, expending its stored energy and dying in the process. The resulting seeds, however, form the nucleus of the next generation of plants in the new season. The "process of planetary life," he wrote, is governed by the law that the "plant must die in order that the seed be fruitful."[53] And, as Rudhyar intended his metaphor to suggest, the seed from the previous root race gives the next a basis from which to build and further evolve—without the contributions of past eras, every new iteration of humanity would have to begin completely anew.

Emphasizing this concept in *Evensong,* Pelton included a symbol that she employed in several other works—Venus, the bright star in the upper right-hand corner.[54] In Theosophical literature, the planet was an emblem of eternal life, as it was both the evening star and the morning star, heralding the close of day but also the return of the sun in the morning, and, by extension, the cycle of death and rebirth through reincarnation.[55] Pelton's use of this symbol fits closely with the theme of *Evensong,* the evening star signaling the promise of the eventual return of the morning.

Venus also alludes to themes of fertility, generation, and renewal, associations that the planet carried even outside of a Theosophical context. In classical mythology, Venus was associated with love and sexual passion, but also with fertility and childbirth.[56] Theosophists argued that a range of female deities with similar associations were actually different manifestations of the same original archetype; Blavatsky held that Isis, Ishtar, Venus, and the Virgin Mary were all expressions of the same entity, representations of the generative principle in nature, the force driving the evolutionary progress of the cosmos.[57]

In *Evensong,* this significance is apparent in the combined symbolism of the planet Venus alongside the vessel; pots and other open, concave containers had been employed as symbols of female sexuality from the early medieval era in Western art, and thus associated with themes of creation, generation, and fertility. Zakian described the vessel in *Evensong* as "a clear association of nature's abundance with a feminine, procreative force."[58] In a similar vein, Nancy Strow Sheley wrote that "Pelton saw the vessel as a feminine procreative force, as a womb-like shape giving birth to flowing waters."[59] Both the planet and the vessel operate as potent symbols of the generative force driving the process of natural and cosmic evolution, orchestrating the progression of root races on the earth.

Evensong represents the waning of the fifth root race and the anticipated advent of the sixth, but Pelton's inclusion of the planet Venus also arguably references the previous stage in this evolutionary cycle, in which the fourth root race gave way to the fifth. Blavatsky wrote that Venus was an emblem of the fourth root race; the "preceptor of the Daityas, the giants of the Fourth Race," was represented by Shukra, or Venus, in her account of Hindu tradition. Further, she asserted that the flood that destroyed the Atlanteans had been presaged by a celestial omen involving Venus changing its size and color.[60] Numerous subsequent writers alluded to the association of Venus with the fourth root race—some even argued that advanced beings from the planet had traveled to the Earth during the Atlantean era to help spur intellectual and technological development.[61] Helena Roerich, coauthor of the Agni Yoga texts, which Pelton avidly read, wrote that Christ, Buddha, and Lord Maitreya (the future Buddha) "came from Venus at the dawn of the formation of physical man."[62]

Pelton's emblematic use of the planet Venus in *Evensong* secures her reference to the fourth root race as a source of the knowledge that would allow the fifth to ascend out of the mire of materialist philosophy and evolve into the next era. The vessel alludes to the peoples that Theosophical writers associated with this ancient wisdom—without any decoration or details to align it with any particular cultural tradition, it represents a generalized antiquity, according with the Theosophical tenet that all ancient religions expressed the same fundamental truth. Pelton's views on pottery as an art form, however, suggest a connection between *Evensong* and the ancient cultures that Theosophists specifically associated with the fourth root race: the Native Americans.

As Arthur Wesley Dow's student and teaching assistant at the Pratt Institute, Pelton would have been familiar with his belief that pottery was among the most important forms of art because of its direct and immediate connection with the earth. As Elizabeth Hutchinson has written, Dow learned Pueblo pottery techniques from Frank Hamilton Cushing, an early Southwestern anthropologist famous for his work with the Zuni, as well as for his advocacy of "participant observation," the idea that an ethnographer could learn best by actually participating in the culture he or she was observing. Dow took this approach with his students, asserting that they could learn from the same "primal instincts" that had inspired primitive artists if they practiced similar techniques and means of production. At the summer school in Ipswich, Massachusetts, where Pelton served as his teaching assistant in 1900, Dow used Native American pottery as examples for his students to copy, using ostensibly accurate indigenous methods of production.[63] Pelton must have absorbed Dow's lessons on the importance of pottery within Native American cultures, as an art that exemplified their alleged closeness to the earth and its generative powers. Her image of a vessel as a repository of ancient wisdom shares in this significance, suggesting that the people who were presumed to be the last remnants of the Atlantean root race could contribute spiritual knowledge that was vital to the continued evolutionary progression of humanity.

Pelton believed that wisdom from Native Americans and other ancient cultures around the world would, like the light preserved in the vessel in *Evensong,* be instrumental in bringing about the Earth's next evolutionary stage. The synthesis of knowledge that characterized the work of Theosophy and other metaphysical religions, she held, would ultimately result in a new age of enlightenment, marked by the ascendance of spirituality over materialism. Inherent in the belief that American Indians preserved knowledge from the fourth root race, however, was the supposition that they were bound to gradually diminish through acculturation. Blavatsky asserted that "in character and external type the elder [root race] loses its characteristics, and assumes the new features of the younger race," until the older root race vanishes entirely.[64] Thus, Theosophy provided both the impetus for learning from and preserving Native American cultures and a religious explanation for the inevitability of their decline. Pelton's paintings evoke this sentiment, representing Native Americans with ancient ruins and artifacts, not images of their thriving contemporary cultures.

Pelton's work reflects a sense of ambivalence underlying liberal religious attitudes toward world religions. The promotion of the study of alternate religious traditions marked an important step toward cultural preservation and the self-determination of numerous societies then under oppressive colonial rule. At the same time, however, American liberal religious leaders were generally unwilling to cede any interpretative authority, seldom allowing non-Western peoples the opportunity to represent their own religious ideas. Historian Carrie Bramen has criticized liberal Christian advocates of religious fusion in the late nineteenth century as practicing a syncretism "from above," in which Western power structures maintained both their identity and their preeminence by advocating limited forms of transculturation.[65] Proponents of "hegemonic syncretism" accepted the incorporation of ideas from other systems of belief, but only to an extent that would not threaten their own cultural boundaries or allow other groups a position of power.

Similarly, Pelton's works alluding to the Native Americans of the Southwest advocate a progressive understanding of American Indian cultural practices as valid forms of religious expression, but nonetheless presuppose the preeminence of Theosophy. Pelton followed metaphysical writers in celebrating the supposed ancient spiritual authenticity of American Indian religions, but always under the unspoken supposition that Theosophists had more authority to interpret their beliefs than the Indians themselves. Pelton intended her references to Native Americans not to impart any knowledge of their actual religions, but to convey her own metaphysical understanding of progressive evolution. Pelton's works portray American Indian cultures as important sources of religious truth, but in her evolutionary view, they contributed to the new synthetic religion only as representatives of a past age.

NOTES

1. Quoted in Nancy Strow Sheley, "Bringing Light to Life: The Art of Agnes Pelton" (Ph.D. diss., University of Kansas, 2000), ii.

2. Agnes Pelton notebooks, Agnes Pelton Papers, Archives of American Art, Smithsonian Institution, 3427:192, 3426:805.

3. For Dow, "synthesis" described both a compositional strategy and a combination of Eastern and Western aesthetic ideals. See Arthur Wesley Dow, *Composition* (New York: Baker and Taylor, 1903). For Dow's involvement with metaphysical religion, see Frederick C. Moffat, *Arthur Wesley Dow* (Washington, D.C.: Smithsonian Institution Press, 1977), 103; and Lawrence W. Chisolm, *Fenollosa: The Far East and American Culture* (New Haven: Yale University Press, 1963), 179–83.

4. Will Levington Comfort, *Midstream: A Chronicle at Halfway* (New York: George H. Doran, 1914), 309.

5. Wassily Kandinsky, *Concerning the Spiritual in Art,* trans. Michael T. H. Sadler (1911; London: Tate, 2006), 103; and Pelton to Rudhyar, August 22, 1938, "Pelton, Agnes: Correspondence" file, Raymond Jonson Collection, University of New Mexico Art Museum.

6. Pelton, "To Introduce My Oil Painting, *Illumination,*" June 12, 1957, "Pelton, Agnes: Correspondence" file, Raymond Jonson Collection.

7. Pelton was born in Stuttgart, Germany, but spent most of her youth in Brooklyn. She remained there until after her mother's death. In 1921, she moved to the relative seclusion of a windmill in Southampton, Long Island, where she spent ten years before moving to California. See Michael Zakian's detailed biography in *Agnes Pelton, Poet of Nature* (Palm Springs, Calif.: Palm Springs Desert Museum, 1995), 39.

8. Agnes Pelton journal, August 28, 1930, Agnes Pelton Papers, 3426:0584.

9. Will Levington Comfort, *The Hive* (New York: George H. Doran, 1914), 8, 208.

10. Quoted in Sheley, "Bringing Light to Life," 51. Pelton's application was denied, as she was apparently unaware that the purpose of the grant was to fund a year of work outside of the United States.

11. Pelton to Jane Levington Comfort, November 26, 1944, Letters from Agnes Pelton to Jane Levington Comfort (Jane Annixter), 1934–1959, Archives of American Art, Smithsonian Institution.

12. Zakian, *Agnes Pelton,* 67.

13. Helena Blavatsky, *The Key to Theosophy* (London: Theosophical Publishing Company, 1893), 107, 148.

14. Paul F. Case, "The Secret Doctrine of the Tarot," *Word* 25, no. 1 (April 1917): 18.

15. Zakian, *Agnes Pelton,* 93.

16. See Lowell John Bean and Lisa Bourgeault, *The Cahuilla* (New York: Chelsea House, 1989).

17. Karen Moss, "Art and Life Illuminated: Georgia O'Keeffe and Agnes Pelton, Agnes Martin and Florence Miller Pierce," in *Illumination: The Paintings of Georgia O'Keeffe, Agnes Pelton, Agnes Martin, and Florence Miller Pierce,* ed. Karen Moss (London: Merrell, 2009), 17. Pelton's papers give regrettably few details about her relationships with individuals on the Cahuilla reservation, but they do show that she knew some of them on a first-name basis: she identified those shown with her in a photograph that she sent to a friend in 1934. See Pelton to Vera Jonson, February 6, 1934, "Pelton, Agnes: Correspondence" file, Raymond Jonson Collection.

18. Edward S. Curtis, *The North American Indian,* vol. 15, *Southern California Shoshoneans: The Diegueños; Plateau Shoshoneans; The Washo* (Seattle, Wash.: Curtis, 1924), 27.

19. See, for example, William E. Gates, "Copan, and Its Position in American History," *Theosophical Path* 1 (July–December 1911): 419–26; and William E. Gates, "Ancient America," *Theosophical Path* 1 (July–December 1911): 323–27.

20. Helen Carr, *Inventing the American Primitive: Politics, Gender and the Representation of Native American Literary Traditions, 1789–1936* (Cork, Ireland: Cork University Press, 1996), 202.

21. See Mark Bevir, "The West Turns Eastward: Madame Blavatsky and the Transformation of the Occult Tradition," *Journal of the American Academy of Religion* 62, no. 3 (autumn 1994): 747–67.

22. Stephen R. Prothero, *The White Buddhist: The Asian Odyssey of Henry Steel Olcott* (Bloomington: Indiana University Press, 1996), 100–101, 134.

23. Ibid., 144.

24. Ibid., 101.

25. Olav Hammer, *Claiming Knowledge: Strategies of Epistemology from Theosophy to the New Age* (Leiden: Brill, 2001), 51–54.

26. Philip Jenkins, *Dream Catchers: How Mainstream America Discovered Native Spirituality* (Oxford: Oxford University Press, 2004), 136–40.

27. Hammer, *Claiming Knowledge*, 51, 41.

28. Helena Blavatsky, *The Secret Doctrine*, 2 vols. (London: Theosophical Publishing Company, 1888), 2:146.

29. Ibid., 1:218–19, 225.

30. Ibid., 2:190, 300.

31. Blavatsky, *Key to Theosophy*, 28.

32. Blavatsky, *Secret Doctrine*, 2:249–50, 443–44. On Blavatsky's use of the term "Aryan," see Robert Cowan, *The Indo-German Identification: Reconciling South Asian Origins and European Destinies, 1765–1885* (Rochester, N.Y.: Camden House, 2010), 178.

33. Adam Kuper, *The Reinvention of Primitive Society: Transformations of a Myth* (Oxford: Routledge, 2005), 133.

34. See Annie Besant, *A Study in Consciousness* (Los Angeles: Theosophical Publishing House, 1918), 109–10.

35. See Aldona Jonaitis, introduction to *A Wealth of Thought: Franz Boas on Native American Art*, by Franz Boas, ed. Aldona Jonaitis (Seattle: University of Washington Press, 1995), esp. 4–9.

36. Alan Trachtenberg, *Shades of Hiawatha: Staging Indians, Making Americans, 1880–1930* (New York: Hill and Wang, 2004), xxiii.

37. Robert F. Berkhofer Jr., *The White Man's Indian: Images of the American Indian from Columbus to the Present* (New York: Knopf, 1973), 67.

38. See T. J. Jackson Lears's description of neurasthenia as an illness indicative of antimodern dissatisfaction with Western society in *No Place of Grace: Antimodernism and the Transformation of American Culture, 1880–1920* (New York: Pantheon, 1981), 47–58.

39. Tisa Wenger, *We Have a Religion: The 1920s Pueblo Indian Dance Controversy and American Religious Freedom* (Chapel Hill: University of North Carolina Press, 2009), 62.

40. Ernest Thompson Seton and Julia M. Seton, *The Gospel of the Red Man: An Indian Bible* (New York: Doubleday and Doran, 1936).

41. Charles Alexander Eastman, *The Soul of the Indian* (Boston: Houghton Mifflin, 1911), 24.

42. Quoted in *The Theosophic Messenger* 21 (1911): 567, 576; and Blavatsky, *Secret Doctrine*, 1:391.

43. Annie Besant, *Esoteric Christianity* (Adyar, India: Theosophical Publishing House, 1966), 12–13.

44. See Lois Palken Rudnick, *Utopian Vistas: The Mabel Dodge Luhan House and the American Counterculture* (Albuquerque: University of New Mexico Press, 1996).

45. Quoted in Flannery Burke, *From Greenwich Village to Taos: Primitivism and Place at Mabel Dodge Luhan's* (Lawrence: University Press of Kansas, 2008), 108.

46. Blavatsky, *Secret Doctrine,* 2:444.

47. Percy Dearmer, *Everyman's History of the Prayer Book* (Milwaukee, Wisc.: Young Churchman, 1915), 173.

48. Emmett Small Jr., "Sunset Reflexions," *Theosophical Path* 30 (January–June 1926): 85.

49. See Blavatsky, *Key to Theosophy,* 148.

50. "Agnes Pelton Paintings," c. 1956, "Pelton, Agnes: Exhibition Related Materials" file, Raymond Jonson Collection.

51. In addition to its frequent use as a funereal symbol, the urn had particular significance for Theosophists. The Theosophical Society elicited significant public attention by advocating cremation in the late nineteenth century; it was among the first groups to do so in the United States. See Peter Washington, *Madame Blavatsky's Baboon* (New York: Schocken, 1995), 56–57. Pelton subscribed to a similar view; before her death, she arranged to have her body cremated, and her ashes buried in the San Jacinto Mountains. See Zakian, *Agnes Pelton,* 106.

52. Small, "Sunset Reflexions," 82.

53. Dane Rudhyar, *The Transcendental Movement in Painting,* unpublished manuscript, 1938, Raymond Jonson Collection.

54. Pelton identified Venus in the painting in a sketch in her notebook. Agnes Pelton Papers, 3426:698.

55. See Blavatsky, *Secret Doctrine,* 2:36.

56. See the extensive contemporary bibliography on this subject in H. J. Rose, *A Handbook of Greek Mythology, Including Its Extension to Rome* (New York: E. P. Dutton, 1929).

57. Helena Blavatsky, *Isis Unveiled,* 2 vols. (Adyar, India: Theosophical Publishing Company, 1972), 2:95–97.

58. Michael Zakian, "Agnes Pelton and Georgia O'Keeffe: The Window and the Wall," in Moss, *Illumination,* 80.

59. Sheley, "Bringing Light to Life," 105.

60. Blavatsky, *Secret Doctrine,* 2:35.

61. See, for example, C. W. Leadbeater, *A Textbook of Theosophy* (Los Angeles: Theosophical Publishing House, 1918), 130–33.

62. *Letters of Helena Roerich,* 2 vols., ed. V. L. Dutko (New York: Agni Yoga Society, 1954), 2:27.

63. Elizabeth Hutchinson, *The Indian Craze: Primitivism, Modernism, and Transculturation in American Art, 1890–1915* (Durham, N.C.: Duke University Press, 2009), 110–13. Sheley describes Pelton's work with Dow in "Bringing Light to Life," 20, 44.

64. Blavatsky, *Secret Doctrine,* 2:444.

65. Carrie Tirado Bramen, *The Uses of Variety: Modern Americanism and the Quest for National Distinctiveness* (Cambridge, Mass.: Harvard University Press, 2000), 276–80.

PART TWO

The Piety and Politics of Liberal Ecumenism

SIX

"Citizens of All the World's Temples"

Cosmopolitan Religion at Bell Street Chapel

EMILY R. MACE

On December 1, 1889, Bell Street Chapel held its dedication ceremony, fourteen years after James Eddy built it in 1875. Anna Garlin Spencer gave the dedicatory address, describing both Eddy's ideals and the principles according to which the chapel would now be put to use. She alluded clearly to a cosmopolitan understanding of religion: "To Mr. Eddy's thought, as to that of many of the world's greatest minds, the word religion connoted more than the name of any one system of religion, whether Christian or other. Hence the society which we trust will here be inaugurated must be a church of the Universal Spirit, and not a band of followers of any one religious leader." In citing this belief of Eddy's, Spencer aligned the new congregation with a broad religious perspective, one that eschewed differences of creed in favor of a transcending religious unity. As Edwin D. Mead articulated later that afternoon, Bell Street Chapel "was stamped with no seal of creed, and was without the customary label of dogma."[1] The universalism cultivated by Bell Street Chapel aspired to move beyond the names usually assigned to denominations or dogmas.

To Spencer, a church of the universal spirit pointed to a cosmopolitan ideal, through which each of its participants could become "a citizen of the World's Temples," akin to the cosmopolitan individuals who felt themselves to be citizens of the world.[2] The phrase implied a broad understanding of religion, one that emphasized the "universal" features shared by many traditions over the teachings of any particular leader or sect. The chapel's founding and dedication, however, illustrated that this understanding of religion existed more easily as an ideal for religious liberals than a practiced reality. James Eddy, the chapel's benefactor, had used his will to found a community dedicated to his own understanding of religious liberalism, one that emphasized theism and people's moral duties to each other and to God. His own goals for the community whose home would be Bell Street Chapel did not forefront a broad-minded eclecticism; instead, his vision of a liberal religious chapel movement remained much more obviously Christian and Protestant. In contrast, the trustees of Eddy's will, particularly Anna Garlin Spencer (who became the editor of Eddy's writings and the agent of the trustees as well as the resident minister and president of the Religious Society of Bell Street Chapel), brought a different emphasis to the work; they hoped to establish a more cosmopolitan basis of union than the one Eddy had called for. The tensions between these two visions of the chapel movement reflected American religious liberalism's Protestant heritage and its increasing cosmopolitan and ecumenical impulses. This difference of opinion ran throughout the chapel's founding and dedication, imbuing the group's formative moments with creative tension.

"A VOLUNTARY MONUMENT OF PRAISE AND GRATITUDE"

In the standard Protestant process, congregations form when individuals sharing religious perspectives or practices come together. But the Religious Society of Bell Street Chapel came into being in an unusual way: through the will and testament of a single person, James Eddy. The congregation was founded by a board of trustees acting under his instructions as set forth in his will. Born in 1806 in Providence, James Eddy made a name and fortune for himself as a portrait painter and an importer of classic European works of art. In particular, according to the *New York Times,* he became one of the first Americans to work in the "novel business . . . of copying in oil important works of the old masters for a market in this country." After marrying at age forty, Eddy moved to Boston and lived there for some years before returning to Providence, where he remained until his death. Few, it seems, knew him very well during his life, though many knew him by reputation; he was, by one account, "a widely-known and little-understood man."[3] Anna Garlin Spencer recalled, "I knew him in his hospitable home. I knew him in his vital and glowing old age. . . . I knew him better after he had passed onward than I did in his person as he stood among us, because to me was committed the task of looking over his writings, coming close to his inmost soul."[4] What Spencer found in his writings confirmed his liberal religious inclinations and indicated the deep sincerity of his hope that a religious community would be established at Bell Street Chapel.

The Eddy estate connected to Broadway Street in Providence by a small lane, known as "Bell-Street." Eddy built the two-story chapel beside the gates of his estate "as a voluntary monument of praise and gratitude to God for the life and many attendant blessings that had been given him."[5] The brick building cost a total of $40,000 to build. Its façade exhibited a neoclassical influence, the colonnaded porch and angled roof suggesting the Parthenon in Athens. Inside, its relatively plain, simple auditorium sat on the second floor, where the architecture of the room focused attention on an unadorned platform and reading desk. Eddy's will provided guides to the decoration of the building: he left to the management of the trustees "all furniture and equipments, paintings, sculptures, busts, bas relief statues, objects of art and nature in said chapel and vestry at the time of my decease, except such as are temporarily stored there from my gallery in Westminster Street."[6] At the rear of the chapel, the doors had leather panels with inscriptions of Eddy's beliefs written out in brass tacks; the walls of the auditorium also spoke of Eddy's religious commitments. One read, "Many Christian beliefs of to-day will become the rejected heathenism of the future," and another appealed (in overtly gendered language), "Give us a true and manly religion that covers the whole field of duty to God and humanity."[7]

James Eddy built Bell Street Chapel in 1875, but for years the building remained "a church without a people," with one small exception. During the summer and fall of 1876, the Providence Free Religious Society used it, but it and he parted ways over the organization's unwillingness to express belief in a divine God. Afterward, the chapel remained unused until James Eddy's own funeral service was held there following his death on May 18, 1888. Notably, the chapel Eddy built to express his religious beliefs had to wait until after his death to house a permanent religious community. His will provided for the maintenance of the unused chapel and specified his desire that it be put to productive religious use. He willed it and its surrounding land, together with the "objects of art and nature" it contained, to his two daughters, Sarah J. Eddy and Amy E. Harris, his son-in-law Edward M. Harris, and his friend Barton A. Ballou, a Providence goldsmith and jeweler, who together formed a board of trustees to manage the trust he established for it.

Eddy had appointed Bell Street Chapel with artifacts of cultural sophistication. In addition to these purely physical endowments, however, he hoped that his chapel would no longer be without a people. In his will, he wrote that he hoped a religious society would occupy it, and added, "it is my earnest wish and desire that the purest and truest religious and moral duties be taught and practiced by the members of this church or society. In true religion every moral duty should be comprised. I hope that the great principles of justice, kindness, and a reasonable charity to all will be recognized, taught, and practiced" (2). He believed strongly in the importance of communal religious worship in pursuit of the truths of religion and morality. "Sunday is an excellent institution, may it always exist!" he said. Eddy did not want any ordinary church, however, but a church that would express the religion of the future as he saw it. "May we have finer temples than now exist. . . . And may all, young and old, with inspiring music, with grateful hearts and humble acknowledgments to God, meet therein in a truer worship than any yet known to man!"[8] Eddy's ideal church put both God and humanity at its core. His words suggested a religious society that recognized humanity's rational potential and emphasized the necessity of thanking and praising God through uplifting worship.

Eddy left few specific instructions regarding the society his money would found. His later writings, collected in the posthumously published *Thoughts on Religion and Morality* (1891), offered perhaps the clearest indication of his desires. While he did want "a reasonable sympathy with, and adherence to my views from those who may found such Society," he added, with a liberal's valuing of freedom and tolerance, that "I should violate my own convictions of freedom and duty if I sought in any way to prevent the exercise of any other person's reason and individual judgment of what is right and true."[9] These instructions allowed the trustees flexibility in their creation of a religious society. Indeed, the will itself could only accomplish so much. It could stipulate, grant, and desire, but it, itself, could not put together a religious community. In order to actually start holding services in the chapel, the trustees needed to take action.

As a first step in carrying out Eddy's wishes, the trustees employed the services of Anna Garlin Spencer to edit Eddy's writings as called for by the will; they also hired Spencer to help establish services in the chapel (2, 4). Anna Garlin Spencer was born in Attleboro, Massachusetts, in 1851, and spent her early years in Providence. As a young woman, Spencer tutored privately for local colleges, joined the Providence women's suffrage organization, and started speaking in public. During the mid-1870s, she left the Congregational church and joined the Providence Free Religious Society, possibly affiliating with them during their brief stay in Bell Street Chapel. She spoke before gatherings of the Progressive Friends, the Providence Free Religious Society, and the Parker Memorial in Boston. In May 1878, she spoke to the Free Religious Association's annual meeting, becoming acquainted there with William Henry Spencer, whom she married on August 15 that year.[10]

Over the course of the next several years, Spencer assisted her husband in congregations in Haverhill and Florence, Massachusetts, and in Troy, New York. In 1889, the family moved to Waupaca, Wisconsin, where William became a partner in the family's loan collection business; his agnosticism had made it increasingly difficult for him to find pulpits. Coincidentally, however, James Eddy died that year in Providence; the trustees of Eddy's estate wrote to Spencer and requested that she return to assist them. What was supposed to be a short stay of only a few months turned into fourteen years, during which time Spencer guided the Religious Society of Bell Street Chapel into institutional maturity as the resident minister and president. After she resigned in 1902, Spencer worked as a religious leader, a suffrage and peace advocate, a professor, and a professional lecturer. Her classes at the University of Wisconsin, the University of Chicago, Meadville-Lombard Theological Seminary, and Teacher's College at Columbia University focused on social ethics and on issues of women, family, and marriage.

In addition to hiring Spencer to work on the trust, the board also consulted with the Supreme Court of Rhode Island to confirm the legality of their actions and plans according to Eddy's will. They used the legal services of Thomas C. Greene, Esq., to prepare their brief. Although the Supreme Court did not issue its confirmatory ruling until July 26, 1890, half a year after the dedication services, it confirmed the necessity of holding services in the chapel and of creating an ongoing religious society. The Court paid careful attention to the "the form of worship contemplated by the testator," which it saw as intended to be "monotheistic and not trinitheistic or trinitarian in doctrine" (40). The word "monotheism" suggests a broad understanding of belief in God, rather than a narrower creed, such as would have been implied by a denominational word such as "Unitarian." Other than this, the Court did not rule on the style of worship to be held. Finally, the Court recognized the necessity of using the bequest to cover "the expenses incident to preaching and devotional services and to the maintenance of a Sunday school and other like expenses" (41).

A "FINER TEMPLE THAN NOW EXISTS"

A year and a half after Eddy's death, on December 1, 1889, the Bell Street Chapel held its formal dedication ceremony. The *Providence Journal* reported that "the auditorium was filled to its utmost capacity and chairs were placed in the aisles, ante-room, and corridor to accommodate the large congregation." The ceremony's organizers had furnished the room with flowers for this significant event, the inauguration of ongoing religious services in a chapel that had stood unused for over a decade. "The pulpit and chancel were prettily decorated with plants and flowers wrought into artistic designs, and each of the clergymen and laity participating in the exercises received a fragrant cluster of blue violets."[11]

At half past two-o'clock, an overflowing congregation gathered in Eddy's chapel. In both its content and its structure, the dedication ceremony merged Eddy's theism with the cosmopolitan universalism that featured so prominently in Spencer's own thought. The dedicatory services started with choral music, and immediately thereafter Anna Garlin Spencer offered an address "on behalf of the Trustees of Bell Street Chapel, Under the Will of James Eddy," during which she called for Eddy's hoped-for "church of the Universal Spirit." She referred to the potential for cosmopolitan inclusivity in Eddy's vision, saying that this church would be "not so much against the thoughtful agnostic or the earnest Ethical Culturist, as for and with the scientific theism of the Reformed Hebrew faith, of the Brahmo Samaj of India, and of that rationalized Christianity which Japan to-day seeks to engraft upon her ancient civilization. Not so much against these as for and with those in all religions who both affirm God in prose and picture him in poetry."[12] The chapel would share the same spirit as kindred liberal religious movements, she explained; this new movement sought not to antagonize other movements, but, in the spirit of inclusion, to join them. Where Eddy emphasized the moral duty of worshipping God, Spencer highlighted an ecumenical inclusivity that embraced not only liberal Judaism and Christianity, but liberal movements in Asia as well.

After Spencer's address, the choir sang a hymn of dedication, declaring the intention of the assembled gathering:

> "We rear not a temple, like Judah's of old
> Whose portals were marble, whose vaultings were gold;
> No incense is lighted, no victims are slain,
> No monarch kneels praying to hallow the fane.

> More simple and lowly the walls that we raise,
> And humbler the pomp of procession and praise;
> Where the heart is the altar whence incense shall roll,
> And the Truth sheds its light on each questioning soul." (15)

The Rev. Henry Ware Jr., a Unitarian minister and professor at Harvard Divinity School during the 1830s, wrote the lyrics of this hymn. Consistent with Eddy's beliefs, its words emphasized several prominent tenets of Protestant liberalism. It described a God worshipped because of his rational nature, which he shared with his human creations, rather than a God worshipped because of his supernatural differences from his creations. The hymn also underscored the idea of an enlightened, progressive religious temple, one in which a rational, just, and loving God, the father of all humanity, was worshipped. At the same time, it deemphasized formal worship and indicated that the only altar that mattered could be found in the heart, a liberal ideal celebrated by such lights as Ralph Waldo Emerson.

Following the hymn, the ceremony featured a "responsive service." Spencer called on the assembled people to, in the words of their benefactor, "consecrate this Temple to God, to Truth, and to all that dignifies and ennobles humanity" (16). They dedicated the chapel to five ideals: Truth, Righteousness, Brotherhood and Fellowship, Faith, and Reverence to God as the father of all human existence. In keeping with the trustees' fidelity to Eddy's wishes, the words echoed Eddy's central beliefs: that God is the father and power which gives us our very lives, that he demands no worship from us, but that we are bound by the duty of morality to worship him for his gifts to us, as we are bound to treat each other justly as children of God.

The responsive service also highlighted its liberal perspectives. The assembly dedicated the chapel "to the mind which reconsiders and re-states and confesses error, which seeks for substance under forms and symbols." The words alluded to liberalism's embrace of progressive approaches to biblical criticism and to religion more generally. They also suggested an understanding of religion grounded in the "substance" of new theories of religion's origins, rather than in supernatural assumptions. The chapel was dedicated "to the spirit . . . which seeks for unity beneath all differences; to this spirit we would dedicate this House, gratefully honoring here all teachers, scriptures, lives, that in all ages have revealed the truth to men" (16). In keeping with Spencer's earlier statement of sympathy with kindred liberal movements, the new chapel movement emphasized unity rather than difference and a positive attitude to diverse religious “teachers, scriptures, lives.” The call stated clearly that inclusion of diverse religious traditions would be a guiding principle of the community’s shared life, and that these differences only concealed the essential unity of “truth.” Interestingly, “truth” meant an inclusive vision of “all teachers, scriptures, lives” as well as the consideration of error and careful study of symbolic life.

The service centered on a series of addresses by local Providence clergy. Their words stood in for the sermon that was usually given toward the end of a Protestant service, offering several voices in the place of one. Both Spencer and local newspapers felt that the presence of these leaders from different denominations indicated the new chapel’s broad-minded spirit. Describing the service in *The History of the Bell Street Chapel Movement,* Spencer wrote that the trustees hoped that the services of dedication would have “such a varied representation of religious opinion and moral effort by the invited speakers as would illustrate the hospitality of that movement toward all sincere and noble effort for truth and righteousness” (14). The voices of the different ministers added an element of variety to a ceremony that honored a multiplicity of religious truths, what Spencer called “a varied representation.” The *Providence Journal* agreed, explaining that “the addresses by the clergymen, representing various denominational churches, was [*sic*] in keeping with the purpose and spirit of the eventful period in the history of the movement inaugurated and stimulated by the liberality and religious devotion of its founder.”[13] Even though all of the speakers hailed from liberal Protestant denominations and causes (none represented, for instance, the Jewish or Hindu liberal movements with which Spencer had expressed explicit sympathy), contemporaneous interpreters understood the presence of clergy from different Christian traditions to be a notably ecumenical feature of the event.

In their addresses, Thomas R. Slicer (called Unitarian in the chapel’s publications, but listed as Congregationalist in local newspapers) and E. Benjamin Andrews (a Baptist minister and the president of Brown University) both praised the movement and wished it “godspeed.” H. W. Rugg, minister of the Universalist Church of the Mediator in Providence, admitted to one doubt concerning the chapel’s move toward breadth and inclusivity, namely its lack of a specific devotion to Jesus. “I believe [the chapel movement] to be good work; work that is needed in this community. It may not include all the elements that I would like to see incorporated in a ministry of spiritual culture, but I have sympathy with the movement as being in the right direction,” he said. Finally, H. C. Hay, pastor of the Swedenborgian Church of the New Jerusalem, expressed his belief "in a religion which ignored denominational lines and broadened a man."[14]

The final speaker, Edwin D. Mead, the New England writer and lecturer, spoke the longest of all the clergy, and his words came closest to matching the spirit of both Eddy's and Spencer's perspectives. "The dedication of this chapel is a brave and noble step in the right direction. I think that it will be seen to be a true step in the road that leads to the religion of the future," Mead began. The breadth toward which the other speakers had pointed Mead saw as leading toward the "universal spirit" that Spencer cited in her opening address. "The religion of the future, the church of the future, will make no philosophy, no belief, a condition of fellowship; it will welcome to itself every soul that strives to advance truth, righteousness, and love in the world," said Mead. Eddy's own hope for the church of the future, Mead implied, might well find a foothold in the endeavor he funded. Mead also highlighted the humanism of Eddy's project: "For himself he [Mead] believes that as Judaism was a schoolmaster that led men to Christ, so Christianity is no finality, but only a great object lesson, a schoolmaster to lead men into their own souls, into a worthy and true appreciation of humanity." In calling for men to turn to their own souls, Mead echoed the sentiments of Ralph Waldo Emerson in his by-then-famous "Divinity School Address"; his liberal outlook could also be seen in his hope for the advance of religious thought in the "onward and upward" progress of humanity. In Mead's supersessionist system, Judaism replaced Christianity, but Christianity also stood to be replaced by a post-Christian and post-Protestant religion of the future.

Mead's address concluded, finally, with words that can only be understood as a call for religious cosmopolitanism.

> We come to see that this divine birthright and heritage is no limited thing, not something true only of the children of certain churches, of those who have the Christian name or any name, but true of the whole family of God, which is all humanity. Simply as citizens, simply by virtue of being here in this world as men with minds and consciences, we are as truly our brother's keepers, keepers of every brother, responsible for the highest welfare and development of all.

Without using the phrase "citizen of the world," Mead spoke of a similar ideal. He described citizenship in the whole of humanity as a higher standard than membership of "certain churches." Mead saw all people as united in the embrace of a shared religiosity linked by common humanity. "No less a definition of citizenship, no less a definition of man, of religion, of politics which rightly is applied religion, is from now on possible. In the light of this great truth, all history, all Bibles, all churches and religions must be interpreted in new and broader relation." The repeated emphasis provided by the word "all" highlighted the universalist and pluralist intent of Mead's words. Nevertheless, religious cosmopolitanism remained complicated as well as implicated by Mead's use of specifically Christian and Protestant terms (including "Bibles" and "churches") to describe a post-Protestantism broader than Christianity itself.

Bell Street Chapel's dedication service closed with music from the choir and a benediction. The trustees assured the audience that services at Bell Street Chapel would continue through the winter season.

DEDICATED TO AN IDEAL

The liturgy for Bell Street Chapel's dedication ceremony did not emerge out of a vacuum. In planning the ceremony, Spencer and the trustees drew from hymnals and service books in use throughout the Western Unitarian Conference (WUC) between 1880 and the first decades of the twentieth century. The WUC had been formed in 1852 in response to what its members perceived as an Eastern bias in the American Unitarian Association. By the 1880s, the divide between the two organizations had become theological as well, as Unitarian leaders addressed the question of whether Unitarianism meant Christian theism or a broader ethical fellowship beyond allegiance to Jesus Christ.[15] The WUC chose to identify with the latter perspective. Its collection *Unity Services and Songs,* with editions issued in 1878, 1881, 1894 and 1901, served as a main source for Spencer and the trustees. This volume incorporated a service of "Fellowship" alongside services on the other two watchwords of their motto, "Freedom, Fellowship, and Character in Religion."

The Fellowship service in *Unity Services and Songs* celebrated human bonds that both transcended particularist divisions and brought all of humanity together under the "fathership" of a shared God and creator. An introduction to the service explained the word's meaning: "Fellowship in Religion is to bring the brotherhood of man into religion, so that the bond of humanity is put above that of creed or church or any other thing. This will teach us not to set bounds anywhere, as to say, We will receive all Christians, but not a Jew, or, We will receive Jews and Christians, but no others; but to say, as Paul did, that we receive all, being made of one blood, and walking under the common sky of the One Creator and Father."[16] The service celebrated the unity of all humanity, a unity that existed because of the embracing canopy of a single, universal God. True religious fellowship admitted of no differences of creed or nation, emphasizing instead the cosmopolitan ideal of a unity that transcended diversity, a unity applicable to religious faiths as well as to the more mundane and human divisions of race and nation.

The Fellowship service began with three quotations, one from the Talmud, one from "Chinese scripture," and one from the New Testament. The selection from the Talmud stated, "Say not, I will love the wise and hate the unwise; thou shalt love all mankind." The Chinese selection read, "Religions are many and different, but reason is one. We are all brethren." Later in the service, between verses of a hymn, the WUC's interest in eclecticism was again indicated by readings from an unspecified Persian source, Socrates, and Paul. The Persian quotation read, "Difference of worship has divided men into many nations; from all their doctrines I have chosen one—the Love of God."[17]

Taken together, the elements of the Fellowship service presented an intricate mix of sources and intentions, some explicit, some only implicit. In the preface, the editors explained the rules guiding their choice of readings: "1. To use all Scriptures, of whatever race or tongue," and "2. To use most our own Bible, because to us the most dear, familiar, and beautiful."[18] These two principles worked against each other, of course: the editors intended a certain measure of diversity but they also felt a need to affirm their closeness to Christian scriptural traditions. The Fellowship service expressed both their Christian heritage and their interest in exploring other sources of religious truth. Ultimately, the Fellowship service retained an overall Christian, Protestant emphasis: the words, no matter what their origin, came together in a largely Protestant formulation of readings, hymns, and prayers, sitting and standing, reading responsively and listening to a minister.

The Religious Society of Bell Street Chapel published a "Service of Dedication and Consecration," a variation on its own dedication ceremony, in its hymn and service book, *Orders of Service for Public Worship*, edited by Anna Garlin Spencer and funded by the bequest from James Eddy. Like the Fellowship service, the Dedication service followed established Protestant practice: an opening hymn, uplifting spoken words to set the tone of the service, music (whether instrumental, choral, or congregational is unspecified), another reading, and then a hymn. A responsive reading came after the hymn, allowing for congregational participation. The service continued with several more readings and musical selections before reaching a discourse or sermon. After this discourse, the service finished quickly with a hymn, a benediction, and a concluding hymn.

While this brief description of the service reveals a basically Protestant structure, the descriptive titles and the contents of the readings suggested more post-Protestant intentions. Like those in the Fellowship service in *Unity Services and Songs*, the scriptural sources in *Orders of Service* were remarkably diverse. Spencer's description of the Dedication service in her preface emphasized its general universalism; in addition to being appropriate for church dedications, the service "also offers a setting for discourses which treat of the universal and eternal elements in religion." The first section of readings used the words of James Martineau, A. Coquerel, Lucretia Mott, Jeremy Taylor, Theodore Parker, and William Channing Gannett. Their statements revealed that the source of true religion, as they saw it, was "Love Divine." The second set of readings, under the heading "Silent Worship," drew from Plutarch, Ralph Waldo Emerson, Omar Khayyam, the Buddha, Max Müller, Thomas Wentworth Higginson, Keshub Chunder Sen, and Samuel Longfellow. The printed text shows that worshippers were expected to be more familiar with some figures than with others; Emerson and Longfellow, as leading lights in religious liberalism, were identified only by their last names, but the Buddha lacked a titulary "the" in front of the word "Buddha." This set of readings followed thematically from the previous one, developing the theme of the essential unity of the world's diverse religious sources. The quotation from Max Müller explained, "Every religion has in it something which should be sacred to us, for there is in all religions a secret yearning after the true and unknown God."[19]

The other thirty-two services in *Orders of Service for Public Worship* drew from similarly eclectic sources. In *The History of the Bell Street Chapel Movement* Spencer described the texts as coming "largely from the Old and New Testament of our Bible, but selections were included, also, from the sacred writings of the Hindoo, the Buddhist, and other scriptures, from the devout thinkers of many ages and countries (including modern poets) whose words have not been canonized by any church but are luminous with inspiration to duty and with trust in the Divine" (134). As did the Fellowship service and Edwin Mead's address, Spencer's words indicated the ironies inherent in their cosmopolitanism. She used the possessive to speak of "our Bible," revealing a closer allegiance to it than to other sacred writings. Yet she also included sources beyond the specifically scriptural, including thinkers (such as prominent philosophers) not canonized by any recognized tradition who nevertheless had inspiring words to offer.

This sample dedication service offered no clear instructions on how, exactly, to use its eclectic sources in practice. Spencer's preface provided one suggestion; she stated that the rather long service (eight pages long, in comparison to the approximately three pages of the other services in the collection) was "not intended to be used as a whole at any one service, but to be selected from according to the occasion."[20] Each religious society, in other words, had complete freedom of practice and could pick among the readings and service elements as it preferred. A congregation could remain within the comfortable Unitarian Christianity of James Martineau, embrace the more radical liberalism of Theodore Parker or William Channing Gannett, or include the more "exotic" sentiments of the poets and spokespeople from the "the East." The service also did not determine who should speak when, or make clear whether the title "Silent Prayer" referred to the readings which followed the heading or merely signified that, during that part of the service, the congregation should be silent, each person pursuing her or his own private meditations. The use of music other than hymns also remained unspecified.

In contrast to the diversity represented by the readings, the hymns in the Dedication service were much more explicitly Christian (as they were in the Fellowship service in *Unity Services and Songs*). They included "many . . . of those most prized and most familiar in the hymnology of the Christian Church" (134). In keeping with the theistic, but not Christological, focus of *Orders of Service,* the hymns made scant reference to Jesus, but referred amply to God as Holy, Lord, and Father. "Holy, holy, holy, Lord God Almighty! Who wert and art, and ever more shalt be," concludes the opening hymn. Sandwiched between the two sections of liberal and eclectic readings, the hymn "The Rest Day" (translated from the German by James Vila Blake, a prominent Western Unitarian hymnist) celebrated the coming of Sunday. Finally, immediately following the discourse, one finds the ever-popular tune "Nearer, My God, to Thee." The words of these hymns did not speak of religion's universal sources, but instead drew on familiar Christian hymns. The presence of the particularly Christian language and rhythm of the service contrasted and contended with its aim, as expressed in the service in the words of Longfellow, "to build the Universal Church, Lofty as the love of God, and ample as the wants of man."[21] These two services, the Fellowship service and the Dedication service, highlight the ways that the Protestant liturgical structure gave shape and form to an ideal of cosmopolitan universalism and diversity. Their religious liberalism, in other words, alluded to post-Protestant ideals, but, ironically, did so from a Protestant frame of reference.

FOUNDING THE RELIGION OF THE FUTURE

The Religious Society of Bell Street Chapel took shape over the course of several months after the chapel's dedication ceremony. During the year 1890, the trustees discussed the best way to create a religious society according to the directions of Eddy's will, but as they did so, they also reformulated his monotheistic intentions as a broader statement of ecumenical inclusion. The trustees had drawn up a "statement of principles" that guided their efforts in creating the society. They took as their motto a favorite phrase of Eddy's, found in his *Thoughts on Religion and Morality:* "I would consecrate a Temple to God, to Truth, and to all that dignifies and ennobles Humanity!"[22] The trustees believed that this statement indicated "a worshipful, a rationalistic and a nonsectarian effort to better the world" (6).

First, since Eddy strongly believed that worship of God was humanity's moral duty, the trustees dwelt on the need "to limit the representative teachers" (meaning "the resident speaker or settled minister of the society receiving the benefits of the trust"). The teachers, they laid down, "must believe in the possibility of a conscious 'relationship' between man and the source of all life and law," and they "must be able heartily to lead in public worship of 'that Power whom we designate as God.'" Further, "such representative teachers must not be 'trinitarians'; must not be believers in 'everlasting punishment' in the present accepted meaning of that term; or bound to any system of theology, Christian or other, which forbids the subjection of any book, or person, or historic religion, to the test of scientific criticism and the judgment of human reason." And they were not to "advocate the special doctrines of 'spiritualism' in the present accepted meaning of that word" (7–8). All of these requirements situated Eddy's beliefs in nineteenth-century religious liberalism: lower-case unitarian theology, acceptance of biblical criticism, and rejection of predestination and the alternative religious movement of Spiritualism.

While representative teachers could not maintain Spiritualism or Trinitarianism, the trustees extended greater freedom to occasional speakers at the society and to its members (7–8). They affirmed that membership would be open to anyone of good moral character who could subscribe to the Bond of Union, a statement of the society's beliefs and principles written by the trustees and based closely on Eddy's writings. "Those of all shades of opinion, from the most 'orthodox' Christian to the most pronounced 'atheist,' 'agnostic,' 'materialist' or 'spiritualist,' are alike welcome, and should forever be, to the general benefits of the trust" (8–9). The open, accepting spirit that the trustees hoped to encourage at Bell Street Chapel could be seen far more easily in their permissive attitude toward membership. In a footnote to their statement, the trustees concluded that the different requirements for leaders, speakers, and members reflected "both the *fraternal spirit*" of their movement and its "*distinctive character* [as] a rationalistic, yet devout, a free yet reverent movement" (11). Within the guidelines set by Eddy's beliefs and preferences, the chapel trustees had the freedom to develop their movement in a spirit of breadth and generosity.

The trustees also worked to illustrate Eddy's beliefs in the services that followed the dedication ceremony in the winter of 1889–90. The first of the series of continuing services took place on December 8, 1889, one week after the chapel's dedication. Each service began on Sunday afternoon at 3 PM. In successive weeks, Spencer treated the topics "Man's Ideal of God," "Gratitude and Trust in the Powers Above," "How Religions Grow," "Reason in Religion," "Man's Freedom and Responsibility, or Character in Religion," and "Human Brotherhood in Religion" (19). Taken together, the discourses touched on what Eddy called his "four cardinal points": "Loyalty to Truth as revealed by each day's growing experience: Reverent love toward God expressed in Worship: Earnest devotion to personal and social ethics: and the Spirit of Fellowship in the Religious life."[23] Once Spencer had completed this series, outside speakers lectured on the same themes in the same order; these speakers were Frederick L. Hosmer, then serving a Unitarian congregation in Cleveland; Ednah D. Cheney, an author, lecturer, and prominent member of the Free Religious Association; Dr. Felix Adler of the Ethical Culture Society; Professor Joseph H. Allen, editor of the *Unitarian Review* and professor at Harvard Divinity School; and finally, the Rev. Samuel J. Barrows, a Unitarian minister and editor of the Unitarian periodical *The Christian Register.* All of the speakers built upon Spencer's initial discourses, together establishing Bell Street Chapel as a liberal, progressive congregation.

Through these services the trustees, with Anna Garlin Spencer at the helm, gave shape and definition to the aims of the young Chapel Society. Spencer drew extensively from the writings of James Eddy in her addresses, often devoting at least half of each discourse to quotations from Eddy's writings. This combination of her own words with those of its founder stamped the young chapel movement with Eddy's pattern, but also permitted it to move toward Spencer's own perspectives, including cosmopolitan religion, which Eddy neither rejected nor called for explicitly. In "Man's Ideal of God," Spencer explained that she saw the chapel's work as a step toward that "religion of the future" Edwin Mead had mentioned in his dedication ceremony address.[24] Spencer articulated this goal in her discourse on fellowship in religion, the last of the six:

> To me the position in the Liberal Religious world, not most practically, but most *philosophically* strong is that of a citizen of the World's Temples whose sentiment soars in all higher forms of aspiration known to men, but who so separates religious sentiment from dogma that his chosen bond of union with others is as impersonal and abstract an allegiance to the Best in Life as can be framed.[25]

Spencer's words indicated the degree to which cosmopolitan religion was indeed stronger as a concept than as a practice. She described it as separating sentiment from dogma, as an impersonal bond of union with others, all of which are ideas rather than practices. She did not rule out the possibility of practicing cosmopolitanism, however. In an earlier address, she used the term "citizens" and spoke more clearly of religious cosmopolitanism as a practice: "There is no form of worship but has something sacred in it. And the freer a man's thought is in religion the more his religious sentiment can become a citizen of all the world's temples."[26] Here again, however, acts of worship quickly became acts of thought and sentiment. Spencer believed that religious liberals should strive for the cosmopolitan ideal, an ideal best attained in the bonds of union formed among fellow liberal travelers.

"A PROPHETIC WORD HAS HAD UTTERANCE"

Bell Street Chapel's dedication ceremony and founding successfully enshrined the cosmopolitan religious ideal in the fledgling congregation, as the ensuing decade of activity reveals. Anna Garlin Spencer's summary in her tenth anniversary sermon emphasized this point. "I believe," she said, "that a prophetic word has had utterance at Bell Street Chapel, one which places a deeper emphasis on the universal and the eternal in religion than is generally heard" (121). By that time, the chapel had developed a small but active congregation, with approximately one hundred member families.[27] Spencer served as the resident minister until 1902, establishing many thriving programs during her tenure. These included many committees common to Protestant congregations, such as committees on membership, Sunday services, the Sunday school, social meetings, finances, and "practical work."

Spencer and distinguished visitors to the chapel lectured on a wide variety of topics befitting an audience of prospective citizens of the world's temples. Their discourses focused on the dominant social issues of the day, on the social roles of men, women, children, and youth, and on Christian theological concepts. In preparation for the 1893 World's Columbian Exposition and the Parliament of Religions that September, the year 1892–93 featured sermons on the evolution of religion and of specific traditions, including Judaism, Christianity, Hinduism, Confucianism, Zoroastrianism, and Buddhism, as well as "our duty to the Chinese," "the new mission to Japan," and "the roots and latest flowers of religion." Visits from distinguished outside speakers continued throughout the chapel's first decade. The usual radical religious suspects—William J. Potter, Edward Everett Hale, Lewis G. Janes, Ednah D. Cheney, and Thomas Wentworth Higginson, among others—spoke at the chapel and echoed its ecumenical vision of liberalism. Figures of international renown, such as William Lloyd Garrison, Booker T. Washington, Julia Ward Howe, and Anagarika Dharmapala, connected this small movement to a worldwide network of cosmopolitan religious liberals.[28]

In 1899, the tenth anniversary of the dedication of Bell Street Chapel inspired those affiliated with the movement to reflect on its progress. Letters written by ministers and laypersons to Spencer about the anniversary indicated the success the chapel had had in introducing a cosmopolitan perspective to the religious life of Providence. She read aloud selections from many of these letters on the Sunday falling closest to the dedication ceremony's tenth anniversary. Some correspondents wrote in general terms about the value the chapel had had in their lives. Fanny Purdy Palmer wrote "to express my allegiance to the forms of endeavor into which you have shaped the noble thoughts which filled the mind of the Chapel's founder."[29] Charlotte Tillinghast, a member of the Sunday school committee, told Spencer that "there has been nothing in my life during the last four years which has given me so much constant inspiration as the Chapel meetings." She emphasized the broadening of perspective that participation in the chapel movement had given her and, she assumed, others as well. "It is easy to become unresponsive to what does not come directly into one's experience, and the emphasis laid at the Chapel on what is vital in outside thought and current life has helped me many times to correct the poor perspective in my own view of the world."[30] Tillinghast highlighted the chapel's role in expanding her views, making her feel more like of a citizen of the world.

While these more everyday affiliates of the chapel expressed their appreciation for the broadening influence the chapel had had on their lives, leaders of the movement for universal religion praised the chapel explicitly for the breadth of its vision. Lewis G. Janes, then serving as the president of the Free Religious Association (which had long advocated for the religion of humanity), wrote a congratulatory note. "Most of all, may we not exchange mutual congratulations on the marvelous growth of the spirit of Free Religion, which, with mutual respect for intellectual differences, finds a basis for fellowship transcending sectarian limitations in common ethical aspirations, and united service for common social ends?"[31]

Jenkin Lloyd Jones, who had by 1899 separated his All Souls Church in Chicago from affiliation with the Unitarian denomination, spoke of All Souls' and Bell Street Chapel's shared position as independent liberal churches, writing that "now it begins to be seen that [independence] is an attitude of hospitality towards all forms of religious organization. We cannot belong to any one because we desire to belong to every one." Jones drew on a traditional Christian image, that of a cathedral, to describe the emerging movement he envisioned: "You began unwittingly to lay the foundations of the new cathedral that is to represent the inspirations of the new and ever old holy catholic church, the Catholic church of humanity which includes the Catholic Church of Rome and all the rest of them."[32] Jones used the non-religious meaning of the word "catholic"—"universal" or "general"—to describe the coming religion of the future. When placed next to the physical images of a cathedral and its stone foundations, the usage further revealed the Christian underpinnings of this essentially post-Christian ideal.

In 1902, after fourteen years of work for Bell Street Chapel as an agent of the trustees of James Eddy's will, as the president of the Chapel Society, and as the chapel's resident minister, Spencer stepped down to take a rest. The society secured the services of Clay MacCauley, a Unitarian minister, for the congregation; MacCauley had worked for the American Unitarian Association, helping to found a liberal religious movement in Japan. Spencer's description of his coming to Bell Street Chapel cited his familiarity with non-Western traditions as one rationale for his selection. "By this leadership in a foreign field Mr. MacCauley has shown that breadth of view and sympathy with all the higher faiths of mankind, which is peculiarly the requirement of one who leads the chapel movement," she explained in a parenthetical remark on his background (159). Turning over the reins to her successor, Anna Garlin Spencer ensured that, through his presence, the cosmopolitan religious vision of Bell Street Chapel would endure after her departure. The phrase "citizens of the world's temples," with which Spencer had launched Bell Street Chapel on its mission, continued to describe the ideals toward which it strived, even as Spencer herself moved on to other projects.

Over the course of her fourteen years of involvement with the Society, Anna Garlin Spencer worked to dedicate Bell Street Chapel to the ideal of cosmopolitan religion. Yet as Spencer herself pointed out, religious cosmopolitanism existed most easily as an ideal for religious liberals, one not easily put into practice. Bell Street Chapel's attempt to do so revealed its inherent contradictions. The chapel's dedication ceremony and founding revealed both the ecumenical vision of post-Protestant and post-Christian religious liberalism and liberalism's Protestant heritage and impulses, represented by their benefactor James Eddy, that shaped the chapel movement. Jenkin Lloyd Jones could speak of a post-Christian "catholic church of humanity" and Spencer could read quotations from "all teachers, scriptures, lives, that in all ages have revealed the truth to men," but translating this inclusive vision into a cosmopolitan religion that escaped its Protestant background remained a difficult task.

NOTES

1. "Love to God and Man," *Providence Journal,* December 2, 1889.

2. Anna Garlin Spencer and James Eddy, *Bell Street Chapel Discourses* (Providence, R.I., 1899), 106.

3. "A Church for Everybody," *New York Times,* December 2, 1889. More biographical information on Eddy can be found in *The New-York Historical Society's Dictionary of Artists in America, 1564–1860,* ed. George C. Groce and David H. Wallace (New Haven: Yale University

Press, 1957); and *Mantle Fielding's Dictionary of American Painters, Sculptors, and Engravers*, ed. Mantle Fielding and Glen B. Opitz (Poughkeepsie, N.Y.: Apollo, 1983).

4. *Bell Street Chapel Anniversaries: James Eddy, Born May 29, 1806—Died May 18, 1888 (One Hundredth Anniversary of Birth)* ([Providence, R.I.]: The Chapel, 1916), 19, 21.

5. "A Church for Everybody."

6. Anna Garlin Spencer, *The History of the Bell Street Chapel Movement, May, 1888 to July, 1902* (Providence, R.I.: Robert Grieve, 1903), 1. Subsequent page references are given in the text.

7. "A Church for Everybody." The full set of "axiomatic statements" can be found on the closing pages of James Eddy, *Thoughts on Religion and Morality: The Existence of God, His Character and Relations to Humanity, Religious Duties Growing out of Human Relations with God, Morality and Our Relations with Each Other* (Providence, R.I., 1891).

8. Eddy, *Thoughts*, 63–64.

9. Ibid., 32.

10. Few extensive biographical sources on Anna Garlin Spencer yet exist. The most comprehensive source, of course, are the Anna Garlin Spencer Papers in the Swarthmore College Peace Collection in Swarthmore, Penn. Particularly useful items include "A Providence Woman Minister," *Providence Sunday Journal*, August 26, 1902 (box 5, folder 1); "Parting Words of Anna Garlin Spencer at Bell Street Chapel, June 15, 1902" (box 5, folder 10); and "Addresses at the Anna Garlin Spencer Celebratory Dinner, 1926" (box 4, folder 7). See also Tanya C. Sikes, "Balancing the Vocational Divide: Anna Garlin Spencer on Women, Work, and Family," Unitarian Universalist Women's Heritage Society, 1995, http://www.uuwhs.org/balancing.php (accessed January 9, 2010). For information about other biographical sources, see Lawrence W. Snyder, "Spencer, Anna Garlin," American National Biography Online, February 2000, http://www.anb.org/articles/15/15-00637.html (accessed May 3, 2007).

11. "Love to God and Man."

12. Ibid.

13. Ibid.

14. These and all subsequent quotations from the ministers' addresses also come from "Love to God and Man."

15. On this issue, see Charles Harold Lyttle, *Freedom Moves West: A History of the Western Unitarian Conference, 1852–1952* (Boston: Beacon, 1952), chapter 11, "The Western Issue."

16. *Unity Services and Songs* (Chicago: Western Unitarian Sunday School Society, 1894), 32.

17. Ibid., 34.

18. Ibid., iii.

19. Anna G. Spencer, *Orders of Service for Public Worship* (Providence, R.I., 1896), iii, 2, 5.

20. Ibid., iii.

21. Ibid., 6.

22. Eddy, *Thoughts*, 32.

23. Anna Garlin Spencer, *What Could a Church at Bell St. Chapel Do for Providence?* (Providence, R.I.: Bell Street Chapel, 1890), 13.

24. Spencer and Eddy, *Bell Street Chapel Discourses*, 8.

25. Ibid., 106, italics in original.

26. Ibid., 73–74.

27. "Bell Street Chapel, Ten Years of an Interesting Religious Experiment," Anna Garlin Spencer Papers, box 5, folder 1.

28. For a full list of speakers, see ibid.

29. Letter from Fanny Purdy Palmer to AGS, December 15, 1899, Anna Garlin Spencer Papers, box 10, folder 5.

30. Letter from Charlotte Tillinghast to AGS, September 13, 1899, ibid.

31. Letter from Lewis G. Janes to AGS, November 29, 1899, ibid.

32. Letter from Jenkin Lloyd Jones to AGS, November 30, 1899, ibid.

SEVEN

Spiritual Border-Crossings in the U.S. Women's Rights Movement

KATHI KERN

> The assumption that woman is naturally and inevitably the inferior half of the race is found in every religion as soon as it crystallizes into dogma, but if we go far enough back we find that the esoteric teaching of all the ancient wisdom was that the Divine Feminine was that out of which all things were evolved or created. . . . In the Bhagavad Gita, Krishna says: 'I am the Father and the Mother of the Universe.' . . . If we could get men to understand the place of the Divine Feminine in the order of the universe, they would cease to think that by holding women in subjection in Church and State, they are helping the Creator to carry out the original plan.
>
> —*Clara Colby, 1914*

For Clara Colby, the long-time editor of the suffrage paper *The Woman's Tribune,* an intervention was necessary. Men of the United States, who denied women their full equality, were mired in a Christian tradition that had muted its most radical message: the Divine Feminine. Colby, a spiritual seeker and a feminist, sought both ancient sources and new voices to counteract the reigning assumption that the subjection of women was of divine design. Her story raises the larger question: To what extent did religious liberalism provide a space for more cosmopolitan thinking in the early twentieth-century women's rights movement? From the work of scholars of the transnational women's rights movement, we know that the Gilded Age and Progressive Era movement was shaped by the growth of international women's organizations and by the movement of people and ideas across national borders. In this essay, I explore one such exchange: Clara Colby's immersion in the work of the early twentieth-century Bengali poet-philosopher Rabindranath Tagore.[1] Like other religious liberals engaged in metaphysical "border-crossings," Colby drew upon a discourse of "affirmative" or "romantic" Orientalism, whereby the insights of the "East" might counteract the spiritual poverty of the "West." In particular, Colby mined the writings of Tagore to challenge the hegemony of Western gender relations. In her effort to apply her reading of Tagore to the problems of a Western democracy, Colby took her place in a long line of Americans—from Transcendentalists to Martin Luther King Jr.—who, in conversation with Indian writers, philosophers, and spiritual leaders, collaborated on essentializing a powerful, persistent idea of "Indian spirituality" and its potential to transform the West. These ideas were seductive to many Americans, perhaps none more so than American women at the turn of the century. Clara Colby, then, can help us to understand both the nature of that collaboration and its appeal to American feminists of the early twentieth century.[2]

CLARA COLBY AND THE CONTEXT OF ANGLO-AMERICAN FEMINISM

As Anglo-American suffragists engaged in a transnational women's movement, encountering new ideas and accommodating and co-opting new religious practices, they responded with varying degrees of skepticism, ambivalence, and fervor. Clearly, many responded with what Edward Said has famously delineated as "Orientalism" and interpreted the "barbaric" religious practices of people around the world as prime evidence of the urgency of Western imperialism. In the tradition of Orientalism, the East and the West emerge as polar opposites. An irrational, exotic, heathen East is set off by its countervailing opposite: the rational, familiar, Christian West.[3] Suffragists' encounters with new religions provide rich opportunities to explore Orientalist discourse. Take, for example, Carrie Chapman Catt, the successor to Susan B. Anthony, a national and international feminist and an advocate of evolution, who carefully documented the "barbaric" practices of "Eastern" cultures in her 1912 world suffrage tour. Catt, like many European and American observers, trained her eye on the cultural practices that came to stand for what was "traditional" about Indian society: religion and gender relations.[4] In Catt's estimation, religion was a curious vestige of Indian culture, one that could be stimulated and improved, but probably not eliminated, by exposure to Western civilization. She observed people bathing in the Ganges and remarked, "There are also some fools called holy men—too disgusting for words." At a later moment in the trip, she encountered Buddhist priests, whom she described as shaving their heads and wearing yellow robes. "I never saw one with a holy or spiritual face."[5]

A "Reform Darwinist," Catt believed "the world moves ever onward and upward." The elevation of women to a position of equality was simply a natural byproduct of evolution, an illustration of the world's continuous upward motion. This scientific transformation was best evidenced in the "advanced nations." In fact, while it was clear to her that American women had evolved beyond the tyrannies of the past, women around the world had not been so fortunate. She found ample evidence of resistance to the natural law of evolution in "the lands of Mohammed" and in India, where "the miserable women of that land [are denied] the hope of inheritance of heaven unless she shall be born again and be born in the form of a man."[6] Catt was typical of Anglo-American women suffragists, much like women reformers in Western Europe, who manipulated the language of "civilization" to bolster their own cause.

But what are we to make of others, like Clara Colby, who found support and vision for feminism in their engagement with foreign cultures and spiritual practices? Suffragists like Colby carved out a more nuanced position, arguing that American women and their campaign for emancipation could be positively influenced by the spiritual ideas of other nations. Is this just another "side" of Orientalism, more appreciative but ultimately just as dualistic?[7] The Indologist Ronald Inden has identified Western thinkers who championed an alternative view of India as "romantic, spiritualistic, or idealistic" as "the loyal opposition." Unlike more positivist thinkers who viewed India as irrational and in need of Western uplift, the romantic, affirmative Orientalists saw the silver lining in the differences they perceived between "East" and "West." The romantic, according to Inden, "typically takes the stance not of a supporter of Western values and institutions, but of a critic of them." Romantics, however, were equally invested in sustaining the "Otherness" of India. They "have a vested interest in seeing that the Orientalist view of India as 'spiritual,' 'mysterious,' and 'exotic' is perpetuated."[8] But for Colby, the spiritual wealth of India, which she mined in both its ancient texts and its modern, nationalist writers, resonated deeply with her own spiritual and political aspirations.

While Carrie Chapman Catt was making her trip around the world, Clara Colby was trying to cobble together a living as a lecturer. In fact, she was one of the few women of her generation who managed to make the transition to a new style of political stumping. In 1912, at age sixty-six, she made fifty-six speeches in Kansas in the single month of September, reporting to a friend, "You know the modern methods are more strenuous, and include speaking at men's Clubs, Unions, at their shops and factories, and on the street corners. Then to make sure that none escape we go to Air-domes and moving-picture shows."[9] Colby supported herself, and not very well, by delivering lectures for pay. "Very little money in," she remarked in her diary in 1914, summarizing the response to her lectures on New Thought, a lack of interest she attributed to ignorance and the "icy indifference of society."[10]

Colby's interest in New Thought was not unusual. In fact, the turn of the century witnessed a spiritual revolution in American life that was frequently commented upon in the press. The growth of "new religions"—including Theosophy and New Thought as well as the Vedanta philosophy, introduced by Swami Vivekananda—was all part of "the new spiritual America emerging." These varied faiths all pointed toward "the growing need of the nation for a more truly religious life."[11] While it might be tempting to write off Americans' collective dabbling in Eastern religions as a minor detour in the inexorable march of a Protestant nation, this dissident critique deserves more careful analysis. What was at stake in the "new Spiritual America" was the very claim to national identity.

As scholars of colonialism have written, the nineteenth-century narratives of nationalism rely upon a series of "national traits"—of gender, race, religion, language—that were invoked to explain the success or failure of a nation. Champions of empire pointed with pride to the West's engagement with science and secularism as proof of its superior modernity. But religion also figured in this discussion, particularly among critics of empire. In contrast to India's spiritual wealth, the relative spiritual poverty of the United States was a cause for concern. Consequently, the spiritual practices of New Thought animated quite a few women suffragists at the turn of the century.[12] With roots in Christian Science, the New Thought movement combined a commitment to metaphysical healing with a theology that privileged women's "moral power" and criticized male desire. The problem of male desire preoccupied Anglo-Americans at the turn of the century. Was male sexual desire the driving force behind civilization, as Social Darwinists argued? Or was it, as the practitioners of New Thought maintained, an obstacle to spiritual progress? By the 1890s, a new idea had emerged to challenge the Victorian commitment to keeping male desire in check. Led by the psychologist G. Stanley Hall, theorists began to argue that a certain "primitive" instinct at the heart of Anglo-Saxon manhood actually infused it with vitality. Hall attributed the success of Anglo-Saxon civilization—its wealth, as well as its republican institutions—to men's ability to channel this touch of savagery into productive accomplishment.[13] As Beryl Satter has argued, the New Thought movement was virtually fixated on the question of women's moral power and the millennial belief in an impending "Woman's era." This revolution would "only come about if the 'carnal' . . . was crushed by an assertion of spiritual power."[14]

Clara Colby subscribed to the view that male passion had lost its spiritual anchor. In her writings on the Gnostic Gospels, Colby narrated "the struggles of the soul" that contended with the three powers of evil: "the Love of Dominion; the Love of Self; and the Love of Lust." The Soul fell into chaos, according to Colby's reading of the Gnostics, because it "mistook the false astral light of sensual love for the pure light."[15] She applied this theory in a concrete way when she took on Theodore Schroeder, a free speech attorney. Although best remembered for his civil-liberties-based critique of Anthony Comstock, Schroeder by 1915 had launched a parallel career as a dabbler in psychoanalysis. He was virtually obsessed with revealing the sexual roots of all religious experience. "Religious ecstasy," for Schroeder, was a misnomer; sexual urges masqueraded as religion.[16] Colby was confronted with Schroeder's views when he addressed the Secular League of Washington, D.C., in 1915 on the topic "Religion and Sex." "I did not like the way he treated either & I spoke from red hot inspiration on the two great facts of life. I said that everyone with respect for the facts of history, with any tenderness for human relationships, with any reverence for life should treat the subject of sex seriously & sacredly." Schroeder had apparently asserted that religious experience had sexual roots, a narrative that Colby rejected as profane. She corrected him, explaining that the common sensual experience of feeling "that relation to something outside of himself that is greater than himself is *religion*."[17]

RABINDRANATH TAGORE, THE INSPIRATION

Colby gained inspiration and theoretical support for her critique of male sexual desire from a seemingly unlikely source: the romantic poetry and plays of the Bengali poet Rabindranath Tagore. Tagore visited the United States on several occasions between 1912 and 1930. While he had nurtured a lifelong interest in American literature, being drawn particularly to Emerson and Whitman, Tagore's impetus for making his first trip was more personal. He sought a homeopathic treatment for an illness. In late October of 1912, Tagore landed in New York City, where he endured the trials of the custom house. "My turban attracted the notice of a newspaper interviewer and he attacked me with questions but I was almost as silent as my turban. This was my first taste of America—the custom house and the interviewer." Tagore took an immediate dislike to the pressures and rhythms of urban life: "Each time I come to a city like New York or London I discover afresh that in my veins courses the blood of my ancestors who were forest-dwellers."[18] For two months in 1912, he set up housekeeping in Urbana, Illinois, close to the university campus, small-town life being more to his preference. Before long, his talents as a lecturer were discovered, although he resisted the public eye, claiming, "I have not come to discover America or to be discovered by Americans." He wrote to a friend, the English portrait artist William Rothenstein, "American people have an unhealthy appetite for sugar candy and for lectures on any subject from anybody. . . . I am afraid they have spotted me,—I am being stalked."[19]

In many ways, Tagore was hard to miss. His long hair and beard, his turban, his white, flowing garments certainly contributed to the popular perception of Tagore as a mystical guru, or, in the words of one female observer, "a powerful and gentle Christ."[20] Basanta Koomar Roy's book *Rabindranath Tagore, the Man and His Poetry,* published in New York in 1916, introduced readers to Tagore in several poses, including a "devotional posture" in which Tagore sits cross-legged on the floor, staring off into the distance.[21]

Despite his popularity as a guru, Tagore considered himself first and foremost a writer, not a religious or spiritual leader. In 2009 the Guggenheim Museum mounted an exhibit entitled "The Third Mind," which traced how "art, literature, and philosophical systems of 'The East' became known, reconstructed and transformed within American cultural and intellectual currents."[22] Included in the exhibit was a small display on Tagore that credited him, much as Colby had, with transmitting Indian spirituality to the West in the early twentieth century. Yet this narrative flattens Tagore into a single dimension, reducing the complexity of his historical context and the wide range of his intellectual and artistic pursuits.

From his family, Tagore inherited a commitment to the Brahmo Samaj, a new religious reform movement in nineteenth-century Bengal, steeped in a rationalist tradition and committed to a revival of the Upanishads.[23] In narrating his own history, Tagore saw his Bengali family emerging from the "confluence of three cultures, Hindu, Mohammedan and British." The exact parameters of Tagore's theology, however, continue to stimulate sharp scholarly debate. As Amartya Sen has argued, the point is not that Tagore failed to offer compelling religious ideas, but rather that he was prematurely "pigeonholed," marketed (and later rejected) as a "spiritual guru" by his Western popularizers, William Butler Yeats and Ezra Pound. In Indian literary history, in contrast, Tagore is known as a profoundly original and wide-ranging artist whose genres included poetry, novels, plays, essays, paintings, and musical compositions. His topics ranged widely as well. Tagore was deeply interested in conceptions of freedom, war and peace, and the limits of nationalism. Unlike Mahatma Gandhi, his highly regarded colleague and friend with whom he is often compared, Tagore rejected a romantic embrace of tradition. He scoffed at Gandhi's call to the spinning wheel; while Gandhi recommended abstinence, Tagore advocated birth control. Although he had much to offer on questions of religion, Tagore was much more than the "remote and repetitive" spiritual guru he has become in American history.[24]

Among his compelling religious ideas, Tagore championed the concept of a universal religion, like that advocated at the World's Parliament of Religions by Swami Vivekananda in 1893. According to Hugh Urban, Tagore "shifted his ideal for society from an explicitly political one to a vision of a new humanism and universalism, rooted in a non-sectarian religion of man."[25] In the series of lectures he delivered at Oxford University in 1930, which were subsequently published under the title *The Religion of Man,* Tagore declared Truth to be the "perfect comprehension of the Universal Mind." An individual engaged in a search for truth and perfection "by extending his limits in knowledge, power, love, enjoyment, thus approaching the universal." For Tagore, there was a reigning spirit: "The *Isha* of our Upanishad, the Super Soul, which permeates all moving things, is the God of this human universe, whose mind we share in all our true knowledge, love and service, and whom to reveal in ourselves through renunciation of self is the highest end of life."[26] Politically, Tagore believed that the "problem of Europe" and its dangerous "egocentric nationalism" was "a disease cured only by a universal ideal of humanity."[27] He extended his critique to India as well, warning that "patriotism cannot be our final spiritual shelter.... I will never allow patriotism to triumph over humanity as long as I live."[28]

By all accounts, Tagore was extremely popular with both Anglo-American and English women. His published work, for which he was awarded the Nobel

Prize in Literature in 1913, coupled with his pilgrimages to England and the United States, touched off a "Tagore craze" among women that merited considerable comment in the press. Most critics agreed that Tagore was "an able literary craftsman." But the enthusiastic response to his work clearly raised the collective anxiety of male commentators. They chalked it up to exoticism: "It is because, in the first place, he is an East-Indian: like that dear, dear Swami who tells you all about your 'aura' at those wonderful afternoon teas at Mrs. Van Dusenbury's! If Tagore had been born in Brooklyn, he would never be a fashionable poet."[29] While an Orientalist preoccupation with Tagore's exoticism can certainly be detected in women's commentary on his work, the critic's claim that readers were merely caught up in the fashionable appeal of an Indian writer underestimates the substantive connections women made to his work. Women were drawn to Tagore because they found his work compelling. His ability to infuse daily life with sacred meaning, his interpretation of human passion as an expression of divine love, his creation of complex, rebellious female characters, all found a ready audience among his women readers. In the process, he offered fresh, progressive ideas about gender.[30]

In his one-act play *Chitra,* Tagore created one of the many strong female characters for which he became legendary.[31] Basing his title character loosely on Chitrangada, a character in the Mahabharata, Tagore offered readers a modern spin on an ancient plot. For his English translation, Tagore additionally anglicized the character's name. As he explained to an English friend, "The name of the heroine in Mahabharata is Chitrangada but as you have no soft dental d in your alphabet and as your readers are sure to put [the] accent in the wrong place making it sound very unmusical I have ventured to cut it short, retaining the first portion of it which I am sure was the only portion used by her parents if she ever did have any name and parents to boot."[32] Tagore shortened the character's name but otherwise embellished her story. The ancient Chitrangada, whose tale is told in only nine verses of the Mahabharata, is recast by Tagore as Chitra, whose story unveils decidedly modern questions of gender and sexuality.

Tagore makes two critical interventions in his effort to update the epic character. Chitra, who is the daughter of the king of Manipur, has been raised as a boy so that she can technically maintain her family's "unbroken line of male descent." Gender inversion, while not unheard of in the Mahabharata, is not found in Chitrangada's original epic. Rather, the king of Manipur followed the tradition of choosing his daughter's son as his male heir. Also, Chitrangada loses her great beauty in Tagore's retelling. Chitra takes on a masculine appearance. Her seamless male identity only becomes problematic when she encounters the man destined to be her soulmate, the famed military hero of the Mahabharata, Arjuna, a member of the Ksatriya or "warrior class."[33] Confronted with her attraction to Arjuna, Chitra regrets her masculine strength, hating [her] strong, lithe arm." While she recognizes that she has the skills and strength to be the perfect companion to Arjuna in his warrior pursuits, she ultimately asks the gods for divine intervention: "Take from my young body this primal injustice, an unattractive plainness. For a single day make me superbly beautiful, even as beautiful as was the sudden blooming of love in my heart. Give me but one brief day of perfect beauty, and I will answer for the days that follow." Chitra appears before Arjuna, not as herself, but as a nameless beautiful woman who lives in a temple. In the course of the play, Chitra wrestles with her "borrowed beauty, this falsehood that enwraps" her. She calls the beautiful body that elicits Arjuna's praise "my own rival" and resolves, "I will reveal my true self to him, a nobler thing than this disguise."

When Arjuna begins to feel the pull of the warrior life, an urge to return to his military pursuits, he requires of Chitra something more significant than beauty: "Give me something to clasp, something that can last longer than pleasure, that can endure even through suffering." Trouble emerges in the plot when the villagers of the kingdom of Manipur, normally protected by the princess-warrior Chitra, report that, in her absence, they have been everywhere despoiled by robbers. Arjuna finds this curious: a kingdom protected by a woman? Chitra warns him that he would be disappointed in Chitra if he met her, owing to her lack of beauty. "But have you grown so weary of woman's beauty that you seek in her for a man's strength?" But Arjuna is not to be dissuaded. He wants to learn everything about this woman warrior who protects the village, who combines the strength of a man with the tenderness of a woman, declaring, "Woman's arms, though adorned with naught but unfettered strength, are beautiful!" Sensing Arjuna's restless heart, Chitra takes a first, hesitant step: "Arjuna, tell me true, if, now at once, by some magic I could shake myself free from this voluptuous softness, this timid bloom of beauty shrinking from the rude and healthy touch of the world, and fling it from my body like borrowed clothes, would you be able to bear it?" Indeed, Arjuna wants to know the truth, to move beyond appearances, seeking in her a woman shorn of ornaments and veils who "stands clothed in naked dignity. I grope for that ultimate *you,* that bare simplicity of truth." The play is resolved when Chitra appears before Arjuna in her manly attire, with her "many flaws and blemishes" fully exposed. She recounts their first meeting, confesses to the divinely obtained beauty that initially seduced him, and concludes, "The gift that I proudly bring you is the heart of a woman. Here have all pains and joys gathered, the hopes and fears and shames of a daughter of the dust; here love springs up struggling toward immortal life." And Arjuna replies, "Beloved, my life is full."

Tagore's decision to translate this play, and particularly to shorten the name of the title character, is an example of how Tagore collaborated in the infusion of "Indian spirituality" into the West. Through his play, Tagore updated and reimagined a character from classical Hinduism, rendering her legible, appealing, and accessible (English-language readers could manage "Chitra") to a twentieth-century American audience. Tagore's message was understood in 1914 as an endorsement of feminism and the New Woman. As one magazine writer put it, "Tagore's message to women seems to be: 'Do not pretend to possess a femininity which you have lost. Be yourself, be what you are, irrespective of the accident of sex.'"[34] But women readers may have also found in *Chitra* an even more compelling message. Tagore's drama was not so much about a femininity "lost" as it was about the absolute artifice of femininity and the comparative substance of true companionship and strength. Chitra compels Arjuna's attention through her temporary remarkable beauty. But his attention is easily distracted by tales of the heroic Princess Chitra, whose value lies not in her ornamental status but rather in her courageous acts, the protection she offers the villagers. Ultimately, Arjuna is drawn to the "real" Chitra because she embodies the strength of a man, destined to be his equal.

At the time of the play's publication, at least one Indian author declared that Tagore's vision of feminism, as embodied in Chitra, "may seem too radical even to the radical feminists of the West."[35] Clara Colby, however, was so persuaded by her reading of *Chitra* and other work by Tagore that she entitled one of her manuscripts "Tagore the Feminist."[36] In preparation for her lecture series, Colby made an in-depth study of Tagore, examining his life as well as his writings published in English. Tagore was a featured subject of her lectures between 1913 and 1915.

As a result of the difficulties she had encountered in her own life, including the secret humiliation of her husband impregnating a household servant and her much-publicized divorce, Colby was drawn to Tagore's sense that suffering was "the other side of joy." According to Tagore, true freedom came only when "we realize that our individual self is not the highest meaning of our being, that in us we have the world-man who is immortal, who is not afraid of death or sufferings."[37] The very act of loving another was steeped in the sacred: "I believe that to love is to worship the mysterious one. Only we do it unconsciously. Every kind of love is the direct outcome of a universal force that tries to express itself through the human heart. Love is the temporary realisation of that bliss which is at the very root of the universe. Otherwise love has no meaning."[38] The idea of the loving, human heart pointing beyond itself to the immortal resonated with readers and critics, particularly Colby. In her collection of clippings on Tagore, Colby preserved one that declared, "A lover, for instance, whether man or woman, usually serves to typify the soul in a passionate search for the beloved—that something higher than itself which may transfigure its very essence, as love may sometimes transfigure a man or woman."[39] Critics agreed that in Tagore's poetry sexual love was generally a metaphor for the search for God. But in Colby's reading of Tagore, the relationship was not just metaphorical. After reading Tagore's poem "The Beloved at Night & in the Morning," Colby reflected that the poem "shows that even in that riotous passionate period of life the sensual was touched with the spiritual, and that he felt even then the spiritual was the permanent and that to which the sensual must lead for its satisfaction."[40]

Colby was able to harmonize her reading of Tagore with her New Thought critique of male desire. In her notes on Tagore, she articulated her grasp of Tagore's analysis of gender relations. Women, because of their traditional roles of serving, loving, and comforting, had throughout time "developed harmony and beauty." Man, on the other hand, was stymied by "diverse, untamed passions [that] stood in the way of his development."[41] Especially in the West, Tagore argued, this essential difference in orientation wreaked havoc. Men's passions drive imperialism, Tagore suggested, so that men of the West seek "shelter in distant nooks & corners on the earth" in a "crushing struggle for existence which is partly due to wants artificially created."[42] This imbalance, this "social discord," is what necessitated the campaign for women's rights in the West. Finally, Tagore stressed the irony of Western preoccupation with the status of the "Hindu woman" in India: "I feel mortified at the waste of sympathy."[43] In Tagore's analysis, to be "Western" was to be materialistic—Tagore attested that "the Western people love furniture"—imperialistic, and sexually undisciplined. In Tagore's view, men's (not women's) behavior and status should be the object of scrutiny. A feminist reader like Colby was able to absorb Tagore's critique of "Western" men and use it to shift the terms of the debate, away from the well-worn narrative of the deprivation of the "Hindu woman" and toward the degradation of the Western man. Inspired by Tagore, Colby challenged citizens of the United States to take stock, to get spiritually and sexually realigned. In so doing, she harnessed a uniquely American narrative of Orientalism in which, in the words of Vijay Prashad, "the cultural wealth of India could transform the alienated American into a spiritual yet material being."[44]

To return to my opening question: To what extent did religious liberalism provide a space for more cosmopolitan thinking in the early twentieth-century women's rights movement? As my brief discussion of Carrie Chapman Catt illustrated, religious cosmopolitanism was far from universally embraced within the movement.[45] And even a comparatively progressive thinker like Colby sometimes retreated defensively from cosmopolitanism when the challenges struck too close to home. Perhaps the best example of such a retreat can be seen in Colby's troubled relationship with her daughter Zintka, a Lakota Indian whom the Colbys adopted and raised from infancy. When Zintka proved to be an undisciplined child who ran "with the colored children" in the alley and showed signs of sexual precociousness, Colby sought the advice of Richard H. Pratt, the founder of the Carlisle Indian Industrial School. Zintka's "rebellion in her blood" proved embarrassing and had to be suppressed; it did not provide Colby with an exotic source of inspiration, or a new way of imagining women's freedom.[46]

Clara Colby's childrearing practices may betray the limits of her cosmopolitanism. In many ways, however, Colby distinguished herself from the champions of American empire by the causes she supported. She believed that the solutions to the problems of modern America might well lie in unexpected places. What was needed was a spiritual realignment, and many Americans, including her, believed that the "West" was unable to achieve that without assistance. In particular, Colby found it possible to locate within the writings of Tagore a model for improving gender relations in her own culture. Western men could be rehabilitated by exposure to the more spiritually refined concepts of sexual desire found in Tagore's writings.

We might pause to consider more fully the significance of seekers like Clara Colby who succeeded in melding political commitments to the oppressed with their spiritual "border-crossing." Clearly, even radical suffragists like Colby succeeded only in manipulating the binaries of Orientalist logic, not in escaping it. Adherents of Eastern religions were either morally retrograde and in need of Western intervention, as Catt would have it, or they were spiritually endowed and capable of benefiting the "West" with their mystical gifts. The dualism may be inverted, but the East remains the mysterious, irrational "Other." Still, perhaps there is something worth pondering more fully in suffragists' use of Eastern ideas to critique the gendered oppression of Western culture. After all, their respect for the insights of ambassadors from abroad—albeit steeped in the dualism of Orientalism—still ran counter to the views that dominated Anglo-American life, according to which the East was perpetually to be the recipient of uplift and knowledge from the West. While I acknowledge Colby's romantic Orientalism, I do not think the conversation should stop at its assertion. Since the publication of Said's *Orientalism,* some scholars have called for a more nuanced paradigm that recognizes the "affirmative" or "sympathetic non-reductive" potential of some of the salient ideas contained within "Orientalism."[47] Nineteenth-century Indian nationalists, for example, capitalized on the idea that India was inherently "more spiritual" and redirected that idea toward anti-colonial aims. As Partha Chatterjee has argued, nationalists at the turn of the century distinguished between the material and the spiritual. The West was worthy of imitation only in the most material, rational sphere: the business of statecraft, science, and technology. Here, according to nationalist logic, European cultures had successfully subjugated non-European cultures. But Europe had "failed to colonize the inner, essential, identity of the East, which lay in its distinctive, and superior, spiritual culture." For Indian nationalists, a crucial part of the nation-building project was to wrest away from "the West" the power to define and elaborate these crucial national traits, to "protect, preserve, and strengthen the inner core of the national culture, its spiritual essence."[48]

This romantic view of a superior spirituality as a distinctively "Indian" trait reflected the collaborative project of colonizers and colonized. While some Americans, like Carrie Chapman Catt, could see in Indian spiritual practices only evidence of the "barbaric," others, like Colby, could align with Indian nationalists and point to the distinctive benefit India offered to Europe and the United States. But how much should we make of this stance? This brand of spiritual border-crossing, while trafficking in Orientalist tropes, opened an interpretive space where American suffragists like Colby would offer a rare and largely unwelcomed critique of their nation's untroubled path to imperial power. Some scholars of postcolonial theory have lamented that postcolonialism has "remained tentative in its appreciation of individuals and groups that have renounced the privileges of imperialism and elected affinity with victims of their own expansionist culture."[49] This is a discussion that we, as scholars committed to renarrating the history of religious liberalism, need to participate in. We need to interrogate the particular circumstances under which the historical actors we study came to see faith and political engagement as inseparable. Too often the conventions of our disciplinary training permit us to do something less than this.

By way of example, I cite a news story from 1894 that was a favorite topic for Clara Colby and, more importantly, has made its way into virtually every American history textbook. In the midst of a lingering depression, in March of 1894, an Ohio businessman and farmer, Jacob Coxey, led an "army" of unemployed on what is often considered the first march on Washington. This direct action of the Gilded Age dispossessed has a particularly "modern," populist familiarity to it; it foreshadows the great protests of the century to come. But it can be seen as a crucial precedent in modern American history only when the religious proclivities of its main actors are obscured. And while I cannot explore at length the complicated religious dimensions of this campaign, I can perhaps hint at them by pointing out that Jacob Coxey, the commander of "Coxey's Army," revealed that "he had discovered traces in his spirit of the reincarnated soul of Andrew Jackson."[50] Coxey's professed spiritual state has the potential to render this neat historical narrative unrecognizable. Can Coxey's Army still "represent" the great tradition of grass-roots political protest when it is revealed that the lauded populist leader of the dispossessed shared a spirit with the architect of the Trail of Tears, a march of a wholly different order? The incomprehensible weirdness this claim introduces to the story disrupts the narrative's central purpose; the leader of Coxey's Army ought to be a rational historical actor. If he is proven not to be, the essence of the story (Americans confronted economic injustice and protested the capitalist order) is hopelessly scrambled, and its potential is derailed. One might argue that Jacob Coxey's embodiment of the spirit of Andrew Jackson threatens to disqualify Coxey's March as a legitimate populist protest of the depression. Rather, it becomes a delusional act of a compromised political actor.

For turn-of-the-century reformers, and for their subsequent historians, spiritual proclivities have sometimes served, in the words of Leela Gandhi, "as a disqualifying mark against the maturity or seriousness" of political commitments.[51] This was certainly the case for Clara Colby, whose financial prospects both as a newspaper editor and as a public lecturer suffered because of her political and metaphysical border-crossing. Susan B. Anthony continually complained that Colby's financial problems were of her own making, a result of straying too far, in the columns of her paper, from the issue of woman suffrage. Colby's problem, in Anthony's words, was that "she won't abate one jot or trifle of her own personality—on Ghandi [*sic*] or Coxey."[52] Anthony's critique nicely couples Colby's commitments to Indian nationalism with the problems of Coxey's army of the unemployed. Clearly, Colby suffered discrimination within the movement for her particular blend of religious experimentation and political radicalism. At one point, the secretary of the national suffrage organization, Rachel Foster Avery, began assigning speech topics to Colby and other religious cosmopolitans in an effort, as Avery put it, "to keep Mzoomdar and all of the Orientals" off of the platform, a comment that highlights the difference between Colby's "Orientalism" and more pernicious versions.[53]

While her spiritual proclivities rendered Colby a liability to a national political movement bent on gaining respectability, it was perhaps these very proclivities that enabled her to stand in opposition to the growing imperial power of her country. Scholars have placed a disqualifying asterisk beside the names of Spiritualists and other cosmopolitan seekers, asking us, their readers, to accept their political radicalism despite their religious quirks (or, as the example of Jacob Coxey illustrates, to simply omit their religious motivations entirely from our historical narratives). But this is not our only interpretive option. Seekers like Colby, who championed an intimate God, who understood sexual desire as an expression of divinity, who believed in the unity of all faiths, who believed that the spirit was not encapsulated in the body—these seekers may have been particularly well situated to transcend their own privilege and find solidarity with people who were different from them. As Leela Gandhi has argued, "Once we concede the varieties in religious experience, the metaphysical may often prove to have much more in common with those questions of multiculturalism, pluralism, and complex equality which constitute the positive ethical preoccupations of our own time."[54] This much is clear: at the height of American xenophobia, some Anglo-American suffragists, including Clara Colby, looked beyond their borders for guidance on the issues they held most dear—their own salvation and, even more importantly, the spiritual regeneration of a country that they firmly believed had lost its soul.

NOTES

I wish to thank my friends and colleagues who offered useful commentary, including Srimati Basu, Kate Black, Susan Bordo, Jessica Delgado, Jeffrey Kripal, David Lai, Rachel Lindsey Helene Quanquin, Ellen Rosenman, Mrinalini Sinha, and the members of the American Religions Workshop at Princeton University. I owe a special debt to Jonathan Gold, whose keen eye and thoughtful commentary broadened my perspective and sharpened my analysis.

The epigraph is from Clara Colby, "What the Gnostics Taught about the 'Divine Feminine,'" box 6, folder 1, Clara Bewick Colby Papers, Wisconsin Historical Society, Madison, Wisconsin. A handwritten date on this document places it in 1914. Here Colby is influenced by a Theosophical interpretation of the Bhagavad Gita. The point in the original text is that Krishna claims he is everything, not that he is a divinity in which male and female are equal.

1. This project draws upon scholarly discussions of postcolonial studies of feminism and empire. The literature on feminism and empire, especially concerning the British empire, is voluminous. See especially Antoinette Burton, *Burdens of History: British Feminists, Indian Women, and Imperial Culture, 1865–1915* (Chapel Hill: University of North Carolina Press, 1994); Joy Dixon, *Divine Feminine: Theosophy and Feminism in England* (Baltimore: Johns Hopkins University Press, 2001); Kumari Jayawardena, *The White Woman's Other Burden: Western Women and South Asia during British Rule* (New York: Routledge, 1995); the introductory essay by Meera Kosambi in *Pandita Ramabai's American Encounter: The Peoples of the United States (1889),* by Pandita Ramabai, translated and edited by Meera Kosambi (Bloomington: Indiana University Press, 2003); and Mrinalini Sinha, *Specters of Mother India: The Global Restructuring of an Empire* (Durham, N.C.: Duke University Press, 2006).

2. On the collaborative nature of colonial discourses of religion and spirituality, see Peter van der Veer, *Imperial Encounters: Religion and Modernity in India and Britain* (Princeton: Princeton University Press, 2001).

3. Edward W. Said, *Orientalism* (New York: Vintage, 1978). Said emphasizes that such statements operate "as representations usually do, for a purpose, according to a tendency, in a specific historical, intellectual, and even economic setting" (273). In laying out the scope of Orientalism, Said argues that European Orientalists were committed to rescuing a "past classical Oriental grandeur" in the service of ameliorating the perceived problems of the present (79).

4. See Partha Chatterjee's discussion of the invention of Indian "tradition" by European observers and the concomitant resistance to these constructions by Indian nationalists. Partha Chatterjee, *The Nation and Its Fragments: Colonial and Postcolonial Histories* (Princeton: Princeton University Press, 1993), 8–11, 119–21.

5. Carrie Chapman Catt, Diary, February 1–April 1, 1912, 36, 41, Carrie Chapman Catt Papers, Library of Congress, Washington, D.C. Repeatedly throughout her "world tour," Catt expressed disdain for missionaries. Yet her commitment to an essentially Protestant, Westernizing impulse as the force that would lift women to equality resonated with a missionary agenda. See Barbara Reeves-Ellington, Kathryn Kish Sklar, and Connie A. Shemo, eds., *Competing Kingdoms: Women, Mission, Nation and the American Protestant Empire, 1812–1960* (Durham, N.C.: Duke University Press, 2010).

6. Carrie Chapman Catt, "Evolution and Woman's Suffrage," May 18, 1893, 2, 3, 4, Carrie Chapman Catt Collection, box 4, folder 5, Manuscripts and Archives Division, New York Public Library.

7. Richard Fox refers to "affirmative Orientalism" in "East of Said," in *Edward Said: A Critical Reader,* ed. Michael Sprinkler (Oxford: Blackwell, 1992), 144–56. James Clifford analyzes "a sympathetic non-reductive Orientalist tradition" in "On Orientalism," in *The Predicament of Culture: Twentieth-Century Ethnography, Literature and Art* (Cambridge: Cambridge University Press, 1988); see also Leela Gandhi, *Affective Communities: Anticolonial Thought, Fin-de-Siècle Radicalism, and the Politics of Friendship* (Durham, N.C.: Duke University Press, 2006).

8. Ronald Inden, "Orientalist Constructions of India," *Modern Asian Studies* 20, no. 3 (July 1986): 429–30, 433, 442.

9. Clara Colby to Elizabeth Boynton Harbert, October 11, 1912, Elizabeth Boynton Harbert Collection, box 3, folder 34, Henry E. Huntington Library, Pasadena, Calif.

10. Clara Colby, Diary, February 6, 1914, Clara Bewick Colby Papers, box 1, folder 5, Wisconsin Historical Society, Madison.

11. "The New Spiritual America Emerging," *Current Literature* 46, no. 2 (February 1909), 181.

12. See especially Beryl Satter's study of gender and New Thought, *Each Mind a Kingdom: American Women, Sexual Purity, and the New Thought Movement, 1875–1920* (Berkeley: University of California Press, 1999).

13. See Gail Bederman, *Manliness and Civilization: A Cultural History of Gender and Race in the United States, 1880–1917* (Chicago: University of Chicago Press, 1995), 16–17; and Satter, *Each Mind a Kingdom,* 38–39.

14. Satter, *Each Mind a Kingdom,* 110.

15. Clara Colby, "What the Gnostics Taught about the 'Divine Feminine,'" Clara Bewick Colby Papers, box 6, folder 1. British Theosophists tended to push the "anti-desire" position even further, arguing that sexual desire "disturbed the astral body." According to Joy Dixon, "spiritual progress involved a literal sublimation of sexual energy, the transmutation of the base metal of sexual desire into purer and higher forms of creativity." See Dixon, *Divine Feminine,* 106–107.

16. As an attorney, Schroeder took on freedom of expression, blasphemy, and censorship cases. In addition to his anti-Comstock work, he was known for defending Emma Goldman and for establishing the Free Speech League with Lincoln Steffins. For coverage of Schroeder's work on the sexual basis of religion, see Leigh Eric Schmidt, *Heaven's Bride: The Unprintable Life of Ida C. Craddock, American Mystic, Scholar, Sexologist, Martyr and Madwoman* (New York: Basic Books, 2010), 232–39.

17. Clara Colby, Diary, February 21, 1915, Clara Bewick Colby Papers, box 1, folder 6, italics added. For a fascinating discussion of New Thought and sexuality, see R. Marie Griffith, *Born Again Bodies: Flesh and Spirit in American Christianity* (Berkeley: University of California Press, 2004), 91–97.

18. Rabindranath Tagore to William Rothenstein, October 27, 1912, William Rothenstein Collection (1148), Houghton Library, Harvard University.

19. Rabindranath Tagore to William Rothenstein, December 30, 1912, December 2, 1912, William Rothenstein Collection (1148). For an edited collection of the extensive correspondence between Tagore and Rothenstein, see Mary M. Lago, ed., *Imperfect Encounter: Letters of William Rothenstein and Rabindranath Tagore, 1911–1941* (Cambridge, Mass: Harvard University Press, 1972). See also Stephen N. Hay, "Rabindranath Tagore in America," *American Quarterly* 14, no. 3 (autumn 1962): 439–63.

20. These are the words of the English poet Frances Cornford, quoted in Amartya Sen, *The Argumentative Indian: Writings on Indian History, Culture and Identity* (New York: Picador, 2005), 94.

21. Basanta Koomar Roy, *Rabindranath Tagore, the Man and His Poetry* (New York: Dodd, Mead, 1915), 120. This, in fact, appears to have been Colby's primary source for Tagore's biography.

22. Alexandra Munroe, *The Third Mind: American Artists Contemplate Asia, 1860–1989* (New York: Guggenheim Museum Publications, 2009), 21.

23. Founded in Calcutta in 1828 by Ram Mohum Roy, Brahmo Samaj was influenced by Islam and Christianity. It rejected polytheism, idol worship, and the caste system.

24. Sen, *The Argumentative Indian,* 90–91.

25. Hugh Urban, *Tantra: Sex, Secrecy, Politics, and Power in the Study of Religion* (Berkeley: University of California Press, 2003), 127.

26. Rabindranath Tagore, *The Religion of Man* (London: Macmillan, 1931), 10–11.

27. "Rabindranath Tagore (1861–1941)," *Founding Fathers,* http://www.thebrahmosamaj.net/founders/rabindra.html.

28. Quoted in Sen, *The Argumentative Indian,* 108.

29. "An Attack on the Tagore 'Craze,'" *Literary Digest,* August 21, 1915, 352, clipping in the Clara Bewick Colby Papers, box 5, folder 11.

30. "Rabindranath Tagore, as a Playwright, Issues a Message to Women," *Current Opinion* 56, no. 5 (May 1914): 358. For women's commentary on and interpretation of Tagore, see May Sinclair, "The 'Gitanjali,' or, Song-Offerings of Rabindra Nath Tagore," *North American Review* 197, no. 690 (May 1913): 659–76; Mary Carolyn Davies, "Rabindranath Tagore: India's Shakespeare and Tasso in One," *Forum* 50 (January 1914): 140–45; and Elizabeth Carpenter, "Has the Gentlewoman Passed," *North American Review* 200, no. 706 (September 1914): 450–58.

31. Rabindranath Tagore, *Chitra,* http://theatrehistory.com/plays/chitra001.html; all quotations are from this text. See also Colby's notes and plot summary in "Chitra," Clara Bewick Colby Papers, box 5, folder 11. Female characters in Tagore's novels and plays sought education, challenged men, took initiative in expressing desire, and sometimes remained unmarried (without penalty). See Bimanbehari Majumdar, *Heroines of Tagore: A Study in the Transformation of Indian Society, 1875–1941* (Calcutta: Firma K. L. Mukhaopadhyay, 1968); and Mary Thundyil Mathew, *Female Development in the Novels of Rabindranath Tagore: A Cross-Cultural Analysis of Gender and Literature in British India* (Lewiston, N.Y.: Mellen University Press, 1995).

32. Tagore to Rothenstein, November 7, 1913, William Rothenstein Collection (1148). Tagore translated the play himself at age fifty, nearly two decades after its original publication in Bengali. See Majumdar, *Heroines of Tagore,* 149.

33. Readers familiar with the Mahabharata would recognize Arjuna as one of the central figures of the sacred text. In the Bhagavad Gita, it is to Arjuna that Krishna reveals his true identity as the supreme deity. Arjuna and his four brothers, the five sons of Pandu, battle their cousins for the right to control the Kuru kingdom. Arjuna is praised for his military prowess. Within these epics, he serves (despite spending a year disguised as a eunuch) as an uncontested icon of masculinity. For English readers unfamiliar with the Mahabharata, however, his background is presented only minimally in the play. He is identified simply as a member of a warrior caste, retired and living as a hermit in the forest. No mention is made of

his countless previous marriages, a detail that would have disrupted the romantic tale of monogamy within the play and perhaps its appeal to American feminists like Colby.

34. "Rabindranath Tagore . . . Issues a Message," 358.

35. Roy, *Rabindranath Tagore,* 130.

36. Clara Colby, "Tagore the Feminist," handwritten manuscript, Clara Bewick Colby Papers, box 5, folder 11. It seems that Colby was basing her lecture on Roy, *Rabindranath Tagore.* Roy includes a chapter with the title "Tagore the Feminist."

37. Clara Colby, "Rabindranath Tagore," handwritten manuscript, Clara Bewick Colby Papers, box 5, folder 11.

38. Rabindranath Tagore, quoted in Roy, *Rabindranath Tagore,* 129.

39. H. W. N., "The Gift of the Sword," unidentified clipping, Clara Bewick Colby Papers, box 5, folder 11.

40. Clara Colby, "The Gardener," handwritten manuscript, Clara Bewick Colby Papers, box 5, folder 11.

41. Colby, "Tagore the Feminist."

42. Quoted in ibid. In Tagore's correspondence, it is not entirely clear that he meant to indict the United States when he critiqued "Western" culture, although clearly Colby understood him to do so. Take, for example, this statement: "Somehow I have an impression that America has a great mission in the history of the Western civilization; for it is rich enough not to concern itself in the greedy exploitation of weaker nations. Its hands are free and perhaps it will hold up the torch of freedom before the world." Rabindranath Tagore to William Rothenstein, 1913, William Rothenstein Collection (1148).

43. Quoted in Colby, "Tagore the Feminist."

44. Vijay Prashad, *The Karma of Brown Folk* (Minneapolis: University of Minnesota Press, 2000), 18.

45. Carrie Chapman Catt, who maintained her international leadership in human rights issues until her death in 1947, commented that she made some progress overcoming, in her own words, "her jingoism." Catt became one of the leading advocates for peace and disarmament. Although she shied away from public pronouncements about religion, she firmly believed that women had a particular mission of a spiritual nature: to bring peace to the globe. In her own evolution, she loosened her grip on the idea that Eastern cultures and religious practices were "barbaric," becoming convinced that the true source of "barbarism" was the war machine in her own country.

46. Clara Colby, letter to Richard H. Pratt, October 14, 1902, quoted in Renee Samson Flood, *Lost Bird of Wounded Knee* (New York: Scribner, 1995), 218.

47. The counter to this call for more attention to the "sympathetic Orientalism" is the suggestion, by such scholars as Richard King, that the point of studying Orientalism is not to interrogate the occasional good intentions of people and institutions. "That is not what an analysis of Orientalism as a discourse is fundamentally concerned with, highlighting as it does the wider structural and political context in which the work of Orientalists occurs." See Richard King, *Orientalism and Religion: Postcolonial Theory, India and "The Mystic East"* (London: Routledge, 1999), 89.

48. Chatterjee, *The Nation and Its Fragments,* 121.

49. Gandhi, *Affective Communities,* 1.

50. *New York Times,* March 23, 1894.

51. Gandhi, *Affective Communities,* 115.

52. Susan B. Anthony to Elizabeth Cady Stanton, January 8, 1897, Anthony Family Papers, Henry E. Huntington Library, San Marino, Calif.

53. Rachel Foster Anthony to Susan B. Anthony, November 24, 1897, Susan B. Anthony–Rachel Foster Avery Papers, University of Rochester Library, Rochester, N.Y. Avery is referring to the Brahmo Samaj leader Pratap Mozoomdar, who visited the United States in the 1880s.

54. Gandhi, *Affective Communities,* 141.

FIGURE 12. Juliet Thompson as a young woman. "There is a magic in Juliet's eyes," her friend Dimitri Marianoff once said. Juliet Thompson, *The Diary of Juliet Thompson* (Los Angeles: Kalimat Press, 1983), viii, xxiii.

FIGURE 13. Juliet Thompson, *Shop Window.*
Frick Art Reference Library, New York, New York.

FIGURE 14. Images of carriages on the Akka beach. Archie Bell, *The Spell of the Holy Land* (Boston: The Page Co., 1915), 306.

FIGURE 15. Thompson's portrait of Abdu'l-Bahá. Juliet Thompson, *The Diary of Juliet Thompson* (Los Angeles: Kalimat Press, 1983), 312.

FIGURE 16. Kahlil Gibran's portrait of Abdu'l-Baha, April 1912.
Private Collection.

Delphic Studios,

44 WEST 56th STREET
NEW YORK, N. Y.

Please send me .... copies of

"I, MARY MAGDALEN"
by JULIET THOMPSON.

I enclose ☐ cash ; ☐ check ; or ☐ money order.

Pre-publication subscription....$2.50

Name ....

Address ....

FIGURE 17. Order form for Juliet Thompson's *I, Mary Magdalen. Office of the Secretary, Records, Files on Individuals, 1940s, Bahá'í National Archives, Wilmette, Illinois.*

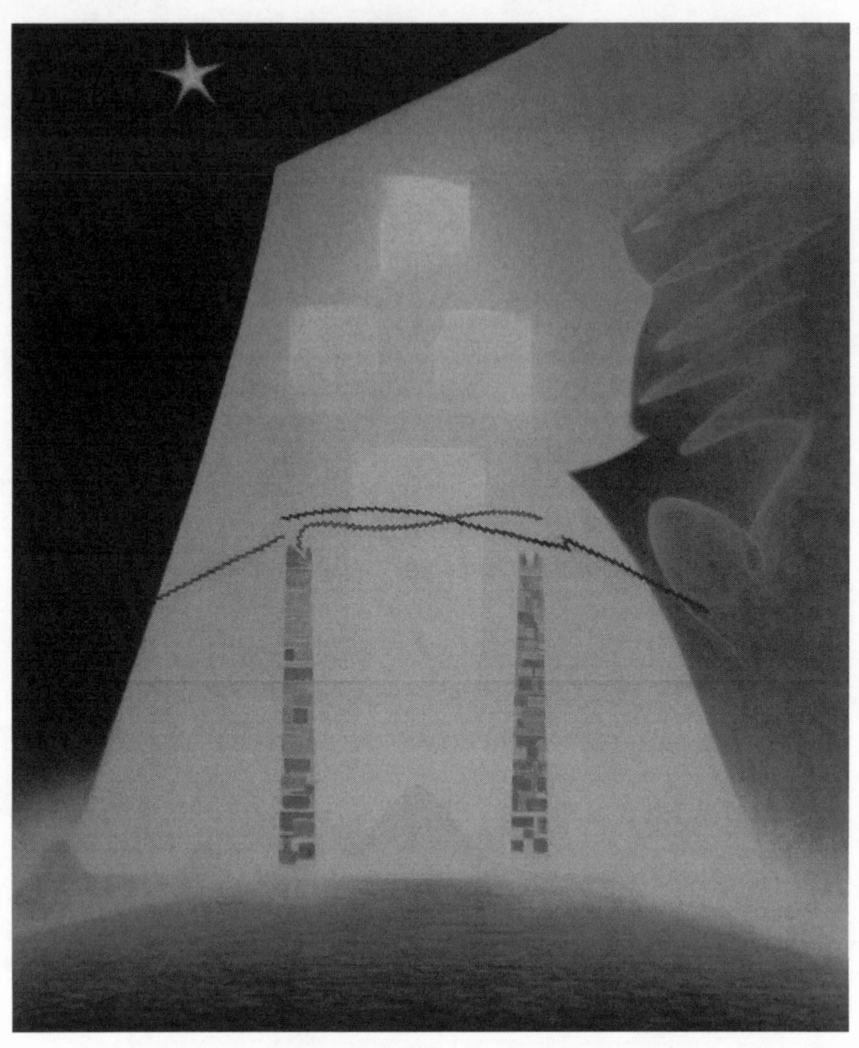

FIGURE 18. Agnes Pelton, *Future*, 1941.
The Buck Collection, Laguna Beach, California.

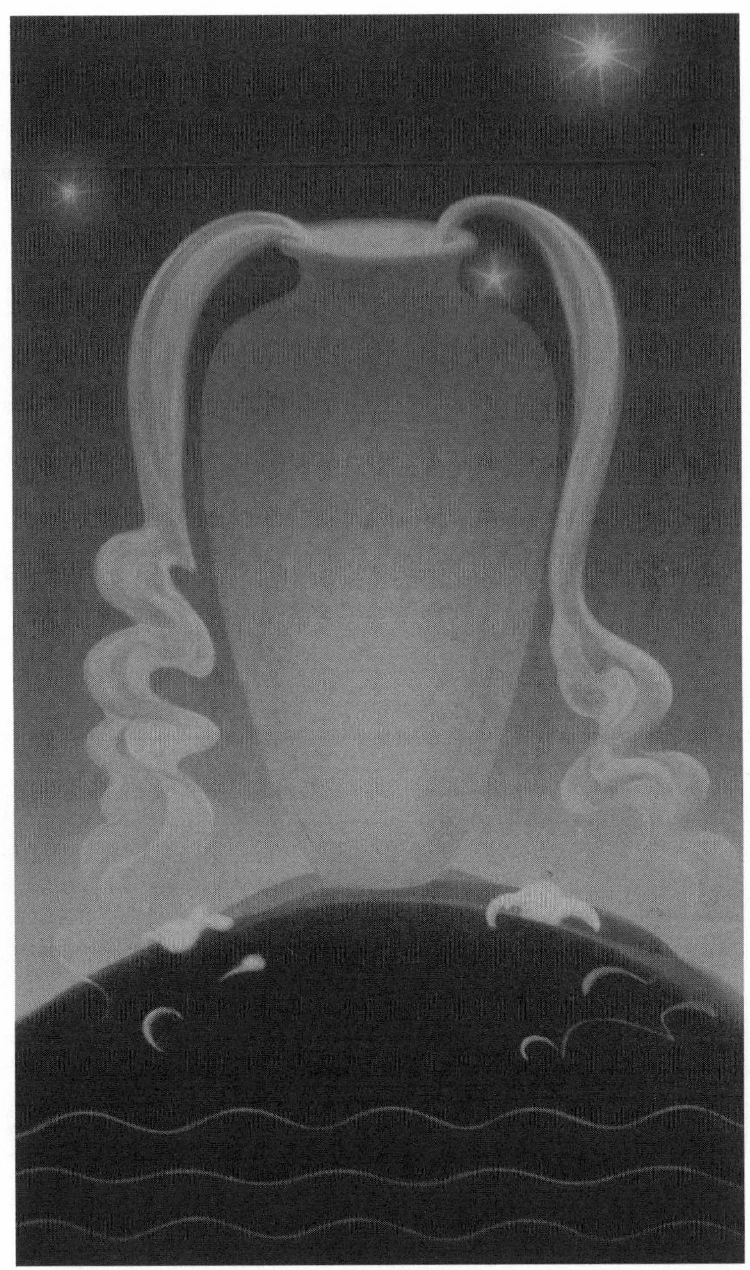

FIGURE 19. Agnes Pelton, *Evensong,* 1934.
Collection of Leighanne Stainer, Fremont, California.
Photograph courtesy of Palm Springs Art Museum.

EIGHT

"We Build Our Temples for Tomorrow"

Racial Ecumenism and Religious Liberalism in the Harlem Renaissance

JOSEF SORETT

INTRODUCTION

In 1926 the National Association for the Advancement of Colored People (NAACP) sponsored a yearlong conversation regarding the relationship between race, the arts, and popular culture. Hosted on the pages of *Crisis,* this discussion included such topics as representations of "the Negro" in American literature, the appropriate aims for African American artists, and the possibility of a black artistic tradition in the United States. Of course, this dialogue was not an isolated event, but an outgrowth of what is now commonly referred to as the Harlem Renaissance, a moment of tremendous black cultural flourishing and the most celebrated phase in a longer New Negro movement that began near the end of the nineteenth century.[1] Regardless of nomenclature, during the 1920s the world witnessed a flurry of black cultural production never before imagined, which achieved such popularity that Langston Hughes—commonly considered Harlem's poet laureate—referred to it as the moment "when the Negro was in vogue."[2] Beyond the pages of black periodicals like *Crisis,* debates regarding black art and culture appeared in mainstream publications like *Survey Graphic,* which featured a special issue on Harlem in 1925, and *The Nation,* which staged a debate between two of Harlem's most promising young black writers—George Schuyler and Langston Hughes—in June of 1926.

George Schuyler, a disciple of H. L. Mencken who would come to be known as the sage of Sugar Hill, wrote first with a sharp-witted essay entitled "The Negro-Art Hokum." In it he sardonically dismissed the idea of "aframerican" art as ludicrous, because of how long blacks had been in the United States. If a racial art were to ever develop, he opined, it could do so only in Africa; such talk on American soil was "self-evident foolishness." He insisted that artistic expressions credited to black people, such as spirituals, blues, and jazz, were more accurately attributable to regional and class variations than to any particular racial characteristic. According to Schuyler, "This, of course, is easily understood if one stops to realize that the Aframerican is merely a lampblacked Anglo-Saxon. . . . Aside from his color, which ranges from very dark brown to pink, your American Negro is just plain American." Schuyler found African American religious life to be especially illustrative of this fact. He explained, "He reads the same Bible and belongs to the Baptist, Methodist and Episcopal and Catholic church. . . . It is sheer nonsense to talk about 'racial differences' as between the American black man and the American white man."[3] Schuyler did not discount the reality of the United States' racial history, or the continued impact of slavery and segregation. Yet what mattered in discussions of art was that blacks and whites alike were contributors, as well as heirs, to a shared American cultural heritage defined more by what David Wills has termed "the encounter of black and white" than by any distinct traditions identifiable as black or white.[4] Moreover, that New Negro artists were well versed in European and American aesthetic traditions was, for Schuyler, of greater significance than any common racial classification.

Offering a rebuttal to Schuyler the following week, in "The Negro Artist and the Racial Mountain," Langston Hughes insisted that there was a distinct racial aesthetic, and it could be discerned in black folk cultures. Perhaps taking a cue from Schuyler, he too pointed to churches as evidence. Where Schuyler argued that a shared American Christianity made the case for a unique black cultural sensibility unfeasible, Hughes explained that "the Negro Church" was not a monolith. He agreed that there were black churches modeled after "Caucasian patterns," but Hughes attributed this to black bourgeois impulses toward respectability. He further described the churches of black elites (i.e., mainline denominational churches) as inclined toward an "aping of things white," and conceded that they were ill-suited for the cultivation of a racial art.[5] However, Hughes implicitly clarified the classed nature of his claims by then shifting attention to the churches of "the low-down folks." For him, such churches (i.e., storefronts) were among the best places to espy the stylings of a distinctive racial culture. In these churches, Hughes argued,

> Their joy runs, bang! Into ecstasy. Their religion soars to a shout. . . . They furnish a wealth of colorful, distinctive material for any artist because they still hold their own individuality in the face of American standardizations. And perhaps these common people will give to the world its truly great Negro artist, the one who is not afraid to be himself.[6]

To be sure, Hughes's romance with folk culture—a common source of inspiration for artists and intellectuals, black and white, in the United States during the 1920s—in part confirmed Schuyler's stressing of a shared American sensibility.[7] However, the religious communities sustained by black people of "the so-called common element" represented, for Hughes, a rich resource to mine for New Negro artists. Claiming black folk churches as a model, his vision both advanced racial particularism and resisted racial provincialism. Near the essay's end Hughes summed up his position as follows:

> We younger Negro artists who create now intend to express our individual dark-skinned selves without fear or shame. If white people are pleased we are glad. If they are not, it doesn't matter. We know we are beautiful. And ugly too. The tom-tom cries and the tom-tom laughs. If colored people are pleased we are glad. If they are not, their displeasure doesn't matter either. We build our temples for tomorrow, strong as we know how, and we stand on top of the mountain, free within ourselves.[8]

The poet critiqued black middle-class cultural politics, wherein he located an "urge within the race towards whiteness." But for Hughes, the distinctiveness of black folk culture was not to be disdained; and he refused to relinquish his interest in it even if it led to an art that was, at times, perceived to confirm a white public's plea for "the primitive." In doing so, Langston Hughes embraced the idea of a racial aesthetic, but he also imagined an artistic plane that privileged human individuality, one on which black people were recognized as "beautiful. And ugly too," irrespective of racial differences or audience reception.

Alongside the obvious concern with race that framed Hughes's discussion of churches, his choice of the term "temple"—suggestive of a spiritual sanctuary, though not explicitly religious—to chart a trajectory for a racial aesthetic indicates the degree to which religion shaped the vision of many New Negro artists. That is, Hughes's attention to the range of black churches helps to reveal a broader spiritual impulse that undergirded much of the political and cultural ambitions of the Harlem Renaissance.[9] That religion figured centrally in Hughes's exchange with George Schuyler calls attention to a critical dimension of the Harlem Renaissance that has been oft overlooked by scholars of African American history and culture, and suggests a fruitful site for research in the field of American religion. Moreover, in the critical debates connected to the New Negro movement, several points of resonance can be discerned between a brand of racial ecumenism articulated by black artists and the rhetorics of religious liberalism, both of which animated America's spiritual and cultural landscape during the interwar period.

THE NEW NEGRO'S SPIRIT: ON RELIGIOUS LIBERALISM AND RACIAL ECUMENISM

Grounded in both historical and theoretical questions, my arguments in this essay are twofold. First, I claim that religion, as it figured into aesthetic debates central to the Harlem Renaissance, is best viewed along a spectrum that has competing appeals to a nascent racial spirit at one end, and varied interpretations of black churches at the other, thus revealing religion to be a crucial battleground. Second, I suggest that the distinction that New Negro artists repeatedly drew between a racial spirit and black churches resonated with (and arguably was indebted to) ideas that are best located within the traditions of American religious liberalism. Such claims are not self-evident, for a number of reasons. First, the relationship between black cultural traditions (in the United States) and the broader American terrain, whether in the realm of religion or aesthetics, is a continued site of scholarly debate. That is, the positions put forward by George Schuyler and Langston Hughes reflect analytical frames that are still in competition: the question of whether to tell a tale of black culture as one of similarity or particularity in relationship to its North American context is still contested. Second, the histories of African American religious and artistic traditions are typically told as mutually exclusive. While some might claim that the Western distinction between sacred and secular does not apply in black cultures, it nonetheless appears to have had a strong influence upon our highly specialized academic work. Perhaps even more pointedly, the latter (the arts) is often envisioned to be the secular foil of the former (religion), or as the inheritor of the cultural authority that had historically been granted to churches within black communities. It was at least in part as a response to the perceived irreligious attitudes of Harlem Renaissance writers that Benjamin E. Mays—arguably the most prominent black liberal Protestant of the twentieth century—wrote his 1938 book, *The Negro's God as Reflected in His Literature.* For Mays, black churches required a defense against the frequent claim that their "other-worldliness" made them irrelevant in the modern world, and literature served as evidence of the degree to which African American ideas of God were tied to the circumstances of particular historical—that is, pressing "this-worldly"—concerns.[10]

Certainly, if black religion and art are understood to run along independent tracks, perhaps even to be opposed to each other, than there is little cause to assume a relationship between racial aesthetics and religious liberalisms more generally. However, as the title of Mays's book suggests, artistic and religious traditions are never experienced as entirely separate entities in history. And, especially at this moment in American history, the relationship between religious traditions and artistic formations was richly debated, and the two were certainly not accepted either as fixed or as unrelated or oppositional realms. For instance, the arts figured as a critical space for both sides in the Fundamentalist-modernist clash of the 1920s, perhaps the most prominent religious drama of the day.[11] While scholarship on the Harlem Renaissance has sought to move past the political metanarrative (i.e., seeing art as politics) that overdetermined early historiography, one might also reexamine the artistic formations of the New Negro movement in light of the era's religious ferment.[12] In doing so, one rediscovers debates regarding racial aesthetics as an intellectual vista for the study of African American (and thus American) religion. More specifically, one finds all the elements that Leigh Schmidt identifies as essential to the cultures of American religious liberalism, including efforts to negotiate tensions between the religious and secular and a certain spiritualization of the arts that embraced cosmopolitanism and ecumenism in order to address the persistent, if changing, "problem of the color line."[13]

If the Fundamentalist side of this equation is readily identifiable by its position on Christian doctrine laid out in the pamphlets that formed *The Fundamentals,* the modernist position has always been somewhat less clear.[14] In his definitive work on the subject, William Hutchison locates "Protestant modernism" within "a cluster of beliefs—in adaptation, cultural immanentism, and a religiously based progressivism."[15] Hutchison's story is largely organized around debates within white mainline Protestant denominations that took place during the first two decades of the twentieth century. However, one also finds ready evidence of the "modernist impulse" in efforts to theorize the New Negro. In 1922 Harry Emerson Fosdick preached a sermon entitled "Shall the Fundamentalists Win?" that would come to stand in more generally for the modernist position.[16] Just one year later Reverdy Ransom wed racial and religious discourses in a poem that revealed his own "Protestant modernism." An African Methodist Episcopal (A.M.E.) clergyman and a leading figure in the Niagara Movement, Ransom was but one of many American preachers of the day who, like Fosdick, deliberately worked to reconcile Christian dogma with the demands of modernity.[17]

A year before his election as a bishop in the A.M.E. Church, and two years before the publication of Alain Locke's definitive anthology of the same title, Ransom's poem "The New Negro" appeared on the pages of New York's *Amsterdam News:*

> Rough hewn from the jungle and the desert's sands,
> Slavery was the chisel that fashioned him to form,
> And gave him all the arts and sciences had won.
> The lyncher, mob, and stake have been his emery wheel.
> TO MAKE A POLISHED MAN of strength and power.
> In him, the latest birth of freedom,
> God hath again made all things new.[18]

Reflecting debates regarding Negro art, the poem balanced emphases on the significance of Africa, on one hand, and the impact of slavery and segregation, on the other, in the development of black culture in America. While much of the imagery in the poem perpetuated a view of "primitive" Africa popular at the time, Ransom posited a triumphalist vision of the New Negro as the "last reserve of God on earth."[19] He claimed that the "the lyncher, mob, and stake" had prepared black people for a special role in America; but only through Christian love would they achieve their place, "ON EQUAL FOOTING everywhere with all mankind." Together, cultural inheritances and the conditions occasioned by white supremacy were the sources of Ransom's redemptive black identity. For him, the New Negro represented a form of racial ecumenism. It implied a shared racial community that transcended the regional, class, and cultural divisions inherent to black life in North America, which had been recently heightened as a result of the Great Migration. Equally significant for my purposes, the poem is illustrative of the commitments of religious modernism, in that Ransom locates the New Negro within a theological rubric that both reconciled "science, religion, poetry and song" and addressed such contemporary concerns as "labor and capital."

As a bishop in a black mainline denomination, Reverdy Ransom embodied the religious, and specifically the liberal Protestant, aspirations of the New Negro movement.[20] Yet, like religious liberalism more generally, the New Negro's spiritual sensibilities were not to be contained within the boundaries of a black Christian modernism. As Leigh Schmidt argues, American religious liberalism, often simply identified with liberal Protestant churches, extended well beyond the bounds of that Protestant denominationalism.[21] So it was, too, for the religious dimensions of the Harlem Renaissance. In fact, as this essay will show, the aesthetic vision of key New Negro artists and intellectuals included a tension between the liberal Protestantism of figures like Reverdy Ransom and the religious liberalism exemplified by Alain Locke, who will be discussed in a moment. Ultimately, Locke—who played a more prominent role in shaping the reception of the New Negro—minimized the significance of the former in favor of the interreligious ecumenism of the latter. So while individual black artists paid attention to a range of practices and ideas associated with black churches, the New Negro movement downplayed differences (such as those of religion) between black peoples by presenting a unified image of modern black life. In this regard, what Henry Louis Gates Jr. identifies as "the trope of a New Negro"—a "coded system of signs complete with masks and mythology"[22]—functioned like the rhetorics of religious liberalism in emphasizing a common racial (and spiritual, depending on who was deploying it) core that sought to unite a diversity of cultural and religious particularities and was tied to a program of political engagement.[23]

Within the circles of American religious liberalism, composed primarily of whites, the aim was to embrace a spirituality that was more expansive and inclusive than that articulated by the Protestant establishment. For African Americans religious liberalism served this purpose as well—one thinks of such figures as W. E. B. Du Bois and Howard Thurman, most immediately.[24] However, for "race men" such as Du Bois and Thurman, it also functioned as a strategy for gaining social inclusion. The egalitarianism preached by religious liberals squared well with the goal of racial equality articulated by black artists, intellectuals, and leaders of civil rights organizations like the NAACP.[25] While religious liberals were often concerned with expanding faith and democracy, if you will, toward the goal of "human brotherhood," beginning from the place of racial alterity requires reimagining the direction of this logic. As Barbara Johnson has argued, "To be a subject means to activate the network of discourse from *where one stands*. . . . To be a subject also means to take nourishment from more than one source, to construct a new synthesis."[26] So for persons who were racial subjects in Jim Crow America, the aim was also to insert themselves into the master narrative by embracing the inclusive ethics of religious liberalism. Now, to clarify, my aim here is not to reduce religious complexities to questions of race politics. Rather, it is to highlight the tradition within black communities of reconfiguring the master tropes of American religion—what might be called "signifying."[27] Such a perspective calls attention to the multiple levels of meaning in the very categories of "race" and "spirituality," both of which were central to the cultures of the New Negro *and* American religious liberalism. It also suggests that what each term signifies in specific instances reflects the social location of the individual invoking the term. Perhaps the best way to make this case is through illustration.

EDITING *THE NEW NEGRO:* CHURCH AND SPIRIT IN THE MAKING OF A RACIAL BIBLE

One year after George Schuyler and Langston Hughes's debate in *The Nation,* James Weldon Johnson turned readers' attention to the sermons of the "old-time Negro preacher," arguing that they were an original artifact of a black aesthetic tradition.[28] And in 1925 Alain Locke framed the aspirations of the Harlem Renaissance as distinctly spiritual. The most familiar document of the era, Locke's edited volume *The New Negro,* is commonly considered the movement's "Bible."[29] While Locke was a philosopher by training, his task as anthologist of *The New Negro* required its own brand of artistic ingenuity. The collection was a virtual Who's Who of black artists and intellectuals of the 1920s. It included poetry, fiction, drama, music, and the visual arts, as well as interpretive and historical essays. Months prior to compiling hundreds of submissions into the more than four hundred pages of the anthology, Locke edited a special issue of the monthly periodical *Survey Graphic,* entitled "Harlem: Mecca of the New Negro," which became the core of the much larger book.[30] One of the most interesting stories of the New Negro movement concerns the process of expanding the journal issue into the anthology. In his account of the interracial exchanges that shaped the Harlem Renaissance, George Hutchinson provides a detailed treatment of the politics involved in Locke's editing efforts. Interestingly, while Hutchinson thoroughly deconstructs Locke's labors to produce *The New Negro,* he does not address the one contribution explicitly on religion in the *Survey Graphic* issue—an essay by George Edmund Haynes that did not make the cut for the larger book. Hutchinson's analysis helpfully frames the anthology as "a field of commerce and conflict"; but he, like most scholars of the Harlem Renaissance, does not address how religion figured as a site of contestation for Locke and New Negro artists and intellectuals more generally.[31]

To illumine the religious dimensions of *The New Negro,* it is helpful to first consider contributions that mentioned religion in some form and were carried over from the *Survey Graphic* issue. Rudolph Fisher's group of short stories, "Vestiges," offer perhaps the most sustained attention to religion in *The New Negro.*[32] Religion stands at the center of the first and last of the four. The first, "Shepherd! Lead Us!" tells the story of an old Southern pastor, Ezekiel Taylor, who has come North in search of his migrating members. Having initially resisted the urge to move with the masses, Taylor now finds himself combing Harlem's streets for his congregation. Lured into a storefront by the sounds of a familiar song, the migrant minister is reunited with his former church, now worshipping under the direction of a new preacher, Shackleton Ealey. In contrast to the naïve Southern sincerity attributed to Taylor, Ealey is portrayed as a prototypical Northern con man who, Fisher tells us, was "inspired to preach the Gospel by the draft laws of 1917" and sought "to make capital out of his conversion." Ealey's efforts are soon undone, as he learns that his congregants will be leaving to reconstitute their old church under Taylor's leadership. In this story, the North figures as the place where faith becomes a financial hustle, but this hustle is ultimately trumped by a religion deeply shaped by Southern kinship ties.[33] Fisher continues this line of thinking in the final story, which features Pete and Lucky, bootleggers who end up at a revival because it presents the prospect of a "pretty good show." As the preacher's talk turns to hell, Lucky, who happens to be the wayward son of a preacher, feels compelled to leave the service. Upon Pete's probing, Lucky explains, "Dam' 'f I know what it is—maybe because it makes me think of the old folks or somethin'—but—hell—it just sorter—gets me—"[34] In contrast to the first story, where the Northern preacher is described as a con man, here the man who profits from vice proves unable to escape the ghosts of his religious past.

As quintessential migration narratives, Fisher's stories provide an image of African American religion as a relic of an authentic Southern folk past that still exerted significant cultural and theological power.[35] Yet religion in the North is also simultaneously critiqued as a con, an absence of reason, and a site of ridicule. Additionally, the syntax that Fisher employs in the dialogue between the bootleggers raises the question of whether Lucky's reluctant religious experience is more a matter of familial ties or theological formation—a question of kinship or creed. Even Lucky appears uncertain whether the hellfire sermon preached at the revival provoked him because it made him think of damnation (he was a bootlegger, after all!) or because it reminded him of "the old folks," presumably his parents and a Southern past. For Locke, these fictional accounts of black folk religion figured as the foil—the ghost of Negro past, if you will—from which New Negro aspirations departed.

In contrast to Fisher's "Vestiges," Locke's own discussion of religion elsewhere in *The New Negro* helps to explain his omission of Haynes's essay. In "The Legacy of the Ancestral Arts," Locke describes Christianity as a particular challenge to his efforts to encourage black artists to draw inspiration from Africa. According to Locke,

> the American Negro, even when he confronts the various forms of African art expression with a sense of its ethnic claims upon him, meets them in as alienated and misunderstanding an attitude as the average European westerner. Christianity and all of the other European conventions operate to make this inevitable.[36]

In Locke's view, churches socialized black people into cultural worlds that privileged Western aesthetics and perpetuated a warped perspective on African culture. Convinced that the "ancestral arts" of Africa should direct New Negro artists, he argued that Christianity, a "European convention," was a significant impediment to their embracing an "African spirit."[37] Together with Fisher's short stories, Locke's essay captures the degree to which *The New Negro* portrayed African American religion, and Christianity in particular, as a remnant of the past, an ingredient that needed to be extricated from black culture, or at least refined, in order for New Negroes to be fully born. Locke imagined that an emerging racial spirit would be informed not by Christianity but by the West African cultural worlds from which enslaved blacks had been extracted.

Locke's looking to Africa as the source of a "racial spirit" is indicative of the New Negro movement's concern with distancing itself from the stigma of American slavery. By doing so, he circumvented the painfully intimate system of oppression that had produced the "invisible institution," a forerunner of the independent black churches.[38] Moreover, he was also able to elude the primarily evangelical ethos of these congregations; evangelicalism was a sure theological and cultural fault line during the 1920s. As Henry Louis Gates Jr. has argued, the trope of the New Negro was a concerted effort to represent black people to the world in a new light.[39] As part of this strategy, Locke's *The New Negro* was as much an exercise in mythmaking as it was an effort to objectively portray black life. This becomes more evident when we examine the article on religion in the *Survey Graphic* issue that was omitted from the book: George Haynes's interpretive essay on Harlem's churches, "The Church and the Negro Spirit." Haynes had degrees from Fisk and Yale, and in 1912 he had become the first African American to receive a Ph.D. from Columbia University. There he studied sociology, while playing an instrumental role in the 1910 founding of the National Urban League. Highly active in the Presbyterian church, when he penned his essay for Locke's *Survey Graphic* issue Haynes was also serving as secretary of the Federal Council of Churches' Commission on Church and Race Relations. Haynes was as much a part of the Protestant establishment as any other African American of his day.[40]

In contrast to Locke's casting of Christianity as a source of "alienation," Haynes argued that "the Negro Church is at once the most resourceful and the most characteristic organized force in the life of Negroes of the Northern cities[,] as it was in the Southern communities from which they come." Extolling the educational, social, and financial capital of black churches, Haynes affirmed that they were "visible evidence of the struggle of an aspiring people to express the best of life within them."[41] As these passages (and the essay's title) indicate, Haynes's analysis led in two distinct directions. First, he lauded churches as the "most resourceful and most characteristic organized force in the life of the Negro." Second, he argued that "the Negro Church" grew out of "the best of life within" black people. In short, black churches were the institutional embodiment of black inner life. To borrow the popular church refrain, "the Negro Church," for Haynes, was evidence of "something on the inside, working on the outside." This distinction that he made between "the Church and the Negro Spirit" was employed by many of the movement's most celebrated figures, including Alain Locke.[42]

The inclusion of Rudolph Fisher's "Vestiges" and the omission of George Haynes's "The Church and the Negro Spirit" together provide a portrait of Alain Locke's take on the limits of black Christian modernism, in both its folk and liberal Protestant forms. However, his introductory essay in *The New Negro* reveals his religious vision to also have been shaped by this trope of church and spirit. I have already argued that Locke's vision for *The New Negro,* as witnessed in his editorial decisions, called attention away from the significance of Christianity in African American culture. Such strategies have helped to put forward an image of the New Negro Movement as primarily secularist in its orientation. However, in his foreword and in the introductory essay of *The New Negro,* Locke repeatedly employed a "grammar of spirit" to interpret the forces animating Harlem's artists. Tarrying here helps to more accurately locate him in the traditions of American religious liberalism, making powerfully clear his sense that the artistic developments taking shape among blacks were decidedly spiritual. While ample attention has been paid to Locke's intellectual heritage, less consideration has been given to his religious background.

Alain Locke was raised in the worlds of Ethical Culture and was a lifelong Episcopalian, but from the teen years of the twentieth century until his death in 1954 he maintained connections to the American Bahá'í community, including serving on their National Interracial Amity committee, writing for Bahá'í publications, and eventually making a pilgrimage to Bahá'í holy places in Haifa. Locke's belief that blacks would make a unique cultural contribution to the Western world squared well with the Bahá'í notion of "unity in diversity," wherein all cultures are esteemed contributors to the human community. In the cultural and political ambitions of the Harlem Renaissance, Locke was able to wed emerging intellectual discourses with the theological commitment to racial equality espoused by the Bahá'í faith.[43] While Locke does not explicitly invoke the Bahá'í tradition in *The New Negro,* it may very well have provided a religious framework for the racial ecumenism and spiritual cosmopolitanism espoused in his introductory essay to the volume, in which he writes, "Negro life is not only establishing new contacts and founding new centers, it is finding a new soul. There is a fresh spiritual and cultural flourishing."[44] Just as he aimed to transform "low" to "high" in the arts, Locke asserts that black people in America are undergoing an analogous transformation from "more of a myth than a man . . . more of a formula than a human being" into New Negroes. For him, this "sudden reorientation of view" amounted to no less than a "spiritual emancipation."[45]

In 1920s Harlem, Locke articulated a vision of racial ecumenism, claiming that a shared racial identity was trumping the demands of ethnic, class, and geographic differences; and he did so by deploying what I have called a "grammar of spirit."[46] "Each group has come with its own separate motives for its own special ends, but their greatest experience has been the finding of one another. . . . Harlem, I grant you, isn't typical—but it is significant, it is prophetic."[47] In light of the urban pluralism fostered by the migrations, he imagined a black diasporic community oriented by a "common consciousness," a concept at the core of what he identified as a "race-spirit."[48] According to Locke, the "new spirit . . . awake in the masses" was prophetic because it predicted that a "deep feeling of race" was becoming the "mainspring of Negro life." And he specifically identified religion (i.e., church) as being supplanted by this nascent racial spirit.[49] His article was no doubt an inaccurate assessment of the role of black churches in the North. Indeed, Locke's claim that a "race-spirit" was replacing religion confirms that *The New Negro* was produced as an act of mythmaking.[50] For while he insisted that the migrations were producing a "new spirit" among the masses, the migrants themselves more often than not interpreted their experience in the language of the Christian churches to which they belonged.[51]

Nonetheless, Locke's introduction to the book, and New Negro aesthetic debates more generally, reveal that traditional notions of religion and an emerging racial sensibility competed for black people's allegiance. Moreover, various constructions of this "race-spirit" were informed by competing definitions of religion, which accented a variety of features of black life, such as Christian churches, the experience of slavery and segregation in the United States, and West African culture. Black artists and critics were shaped by a dynamic cultural field that included debates on the changing nature of institutional religion, the social demands imposed by migration and urbanization, the emergence of a range of new intellectual discourses, and the rise of Marxism as a popular ideology and powerful organizing force in black life. But the New Negro movement also evinced an explicit concern with spirituality that was informed by (but not limited to) church history, indigenous artistic traditions, and the general question of America's national identity. Specifically, New Negro artists and intellectuals often read race through rhetorics indebted to religious liberalism.[52] Moreover, because of the crisis posed by World War I, many Americans in this historical moment looked to the arts to replace organized religion as a source of spiritual authority.[53] As such, religion was repeatedly relied upon in arguments both for and against the possibility of a unique tradition of African American art and culture. While identifying the tension between appeals to churches and a racial spirit helps to organize these arguments, the relationship of these two categories was anything but neat, and they were certainly not mutually exclusive.

Not only did New Negro artists and intellectuals negotiate these tensions between church and spirit differently, but the very meanings assigned to these respective categories were neither fixed nor agreed upon or accepted by all. In fact, black churches were simultaneously imagined to sustain uniquely racial sensibilities, support the uplift efforts of the race, frustrate black creative freedom, and provide a shared social fabric that bound blacks and whites together as simply Americans. Additionally, how the cultural work of churches was perceived often corresponded to an implicit class analysis, as large denominational churches were commonly described as "white" and storefront churches were deemed "black." Clearly, the concrete institution of "church" could be cast in any number of lights. "Spirit" could signify race, or vice versa, and "church" could carry the meaning of both categories. New Negro artists and intellectuals developed what I have called a grammar of spirit, and in doing so celebrated spirit as definitive of the New Negro's novelty. While they might draw on everything from European Romanticism to a romanticized view of Africa to do so, by framing the New Negro through this grammar of spirit they developed race itself as a religious category. As part of the rich history of American religious liberalism, they clearly synthesized racial and religious discourses in complicated ways that at times seemed outright contradictory. But, to paraphrase that infamous elegist of the Harlem Renaissance, Richard Wright, such efforts nonetheless reflected the age in which New Negroes lived, struggled, and died.[54]

NOTES

1. Henry Louis Gates Jr., "The Trope of a New Negro and the Reconstruction of the Image of the Black," *Representations*, no. 24 (autumn 1988): 129–55; and Gerald Early, *"My Soul's High Song": Countee Cullen, Voice of the Harlem Renaissance* (New York: Anchor, 1991).

2. Langston Hughes, *The Big Sea* (New York: Hill and Wang, 1940), 223.

3. George S. Schuyler, "The Negro-Art Hokum," in *The Norton Anthology of African American Literature,* ed. Nellie McKay and Henry Louis Gates Jr. (New York: Norton, 2004), 1221–23. Originally published in *The Nation,* June 16, 1926.

4. David W. Wills, "The Central Themes of American Religious History: Pluralism, Puritanism, and the Encounter of Black and White," in *African American Religion: Interpretive Essays in History and Culture,* ed. Timothy Fulop and Albert Raboteau (New York: Routledge, 1997), 7–20.

5. Langston Hughes, "The Negro Artist and the Racial Mountain," in McKay and Gates, *The Norton Anthology of African American Literature,* 1311–14. Originally published in *The Nation,* June 23, 1926.

6. Ibid., 1312.

7. Ann Douglas, *Terrible Honesty: Mongrel Manhattan in the 1920s* (New York: Farrar, Straus and Giroux, 1995).

8. Hughes, "The Negro Artist and the Racial Mountain," 1314.

9. Leigh E. Schmidt, "Introduction: The Parameters and Problematics of American Religious Liberalism," in this volume.

10. For a discussion of the life and career of Benjamin Mays, see Barbara Dianne Savage, *Your Spirits Walk beside Us: The Politics of Black Religion* (Cambridge, Mass.: Harvard University Press, 2008).

11. Giles Gunn, *The Interpretation of Otherness: Literature, Religion and the American Imagination* (New York: Oxford University Press, 1979), 13–22.

12. The three earliest works on the Harlem Renaissance movement debated its merits in light of its success or failure as a strategy for race politics. See Nathan Huggins, *The Harlem Renaissance* (New York: Oxford University Press, 1971); David Levering Lewis, *When Harlem Was in Vogue* (New York: Oxford University Press, 1979); and Houston Baker, *Modernism and the Harlem Renaissance* (Chicago: University of Chicago Press, 1987).

13. W. E. B. Du Bois, *The Souls of Black Folk* (1903; New York: Norton, 1999), 5.

14. For a seminal scholarly treatment of Fundamentalism, see George Marsden, *Fundamentalism and American Culture: The Shaping of Twentieth-Century Evangelicalism,* 2nd ed. (New York: Oxford University Press, 2006).

15. William R. Hutchison, *The Modernist Impulse in American Protestantism* (1976; Durham, N.C.: Duke University Press, 1992), 2.

16. Harry Emerson Fosdick, "Shall the Fundamentalists Win?" *Christian Work* 102 (June 10, 1922): 716–22.

17. Calvin Morris, *Reverdy C. Ransom: Black Advocate of the Social Gospel* (Lanham, Md.: University Press of America, 1990), 40–72.

18. Reverdy C. Ransom, "The New Negro," *New York Amsterdam News,* January 3, 1923, 12.

19. Interestingly, discussions of primitivism figured prominently in interpretations of African American religion. For a discussion of the significance of primitivism to the aesthetics of the Harlem Renaissance, see Lewis, *When Harlem Was in Vogue,* 224, 239, 257; Douglas, *Terrible Honesty,* 282–88, 506–507; and George Hutchinson, *Harlem Renaissance in Black and White* (Cambridge, Mass.: Belknap Press, 1995), 284–85.

20. Jon Michael Spencer, "The Black Church and the Harlem Renaissance," *African American Review* 30, no. 3 (fall 1996): 453–60.

21. Schmidt, "The Parameters and Problematics of American Religious Liberalism."

22. Gates, "The Trope of a New Negro," 136–40.

23. Leigh Eric Schmidt, *Restless Souls: The Making of American Spirituality* (New York: HarperCollins, 2006), 12.

24. For treatments of the role of spirituality in the lives of Du Bois and Thurman, see Edward Blum, *W. E. B. Du Bois: American Prophet* (Philadelphia: University of Pennsylvania Press, 2007); and Alton Pollard, *Mysticism and Social Change: The Social Witness of Howard Thurman* (New York: Peter Lang, 1992).

25. While a discussion of gender is not this paper's focus, by placing "race men" in quotes I'm calling attention to the gender dynamics of the history of black leadership, as well as citing Hazel Carby's *Race Men* (Cambridge, Mass.: Harvard University Press, 1998).

26. Barbara E. Johnson, "Response" (to Henry Louis Gates Jr. "Canon-Formation, Literary History, and the Afro-American Tradition: From the Seen to the Told"), in *Afro-*

American Literary Study in the 1990s, ed. Houston A. Baker Jr. and Patricia Redmond (Chicago: University of Chicago Press, 1989), 43.

27. My thinking here is informed by Henry Louis Gates Jr.'s notion of the "signifying difference" in black cultural forms. See Gates, *The Signifying Monkey: A Theory of African-American Literary Criticism* (New York: Oxford University Press, 1988). In the realm of religious studies, Charles Long's work remains instructive. See Long, *Significations: Signs, Symbols and Images in the Interpretation of Religion* (Aurora, Colo.: Davies Group, 1995).

28. James Weldon Johnson, *God's Trombones: Seven Negro Sermons in Verse* (1927; New York: Penguin, 2008), 1–8.

29. Alain Locke, ed., *The New Negro: Voices from the Harlem Renaissance* (New York: Simon and Schuster, 1997; originally published in 1925 as *The New Negro: An Interpretation*).

30. Alain Locke, ed., "Harlem: Mecca of the New Negro," special issue of *Survey Graphic* 6, no. 6 (March 1925).

31. Hutchinson, *Harlem Renaissance in Black and White,* 396–433.

32. Collectively entitled "The South Lingers On" in the *Survey Graphic* issue (Locke, "Mecca of the New Negro," 644–47), these stories appeared in *The New Negro* under the umbrella title "Vestiges," and the individual stories were entitled "Shepherd! Lead Us!" "Majutah," "Learnin'," and "Revival."

33. Fisher, "The South Lingers On," 644–45.

34. Ibid., 647.

35. For a definitive treatment of the core tropes and themes that define African American migration narratives, see Farah Jasmine Griffin, *"Who Set You Flowin'?" The African-American Migration Narrative* (New York: Oxford University Press, 1995).

36. Alain Locke, "The Legacy of the Ancestral Arts," in *The New Negro,* 254–55.

37. Ibid. Here I do not mean to equate "African spirit" with spirituality in Locke's thinking. Rather, my aim is to highlight how Locke framed Christianity as a Western rubric that hindered blacks from embracing an African cultural heritage. While Locke's view of aesthetics created space for this younger group of artists to take on more taboo topics (such as class and sexuality) that often offended race leaders, the new guard also took issue with the sources that Locke believed should sustain a racial spirit. Wallace Thurman satirized this generational gap in his novel *Infants of the Spring* (New York: Macaulay, 1932), in which he portrayed a youthful artist's response to an elder figure who strongly resembled Locke. In his efforts to play the role of mentor, the elder suggests that the young writer embrace his African heritage, but the strong-willed youth's response is simply "I ain't got no African spirit." For a critical discussion of Locke's understanding of the place of Africa in inspiring New Negro art, see Hutchinson, *Harlem Renaissance in Black and White,* 183–84.

38. Albert J. Raboteau, *Slave Religion: The "Invisible Institution" in the Antebellum South* (New York: Oxford University Press, 1978).

39. Gates, "The Trope of a New Negro."

40. David Wills, "An Enduring Distance: Black Americans and the Establishment," in *Between the Times: The Travail of the Protestant Establishment in America, 1900–1960,* ed. William R. Hutchinson (Cambridge: Cambridge University Press, 1989), 168–92.

41. George E. Haynes, "The Church and the Negro Spirit," in Locke, "Mecca of the New Negro," 696, 709.

42. Locke, "Introduction: The New Negro," in *The New Negro,* xxv.

43. Locke's Ethical Culture background is discussed in Hutchinson, *Harlem Renaissance*

in Black and White; and Christopher Buck, *Alain Locke: Faith and Philosophy* (Los Angeles: Kalimat, 2005). For explorations of the impact of the Bahá'í tradition on Locke's aesthetics, see Buck, *Alain Locke;* and Derek Jalal Smith, "Love's Lonely Offices: Robert Hayden and the African-American Literary Tradition" (Ph.D. diss., Northwestern University, 2004), 172–203.

44. Without crediting his source, Locke explained, "It has been aptly said, 'For all who read the signs aright, such a dramatic flowering of a new race-spirit is taking place among American Negroes.'" Locke, foreword to *The New Negro,* xxvii.

45. Locke, "The New Negro," in *The New Negro,* 3–4. Here I mean to locate the New Negro movement within current trajectories in African American religious studies. For instance, in order to interpret black cultural production as a site of religious practice, Anthony Pinn defines religion as the "quest for complex subjectivity." In this he shares much with Locke's use of a spiritual grammar to articulate his hope that New Negro identity signaled a breaking out of existing racial stereotypes to acknowledge the full complexity and humanity of black people. See Pinn, "Black Bodies in Pain and Ecstasy: Terror, Subjectivity, and the Nature of Black Religion," *Nova Religio* 7, no. 1 (July 2003): 76–89.

46. To be clear, I use the term "grammar of spirit" as a rubric to place in conversation the many ways that black artists and critics employed spirit-talk (i.e., terms such as "spirit," "spiritual," and "spirituality"); and, in the same way, to reference the range of race-terms (such as "Negro," "darker-skinned," "aframerican," and "African") they used to explain the particular racial quality of black art and culture. This "grammar of spirit" performed a wealth of work in the New Negro movement and continued to do so for black artists and intellectuals throughout the twentieth century, and it simultaneously allowed for a shared terminology and a wide spectrum of positions on both art and race.

47. Locke, "The New Negro," 6–7.

48. Leonard Harris, "Harlem Renaissance and Philosophy," in *A Companion to African-American Philosophy,* ed. Tommy L. Lott and John P. Pittman (Malden, Mass.: Blackwell, 2003), 381–85. On "imagined communities," see Benedict Anderson, *Imagined Communities: Reflections on the Origin and Spread of Nationalism* (London: Verso, 1991).

49. Locke, "The New Negro," 3, 11.

50. Gates, "The Trope of a New Negro."

51. See Milton Sernett, *Bound for the Promised Land: African American Religion and the Great Migration* (Durham, N.C.: Duke University Press, 1997); and Wallace Best, *Passionately Human, No Less Divine: Religion and Culture in Black Chicago, 1915–1952* (Princeton: Princeton University Press, 2005).

52. Hutchinson, *Harlem Renaissance in Black and White,* 1–28. My argument here is informed by George Hutchinson's effort to revise the historiography of the Harlem Renaissance by locating it in the broader context of "the American cultural field." Also, the grammar of spirit that I've identified should be understood in relationship to the history that Leigh Schmidt outlines, wherein "'spirituality' was, in fair measure, a search for a religious world larger than the British Protestant inheritance." Schmidt, *Restless Souls,* 5.

53. Gunn, *The Interpretation of Otherness;* and Douglas, *Terrible Honesty.*

54. Richard Wright, "Blueprint for Negro Writing," in McKay and Gates, *African American Literature,* 1384. Originally published in the inaugural issue of *New Challenge* in 1937.

NINE

Reading across the Divide of Faith

Liberal Protestant Book Culture and Interfaith Encounters in Print, 1921–1948

MATTHEW S. HEDSTROM

When Rabbi Joshua Loth Liebman published his number-one bestseller *Peace of Mind* in 1946, he fulfilled, in many ways, a long-standing dream of liberal Protestantism. Generations of Protestant and post-Protestant intellectuals, after all, had sought a means of disentangling the spiritual heart of Christianity from its religious carapace, and of conveying that heart in words that would move the masses. In addition to countless liberal Protestant clergy and seminary professors, public figures from Ralph Waldo Emerson and William Ellery Channing to William James and John Dewey had searched for the vocabulary to convey liberal religious sensibilities to the widest possible American audience. However, for all their cultural and intellectual influence, these earlier figures often remained esoteric as writers, incapable of finding a voice that would speak to the burgeoning mass market for religious books. In the wake of World War II, an American Jew found that voice.

Though hardly the first liberal religious bestseller, *Peace of Mind* achieved unprecedented commercial success, and soon became the best-selling non-fiction religious book of the twentieth century to that point. Some of this success surely stemmed from Liebman's popularity as a lecturer and radio preacher. Before *Peace of Mind* he was already known across New England for his weekly radio sermons broadcast from Boston's Temple Israel, which by the mid-1940s commanded audiences of between one and two million, 70 to 80 percent of whom were Christians.[1] Only thirty-nine years old when the book appeared, Liebman was quickly becoming a celebrity (his meteoric rise was tragically cut short by a fatal heart attack just two years later). Furthermore, Simon and Schuster, Liebman's publisher, advertised *Peace of Mind* widely. Still, the book's astonishing sales surpassed all expectations. The book's popularity probably stemmed, more than anything, from word-of-mouth praise, and from enthusiastic coverage in newspapers and popular magazines such as *Life, Look, Ladies' Home Journal,* and *Cosmopolitan.*[2] The *Look* piece, for example, included a digest of Liebman's chapter on grief, perhaps the portion most directly relevant to a postwar audience.[3] In venues such as these, Liebman's message reached a vast public.

Liebman was well aware of the book's success in reaching across divides of faith, and was deeply moved that his religious teachings on matters such as grief offered solace to Americans from many backgrounds. The *Boston Post* ran a story on Liebman under the banner headline "Writer of Clean Best-Seller Presents His Views," in which Liebman remarked on his place as a Jewish counselor to an overwhelmingly Christian nation. Liebman told the *Post* reporter of the survivors of a deadly fire in Georgia who requested autographed copies of his book. The reporter recounted, "His eyes moistened, his shoulders sagged a little, as he told about it the other day. 'They are Christian men and women,' he stated softly. 'Here I am, a rabbi and a Jew.'"[4] Such receptivity by Christian readers to the ministering of a rabbi was undoubtedly aided by the wartime climate of unity, and by media attention to the suffering of the Jews of Europe. The term "Judeo-Christian," as Mark Silk reminds us, began to gain meaningful usage in the 1930s in response to fascist appropriations of the label "Christian," and in the wake of the war it emerged as a part of common parlance.[5] A Jewish writer surely commanded newfound spiritual authority in the wake of the Nazi atrocities.

But the Liebman phenomenon, and indeed an entire postwar culture of tradition-crossing religious exploration, of which his book was but the most celebrated example, had deeper roots in American religious liberalism, particularly in liberal Protestant book culture. Indeed, the success of *Peace of Mind* in reaching such a large interfaith audience marks the culmination of decades of developments in the culture of religious liberalism, and indicates the way those developments played out in the religious book business. Most specifically, *Peace of Mind* testifies to the inroads made by the ecumenical movement within liberal Protestantism, a movement that institutionalized the liberal mission to decenter doctrine and focus the faith more fully on ethics and social justice. Furthermore, as David Hollinger contends elsewhere in this volume, liberal Protestantism, as a movement born in dissent against the constraints of orthodoxy, fostered habits of self-interrogation that further eroded barriers between denominations and traditions. Yet, most significantly, regardless of the precise cause and effect relationships at work, the very practice of reaching beyond the boundaries of faith and traditions eventually acquired for nineteenth- and twentieth-century liberals a life and momentum of its own. Openness to otherness was much of what it meant to be a religious liberal.

For many Americans, so often socially insulated from flesh-and-blood religious others by barriers of geography, class, ethnicity, and social convention, reading became the primary venue for such encounters. Liberal Protestant leaders had since the early 1920s engaged in a variety of commercial efforts to influence the reading choices and practices of Americans. Aware of the psychic and spiritual dislocations wrought by the Great War, the theological rancor of the Fundamentalist controversies, increasing consumerism, and the profusion of new scientific and theological knowledge, these cultural leaders sought to guide American moderns through troubled times by offering their expertise in the field of religious reading; in doing so, they created the institutions of a thriving religious middlebrow culture between the wars.[6] Religious middlebrow reading endeavors, including book clubs, book weeks, and other promotional campaigns, encouraged forms of liberal spirituality that sought to rise above narrow sectarianism with a modern faith rooted in the latest scientific and theological thinking—especially psychological and mystical thinking in the tradition of William James's *Varieties of Religious Experience.* The success of Liebman's *Peace of Mind,* a deeply Freudian and deeply Jewish book, testifies to the inroads made by liberal Protestant leaders in breaking down barriers—through ecumenism and a search for religious essences in psychology and mysticism, most especially—and to their efforts in promoting reading that reflected these sensibilities. Even more, *Peace of Mind* speaks of a critical dynamic at the heart of religious liberalism in the twentieth century: how impulses toward ecumenism, cosmopolitanism, and universalism, born in Protestant liberalism, soon became vehicles for the demise of liberal Protestantism as a hegemonic establishment. After all, by 1946 a rabbi had become the most successful ambassador in print for religious liberalism.

THE RELIGIOUS BOOK CLUB

The institution of book culture that best demonstrates liberal Protestant self-transcendence was the Religious Book Club.[7] In 1927, only a year after the founding of the Book-of-the-Month Club, the biggest names and most important institutions of the Protestant establishment opened the Religious Book Club for business. The book club quickly became a critical institution for liberal Protestant readers nationwide, and as part of its middlebrow sensibility of intellectual and spiritual uplift, the book club, from its very beginning, advocated the reading of books from outside the Christian tradition, even as it remained firmly rooted in liberal Protestant cultural and institutional life.

"BOOKS, BOOKS EVERYWHERE! Are you overwhelmed each month by the flood of new books?" screamed an advertisement for the new book club. "Have you the time and eyesight to spare to discover among these volumes the one or two which will minister to your spiritual needs? Have you not often felt that for the sake of your own self-development you ought to read more of the great books on religious life and thought?" Whether you were a pastor or lay reader, living in the country or the city, an answer was now at hand—the Religious Book Club. "Would it not be an ideal situation if you could find in your hands each month a book that is truly significant, truly inspiring, a book whose spiritual worth has been tested and endorsed by five great religious leaders?"[8]

The editorial committee—the "five great religious leaders"—came from the highest ranks of the Protestant establishment: they were the president of the Federal Council of Churches, Dr. S. Parkes Cadman; Harry Emerson Fosdick of Union Theological Seminary; the chief of chaplains of the American Expeditionary Forces during the World War; the president of the Religious Education Association; and the president of Mount Holyoke College. Dr. Cadman, in announcing the formation of the club, captured both the prevailing sense of rapid, disorienting cultural change and the business boosters' optimism. "Some gravely question whether civilization will go down in a crash," while "others give way to an acrid cynicism," he proclaimed. "The sweeping developments in science and world affairs," while not to be feared in their own right, nevertheless require "all thoughtful people to be rethinking constantly the meaning of religion for human life. Unless one does this," Cadman warned, "he is in danger of finding himself swept loose from his moorings and not knowing how to anchor himself to any spiritual realities." Fortunately, in spite of the unsettling pace of modern life and the rapid and confusing profusion of new ideas, new religious thinking offered even disillusioned moderns "faith in the reality of the unseen world" and in the "goodness and righteousness at the heart of the universe." Americans in the 1920s were awakening to the hope offered by the latest religious thinking, insisted Cadman, and the "Religious Book Club is one more indication of the extraordinary interest in religion today."[9]

Cadman's vision for the Religious Book Club placed it squarely alongside *Reader's Digest* and the Book-of-the-Month Club as a tool for earnest, intelligent, and curious readers seeking guidance in confusing times. "The undertaking was born in the conviction that hosts of men and women all over the United States are hungrily seeking for light on the great problems of religious life and thought," Cadman announced. "The Religious Book Club hopes to make a modest contribution, by drawing larger attention to the most worthwhile publications, now too much neglected because of the notoriety achieved by sensational volumes of no enduring significance." The mass market simply overwhelmed readers with hyped bestsellers and sheer consumer excess, leaving those seeking to better themselves helplessly adrift. "The man in the street, who often seems concerned only with the stock market and the World Series, is really immensely interested in religion," Cadman proclaimed. "Such people are eager to avail themselves of the best opportunity to keep abreast of the best insight and scholarship in the realm of religion."[10]

In May 1927, just months before the book club's November debut, the Rev. Joseph Fort Newton, an editor at the *Christian Century,* remarked that "we ought to have some competent guidance in the midst of the maze of books.... It is amazing to me that the Literary Guild and the Book of the Month Club have apparently excluded religious books from their lists."[11] Many others evidently felt such a need as well, as the Religious Book Club grew rapidly in membership and influence in its early years. In only its second month it could boast of members in every state and in China, Mexico, Canada, Switzerland, England, Scotland, Hawaii, and Puerto Rico (most members outside the United States appear to have been American missionaries). Total membership increased more than sixfold in the first seven months, from 980 to nearly 6500.[12] The club regularly lauded its selections for topping the bestseller list of *Church Management,* a leading ecumenical periodical.

Reports also came back of libraries, bookstores, and community reading groups using the book club's selections as guides for choosing their own stock or reading lists. The problem of proper selection was especially critical for libraries, noted one librarian, since the public librarian "represents a non-sectarian institution and therefore shuns the sectarian and highly controversial book." Marcia M. Furnas, chief of circulation of the Indianapolis Public Library, addressed this problem with the assistance of the Religious Book Club. "We have usually prepared for distribution during Lent . . . a list of the most interesting titles," she reported. "In our present list, we have used the appeal which we thought the Religious Book Club selection would have, to advertise the books." With this method of selection, she added, "a title on the list can rarely be found on the shelves even long after the list has gone out."[13] A bookstore in Concord, New Hampshire, sent its clients a card each month, on which were printed the titles selected by the book club. The bookstore "finds that if the titles are good enough to be selected by the committee of the Religious Book Club," they were likely to sell well among its regular customers.[14] The *Religious Book Club Bulletin* called attention to yet another "recent and outstanding trend" in the use of its selections—local reading clubs based on the religious book of the month. "Leading citizens in many communities," the editors noted, "are bending every effort to further the interest already aroused in this excellent method of religious education and group thinking. If you think this idea is a worthy one we shall be glad to send you further information."[15]

The membership of the Religious Book Club never grew terribly large, at least by the standards set by *Readers' Digest* or the Book-of-the-Month Club, but given its celebrity editorial committee, its close ties to the Federal Council of Churches, and its status as the first book club in the nation devoted to religious reading, it nevertheless served for decades as the model institution of religious middlebrow culture. Henry Ormal Severance of the library at the University of Missouri summarized the importance of a Religious Book Club selection when he told a gathering of professional librarians in 1932 that the club was simply "the best source of information for the most readable books" in religion.[16]

The club functioned for decades as perhaps the most influential arbiter of religious reading among mainline Protestants. Endorsement by the Religious Book Club placed a new book, thinker, or idea before the most powerful people in American religious life, especially after October 1930, when the Religious Book Club absorbed the *Christian Century* Book Service, prompting Charles Clayton Morrison, editor of the *Christian Century,* to join an expanded editorial committee.[17] The Religious Book Club serves for the cultural historian, therefore, as a reflection of the Protestant establishment's sense of itself, of its values and the role it imagined for itself in society. The 1920s and 1930s witnessed great campaigns for interreligious cooperation, such as the Interchurch World Movement, the continued expansion of the Federal Council of Churches, and historic global ecumenical gatherings at Stockholm in 1925 and Lausanne, Switzerland, in 1927, all heavily supported by American Protestants. The Religious Book Club, though an independent corporation, functioned as the de facto voice of the Federal Council in the world of books, with Samuel McCrea Cavert, general secretary of the council, serving as its founding editorial secretary, and editorial committee members S. Parkes Cadman (1924–28) and Francis McConnell (1928–32) each serving terms as president of the Federal Council. The Religious Book Club embodied the same spirit of earnest inquiry, high civic-mindedness, social tolerance, and *noblesse oblige* that animated ecumenical Protestantism. In a culture it saw as drifting farther and farther from its steadying influence, the Protestant establishment aimed to use the Religious Book Club and the power of print to define the character of the American spiritual center. Along the way, the Religious Book Club also gave the Protestant establishment's stamp of approval to the kind of interfaith encounters—openness to otherness—that characterized liberal religion in the twentieth century.

With great regularity, in fact, the editorial committee endorsed texts written by non-Protestants. Rabbi Ernest Trattner of Los Angeles wrote the first such book chosen, in April 1929: a work of Biblical scholarship called *Unraveling the Book of Books,* which addressed both the Hebrew and Christian scriptures. The first Catholic book came in June 1932: Abbe Ernest Dimnet's *What We Live By,* a book on how to be happy that soon became a national bestseller. Many more volumes from Jewish and Catholic writers appeared in the ensuing years and decades, and the breadth of the club's selections eventually reached even beyond the Judeo-Christian tradition to include Buddhist and Hindu texts, such as Swami Akhilananda's *Hindu View of Christ* and *Mental Health and Hindu Psychology.*[18] Overall, the diversity of recommended authors was quite remarkable in the decades after the club's founding. Fulton Sheen and Paul Blanshard, Billy Graham and Aldous Huxley, Martin Buber and Karl Barth, Reinhold Niebuhr and Alan Watts, C. S. Lewis and D. T. Suzuki, Kahlil Gibran and Howard Thurman, Ralph Waldo Trine and W. E. B. Du Bois, Theodore Dreiser, Paul Tillich, Kirby Page, Jacques Maritain, William F. Buckley Jr., Carl Jung, Mary Pickford, and Albert Schweitzer all had books chosen as primary or alternate selections between the late 1920s and early 1950s.

In spite of this openness—really, in some ways, precisely because of this openness—the Religious Book Club remained solidly a creature of liberal Protestantism. The openness to new ideas indicated by this remarkable roll call of recommended authors stemmed from the middlebrow project's goal of broadening horizons; it represented an effort on the part of the better educated and more sophisticated editorial committee to inform the club's members of the world beyond the safe confines of Euro-American Protestantism. The committee sometimes signaled quite clearly when it was offering such take-it-it's-good-for-you vitamins to its members. The October 1928 main selection, for example, James Bissett Pratt's *The Pilgrimage of Buddhism,* aimed to teach readers "how it feels to be a Buddhist," but the editorial committee, recognizing that Buddhism was an "alien faith" for its members, drew attention to an alternate selection for those unwilling to try Pratt's volume. Many members accepted this alternate offer, making Pratt's book the most substituted of all main selections in 1928. Pratt's work on Buddhism "was apparently too far removed from the ordinary experience of most Americans," the club's executive director commented, though he found consolation in the fact that, nevertheless, a majority of the members were "ready to explore a realm that a few years ago was almost *terra incognita.*"[19] Reading a work on Buddhism or any other "alien faith," just like reading a book offering challenging new ideas on science, history, politics, or Biblical interpretation, was intrinsic to the middlebrow agenda of reading for self-improvement. Through the reading practices of the club—through this exercise in free intellectual inquiry—the club and its members performed, in their selecting, reviewing, and reading, the liberalism of liberal Protestantism.

By the mid-1940s, the Religious Book Club began to receive very public criticism for its wide-ranging book choices. *Time* magazine, in November 1946, wryly commented, "The Religious Book Club has no Index Librorum Prohibitorum—it is proud of its lack of religious rigidity in the books it recommends to subscribers. But this month many a Christian thought the club's board of editors might well be ashamed of its religious laxity" for its choice of the Robert Graves novel *King Jesus.*[20] The editors of *Time,* in fact, might well have directed their scorn at any one of a number of choices, for in the preceding years the club had chosen as alternates Aldous Huxley's *Ends and Means* (December 1937) and *The Perennial Philosophy* (January 1946), the classic statement of the essential unity of the world's mystical traditions. The club also chose as an alternate selection in April 1944 *A Preface to Prayer,* by Huxley's friend and colleague Gerald Heard. Huxley and Heard had emigrated from England in 1937, and together with the writer Christopher Isherwood had immersed themselves in Vedantism in Southern California.[21] "Mr. Heard," the Religious Book Club's review noted, "draws in part on the Christian mystics but almost as much upon Hindu and Buddhist philosophy." In describing Heard's treatment of prayer, meditation, and "universal Consciousness," the reviewers noted, "Some of these suggestions will seem rather strange to those not familiar with mystical disciplines."[22]

The selection of Jewish and Catholic and Buddhist texts, as well as the eclectically metaphysical writings of Huxley and Heard, demonstrate the way in which the middlebrow culture and ethos of consumerism that characterized the Religious Book Club promoted a culture of reading across the divides of faith. The very mission of the Religious Book Club, in fact, was to introduce readers to new ideas, to challenge staid teachings and practices, to give readers their intellectual and spiritual vitamins. In this way, the religious middlebrow culture of the twentieth century recapitulated the story of Protestantism itself, in which print, from the beginning, has functioned both as an instrument of central authority and as the single most important force in undermining that authority. The priesthood of all believers, in the years after World War I, merged with the kingship of the consumer.

RABBI LIEBMAN AND THE CLIMATE OF WORLD WAR II

Once the United States entered the Second World War, these trends received a tremendous new impetus, for two primary reasons. First, with the war, the drive for national spiritual unity became a wartime imperative. The war was, after all, an ideological struggle, and religious unity not only served practical purposes in the armed forces and in the defense industries, but also exemplified the very notions of tolerance and liberty that were commonly understood to be at stake in the struggle with fascism. In addition, the war legitimated psychology in an unprecedented way in the eyes of the American public, and psychology provided a spiritual *lingua franca* that transcended sect and tradition with the authority of science. The mass cultural phenomenon of Liebman's bestseller, and the larger postwar culture of interfaith spiritual exploration it represents, rode this cresting wave.

The major religious reading campaign conducted during the war years was, in fact, spearheaded by an interfaith organization, the National Conference of

Christians and Jews (NCCJ). Founded in 1927 as a spin-off of the Federal Council of Churches, it quickly grew into the nation's most significant interfaith enterprise.[23] The NCCJ's reading programs, beginning with its first Religious Book Week in 1943, were massive undertakings. The NCCJ coordinated with the Council on Books in Wartime to distribute thousands of book lists, posters, and bookmarks to schools, colleges, libraries, and bookstores. Press releases and reading lists were published in major newspapers across the country. Book week promoters arranged for special displays in bookstores; museums and archives exhibited rare volumes of religious significance. Members of Congress, governors, and mayors regularly issued official proclamations of support. The chief of chaplains of the War Department also lent his support.[24] The International Ladies' Garment Workers Union supplied free kits of Religious Book Week materials to its chapters and libraries. The NCCJ also developed a variety of short radio advertisements that ran on stations across the country.[25] And librarians across the country, mostly public librarians, held readings and panel discussions, erected displays, recommended books to patrons, and even lobbied local religious and civic leaders to support the campaign.

The NCCJ printed its approved book list in pamphlet form, subdivided into four separate lists: Protestant, Catholic, and Jewish, each chosen by a distinct committee, and a final "Good-Will" list chosen by a committee of representatives from each of the traditions. The National Conference's approach to book selection drew heavily on the conventions of middlebrow culture, especially the simultaneous focus on accessibility and enrichment. Overall, the NCCJ announced, it operated with "the aim . . . to select books of interest to the average layman."[26] In general, each of the selection committees strove to find the fine balance between expert guidance and respect for middle-class busyness and autonomy.

Central to the book week project was the clear understanding that a thriving pluralistic democracy required not just better-informed citizens, but better-formed citizens, citizens with spiritual and moral as well as intellectual maturity and sophistication. The centerpiece of the Religious Book Week endeavor, therefore, was the Good-Will List, the list compiled by representatives from the three faith traditions and designed to be read by members of all. The Good-Will lists featured heavy doses of social scientific investigations of racial and religious intolerance, and histories chronicling the contributions of each group to Western civilization, especially to American democracy. In all, the Good-

Will Lists promoted a vision of religious life in the United States deeply rooted in the liberal commitments to tolerance and dispassionate scientific inquiry.

Liebman's *Peace of Mind* appeared in the midst of this massive reading campaign, still going strong the year after the war ended. It was the main selection of the Religious Book Club for May 1946, and was a featured work in the National Conference's Religious Book Week of 1947. It also, of course, came directly on the heels of the war itself, and the Second World War had prepared Americans to accept a psychological message from their religious leaders. Modern psychology had been slowly gaining acceptance among cultural elites since just after the turn of the century, but in the Second World War psychology truly became a mass endeavor. During the war Army hospitals saw one million psychiatric admissions, and yet the reach of the psychological and psychiatric professions extended far beyond the treatment of war trauma. Military officials used psychological assessment as a vital tool in the induction and training of fifteen million draftees—more than 10 percent of the national population—"most of them," according to one historian, "encountering psychological logic for the first time."[27] Throughout the war, civilians back home read reports from the front thick with psychological analysis, such as a *Newsweek* story from the Pacific describing "Guadalcanal neurosis."

The dramatic conclusions of the war in Europe and the Pacific only heightened its psychological impact. The advance of Allied forces into Nazi death camps, in April and May of 1945, forced the American public to confront unfathomable brutality in the heart of Western civilization. This shock and fear grew exponentially in August 1945, when the atomic bombings of Hiroshima and Nagasaki demonstrated a new means of mass extermination that might one day visit American soil. The threat of atomic annihilation meant, declared the psychiatrist Jules H. Masserman, "that no sentient man or woman can really find peace of mind or body."[28]

The postwar setting of Liebman's *Peace of Mind* pervades the text. "It may seem strange," Liebman began the book, "for a man to write . . . about peace of mind in this age of fierce turmoil and harrowing doubts. It may seem doubly strange for a rabbi, a representative of a people that has known so little peace, to engage in such an enterprise."[29] Though Liebman usually mentioned the war only indirectly—the terms "Second World War," "Auschwitz," "Hitler," and "Hiroshima" never appear in the text, for example—he nevertheless made clear that his goal of providing Americans the intellectual tools for achieving spiritual maturity was more important than ever in its wake. He wrote of the war most explicitly in the sections of the book that deal with death, at one point poetically acknowledging the "fathers, mothers, and young wives who remember the songs of youths whose lives were brief in duration" and "the singers of these songs, young aviators and sailors and brave young soldiers at their posts of freedom" (143). Elsewhere in the book he acknowledged the challenge that immense suffering often poses to faith, citing, in particular, a war widow who came to him doubting God's love. Liebman, the pastor, looked at the needs of his flock, and in 1946 he saw them arising most acutely from the hardships of war. Though more background than foreground in the actual text of *Peace of Mind,* the war nevertheless informs nearly every aspect of the book, and Liebman's work clearly represented a direct response to wartime fears, hopes, and anxieties.

Liebman maintained that a "healthier society must be built by healthier human beings," and so *Peace of Mind* must be understood first and foremost as a pastoral, not sociological or political, work. "I wrote 'Peace of Mind,'" he told one audience, "to provide a kind of group-answer for many troubled minds and to show how this new science [psychoanalysis] and prophetic religion can become wonderful partners in a joint program of human health and happiness."[30] His chapter on grief, the book's most pastoral section, soon became its most talked-about as well. In the extensive advertising campaign promoting the book, images often showed it open to the first page of the grief chapter, and a *Readers' Digest* excerpt featured this section extensively. The painful, unavoidable process of grieving was well understood by the mid-1940s, thanks to modern psychology, Liebman thought, yet modern Americans still too often failed to experience grief in healthy ways. "The discoveries of psychiatry . . . remind us that the ancient teachers of Judaism often had an intuitive wisdom about human nature and its needs which our more sophisticated and liberal age has forgotten" (122). The Jewish practice of sitting *shiva,* for example, with its careful ordering of time precisely for the expression of grief, had much to teach "liberal rabbis and liberal ministers alike," Liebman wrote, who "are continually committing psychological fallacies" in their desire to prevent awkward expressions of emotion. Such fear of basic human feeling revealed, Liebman argued, "the whole superficiality of modern civilization" (124).

In many instances throughout *Peace of Mind,* as in his chapter on grief, Liebman's advice took decidedly countercultural forms, as he used the discoveries of psychoanalysis to counter the prevailing assumptions of American liberalism.[31] "Modern liberal religion has shared the mood of the last several centuries—the mood of rationalism," he noted, and these reason-worshipping liberals have, in his words, "built chilly meetinghouses upon the cold pillars of abstract reason" (195). Historian of psychology Nathan Hale notes that most Americans at mid-century—those who paid any attention to Freudianism, anyway—downplayed Freud's emphasis on the darker side of human nature, but Liebman was not so quick to dismiss Freud's gloomier propositions.[32] "Man became half human while worshiping at the shrine of pure reason," he wrote. "The result was that the emotions were captured by perverts and tyrants" (196).

According to Liebman, therefore, psychology and religion together must temper the excesses of Western liberalism and teach humans again how to care for their emotions and spirits. On the very basic matter of fear, for example, Liebman stoutly observed that "man has to pay the price of fear and worry in order to be human"—a price worth paying, since "fear is often the stimulus to growth, the goad to invention" (82). The key to handling the myriad sufferings of the human condition, Liebman thought, was to accept them as part of our limited humanity, yet also to face them unflinchingly so that they do not unhealthily consume our entire existence. In the same way, Liebman observed that many are reluctant to face fears because they "are sometimes like old friends; we are afraid to give them up because they have a certain psychological premium value," and yet he warned his readers that repressed fears might lead to depression, rage, and aggression. Psychological insight can often be invaluable in confronting fear, Liebman noted, and he advised readers to take advantage of the many resources for therapy springing up across the nation, including new counseling centers in churches and synagogues. Ultimately, though, for the most fundamental kind of fear—metaphysical fear, the fear of meaninglessness and oblivion—only faith can provide succor. "Judaism and Christianity," Liebman counseled, "can teach us what we need to know—that we are rooted in the Divine and that we need not fear our destiny either here or in any world yet to come" (103). Liebman's direct acknowledgment of the evil side of human nature—an acknowledgment rooted in his Jewish identity as much as in his Freudianism—may have run against the American grain, but his ultimate admonishment to trust in God surely did not.

Liebman's reaffirmation of human depravity and irrationality must have resonated with Americans in their post-Auschwitz, post-Hiroshima moment, especially those many Americans also grieving lost loved ones. That these words came from a Jew undoubtedly added to their moral authority. Yet central to Liebman's work, right alongside the psychoanalysts and prophets, were those sunnier American giants who also reflected on matters of psyche and soul—Ralph Waldo Emerson and William James. Indeed, for all the countercultural ambition of Liebman's critique of liberal rationalism, *Peace of Mind* nevertheless exhibited a deep debt to the very American tradition of pragmatic and transcendental spirituality, foundational components of American liberalism. In his appropriation of James and Emerson, Liebman accomplished many things: he tempered the pessimism of unmitigated Freudianism, he spoke to the new reality of American global power and its attendant optimism, and he demonstrated that Jewish pastoral wisdom—which always remained central to this book—was also deeply and profoundly American.

Liebman's debt to American pragmatism was evident well before *Peace of Mind* appeared. In a March 1943 sermon broadcast from Temple Israel, called "How to Be Normal in Abnormal Times," Liebman turned to an American rather than the Viennese muse. William James, Liebman remarked,

> taught himself to rise from sick-mindedness to healthy-mindedness. . . . This courageous liberal who suffered so profoundly himself and conquered his dark and wayward spirit can help us to take as the motto of our lives those words from the prophet Ezekiel, which he loved to quote, "Son of man, stand upon thy feet and I will speak unto thee."[33]

In *Peace of Mind* as well, Liebman echoed James—"all men today need the healthy-mindedness of Judaism," he wrote (143)—and cited with great admiration as well the Seer of Concord's admonition to "give all to love . . . nothing refuse" (69).

In ways even more profound than these occasional quotes from James and Emerson suggest, however, Liebman's *Peace of Mind* exhibits a Jamesian and Emersonian ethos, including a pragmatic theology rooted in an expansive sense of American possibilities. "I believe that the time is coming," Liebman rhapsodized, when "the age-old fears of want and poverty, illness and uselessness, will be conquered by the collective conscience of democratic society" (102). Though Freud and the Hebrew scriptures did indeed lead Liebman to acknowledge the inherent evil in humanity, he nevertheless maintained that psychically and spiritually healthy Americans, armed now with knowledge from the latest science and the wisdom of the ages, would transform not only themselves, but their own society and indeed the whole of humanity. "The millions of Americans living far distant from the scenes of carnage," he admonished, must "make the achievement of moral resoluteness and courage in the presence of death a kind of ethical obligation—a determination to keep ourselves sane as the guarantors of the human future" (141). Americans must find peace of mind not just for themselves, in other words, but more critically as a kind of psychic and spiritual Marshall Plan for a war-torn world.

On this foundation of postwar optimism and American exceptionalism Liebman constructed a theological vision he grandiosely called "a new God idea for America." America's new standing in the world required a new idea of God; as Emerson had done in his day, Liebman called upon this new generation of Americans to cast off the God of their parents and grandparents and reconcile afresh with the divine. "We must be brave enough to declare that every culture must create its own God idea rather than rely on outworn tradition" (174). And so, writing to an audience flush with victory, Liebman saw in the power of American democracy a chance not only for a new world order, but for a new divine order as well: "There is a chance here in America for the creation of a new idea of God; a God reflected in the brave creations of self-reliant social pioneers; a religion based not upon surrender to submission, but on a new birth of confidence in life and in the God of life" (173). Here, layered together with Liebman's vigorous advocacy for the wisdom and healthfulness of Jewish traditions, is an equally vigorous reinterpretation of the spiritual tradition of American liberalism. At times the two strands run seamlessly together, and Liebman in fact goes so far as to find in a Jamesian God and an Emersonian democracy the very telos of Judaism itself. "God, according to Judaism, always wanted His children to become His creative partners," Liebman wrote, "but it is only in this age, when democracy has at least a chance of triumphing around the globe, that we human beings can grow truly aware of His eternal yearning for our collaboration" (174).

CONCLUSION

Just over a decade before *Peace of Mind* appeared, the social philosopher John Dewey published a small volume called *A Common Faith,* based on a series of lectures he had delivered at Yale. The book, Dewey told the Unitarian Max Otto, was written "for the people who feel inarticulately that they have the essence of the religious with them and yet are repelled by the religions and are confused."[34] Dewey contended, in fact, that the dogma of religions actually inhibited their adherents from experiencing the religious in life. "Religions now prevent," he wrote, "because of the weight of historic encumbrances, the religious quality of experience from coming to consciousness and finding the expression that is appropriate to present conditions, intellectual and moral." According to Dewey, the debasement of the religious experience by religion could not be altered—"the opposition between the religious values . . . and religions is not to be bridged"—and therefore the monopolistic claims of religions had to be dismantled.[35]

Dewey, like many other liberal intellectuals of his period, had traversed the long road from the evangelicalism of his nineteenth-century New England youth to the hard-won secular rationalism of his maturity. A critical aid in his development, and that of his entire generation, was the emergence of scientific psychology, for in psychology liberal thinkers found the tools to plumb the depths of the soul without resort to an untenable supernaturalism.[36] By embracing scientific methods and recognizing that "the universe has no other existence except as realized in consciousness," Dewey found in psychology a means to encompass all traditional theological concerns, studied now through human experience.[37] By 1934, when *A Common Faith* was published, Dewey had devised a philosophy that both defended the religious as a critical component of human experience and yet, simultaneously, asserted, "religious experience does not require special obedience to specific beliefs or institutions or, by implication, commitment to their permanence."[38] Dewey's *A Common Faith,* with its thoroughgoing rejection of supernaturalism, represents a post-Protestant and post-Christian liberalism, and demonstrates both the remarkable philosophical bravura and the inherent centrifugalism of liberal discontent in the interwar years. In an effort to find a common faith, Dewey and his intellectual comrades instead facilitated the irreparable fracturing of Protestant claims to unique cultural authority.

Dewey's brand of post-religious religious liberalism could never gain a wide following; it was too abstruse, too cool, too heady. After the war, writing in a pastoral rather than a philosophical voice, Rabbi Liebman found that following. In *Peace of Mind,* Liebman used the conventions of middlebrow print culture to offer spiritual guidance based on Jewish wisdom, Freudian psychology, and a reinterpretation of American pragmatic and Transcendentalist spiritual traditions. Remarkably, Liebman managed to continue the liberal assault on Protestant orthodoxy, as he repeatedly criticized Paul, Augustine, Luther, and Calvin as unhealthily obsessed with human beings' natural wickedness—and with repression and atonement as responses—rather than advocating a more psychologically sound focus on growth (24, 123). Yet, unlike Dewey, Liebman felt no need to abandon his faith tradition in light of scientific advances. "Liebman thrilled to the idea that Judaism's insights into human nature matched those of dynamic psychology," writes historian Andrew Heinze. "That idea fueled the Jewish polemic in *Peace of Mind*."[39] Liebman's Judaism, in other words, offered his largely Christian audience the warmth of faith along with the light of science.

The parameters of liberal religion continued to expand in the postwar years, as the kind of interfaith reading that had been the privilege of a spiritual avant-garde in preceding decades became increasingly commonplace. *Peace of Mind* was the first religious book by a non-Christian to reach a mass audience in the United States, but in the years to come ordinary liberals—middle-class Americans with high school and college educations who bought mass-market paperbacks—increasingly turned to the faith of religious others to temper the cold rationality of their own tradition. Sociologists of religion, including Wade Clark Roof in *A Generation of Seekers* and Michele Dillon and Paul Wink in their remarkable longitudinal study of religious practice, have tended to describe the practice of seeking beyond the bounds of one's natal faith as an innovation of the 1960s.[40] Yet as *Peace of Mind* and the Religious Book Club indicate, the movement toward interfaith cosmopolitanism had deep roots in the logic of liberalism. The U.S. Religious Landscape Survey, released by the Pew Forum in 2008, shocked many news pundits with the finding that nearly half of American adults have left the faith they were raised in, either by switching allegiances or by abandoning organized religion altogether. Yet Americans have always been a religiously restless people, and as the Protestant mainstream burst its banks in the middle decades of the twentieth century, new avenues for interfaith exploration emerged.

The interplay of liberal religion and book culture in the 1920s, '30s, and '40s promoted the steady advancement in American culture of psychological and mystical vocabularies, of spiritual exploration across the boundaries of religious traditions, and of practices of spiritual eclecticism. From the broadening impulses of the Religious Book Club and the mass interfaith appeal of Rabbi Liebman's *Peace of Mind,* one can readily comprehend the move in postwar popular religious culture to Jack Kerouac and George Harrison, and later to Deepak Chopra, the immense celebrity of the Dalai Lama, and the ubiquitous yoga centers, full of Jewish and Protestant and Catholic seekers, in strip malls across present-day America. Indeed, in the reading practices and consumer culture of the interwar years grew the roots of a remarkable and ongoing religious revolution, an eruption of liberal spirituality still reverberating in our increasingly open, democratic, and often chaotic religious marketplace.

NOTES

1. Andrew Heinze, *Jews and the American Soul: Human Nature in the Twentieth Century* (Princeton: Princeton University Press, 2004), 205.

2. A national survey of reading habits conducted in 1945–46 indicated that 57 percent of books read were borrowed rather than purchased, a useful reminder of the importance of libraries and social networks in book distribution, and of the need to look with some caution at sales figures as a stand-in for books actually read. Interestingly, the rate of borrowed versus purchased books was consistent across income groups. Henry C. Link and Harry Arthur Hopf, *People and Books: A Study of Reading and Book-Buying Habits* (New York: Book Manufacturers' Institute, 1946), 76–79, 158.

3. Harold B. Clemenko, "The Man behind *Peace of Mind*," *Look*, January 6, 1948, 15–17.

4. Mark Hatch, "Writer of Clean Best-Seller Presents His Views," *Boston Post*, June 22, 1947.

5. The most thorough examination of "Judeo-Christian" as both lexical formulation and social formation is Mark Silk, "Notes on the Judeo-Christian Tradition in America," *American Quarterly* 36, no. 1 (spring 1984): 65–85.

6. The utility of the term "middlebrow," and its relationship to the middle class, are highly contested among scholars of print. Though it is widely employed, most notably by Joan Shelley Rubin in *The Making of Middlebrow Culture* (Chapel Hill: University of North Carolina Press, 1992), some reject the term for its phrenological, and therefore racist, history, and its sociological imprecision. See Gordon Hutner, *What America Read: Taste, Class, and the Novel, 1920–1960* (Chapel Hill: University of North Carolina Press, 2009).

7. For an alternate analysis of the Religious Book Club, see Erin A. Smith, "The Religious Book Club: Print Culture, Consumerism, and the Spiritual Life of American Protestants between the Wars," in *Religion and the Culture of Print in Modern America*, ed. Charles L. Cohen and Paul S. Boyer (Madison: University of Wisconsin Press, 2008), 217–42.

8. Religious Book Club advertisement, Harry Emerson Fosdick Papers, Union Theological Seminary Archives, Burke Library Archives, Columbia University. Although it's not clear when or where this advertisement was published, from context it clearly appeared in the fall of 1927 or the winter of 1927–28, soon after the club debuted in November 1927.

9. "Religious Books of the Month," *Publishers' Weekly*, October 29, 1927, 1641–42.

10. Ibid.

11. J. F. Newton, "Religious Books," *Publishers' Weekly*, May 21, 1927, 2003.

12. As reported in *Religious Book Club Bulletin*, July 1928. By contrast, the Book-of-the-Month Club counted slightly more than 110,000 members in 1929, according to Rubin, *Making of Middlebrow Culture*, 96.

13. Karl Brown, "The Religious Book in the Library," *Publishers' Weekly*, February 20, 1932, 846–47.

14. "Sales Notes," *Publishers' Weekly*, February 20, 1932, 856.

15. *Religious Book Club Bulletin*, August 1928.

16. "Religious Books Round Table," *Bulletin of the American Library Association* 26, no. 8 (August 1932): 621.

17. Announced in the *Religious Book Club Bulletin,* October 1930.

18. Religious Book Club selections in November 1949 and August 1952.

19. Samuel McCrea Cavert, "What Religious Books Are Read," *Publishers' Weekly,* February 16, 1929, 752.

20. "Religious Books?" *Time,* November 4, 1946, 72.

21. On the seeker culture of Huxley, Heard, and others, see Leigh Eric Schmidt, *Restless Souls: The Making of American Spirituality* (San Francisco: HarperSanFrancisco, 2005), 227–68.

22. *Religious Book Club Bulletin,* April 1944.

23. The standard history of the National Conference of Christians and Jews is James E. Pitt, *Adventures in Brotherhood* (New York: Farrar, Straus, 1955).

24. "Religious Book Week Starts May 4," *Publishers' Weekly,* April 26, 1947, 2221–22.

25. "Factsheet: Religious Book Week, October 24–31, 1948," box 6, folder 21, National Conference of Christians and Jews Records, Social Welfare History Archive, University of Minnesota.

26. "Foreword," Religious Book Week pamphlet, National Conference of Christians and Jews, 1944, 3. The complete collection of Religious Book Week pamphlets is located in box 6, folder 21, National Conference of Christians and Jews Records, Social Welfare History Archive, University of Minnesota.

27. Eva S. Moskowitz, *In Therapy We Trust: America's Obsession with Self-Fulfillment* (Baltimore: Johns Hopkins University Press, 2001), 102, 105.

28. Quoted in Paul S. Boyer, *By the Bomb's Early Light: American Thought and Culture at the Dawn of the Atomic Age* (Chapel Hill: University of North Carolina Press, 1994), 277.

29. Joshua Loth Liebman, *Peace of Mind* (New York: Simon and Schuster, 1946), xi. Subsequent citations from this book are indicated in the text.

30. Joshua Loth Liebman, "Reconstructing the Individual for a New Society," address delivered before the Women's City Club in Boston, May 14, 1946, typescript in the Joshua Loth Liebman and Fan Loth Liebman Collection, Howard Gotlieb Archival Research Center, Boston University.

31. Liebman, for example, often quoted with approval the French Catholic philosopher Jacques Maritain, whose own rejection of scientific positivism led him first to Henri Bergson and later, after his conversion to Roman Catholicism, to the writings of St. Thomas Aquinas.

32. Nathan G. Hale Jr., *The Rise and Crisis of Psychoanalysis in the United States: Freud and the Americans, 1917–1985* (New York, Oxford University Press, 1995); Andrew Heinze, "Jews and American Popular Psychology: Reconsidering the Protestant Paradigm of Popular Thought," *Journal of American History* 88, no. 3 (December 2001): 950–78.

33. Joshua Loth Liebman, "How to Be Normal in Abnormal Times," sermon delivered Friday, March 7, 1943, typescript in the Joshua Loth Liebman and Fan Loth Liebman Collection, Howard Gotlieb Archival Research Center, Boston University.

34. Quoted in Melvin L. Rogers, *The Undiscovered Dewey: Religion, Morality, and the Ethos of Democracy* (New York: Columbia University Press, 2009), 110.

35. John Dewey, *A Common Faith* (New Haven: Yale University Press, 1934), 9, 28.

36. See Christopher G. White, *Unsettled Minds: Psychology and the American Search for Spiritual Assurance, 1830–1940* (Berkeley: University of California Press, 2008).

37. Neil Coughlan, *Young John Dewey* (Chicago: University of Chicago Press, 1975), 62.

38. Rogers, *The Undiscovered Dewey*, 111.

39. Heinze, *Jews and the American Soul*, 220.

40. Wade Clark Roof, *A Generation of Seekers: The Spiritual Journeys of the Baby-Boom Generation* (San Francisco: HarperSanFrancisco, 1993); and Michele Dillon and Paul Wink, *In the Course of a Lifetime: Tracing Religious Belief, Practice, and Change* (Berkeley: University of California Press, 2007).

TEN

The Dominant, the Damned, and the Discs

On the Metaphysical Liberalism of Charles Fort and Its Afterlives

JEFFREY J. KRIPAL

> Hydrogen is a light, odorless gas which, given enough time, changes into people.
>
> —*Anonymous, quoted in David Christian, Maps of Time*

Once upon a time, a man named Charles Fort (1874–1932) sat at a table in the New York Public Library or the British Museum in London, spending more or less every working day for a quarter century reading the entire runs of every scientific journal and newspaper he could find, in English or French. "A search for the unexplained," he explained, "became an obsession." That is something of an understatement. Here is how he joked about a typical day at the office: "I was doing one of my relatively minor jobs, which was going through the London *Daily Mail,* for a period of about twenty-five years, when I came upon this—"[1]

What he came upon was certainly unusual enough. In his quite ordinary newspapers and journals he found reports of fish, crabs, periwinkles, and other unidentified biological matter that fell from the sky and piled up in the ditches for anyone to see. Or smell. He found reports of rocks that fell slowly from the ceiling of a farmhouse, or from the sky as if materializing out of nowhere just a few feet up. He found orphaned boys and servant girls who had the curious habit of psychically setting thing on fire, seemingly unconsciously and almost always in broad daylight (so no one, he reasoned, would get hurt). He found objects, animals, even human beings appearing out of nowhere on a cold city street or in the room of a house, apparently "teleported," as he put it, from somewhere else. That word that he coined, "teleportation," would have a long history in later science fiction.

Perhaps most of all, though, Fort found numerous reports of what he called "super-constructions" in the sky. These were essentially spaceships, floating over cities around the world, shining searchlights, baffling witnesses, and otherwise making a mess of the rational order: "One of them about the size of Brooklyn, I should say, offhand. And one or more of them wheel-shaped things a goodly number of square miles in area" (BD 136). These super-constructions float through all of Fort's texts, giving his implied narrative, which he seldom makes explicit, a certain ominous quality.

Within just four pages of his 1923 *New Lands,* for example (468–71), covering only a few months of newspaper clippings, we encounter reports from Oxford and London, England, as well as Nymegen, Holland. But the real action appears to be in the United States, at least in 1897, with what came to be known as the "great airship wave." In these four pages on this year, Fort invokes reports from Kansas City, Chicago, Evanston, New York, Omaha, Dodge City, Brule (in Wisconsin), Sistersville (in West Virginia), and Lake Erie (a "queer-looking boat" rose up out of the waters there [NL 470]). The states of Illinois, Indiana, Missouri, Iowa, and Wisconsin all appear as well, but Texas holds a special place in whatever news Fort is tracking. Reports come in from Benton, Fort Worth, Dallas, Marshall, Ennis, and Beaumont. Here's how the *New York Sun* described the airship seen over Texas: "It was shaped like a Mexican cigar, large in the middle, and small at both ends, with great wings, resembling those of an enormous butterfly. It was brilliantly illuminated by the rays of two great searchlights, and was sailing in a southeasterly direction, with the velocity of the wind, presenting a magnificent appearance" (NL 469).

Geezus.

The possible implications of such impossible stories hardly escape Fort, who had a keenly critical mind and a penchant for questioning pretty much everything. Something of a postcolonial theorist before his time, he invokes the night of October 12, 1492, and the image of Native Americans gazing out over the ocean waters at lights they had never seen before. The earlier inhabitants of the New World, of course, would have explained the unfamiliar in terms of the familiar. Their wise men, Fort explains, would have concluded something along these lines: "So there are three big, old, dead things out in the water—" (NL 471). Not exactly an accurate conclusion, and eventually devastating in its misplaced trust in the predictability of things.

For Fort, what the newspaper stories imply is that we are *all* natives now, and we can no more fathom the intentions and powers of the airships than the American natives could fathom the intentions and powers of the colonial ones. He thus speculates about a certain galactic colonialism going on and wonders whether we are not someone else's farm (this, he points out, may be why they show so little interest in openly communicating with us). He returns to the colonization of the Americas again and again, always to question the wisdom of the familiar and mock the certainty of our own wise men called "scientists":

> I am simply pointing out everybody's inability seriously to spend time upon something, which, according to his preconceptions, is nonsense. Scientists, in matter of our data, have been like somebody in Europe, before the year 1492, hearing stories of lands to the west, going out on the ocean for an hour or so, in a row-boat, and then saying, whether exactly in these words, or not: "Oh, hell! There ain't no America." (LO 625)

Not that he was only interested in such super-constructions. These held a special place in his prose and did special philosophical work for him, as we shall see, but they were hardly the only objects of his eccentric attention.

There was, however, at least one rule guiding his avid search for such reports. Fort chose an arbitrary but admittedly even date of 1800 as the place to end his reading odyssey. He had to stop somewhere. Besides, he reasoned, if the events that fascinated him so were not happening in the modern world, well then, they were of only historical interest. He was not after those ancient mysteries of orthodox religion, now lost to us by thousands of years of political history and cultural reshaping. Even in the modern world, he was only marginally interested in those rare visions glimpsed in fleeting dreams or darkened séance rooms. Oh, he read and thought about such things, a great deal really, mostly as he worked his way through all the issues of the *Journal of the Society for Psychical Research* that he faithfully read in the library. By his own confession, he accepted the reality of psychical phenomena, and he often used the word "occult" to describe his own materials. But he was deeply suspicious of all talk of (or with) departed spirits, and he wanted no part of Spiritualism, which he associated with cranks and Fundamentalism.[2] In the end, his were mostly "sunlight mysteries," as he called them—strange things that come, usually unbidden, to ordinary people in ordinary circumstances in small towns and on city streets, and then show up in the papers, almost always in confused, baffled, and distorted ways (WT 916). Things like giant Mexican cigars with butterfly wings and searchlights floating over Beaumont, Texas, and then showing up in a New York newspaper.

It is precisely this journalistic ordinariness that makes what I want to call Fort's "metaphysical liberalism" so extraordinary. By this phrase, I have something very specific in mind. Fort's reading, after all, was finally neither random nor unfocused. He wore glasses to focus his physical eyes. Similarly, he adopted a quite specific metaphysical system in order to focus his texts and bring their riotous colors and seemingly unorganized bizarreness into a kind of laser-like beam whose burning brightness many readers since have experienced as a veritable "zapping." This metaphysical focus was shaped by a dialectical monism in which nothing was really separate from anything else and opposites were forever changing into one another. Logically speaking, such a monism expresses a world in which it is not so much that nothing is supernatural, but rather that *everything* is (LO 655). This is a world, as our opening epigraph has it, in which hydrogen changes into people, and people, of course, change back into hydrogen.

It is worth repeating, and then underlining: Fort's metaphysical system does not draw on spiritual flights of ecstasy or unions with beloved deities, much less historically distant prophetic revelations or some singular oriental enlightenment. Part of this is because his arbitrary boundary at the year 1800 efficiently prevented him from privileging what had always been privileged, that is, the ancient world and the Bible. As a result, there is little, if anything, that is specifically "Protestant" about his thought, or "Catholic" for that matter, much less "Buddhist," or "Hindu," or anything else. It is true that his family were Dutch immigrants, and probably Dutch Calvinists, but it is difficult to make too much of this. If one, for example, visits the family grave plot north of Albany, New York, one will see a Greek-looking goddess holding a wreath perched atop a central pillar, but not a single Christian cross or biblical passage. The individual gravestones, including Charles's, are decorated with an abstract wreath design—nothing more.

Having said that, it is also true that the psychical and paranormal lineages in which he wrote were indeed somehow "Protestant" in at least one important sense, namely, that the psychical research tradition of the nineteenth century from which the category of the paranormal gradually emerged at the turn of the twentieth—mostly in England, around the London Society for Psychical Research (founded in 1882), but also in France—was dominated by Protestant-born intellectuals struggling with their faith in the aftermath of Darwin and *The Origin of Species*. Indeed, I can think of no English-speaking Catholic student of this material, at least until the British Jesuit Fr. Herbert Thurston in the 1930s and '40s, who mined, at some risk to his own career, Catholic hagiography for data on "the physical phenomena of mysticism."[3]

This point is worth dwelling on, if only for a moment. Despite a fantastically rich hagiographic and mystical vein—with reports of figures like Teresa of Avila levitating off the floor and Joseph of Cupertino flying to the tops of trees—Catholic theology has long been suspicious of what we now call psychical phenomena, unless, of course, they are linked to and disciplined by correct doctrine and the theological virtues. Indeed, it is precisely this theological and moral disciplining of the paranormal that is at issue in many cases of Catholic sanctity and sainthood.

As a means of demonstrating the obvious here, consider the linked phenomenologies of stigmata phenomena and birthmarks suggestive of reincarnation. When the paranormal takes on traditional forms, when it literally writes itself into the flesh in signs that are recognizably orthodox, it can be accepted, or at least contemplated. But what of similar psychosomatic transformations that signal a completely different theology or worldview? For example, what of birthmarks on babies that strongly suggest some kind of reincarnation imprint or memory of a previous life's violent end? It is one thing to bleed from the palms and the forehead on Good Friday in Chicago. It is quite another to be born with entry and exit bullet scars and haunting memories of being shot by your brother in Charlottesville.[4] Obviously, such phenomena are dangerous subjects for anyone attached to a particular belief system. Little wonder, then, that Roman Catholicism and the Protestant churches have generally and effectively "demonized" occult and paranormal phenomena by linking them to the deviances of heterodoxy, heresy, and witchcraft, if not the Devil himself. If one is attached to a particular dogmatic system, *any* system, these are indeed devilish phenomena. They mess up pretty much everything, including every academic materialism, relativism, and contextualism.

In truth, it is exceptionally difficult to locate Charles Fort within standard academic categories and practices, partly because historians of American religion have more or less (mostly more) ignored him in their mappings, partly because Fort himself is deeply suspicious of all systems and hence of all locations. He certainly does not want to be located. But it is also true that he had identifiable ideas, and that these ideas were understood and picked up by different people after him and employed in some rather specific ways. Indeed, Fort had a rather massive influence on later heterodox religious thought, particularly as it found expression in the early and later histories of pulp fiction, science fiction, the French and American countercultures of the 1960s, and various UFO religions and New Age metaphysical systems.

In the light of such a legacy, Fort is probably best located in that broad band of metaphysical religion that historians of American religion such as Catherine Albanese and Leigh Eric Schmidt have begun to map for us. We may have to broaden and detail the map, of course (and make it way, way weirder), but he does seem to fit here. Sort of.

Not only was Fort suspicious of locations and systems. He was also suspicious of explanations. Technically speaking, Fort never explained anything. Indeed, he did not even accept the epistemology of what he called "explanation," which he equated with the current reign of Science. Nor, by the way, did he accept the epistemology of what he called "belief," which he equated with the previous reign of Religion. What he *did* accept, in the coming future reign of Intermediatism (or Witchcraft), was the epistemology of what he called "expression." For Charles Fort, we are all essentially caught in the script of a play. The only way out is to see that everything we assume to be real is more of an expression than an objective reality, more of an act than a fact. The world is ruled by meaning and sign, not matter and cause; by story and plot, not law and mathematics. It is this claim that makes Fort's thought a species of metaphysical liberalism. After all, it is not that he simply conceived the social world, the political scene, or a particular religious system or moral code as open to change and reconstruction in the light of new experience and new data. That would be easy, and common, enough. Rather, it is that he conceived *reality itself* to be fluid, plastic, and ultimately free.

This metaphysical liberalism often expressed itself negatively, that is, through some fairly radical criticisms of previous systems of explanation and ordering. What he was best at was showing, often hilariously, how previous religious and scientific explanations fail miserably to explain the existing data, really how they *ignore* or *deny* the data. Religion and Science were his two great enemies here. He borrowed deeply from both, but he then tried to move beyond belief and beyond reason into a third space that I think we can well call "liberal," though I doubt we can call it "religious," "mystical," or "spiritual." "Occult" or "metaphysical" were his preferred terms, but he also used "paranormal."

Whatever we choose to call it, the fact remains that academic mappings of modern forms of religious liberalism have generally failed to take Fort and his followers into account. Why? Part of the answer, I would suggest, is epistemological. Simply put, paranormal phenomena violate the subject-object split that created the humanities and the sciences in the first place. But mind and matter meet and merge here in ways that simply cannot be fit into the neat manner in which our universities are divided up into departments and divisions. With our present epistemologies and methods, what can we do, really, with a table that taps out messages? All we can do is smile and sneer. All we can do, that is, is call it a fraud. But the table, rudely ignoring our name-calling, goes on tapping away anyway, and sometimes—God forbid—to academics themselves.[5] That is certainly a bit uncomfortable.

Part of the answer also lies in our intellectual practices, and more specifically in our penchant for specialization. Significantly, Fort was particularly hard on what he called the "evil of specialization." He felt that specialization prevents us from seeing the hidden connections between different domains of knowledge. "He knew," his biographer Damon Knight explains, "that we can only see what we are looking for, and he was tantalized by the feeling that there are unsuspected patterns all around us, which would be visible if we only knew where and how to look."[6] Within this kind of global scanning, specialization appears as a type of tunnel vision that effectively blinds people from seeing the hidden patterns of the Big Picture, which emerge only when we perceive the relations or coincidences between material things and mental events (NL 446–47).

Fair enough. So Charles Fort did not think like most professional intellectuals. So how did he think? In a profoundly non-specializing way, we could say that Charles Fort was first and foremost a *collector,* a collector of anomalies reported in his library sources that were inevitably offered forced or bogus explanations by the official intellectuals of the time, or, more likely, simply ignored and passed over until the next day's distractions called "news." He would collect tens of thousands of notes on such anomalies. At one point in 1931, he mentions having written sixty thousand of them (LO 576). Earlier in life, he had burned another twenty-five thousand—before, he explained, they burned him (living in a cramped tenement apartment with tens of thousands of paper scraps is not the safest thing to do). Those he collected again he organized into hundreds of alphabetically arranged shoeboxes in his Bronx apartment.

Charles Fort did not just collect anything, though. He collected *coincidences,* coincidences that he felt—he could not quite say why—signaled some larger, and perhaps literally cosmic, truth. He was on the intuitive trail of, well, *something.* Here is how he put it:

> Sometimes I am a collector of data, and only a collector, and am likely to be gross and miserly, piling up notes, pleased with merely numerically adding to my store. Other times I have joys, when unexpectedly coming upon an outrageous story that may not be altogether a lie, or upon a macabre little thing that may make some reviewer of my more or less good works mad. But always there is present a feeling of unexplained relations of events that I note; and it is this far-away, haunting, or often taunting, awareness, or suspicion, that keeps me piling on— (WT 862)

This is why, beginning in 1906, he began his famous reading practice. Charles generally spent his mornings working at home and his afternoons in the library. He and his wife, Anna, would then often go to the movies in the evenings. This was a nightly ritual that appeared to have only reinforced Charles's most basic conviction that "the imagined and the physical" were deeply intertwined, if not actually identical on some level: "According to some viewpoints," he wrote on this latter point, "I might as well try to think of a villain, in a moving picture, suddenly jumping from the screen, and attacking people in the audience. I haven't tried that, yet" (WT 1010). Which implies, of course, that he had tried other things, or that he might still try this one.

Charles's literary talents early on attracted the attention—stunned worship, really—of one of the era's most respected novelists, Theodore Dreiser, who once told Fort in a letter that he was "the most fascinating literary figure since Poe."[7] Dreiser was not exaggerating. And Dreiser's fascination was echoed by other literary figures, including Booth Tarkington, who described Fort's pen as a "brush dipped in earthquake and eclipse."[8] Buckminster Fuller, who wrote the introduction to Knight's biography; and numerous science fiction writers, who borrowed generously from Fort's data for their own fictional purposes. Indeed, in many cases, later science fiction reads like a series of imaginative riffs on Charles Fort.

But it was Dreiser who published Fort's early humorous short stories and helped him publish his first and most famous "non-fiction" book, *The Book of the Damned,* by basically threatening his own publisher: if he didn't publish Fort, he wouldn't publish Dreiser. Despite his devoted and admiring literary following, none of Fort's books were bestsellers during his lifetime. But they all had fascinating and incredibly productive afterlives, mostly through the subcultures of science fiction and the American, British, and French countercultures. Fort died in 1932 after publishing one novel, *The Outcast Manufacturers* (1909), and four really weird books: *The Book of the Damned* (1919), *New Lands* (1923), *Lo!* (1931), and *Wild Talents* (1932). Advance copies of the last book, on the subject of anomalous human beings and their superpowers or "wild talents," were delivered to Fort as he faded away on his deathbed. He was too weak to hold them in his hands.

It is not, however, quite true to say that *The Book of the Damned* was Fort's first work of non-fiction. To begin with, in 1901 Fort had already completed a draft of a youthful autobiography entitled *Many Parts,* only a portion of which has survived. The title is from Shakespeare's famous lines in *As You Like It:* "All the world's a stage, and all the men and women merely players. They have their exits and their entrances, and one man in his time plays many parts."[9] As with Shakespeare's collapsing of the stage into life and life into the stage, Fort denied in principle any stable distinction between fiction and reality. He especially hated how books were divided up as "fiction" and "non-fiction" in the libraries. "I cannot say that truth is stranger than fiction, because I have never had acquaintance with either." There is only "the hyphenated state of truth-fiction." Nor, as we have already noted, did Fort believe in any stable distinction between the imagined and the physical. The imagination, properly understood in its true scope, is nearly omnipotent in Fort's worldview. Indeed, it is so powerful (and potentially perverse) that Fort suggested in more than one context that we are all living in someone else's novel, which was not even a particularly good one. Life really *is* a stage (WT 863, 864, 1010; BD 79).

Fort was quite serious about the imaginal nature of reality. Hence his two earlier and now lost (or destroyed) book manuscripts, *X* and *Y* (1915–16). Jim Steinmeyer has reconstructed the lost manuscript of *X,* largely through Fort's correspondence with Dreiser in a three-page letter dated May 1, 1915, and it appears that *X* was a more confessional version of the worldview that later would be more agnostically presented in *The Book of the Damned.* Dreiser was stunned by its thesis, which involved the idea that all of earthly biological and social reality is a kind of movie (we would now say "virtual world") from the rays of some unknown alien super-consciousness. Then he had a dream that seemed to confirm the thesis, and he summed up Fort's *X* this way: "The whole thing may have been originated, somehow, somewhere else, worked out beforehand, as it were, in the brain of something or somebody and is now being orthogenetically or chemically directed from somewhere; being thrown on a screen, as it were, like a moving-picture, and we mere dot pictures, mere cell-built-up pictures, like the movies, only we are telegraphed or teleautographed from somewhere else."[10] In short, *we* are the shadows of Someone Else's Platonic cave. Fort would also later suggest that we are the object of other beings' occult experiences, that we constitute their Arcanum, heaven, or afterlife.

Fort would also back down from his thesis that there was a something, an "X," emanating from Mars, which was commonly believed to be inhabited, largely as a result of Percival Lowell's observations from 1906 to 1909 that the planet seemed to show canals. (H. G. Wells was no doubt also a factor here.) The idea that Mars bore life was by no means a new one, and it was shared by many well-known and respected astronomers.[11] Astronomers aside, Steinmeyer notes that Fort's Martian hypothesis "sounds like science fiction." Indeed it does.[12]

But if the world can be thought of as a Martian fiction, it is a fiction out of which we can, conceivably at least, awaken and "step off the page," much like Fort's imagined moving-picture villain stepping out of the movie screen. Fort, it turns out, is not finally bound to a mechanistic Nirvana. Hence his fascinating reference to *X* in a reply to the charge that his writings were inconsistent. "In 'X,'" he mused, "I have pointed out that, though there's nothing wrong with me personally, I am a delusion in super-imagination, and inconsistency must therefore be expected from me—but if I'm so rational as to be aware of my irrationality? Why, then, I have glimmers of the awakening and awareness of super-imagination."[13]

Collection, comparison, and systematization were not simple or banal activities for Charles Fort. They contained awesome power. They constituted a kind of occult meta-practice that could lead, at any moment, to a sudden awakening to just such "super-imagination." Hence Fort's obscure but telling claim that "systematization of pseudo-data is approximation to realness or final awakening" (BD 22). He at least collected, classified, and compared to wake up, to become more fully conscious of reality-as-fiction. He at least was ready to step out of the movie screen.

READING FORT: COMPARISON, HISTORY, AND SELF

How, then, to read Charles Fort, and to read him as an exponent of what I have called a metaphysical liberalism? I want to highlight just three Fortean themes here: his comparative method, his philosophy of history, and the status of the individual in his worldview. I will then treat Fort's legacy in the twentieth century, which is where this liberalism is most richly played out, and end with some thoughts on the continuing relevance of his mischief.

Methodologically speaking, Fort was a kind of occult comparativist who understood perfectly well that knowledge and theory arise from how one collects and classifies data. "By *explanation,*" he pointed out succinctly, "I mean *organization*" (LO 551). But he also knew that the data themselves are never innocent, that much depends upon *which* data the comparativist chooses and selects out of the weltering mass of stuff that is the world of information. Fort's most basic comparative principle worked from the conviction that one should privilege "the data of the damned," that is, all that stuff that had been rejected, facilely explained away, or literally demonized by the two most recent reigning orders of knowledge, Religion and Science.

What this implied, indeed required, was that Fort's thought become inherently and structurally transgressive. If Truth lies outside every system, if every system is only an approximation or partial actualization of this Truth, then a better approach to the Truth can only be had by going outside the present system, that is, by transgressing the proper order of things. "I do not know how to find out anything new," he thus pointed out with faultless logic, "without being offensive" (LO 547). Still within this same offensive logic, Fort is deeply suspicious of any socially sanctioned truth, particularly any such truth that smells of piety or humility. "I am suspicious of all this wisdom," he writes, "because it makes for humility and contentment. These thoughts are community-thoughts, and tend to suppress the individual." Such "wisdom" is nothing but another reduction of the human being to a machine, to a cog in a social wheel. He thus sees such community-thoughts as "corollaries of mechanistic philosophy, and I represent a revolt against mechanistic philosophy" (WT 975).

One of the clearest and most dramatic expressions of this transgressive aspect of Fort's thought occurs in the very first lines of *The Book of the Damned.* These are worth quoting at length, as they introduce Fort's prophetic voice to the world and set down some of the basic terms of his own system. Here is how he begins in 1919, in what is essentially an oracular voice:

> A procession of the damned.
> By the damned, I mean the excluded.
> We shall have a procession of data that Science has excluded.
> Battalions of the accursed, captained by pallid data that I have exhumed, will march. You'll read them—or they'll march.

He goes on to define what he means by "the damned" and comments on the radical relativism of human history, where worlds replace worlds that have replaced other worlds:

> So, by the damned, I mean the excluded.
> But by the excluded I mean that which will some day be the excluding.
> Or everything that is, won't be.
> And everything that isn't, will be—
> But, of course, will be that which won't be—

He then becomes still more abstract as he introduces his dialectical monism through the classical philosophical terms of existence and being:

> It is our expression that the flux between that which isn't and that which won't be, or the state that is commonly and absurdly called "existence," is a rhythm of heavens and hells: that the damned won't stay damned; that salvation only precedes perdition. . . .
>
> It is our expression that nothing can attempt to be, except by attempting to exclude something else: that that which is commonly called "being" is a state that is wrought more or less definitely proportionately to the appearance of positive difference between that which is included and that which is excluded.

At this point, he sounds remarkably like Derrida on difference, or Foucault on the *episteme* as a temporary and relative order of knowledge and power. There are clear resonances here. But then one realizes that these resonances are essentially photographic negatives of one another, that Fort is more like the opposite of Derrida and Foucault, acknowledging both Difference and Sameness but finally privileging Sameness:

> But it is our expression that there are no positive differences: that all things are like a mouse and a bug in the heart of a cheese. Mouse and a bug: no two things could seem more unlike. They're there a week, or they stay there a month: both are then only transmutations of cheese. I think we're all bugs and mice, and are only different expressions of an all-inclusive cheese. (BD 3–4)

Everything genuinely Fortean spins out of this irreverent monism. Every opinion, which is also every mistake, Fort insists, is a result of privileging some aspect of this Oneness over every other aspect. Error results when parts attempt to be wholes, when the bug imagines itself as fundamentally different from the mouse in the same chunk of cheese. "To have any opinion," Fort opined, "one must overlook something" (LO 559).

What Fort is most interested in is how much of the world a system must exclude to form an opinion. He was deeply bothered by how easy it is to disregard or damn a datum. Early in his first book, he introduces a metaphor that will help him explain this strange feature of human beings. It will come to play a more and more central role in his writings. Enter—or swim in—the metaphor of the deep-sea fishes:

> I'd suggest, to start with, that we'd put ourselves in the place of deep-sea fishes:
> How would they account for the fall of animal-matter from above?
> They wouldn't try—
> Or it's easy enough to think of most of us as deep-sea fishes of a kind. (BD 26)

And what, he asks, would such a deep-sea fish learn if it bumped into a steel plate that had fallen from some wrecked ship above? Probably nothing at all. "Sometimes I'm a deep-sea fish with a sore nose" (BD 162). Fort calls the metaphysical ocean "above" us—whatever that means—the Super-Sargasso Sea. It will become a kind of metaphorical space in which he will gather all of his damned data until the waters around the swimming reader are filled with floating and falling debris, "material for the deep-sea fishes to disregard" (BD 119).

It is not simply a matter of stuff randomly falling through the texts, though. Fort is not so simple or so naïve. He has a specific means for locating the steel plates of the ship in the deep-sea waters of his data. He knows exactly what it feels like to bump his fishy nose up against something strange and steely. That feeling, that bump, is called a "coincidence." Here is a typical bump on the nose, this one involving the slow falling of stones from the sky or from a specific point in the ceiling of a house, the classic stuff of poltergeist phenomena:

> Somebody in France, in the year 1842, told of slow-moving stones, and somebody in Sumatra, in the year 1903, told of slow-moving stones. It would be strange, if two liars should invent this circumstance—
>
> And that is where I get, when I reason. (LO 566)

It is easy to disregard one such report. Merely an "anecdote," as the scientists like to say in their pseudo-explanation. But two now? Then three? Then, with enough time in the library, three dozen from different parts of the world and in different decades and centuries? Just how long can we go on like this until we admit that this is real data, and that we haven't the slightest idea where to put it? How long until we see the ship's steel plate bumping up against our bruised noses?

Colin Bennett has read Fort through the prism of postmodern theory. The analogies between Fortean philosophy and contemporary postmodernism are indeed significant and extensive, if not actually astonishing. But it also must be said immediately and up front that Fort is finally far too much for most postmodern writers. Whereas the latter almost always lack a metaphysical base, indeed consciously and vociferously eschew such a thing as the Great Sin, Fort clearly possessed a developed and consistent monist metaphysics through which he read, and into which he subsumed, the "differences" and "gaps" of his anomalous material. Moreover, he fully acknowledged these metaphysical commitments. He sinned boldly.

He may, then, have agreed with, indeed presciently foreseen, the postmodern condition and its deconstructionist penchant for seeing reality as a language game in which every term or concept refers only to other terms and concepts within one huge self-referential web of local meaning, which never arrives. He may have also recognized that every such linguistic system of thought is without a final base or stable standard, that it is more or less arbitrary, that it must exclude or "damn" data to exist at all, but that the damned always return to haunt it and, finally, to collapse it. "All organizations of thought," he wrote, "must be baseless in themselves, and of course be not final, or they could not change, and must bear within themselves those elements that will, in time, destroy them" (NL 368). He may have also recognized, acutely, that every form of knowing is an "era knowing," bound to the concepts and assumptions of the culture and clime. "There is no intelligence except era-intelligence" (LO 428). "My own acceptance," he explained further, "is that ours is an organic existence, and that our thoughts are the phenomena of its eras, quite as its rocks and trees and forms of life are; and that I think as I think, mostly, though not absolutely, because of the era I am living in" (LO 604–605).

But it is precisely that "though not absolutely" that haunts us here. For Fort also suggested that all of these quasi-systems, with their quasi-standards and false senses of completeness, are struggling within a "oneness of allness" or "Continuity" (BD 239). There is thus—and he italicizes this—"*the underlying oneness in all confusions*" (LO 542). By means of the inclusion of ever greater swaths of data, human thought *is* developing for Fort, and this toward what he called "the gossip of angels," that "final utterance [that] would include all things" (BD 249). This final utterance, however, must be "unutterable" in our "quasi-existence, where to think is to include but also to exclude, or be not final" (BD 249).

To think at all, for Fort, is "to localize," to mistake the part for the Whole. But, like the self-described metaphysician that he was, he sought to think into infinity. He even hinted that this infinite Truth (which, yes, he capitalized) could be experienced—or, more accurately, *identified with:* "A seeker of Truth. He will never find it. But the dimmest of possibilities—he may himself become the Truth" (BD 178, 14).

There is, however, one feature of Fort's thought that marks it as distinctly postmodern, that is, his penchant for thinking of intellectual eras in threes. It is this tripartite model of history, along with his 1800 rule, that finally structures his metaphysical liberalism. As introduced above, Fort's entire system works through the neat dialectical progression of three Dominants or Eras: 1) the Old Dominant of Religion, which he associates with the epistemology of *belief* and the professionalism of priests; 2) the present Dominant of Materialistic Science, which he associates with the epistemology of *explanation* and the professionalism of scientists; and 3) the New Dominant of Intermediatism, which he associates with the epistemology of *expression* or *acceptance* and the professionalism of a new brand of individuating wizards and witches. Whereas the first two Dominants work from the systemic principle of Exclusionism, that is, they must exclude data to survive as stable systems, the New Dominant works from the systemic principle of Inclusionism (what he also calls his "philosophy of the hyphen"), that is, it builds an open-ended system and preserves it through the confusing inclusion of data, theoretically *all* data, however bizarre and offending, toward some future awakening.

The gossip of angels.

Fort is brutal on both religion and science, although he makes some crucial concessions to each that end up defining the dialectical contours of his own third system, which is at once religious and scientific, if in highly untraditional ways. Fort, for example, is especially friendly to quantum mechanics, although he was worried about this affection in his usual humorous fashion. Alas, he could hardly find a physicist to argue with any longer, so close were their ideas now to his own pet theories, that is, to "an attempted systematization of the principles of magic." Why, this stuff could "make reasonable almost any miracle," he concluded, like "entering a closed room without penetrating a wall, or jumping from one place to another without traversing the space between" (WT 905). Isn't that exactly what electrons do in the new science?

Which is not to say that Fort was generally friendly to science, or religion. Here is a typical passage on his two great enemies:

> Or my own acceptance that we do not really think at all; that we correlate around super-magnets that I call Dominants—a Spiritual Dominant in one age, and responsibly to it up spring monasteries, and the stake and the cross are its symbols; a Materi-

> alist Dominant, and up spring laboratories, and microscopes and telescopes and crucibles are its ikons—that we're nothing but iron filings relatively to a succession of magnets that displace preceding magnets. (BD 241)

Fort was very serious about our near inability to think freely. Hence his humorous rewriting of Descartes' *Cogito ergo sum*. Here is Fort's version: "I do not think. I have never had a thought. Therefore something or another" (WT 941). Such philosophical humor hides a quite sophisticated notion of mental processes. We do not think. We are thought, particularly by our religious beliefs and scientific reasons.

What the two Dominants of religion and science share is their Exclusionism, a basic intolerance that inevitably leads to real-world violence. But the Old Dominant of religion holds a special place in Fort's rhetoric. It is *the* model of intolerance, delusion, and Exclusionism. Deeply immersed in psychical research and its metaphors, Fort often preferred to see the power of religion as a psychological one akin to hypnosis (BD 12). Religion is also a lie and a laugh:

> Suppose a church had ever been established upon foundations not composed of the stuff of lies and frauds and latent laughter. Let the churchman stand upon other than gibberish and mummery, and there'd be nothing by which to laugh away his despotisms. . . . Then we accept that the solemnest of our existence's phenomena are of a wobbling tissue—rocks of ages that are only hardened muds—or that a lie is the heart of everything sacred— (LO 730)

The present Dominant of Science has taken over and copied the Old Dominant of Religion. The priests have changed their vestments for lab coats and exchanged religious dogmas for scientific ones. Thus Fort can write of a "scientific priestcraft" who shout "Thou shalt not!" in their "frozen textbooks." The spirit and structure of their arguments retain the same, essentially religious dimension. As do everyone else's, for that matter: "Every conversation is a conflict of missionaries," he writes, "each trying to convert the other, to assimilate, or to make the other similar to himself" (NL 315; BD 171). But this does not mean that science has made no advances on religion. It most definitely has. Or that we should stop proselytizing one another. How else could we make any progress?

One way to get at the provocations of Fort's metaphysics is to locate the status of free will within it. Is there, *can* there be such a thing in such a system? By "free will," Fort means Independence, that is, an existence that does not merge away into something else. Because there is a whole spectrum of things that do and do not merge away, there is also a whole spectrum of freedoms for Fort, depending upon how "real" something has become, how much existence it has managed to carve out in the sea of the Universal. This, it turns out, is true of everything within human culture, and not just internal moral or intentional states. All "imaginings that materialize into machines or statutes, buildings, dollars, paintings or books in paper and ink are graduations from unrealness to realness" (BD 212). They are still relative, but they are also progressively free and independent. They exist.

Sort of. Whether it is the psychological building of selves or the cultural building of societies and civilizations, this process is always problematic for Fort, for it speaks of "an attempt by the relative to be the absolute, or by the local to be the universal" (BD 11). This is truly impossible for Fort (which is saying a great deal!). Only the Universal can be truly real, truly Complete. Here he leaves his reader in a state of indecision and metaphysical ambiguity. He denies and affirms within a single tail-biting move:

> I can accept that there may be Super-phenomenal Completeness but not that there can be phenomenal completeness. It may be that the widespread thought that there is God, or Allness, is only an extension of the deceiving process by which to an explanation of a swarm of lady birds, or to a fall of water at St. Kitts, is given a guise of completeness—or it may be the other way around—or that there is a Wholeness—and that attempting completenesses and attempting concepts of completenesses are localizing consciousness of an all-inclusive state, or being—so far as its own phenomena are concerned—that is Complete. (LO 753)

Terms, moreover, are just that for Fort: *terms,* that is, "ends" of a single real spectrum. He can thus sound very much like a Daoist when he writes of existence as "a hyphenated state of goodness-badness, coldness-heat, equilibrium-disequilibrium, certainty-uncertainty." But he is not at all a Daoist when he further insists that all of these hyphenated processes serve a real purpose, that they are the paradoxes through which the Whole evolves or progresses. In a single Fortean word, the opposites are said to be "metabolic" (WT 908).

Such a metabolism can be quite chilling, as when Fort suggests that war between nation-states might serve a balancing or super-metabolic purpose, or when he suggests, in an even chillier mood, that people gather in churches during volcanic eruptions so that they can be more efficiently wiped out. Human beings, he concludes in such passages, "have not existed as individuals any more than have cells in an animal organism existences of their own" (LO 808). Our individual deaths, then, are no more tragic than those of the millions of cells dying each minute in our bodies to keep us alive as relative Wholes

(LO 735). In other places, he reverses this logic and insists that we do exist as individuals, and that virtues are virtues to the extent that they put us into sync with the larger Whole, to the extent that they create a way of life that recognizes its proper place. As such, moral virtues become "imitations of the state of a whole existence, which is very old, good, and beyond reproach" (WT 878). Fort can thus privilege the One over the Many, or the Many over the One. It can go either way—and it *must* go either way—in the philosophy of the hyphen.

LEGACIES: SCI-FI GNOSIS, THE NEW AGE, AND THE RIDERS OF THE CHARIOT

Another way to get at Fort's metaphysical liberalism is to look at its legacies, its enthusiasms, its shadows, and the continuing presence of strange lights in our skies.

Fort's clearest legacy can be found in the pages and on the screens of twentieth-century science fiction productions. Perhaps it is of some note here that Fort was writing during a time in which the terms and rules of this genre had not yet been established. More interestingly, Fort was writing during the exact period in which the genre was coming into clear focus. Emerging from the earlier apotheosis of the imagination within the Romantic movement and the Gothic tales of the occult and the supernatural, but drawing now on the materialist hardware of technology and science, the stories of writers like Jules Verne and H. G. Wells had been marketed as *voyages extraordinaires* or as "scientific romances." It was the American pulp magazines of the 1920s—so named after the thick, cheap, and quickly yellowing paper on which they were published—that science fiction came into its own and was first named. The first pulp appeared in 1919, the very same year as *The Book of the Damned,* but it was not until editor Hugo Gernsback's *Amazing Stories,* which began publication in 1926, that the industry really got off the ground. And it was Gernsback, by his own account, who first coined the expression "science fiction," out of an earlier and not so successful attempt—"scientifiction."

One could easily write an entire book, or a series of books, on Fortean themes in science fiction. Historian and insider to the field Sam Moskowitz has given us at least one chapter along these lines.[14] For our own immediate purposes, a few further observations might be helpful. First, and perhaps most obviously, it is worth pointing out that the pulps turned to Fort's central mythology of the alien invasion or of a galactic colonialism (not, of course, entirely unique to him) as their core obsession and theme. Second, the pulps serialized Fort's writings, referred to him in their editorial pages, and even illustrated his scenes on a few of their covers.[15] Consider, for example, the back cover of *Amazing Stories* from November of 1947. It shows a huge fireball emerging from the ocean in front of a large ship. The explanation reads thus: "Impossible But True. On Nov. 12, 1887, the British steamer *Siberian* saw an enormous ball of fire rise from the sea off Cape Race, move against the wind toward the ship, then move away to be lost from sight in five minutes. What was it? Fire does not rise from the sea, it does not move against the wind. Was it really a submersible-aircraft spaceship the *Siberian* saw?" On the inside, the writer cites Tiffany Thayer's classic edition of *The Books of Charles Fort.*[16] Yes, the pulps loved Charles Fort.

As did many later science fiction writers. Indeed, his most well known biographer until very recently was Damon Knight, a writer of science fiction. And, although I hardly know what to make of this, it is worth observing that one of the greatest sci-fi writers of the last century, Philip K. Dick, experienced a spiritually transforming, year-long metaphysical opening from February of 1974 to February of 1975 that more than resembles Fort's early notion of a Martian X controlling us from afar. During this time, Dick was overwhelmed by a brilliant pink light that "resynthesized" him, beamed ideas, words, and story seeds into his brain, and, perhaps most astonishingly, telepathically communicated to him a perfectly correct diagnosis of the hidden intestinal birth defect of his young son, which, if we are to believe Dick, was then corrected by an immediate surgery inspired by the pink beam.[17] In an eight-thousand-page private journal he called "Exegesis," Dick desperately tried to make sense of his mystical illumination, employing everything from Valentinus and early Christian Gnosticism (with which he spiritually identified) to Jungian depth psychology, quantum physics, and psychopathology. He also wrote out of it, elaborating its elusive meanings through the symbolic forms of science fiction as an alien satellite or super-being named VALIS (for Vast Active Living Intelligent System). The contours of Dick's imaginative reconstructions are particularly evident in his final trilogy: *Valis, Divine Invasion,* and *The Transmigration of Timothy Archer* (the latter based on his friend, the radical Episcopalian bishop James Pike). One of the many things I find remarkable about Dick and his gnostic revelation is how uncannily, impossibly close it was to Fort's X. What to make of this?

Perhaps it goes without saying, but I will say it anyway: science fiction is rife with theological and religious implications, and almost all of them are radically liberal, if not actually devastating to conservative religious worldviews. There are at least five basic strategies at work here: what we might call 1) the Archimedean alien, 2) the historical revisionist, 3) the alternative religious, 4) the technologization of the sacred, and 5) the conspiratorial. As all five of these patterns can easily be found in Fort's text as well, it seems worth describing them as expressions of a metaphysical liberalism that Fort helped bequeath to science fiction.

1. By "the Archimedean alien," I mean to reference the real philosophical work that the mythology of the alien accomplishes in science fiction literature. Basically, the alien, and the cosmic evolutionary scale that this figure always implies, provides an imaginative Archimedean point or assumed transcendent perspective through which to see (and say) how hopelessly naïve, local, and primitive all human, Earth-bound religious systems really are. "One man's theology is another man's belly laugh," Robert A. Heinlein pointed out, correctly, in *Time Enough for Love.* "People believe in God," Aldous Huxley opined in *Brave New World,* "because they've been conditioned to believe in God." Michael Moorcock in *Behold the Man* is more critical, and more psychological: "Religion was the creation of fear. Knowledge destroys fear. Without fear, religion can't survive." Philip K. Dick, himself zapped by Valis, is more critical still, and fundamentally gnostic, in his approach to creator deities:

> 1) God does not exist.
> 2) And anyhow he's stupid.[18]

And so on.

2. The "historical-revisionist strategy" is similar, but somewhat more radical. It does not content itself with relativizing local belief systems as primitive myths, belly laughs, conditionings, or expressions of a stupid creator deity. It rereads them as ancient intuitions or naïve misinterpretations of actual alien interference in human social evolution. There are dozens, if not hundreds, of examples here, but the two most common in the literature are Ezekiel's vision and abduction via the flaming, many-wheeled "chariot" (which the text never calls a chariot) and the 1917 "Miracle of the Sun" of Fatima, Portugal, during

which about fifty thousand people witnessed the sun (or a spinning silver disc that looked like the sun) fall to the earth in a distinct "falling-leaf" motion that would be reproduced dozens of time in later ufological reports. Here the history of religions, that is, the history of superior beings from the sky communicating with humans, is reread as a long alien tutelage or, more darkly, as a kind of mythological control system masterminded by an alien intelligence, cosmic zookeeper, or galactic farmer.

3. By "the alternative religious," I refer to the various heterodox religious systems that the alien mythology spun out over the course of the twentieth century. Hence the long list of UFO religions that dot the alternative religious landscape from the 1950s on: Unarius, the Aetherius Society, the Raelian Church, the book of URANTIA, the United Nuwaubian Nation of Moors, and so on. These, of course, are not all Fortean in structure (many are more Theosophical in orientation, or are related to channeling techniques), but they do generally bear a kind of family resemblance to Fortean tropes. Very much unlike Fort, however, many of these movements have been expertly studied by scholars of religion.

4. Perhaps most interesting of all, science fiction and its UFOs would also become linked to what Michael Lieb has eloquently analyzed as the "technologization of the sacred," which he traces back to the fiery, spinning wheels of Ezekiel's vision. Lieb mines here rabbinic fears concerning the study of this text, the subsequent chariot (*merkabah*) mysticisms of Kabbalah and their "riders of the chariot," and the rare Hebrew word (*hashmal*) of the prophetic book that points to the original vision's "amber," "glowing metal" or *electrum*-like qualities (the "mysterium of *hashmal*," as Lieb puts it). For Lieb at least, the "child of Ezekiel," that is, the new UFO visionary of the New Age, is the "new *merkabah* mystic," the new rider of the chariot. The visionary *sign* has become the machine-like *thing*.[19]

5. Fifthly and finally, it is worth noting that Fort often strikes a potentially conspiratorial note, particularly in his frequent suggestion that the superconstructions in the sky have long been in contact "with a sect, perhaps, or a secret society, or certain esoteric ones of this earth's inhabitants" (BD 136). Related ideas, though with no obvious connection to Fort, would have a long history in later American politics and cultural life. As political scientist Michael Barkun has convincingly shown, although UFOs are not necessarily connected to any particular political platform (and certainly were not in their early his-

tory), this UFO–"secret society" connection was picked up by any number of paranoid, racist, and anti-Semitic political movements in the late 1980s and '90s and developed from there.[20]

Race is also clearly a factor here, from the oft-described "Asian" or "Oriental" eyes of the alien, to the fact that the very first major American abduction case involved a mixed-race couple, Betty and Barney Hill (Betty was white, Barney black). Lieb actually focuses much of his study on what he calls "the crisis of race," particularly as this found expression in the UFO visions and racial politics of the Honorable Louis Farrakhan and the Nation of Islam. Farrakhan has spoken and written bravely about what he and his followers call the Mother Plane or the Mother Wheel, which he claims to have literally entered in an initiatory visionary experience on September 17, 1985, on a mountain in Tepotzlan, Mexico. In sync with the earlier ufological mystics and riders of the chariot, Farrakhan identified the Mother Wheel with the original wheel of Ezekiel's vision.[21]

* * *

Any of these five Fortean themes could be pursued in the pulp fiction, science fiction, and ufological literature for pages and pages. In the end, though, the damned data remain, not perfect or beyond criticism or question, but as data like any other data, open to multiple readings and multiple realities. Fort lays down his challenge:

> Here are the data.
> See for yourself.
> What does it matter what my notions may be?
> Here are the data. (BD 238)

Who in the professional study of religion has taken up that challenge? Who looks, and I mean *really* looks, at this stuff? Better to swim on, pretending that religion and its sky-gods are more or less about power, gender, class, and race, or psychological well-being or social cohesion or money or violence or ethnic identity or colonialism (Fort would agree), or whatever system happens to be in fashion at the time of one's graduate training or has become politically relevant within one's social field (Fort would agree again). Fair enough.

But this can take us only so far, which is not really very far at all with respect to our present subject—the paranormal as another, unexplored, unacknowledged branch of American religious liberalism. The truth is that we do not really have a theory of religion, only theories about religion, and this partly because we have never really taken the paranormal seriously. Regardless, we continue to bump into this damned stuff from time to time.

And swim on.

NOTES

Portions of this essay originally appeared in my *Authors of the Impossible: The Paranormal and the Sacred* (Chicago: University of Chicago Press, 2010) and are used with permission here.

1. Charles Fort, *The Complete Books of Charles Fort,* with a new introduction by Damon Knight (New York: Dover, 1974), 918 (from *Wild Talents*), 631 (from *Lo!*). This omnibus collection, a reissue of *The Books of Charles Fort,* with an introduction by Tiffany Thayer (New York: Henry Holt, 1941), is the standard source for Fort's writings. Further citations are given in the text, with page numbers preceded by an indication of which of the four works in the volume is being cited: BD (*The Book of the Damned,* originally published in 1919), NL (*New Lands,* originally published in 1923), LO (*Lo!,* originally published in 1931), or WT (*Wild Talents,* originally published in 1932).

2. Fort made all of this quite clear in a May 1926 letter to the science fiction writer and Fort fan Edmund Hamilton, quoted in Damon Knight, *Charles Fort: Prophet of the Unexplained* (New York: Doubleday, 1970), 171–72.

3. Herbert Thurston, S.J., *The Physical Phenomena of Mysticism,* ed. J. H. Crehan, S.J. (London: Burns Oates, 1952). I am not suggesting, of course, that there were no Catholic intellectuals interested in psychical research, only that the field as a whole was dominated, particularly in England, by Protestant writers. The French case is no doubt different.

4. I am thinking of the lifework of psychiatrist Ian Stevenson, who spent almost half a century documenting what he called "cases of the reincarnation type" and "the biology of reincarnation." For a summary of Stevenson's work, see my "The Rise of the Imaginal: Psychical Phenomena on the Horizon of Theory (Again)," *Religious Studies Review* 33, no. 3 (July 2007): 179–91.

5. I am thinking here of Stephen E. Braude, an analytical philosopher who has written extensively about paranormal phenomena, including his own experience as a graduate student when he witnessed a table lift off the floor and communicate tapping messages to him and two friends during an impromptu séance session in his own apartment. See his *Immortal Remains: The Evidence for Life after Death* (Lanham, Md.: Rowman & Littlefield, 2003), ix–x.

6. Knight, *Charles Fort,* 65.

7. Letter of August 27, 1930, in Robert H. Elias, ed., *Letters of Theodore Dreiser: A Selection* (Philadelphia: University of Pennsylvania Press, 1959), 507, quoted in Louis Kaplan, *The Damned Universe of Charles Fort* (Brooklyn: Autonomedia, 1993), 8.

8. Quoted in Knight, *Charles Fort,* 70.

9. Cited and contextualized in Steinmeyer, *Charles Fort,* 75.

10. Quoted in ibid., 143. By "orthogenetically," Dreiser referred to his and Fort's belief in a kind of directed evolutionary process, a kind of occult intelligent design, if you will. Fort was very clear, however, that such a seeming design need have no designer. Fort was no theist.

11. For more on this, see R. A. S. Hennesey, *Worlds without End: The Historic Search for Extraterrestrial Life* (Charleston, S.C.: Tempus, 1999), chapter 9, "To the Canals of Mars—and After, 1880–1920."

12. My discussion of *X* relies heavily on Steinmeyer, *Charles Fort,* 137–44.

13. This remark appears in Damon Knight's introduction to *The Complete Books of Charles Fort,* xiii, without a source citation. I assume the letter is addressed to Dreiser.

14. Sam Moskowitz, "Lo! The Poor Forteans," in *Strange Horizons: The Spectrum of Science Fiction* (New York: Scribners, 1976), 218–48.

15. For a pulp serialization of Fort's *Lo!* see *Astounding Stories* 13, no. 6 (August 1934); 14, nos. 1 and 3 (September and November 1934).

16. *Amazing Stories* 21, no. 11 (November 1947): 177.

17. For the details, see Lawrence Sutin's marvelous biography *Divine Invasions: A Life of Philip K. Dick* (New York: Citadel, 1991). For fictionalizations of these events that are barely fictionalizations, see Dick's *Valis.*

18. For these remarks and many more, see the sections on "God," "Belief," and "Religion" in Gary Westfahl, ed., *Science Fiction Quotations: From the Inner Mind to the Outer Limits,* with a foreword by Arthur C. Clarke (New Haven: Yale University Press, 2005).

19. Michael Lieb, *Children of Ezekiel: Aliens, UFOs, the Crisis of Race, and the Advent of End Time* (Durham, N.C.: Duke University Press, 1998), 12, 16. This is a truly gorgeous study, with the haunting beauty of its scholarly prose matched only by the fundamental strangeness of its subject matter.

20. Michael Barkun, *A Culture of Conspiracy: Apocalyptic Visions in Contemporary America* (Berkeley: University of California Press, 2003).

21. See Louis Farrakhan, *The Announcement: A Final Warning to the U.S. Government* (1989; Chicago: Final Call, 1991). My thanks to Stephen Finley for this source and much enlightening discussion of the relevant literature.

ELEVEN

Liberal Sympathies

Morris Jastrow and the Science of Religion

KATHRYN LOFTON

Any review of twenty-first-century scholarship in the study of religion will find that it is an object around which there seems an inordinate amount of disagreement. From journals to monographs, conferences to classrooms, the question of the "what" in what we study continues to elicit frustration. This essay begins, then, with a contemporary concern: Why do we still seem to be asking whether the study of religion is possible? Is this the reasonable self-consciousness of a polymorphic discipline, or the introspective cul-de-sac of an unstructured field? Even as global political concerns and cognate academic disciplines seem needful of the replies an expertise in religion could supply, there remains a good deal of hemming and hawing on the point, even among those located within proper departments or programs of religious studies in America.[1] While self-scrutiny pervades most arts and sciences endeavors, scholars of religion—or, rather, scholars under the organizational and intellectual sway of "religious studies"—return to this uncertainty with surprising frequency. Even after decades of promotional analysis on the subjects of comparative religions, the history of religions, and religious studies, the gathering of those scholars into a collective seems at best an institutional convenience or a tolerated separate peace.[2]

As scholars contemplate their collaborative coexistence within departmental confines, multiple contemporary volumes appraising the field offer tales for the study of religion.[3] From this array of companions, handbooks, and encyclopedias, it becomes clear that whether or not individuals understand their role as religionists, the history of the field supplies several arguments supporting the cause. Why study religion? The answers are familiar: because we have; because we should; because it is the natural evolution of the Enlightenment; because we must deconstruct imperialism; because it is fascinating; because it connects the history of humanity in common patterns of behavior; because it drives men to suicide bombing; because it is beautiful; because it is ugly; because it is the highest form; because it articulates our basest needs; and because if we don't do it, *they* will. It is easy to find scholars of religion defending the importance of the study of religion under any of these principled positions. Yet enthusiasm about these reasons is diffuse, assailed by wariness of a category (religion) and of a category of an academic field (religious studies).

This was not always the case. In 1901, philologist, Semitic scholar, and devoted religionist Morris Jastrow Jr. explained confidently that there were "two main objects of the study of religions." First, he said, the study of religion seeks to determine "the nature, scope, and achievement of the religious spirit in all its various manifestations, from the earliest times to the present." Second, the study of religion will cultivate "that spirit of intense sympathy with one another, which is the basis of mutual esteem, and constitutes an important factor in establishing peace and good-will among individuals and among nations."[4] We study religion, Jastrow argued repeatedly then and throughout his career, because doing so fosters sympathy. He claimed further that we do not study religion merely by spirit, but by a methodical, scientific appraisal of the "nature, scope, and achievement" of those things produced by the "religious spirit." The study of religion makes manifest its subject through science in the pursuit of mutual sympathy. For such claims, Jastrow was heralded in his times as a scholar of the highest caliber. "Truly Jastrow's phenomenology is as representative of religious studies as it appears possible for any one scholar to be at the beginning of the twentieth century," insists one historian of religions.[5]

Current religionists bearing rapiers approach immediately, seizing upon Jastrow's celebration of sympathy and his suspicious confidence in science as vestigial opiates of a bygone Orientalism. In the years since Jastrow's identification of sympathy and science as codependent contributors to and products of the study of religion, scholars of religion have become uneasy with both. This is too flat: we have become kneejerk in our discomfort, rejecting his scientism as an impossible Gilded Age hubris, and his sympathy as a euphemism for a presumptive Edwardian piety, a "progress of the races" from primitive violence and pagan immorality to a patronizing goodwill toward men. Yet Jastrow's certitude about the subject of religion and its study are indistinguishable from the formats of liberalism which propelled the universities he inhabited and the American democracy he occupied. Identifying Jastrow is to identify a liberalism with which contemporary scholars have an awkward relation, even as it was his early twentieth-century intellectual and organizational leadership which fostered the locations of so much of our current work.

In his study of Thomas Wentworth Higginson (1823–1911), Leigh Eric Schmidt focuses on the piety prescribed in Higginson's essay "The Sympathy of Religions." This 1871 article achieved national, then international, influence as a summary text of late nineteenth-century religious liberalism, emphasizing as it did that the foundation of religious unity lay in extending the notion of sympathy into the realm of comparative religions. Sympathy was, therefore, a "practical paradigm" for dealing with a constantly expanding body of information about the religions of the world. "Sympathy was especially viewed as an ethic of compassion and benevolence, a fellow-feeling with those in pain or distress, but it was more than that," Schmidt explains. "Cultivating sympathy was a way of bridging differences and recognizing commonalities; it was a basis of overcoming isolation through affective connection, joining people to shared enterprises, and creating mutuality through identification with others."[6] For Higginson, sympathy was a social hope for the encounter between different people. For Jastrow, the best religions—and the best work in religious studies—bred sympathy. "One of the functions of religious guides," Jastrow wrote, was "to impart this spirit of sympathy."[7] A reconsideration of Jastrow is, in no small way, a reconsideration of sympathy as an academic value drawn from a distinctly liberal tradition which formed the basis of American religious studies. "Liberalism, both theological and political, provided the ground in which [comparative religion] was able to flourish," Eric Sharpe has written.[8]

Jastrow was, by any definition, a liberal—liberal in politics, liberal in academic inclinations, liberal in post-rabbinic Jewish practice. He was also idiosyncratic, and impossible to foist into any simple categorization of liberalism. Returning to Jastrow as an emblem of a certain academic liberalism invites critical inquiry into the nature of such emblematic nominations. Any attempt to revive a name for addition to a canon usually requires retelling something from their life that has been misunderstood, unnoticed, or considered unexceptional by the preexisting scholarly consensus. Someone might, for example, resuscitate a figure from the past because their life indicates something notable about their historical epoch; one might also turn to them because they formed a unique fulcrum in a set of critical social circles; scholars also revive ignored figures because they authored unusually prescient works, whose prescience is only realized far after their time is over. On all three points, Jastrow welcomes resuscitation: he was the intellectually rebellious son of a famous rabbi, he was at the epicenter of multiple cultures of American liberalism, and he did author the first comprehensive American treatment of the study of religion as an academic discipline. Reminding ourselves of his peculiar locality inspires here an interest in his generality, in his passionate, repeated calls for his practices to be adopted by an entire field of study. Through discerning what was then adamant in Jastrow, we learn too what might be subtext in our own scholarly ventures, how we name our scientism, how we renamed our sympathy "pluralism," and why we still don't know what the "we" is in what we do.

In 1902, Morris Jastrow memorialized his friend and intellectual mentor, Cornelis P. Tiele, in an obituary for *The Independent.* "In his estimate of religions past and present his point of view is not coldly scientific but essentially sympathetic; and yet his eloquence and fervor never lead him into the airy regions of sentimentality," Jastrow wrote, concluding, "His frame of mind may best be described as that of a philosopher who is in love with mankind."[9] Such a celebratory emphasis on the stance of the scholar—sympathetic but not fervent, philosophical but not sentimental—might have also been made in Jastrow's own case; he left in his wake a similar spate of obituaries that celebrated his character as much as his vitae, remarking on the earnest decency that surrounded his systematic industry.

Morris Jastrow, Ph.D., Professor of Semitic Languages and Librarian of the University of Pennsylvania, was born in Warsaw on August 13, 1861, where his father, Marcus Jastrow, led the German Jewish pulpit in that city. In 1886 the family came to Philadelphia after Rabbi Jastrow had accepted a call to become the rabbi of Congregation Rodef Shalom. At the age of sixteen Morris entered the University of Pennsylvania, from which he graduated in 1881. For the next four years he pursued extensive studies in language and philosophy at universities in Breslau, Leipzig, Strasburg, and Paris; in 1884 he received his doctorate from the University of Leipzig.

Jastrow's continental years could not have been more fortuitous in their timing. This was a critical epoch in the history of religions, especially at universities like Leipzig where the nascent science of history was under active consideration as the driving methodology for the comparative study of religious origins.[10] Within those transnational debates, Cornelis Tiele dominated. A Dutch scholar, Tiele specialized in Egyptian, Assyrian, and Mesopotamian religions, tracking religion from its animistic origins to the Greco-Roman roots of Christianity. Nietzsche would name Tiele's *Comparative History of the Ancient Religions of Egypt and the Semitic Peoples* (1882) as essential to his "ideal library," and it was one of the most important reference works for scholars of religion at the time. In his description of European religious studies in the late nineteenth century, Hans Kippenberg observed, "Tiele thought there was a development of religions, and he linked this assumption with the claim that the more independent religions were of language and nationality, the more advanced was their development."[11] Tiele's genealogy describing the rise of "ethical religions" out of "natural religions" depended upon evaluation of morphological evidence. "Professor Tiele, in the course of his Gifford Lectures, took occasion to formulate anew his views on the general character of religion, and has, through his lucid presentation, made a contribution of permanent value to the problem," Jastrow wrote. "[Tiele's] distinction between 'the forms in which religion is manifested' and 'the constituents of religion' is an important step towards a determination of what religion really is."[12] Defining religion's essence was only possible through a phenomenological description.

During the time Tiele served as a professor at Leiden (1873–1902), the Dutch study of religion underwent a critical bureaucratic transition. As a Remonstrant professor, Tiele had to teach mainly practical theological disciplines such as homiletics, catechetics, and pastoral theology. Even as he engaged deeply with the theology of the Gospel of John and other critical texts in the history of early Christianity, Tiele railed against theological imperatives within the university curriculum, advocating instead on behalf of the science of religion.[13] Shortly after he began his Leiden appointment, the science of religion was given a formal place in the theological curriculum by the Higher Education Act of 1876. The historiography of religious studies returns to this act time and again as a pivotal moment in the definition of religion as a critical subject of humanist inquiry.[14] Following its passage, the Dutch separated theological courses, to be taught by church-appointed professors, from courses on the scientific study of religion, which were to be taught by state-appointed professors.[15] In this protection of multiple modes of religious studies inquiry, the act stands—in Arie Molendijk's account—as "a victory for the liberal Protestant view on theology."[16] The act restructured theological education within the Dutch university, but it did not eradicate theological perspectives, merely privileging those that could accord with broader humanistic inquiry.

This European sojourn is the only period in Jastrow's biography that has as of yet received any serious academic treatment, since from 1881 to 1884 he also frequented courses in the Jewish Theological Seminary at Breslau. In his brief treatment of Jastrow's fraught decision to choose the professoriate over the pulpit, Harold Wechsler demonstrates Jastrow's conflicted relationship to American Judaism, Reform Jews, and the problem of professionalized religious faith in the modern period.[17] Entangled with other leading American Jews through his family—including Felix Adler, Henrietta Szold, and Isaac Mayer Wise—Morris Jastrow never altogether eschewed his Judaism, nor did he retain a commitment to its ministerial propagation in the New World. Unlike his equally prominent brother, Joseph, Morris could not see his way to any religious practice that made sense alongside his particular scholarly advocacies. The extraordinary success of Morris and Joseph in their chosen academic fields perhaps indicates their shared wrestling with the rabbinate as an alternative professional path. Joseph Jastrow received the first Ph.D. in psychology to be awarded by an American university with a fully functioning psychology laboratory, Johns Hopkins. During his peak research years, Joseph Jastrow wrestled with a variety of problems in the emergent academic study of psychology, including the problem of belief within modern thought.[18] After a nearly forty-year career at the University of Wisconsin, including the inaugural presidency of the new American Psychological Association, Joseph authored a syndicated advice column from 1927 to 1932, "Keeping Mentally Fit."[19] Joseph also became one of the first radio psychologists. "The psychologist must recognize things as they are," Joseph said, remarking that this role contrasted with that of a rabbi. "Fortunate are they who can use the path of prayer. There is little need to advise that path for those who tread it; for they do so of their own accord. But the psychologist, like all other men, knows many who find their codes and creeds in other directions; so he must speak to and for all."[20]

If Joseph named the psychologist as a neutral observer of the human subject, Morris would hallow the historian as a similarly secular observer. "Starting out without bias or preconceived theory, the historical method aims at determining as accurately as possible what are the beliefs, what the rites, what the aspirations of any particular religion or system of religious thought," Jastrow explained. "It is obvious that, for the time being, all such factors as special dispensation and miraculous intervention must be excluded." In a historical moment that included many prophetic utterances and restorationist claims by American religious actors, Morris Jastrow resisted confusing such articulations of belief with the organizing principles of scholasticism. "Unless human history is to be explained by a thorough study of causes and results, and by an exclusive regard to human conditions, no explanation in any real sense of the word is possible."[21] To pose himself rightly toward his subject, to serve best the humanity of his subject, Jastrow seemed to imply that examiners must denude themselves of any directing theology, ritual possession, or partial sectarianism. "One must guard against the predominance of the personal factor, which could easily lead an instructor to impart prejudicial views or to come into more or less violent conflict with the religious sentiments held by a large section of the community," Jastrow wrote, adding that this "danger can be averted by a strict insistence upon a purely historical treatment of religions which belong to the present."[22] Historical method was, for Jastrow and many of his peers, the surest guide because it possessed sympathy and scientism, disclosing data through narrative documentation and inspiring right perspective through the regulated encounter with difference. The inductive technique meant the subject would be treated generously but rigorously.

Upon his return to America in 1885, Jastrow became a lecturer in Semitic languages at the University of Pennsylvania, and in the following year was appointed professor of Arabic and rabbinical literature, a position he retained until 1892, when he became a professor of Semitic languages. "Religion as a subject for speculation is as old as human thought," he would comment not long after his appointment as a full professor. "Religion as an object of investigation is one of the most recent of sciences."[23] With an initial appointment in language programs, Jastrow used his training in comparative philology to publicize the importance of institutionalizing the study of religion both within his home university and through the development of the international scholarly associations. Jastrow's record of service and organizational labor on behalf of the study of religion included membership in the American Philosophical Society, the American Oriental Society, and the Society of Biblical Literature. In every organization, he served in multiple administrative capacities, from president to vice president to secretary to treasurer. He organized the American Convention for Lectures on the History of Religions and served subsequently as its secretary. He was a delegate to multiple International Congresses of Orientalists, International Congresses of Science, and International Congresses for the History of Religions. He edited a series titled Handbooks on the History of Religions, as well as the Semitic Studies Series for Brill. He was an editor of the *American Journal of Semitic Languages* and the *American Journal of Theology.* He was editor of the Semitic department of the *International Encyclopedia* and of the Bible department in the *Jewish Encyclopedia;* he contributed more than fifty entries to the *Encyclopedia Britannica;* he revised the Semitic definitions in *Webster's Dictionary;* he contributed too to *Hasting's Dictionary of the Bible* and the *Encyclopedia Biblica.*

Meanwhile, he continued to publish scholarly work on Arabic, Assyrian, Hebrew, the Old Testament, Judaism, Orientalism, and the study of religion that was described by many of his contemporaries as unparalleled. His book-length studies included *The Religion of Babylonia and Assyria* (1898), *Hebrew and Babylonian Traditions* (1914), *A Gentle Cynic, being the Book of Ecclesiastes* (1919), *The Book of Job* (1920), and *The Song of Songs: Being a Collection of Love Lyrics of Ancient Palestine* (1921). In addition to these sustained examinations of particular texts and traditions, Jastrow contributed shorter studies to popular and academic journals on an array of topics, including the Arabic tradition of writing on clay and the races of the Old Testament; textbooks of the Babylonians and ethics of the Assyrians; cuneiform tablets and Phoenician seals; the palace of Nebuchadnezzar and the Tower of Babel; the religious meanings of the liver, of Mars, and of Saturn; astrological letters and Jewish libraries; the tearing of garments and the baring of shoulders; the books of Daniel, Esther, Lamentations, and Ruth; the modern attitude toward religion; the scope and method of the historical study of religions; and recent movements in the historical study of religions in America.[24]

Throughout this vast corpus of writings, Jastrow modeled a measured perspective, focusing on the connectivity of religious practices with other sociological facts, cultural aspects, and analytic perspectives. "Liver divination has wider bearings also from another point of view," he wrote in his study of the liver as the seat of the soul. "It marks the beginnings of the study of anatomy, for in the effort to note the signs on the liver, the organ itself was studied, and a terminology developed which distinguished its various parts." Here the history of science encounters the history of religions, with the observant Jastrow speculating about the co-creation of belief and medical empiricism. Later in the same essay, Jastrow demonstrates his multiple fields of interest, including archaeology, history, and anthropology. "Clay models of livers, similar to the one above referred to, have been found recently at Boghaz-Keui—the ancient center of a Hittite empire—testifying to the existence of the rite of hepatoscopy at an early period in the very district from which the Etruscans may have come." Excitedly, Jastrow concludes his research with a corporate declaration of historical accomplishment: "We thus obtain an uninterrupted chain of Babylonian influence, embracing Etruscans, Greeks, and Romans, as well as Hittites."[25] Such genealogies were, for Jastrow, the happy result of accumulative scholarship that coordinates material evidence in order to supply a contextual explanation.

Despite the intimacy Jastrow possessed with specific subjects, to a contemporary critic his enormous range of expertise may signal the dilettantism of late nineteenth-century scholarship. Jastrow himself discussed such accusations in his own prescriptions for the future study of religion. "In Germany there is a feeling, which is stronger in some sections of the country than in others, that the study of religion furnishes an open door to dilettantism. This feeling is justified; and I regard the attraction which the subject offers to superficial minds, to those who are fond of taking a little dip into the well of knowledge, as one of its most serious drawbacks."[26] Nothing troubled Jastrow more than the amateur, the uninformed, or the inexpert, especially insofar as he studied a subject—religion—which seemed to attract observers that were, to him, tainted by theology and unversed in the methods of history.

In his positivistic claims on behalf of history and his derogatory descriptions of lay commentators, Jastrow reflects a significant transition in scholarly work, one marked by the professionalization of the scholar and the eclipse of the amateur. "Constantly excoriated by university men, amateur writing in the nineteenth century might additionally be seen as a kind of impurity that the professional eliminated—a thicket of falsehoods he cleared away in order to find an authentic past and objective truth," Bonnie G. Smith writes. "Or . . . was the concept of the amateur only a result of professionalization, a weak and less worthy ('amateurish') imitation of the scientific practitioner embodied by those not up to being professional historians?"[27] As Smith indicates, the very notion of an amateur only had sway once a privileged form of knowledge production was institutionalized. When in May 1911 Jastrow was contacted by a number of newspapers reporting that the Ark of the Covenant had been found beneath the mosque of Omar in Jerusalem by an English expedition, he replied with a categorical dismissal, calling the rumor "absurd." But his justification signaled his loyalty to the relatively new channels of informational legitimacy: "There has been no account in any of the archaeological journals of the reported expedition and none of the names are familiar to me. All archaeological expeditions sent out from England are under the direction of the Palestine Exposition Fund Society, which issues quarterly statements and there has been nothing in them of this great expedition."[28] Knowledge, for Jastrow, was only knowledge if it had traversed the disciplinary mechanism of journals, societies, and familiar names. Only these processes and pathways could assure him, the scientist, that the story was more than mere story: that it could become a fact of religion.

"Every 'historical fact' results from a praxis," Michel de Certeau has written. "It results from procedures which have allowed a mode of comprehension to be articulated as a discourse of 'facts.'"[29] As historians of history have explained, the new procedures associated with a "scientific" historical method like that promoted by Jastrow "produced skilled men with common ways of behaving—a brotherhood, a republic, a peer group."[30] This *Gesellschaft* collaborated on documents, and attended and contributed to academic and area-interest clubs, journals, seminars, and societies, in order to produce consensus on time periods, cultures, and literary genres. By the end of the nineteenth century, the strategies promoted in seminars—especially those emphasizing archival research—gained ascendancy over other historical practices, "setting the standards for historical writing as the investigation of politics and becoming the criteria for success within a powerful profession."[31] "Politics" describes here the dominant trends of intellectual and national history, but also the effects and affects of the specific formats of academic investigation.

"In all countries, proponents of seminars adopted a common, civic language to suggest that the character of a man was transformed and perfected through the new methods of historical study," Bonnie Smith explains. Through its emphasis on language and focused organization the seminar promoted a perfected public sphere, one in which "many traditional hierarchies—estate, age, status—were leveled in the presence of expertise."[32] The creation of scientific methodologies was obviously never a neutral venture, even as it advocated the objectivity of the rationalist examiner. It was, always and ever, an ideal of liberalism, where the classroom was an experimental arena for the expansion of equality and encouragement of mutual sympathy.

Morris Jastrow fought relentlessly to create contexts that would permit religion to be at the epicenter of the emerging modern university, even as religion might seem for many of his colleagues a topic too tainted by amateurism and ideology to be central to a liberal intellectual curriculum. "If adequate provisions were made at our universities for students desirous of investigating the phenomena of religion," Jastrow declared, "the difficulties involved in the proper study would soon be apparent, and would deter those from giving their crude results to the public who are now unrestrained through the lack of a scientific standard which can only be furnished by a college and university curriculum."[33] The institutions he built and buoyed relied upon professional networks and on courses that emphasized perpetual scrutiny, study, and the making of legitimate religious history through those networks and refereed observances. "Professor Jastrow's service to the science of religion was not confined to his own weighty contributions to its literature," wrote one scholarly colleague in 1921. "He rendered an equally great service by organizing enterprises which called forth the contributions of others."[34] Such praise was hardly isolated. Jastrow's obituary in *The Nation* noted that "in the death of Dr. Jastrow we have lost the one man who, since Henry C. Lea's life ended, gave Philadelphia a standing in the learned world of Europe."[35] The science of religion existed as an intellectual possibility, but Jastrow supplied secretarial labor, encyclopedic heft, and methodological consistency to its institutionalization in the American academy.

Just as Jastrow celebrated the project to which he became increasingly linked, so was he complicit in the multifarious implications of that project. Jastrow was, for example, typical among religionists of the day in his promotion of a "universal religion" for all humankind. Theories of universal religion, and optimism about the "unity of all religions," permeated intellectual and popular religious discourse by the close of the nineteenth century.[36] This talk of the "universal" among American religious observers and leaders was as diverse as the religious landscape itself. Some commentators did use talk of the "universal" to promote imperial Christian programs. Others, however, offered a complicated profile for the "universal religion," sincerely attempting to mix and match the best features of world religions to produce an equitable compromise to the world's divisive diversity. Others simply used the word "universal" to identify laudable qualities within particular denominations; they were less interested in a new religion, and more interested in reaffirming the modern logic of the one they had.

The pursuit of universal religion has a longer history in the United States both within and outside formal academic circuits. In an 1872 review, Thomas Wentworth Higginson derided James Freeman Clarke's *Ten Great Religions* (1871) as reliant on outdated scholarship and "imprisoned" by a Judeo-Christian straitjacket. In contrast, Higginson held up the first volume of Samuel Johnson's *Oriental Religions and Their Relation to Universal Religion* (1872) as "a really good book . . . of which any American may speak with pride."[37] Throughout the three-volume *Oriental Religions,* Samuel Johnson refused to center Christianity or privilege its development in the history of religions. "I have written," he wrote in his introduction, "not as an advocate of Christianity or of any other distinctive religion, but as attracted on the one hand by the identity of the religious sentiment under all its great historic forms, and on the other by the movement indicated in their diversities and contrasts towards a higher plane of unity, on which their exclusive claims shall disappear."[38] Johnson's project had two aims: first, to provide a clear and accurate examination of Oriental religions; second, to use this examination to exhume the "Universal in Religion." Johnson thus sought not an amalgamated ideal, but an expansive understanding of universality.[39] "The scholar must identify himself with the social reformer, and demonstrate brotherhood out of the old Bibles and the stammering speech of primitive men," Johnson preached. "It is his duty to show that the human arteries flow everywhere with the same royal blood."[40] The pursuit of universal equality among religions ought to be the primary pursuit of the modern intellectual.

Jastrow tended to participate in dreams of the mix-and-match variety, wherein all the "advanced" religions would contribute their best material to make a system that could provide a "oneness of purpose" directed by a "spirit of love." He was severely skeptical of propositions of universality, writing that assertions of the universal should be "considered a matter of confessional claim rather than a quality that can be descriptively and objectively ascertained."[41] At the 1902 New York State Conference of Religion, he remarked that such a universal religion should be pursued "by the study of religions, one by another, and by the keeping of our minds open for new interpretations of truth, and for the recognition of varying religious forms as different attempts to express truth."[42] Echoing sentiments familiar to his audiences at Ethical Culture Society meetings, Jastrow here seeks to balance a scientist's open-ended research with the religionist's sympathy for human need and social creativity. Presupposed in such dreams of universal religion were hierarchies of religions, dividing the advanced (Christianity, Judaism, Islam, and Buddhism, by Jastrow's rendering) from the naïve. Like many of his epoch, Jastrow had a bigoted impression of certain "primitive" religions, claiming that among them we may see "direct manifestations of man's emotional or religious nature." "The religion of savages and of people living in a primitive condition of culture are," Jastrow concluded, "the more special concern of the student of religions" than those of the advanced.[43] Jastrow's universal religion would begin with people of the advanced races culling from the naïve to find those things which are, in their very base need, universal.

Comments like these proposing a universal religion are not found, however, in Jastrow's climactic contribution: *The Study of Religion* (1901). Published in Scribners' Contemporary Science Series, edited by famed British sexologist Havelock Ellis, *The Study of Religion* offers an introduction to the field of study and a scientific method for its ongoing pursuit. The book walks at an even rate through the history of the development of the science of religion, describes the relation of religion to ethics, philosophy, mythology, psychology, history, and culture, and, in its final third, grapples with the treatment of sources in the study of religion, as well as the status of the subject in colleges, universities, and museums. The book is a textbook without the cartoon caricatures that pervade its contemporaneous peers. To be sure, Jastrow offers stilted analysis, suggesting that it was "inconceivable that Buddhism should ever spread to northern countries with populations marked by great intellectual activity." Yet Jastrow tempers every cultural overstatement with careful specificity, requesting elsewhere, for example, that "we may content ourselves with sounding a note of warning against the present tendency in ethnological science to give undue weight to the factor of race in producing mental traits."[44] *The Study of Religion* (1901) would be, to anyone versed in the history of religions, a relatively unchallenging work of summary and proposition, including responsibly efficient analysis of the religious interpretations available in Hegel, Herder, Kant, Schelling, and Schleiermacher, while nominating Max Müller, Albert Réville, Herbert Spenser, and, of course, Tiele as critical figures for the ongoing definition of religious studies. Rather than propose a new theory of religions, Jastrow provides instead a careful study of religion itself: how it has been imagined, how it has been understood, and how one thinker influenced another.

Over and over Jastrow dismisses easy readings of religious history in favor of a careful ambiguity. He rejects out of hand theories of projection which suggest that religious belief is an "illusion." "The weakness of this position lies in the one-sidedness of the view taken of religion," Jastrow writes, "as though it consisted solely of certain beliefs, and as though these beliefs had been forced upon people through some external influence, instead of being spontaneous growths." He also repudiates social theories "which could see nothing in religion but the cunning devices of priests to keep the masses under their control."[45] Origins could not be reduced to one desire, or to a conceit of the mass. Like his hero Tiele, Jastrow argues that religion is a relentlessly human phenomenon, impossible to reduce to a simple desire or need.[46] Religion was, he argues, a transhistorical phenomenon in which material concerns were explained through material facts. Jastrow never quite defines religion, choosing instead to describe the reasons why religious forms may exist: "Man, in the course of time, developed a more or less extended series of precautionary measures to avoid unpleasant circumstances, and correspondingly, by noting the circumstances which accompany favorable incidents in life, he endeavored to bring about a repetition of them by repeating at the proper time the activity in which he was engaged when some fortune befell him."[47] Religious actions ought to be studied historically because they were, Jastrow explains, acts of historicism themselves, recollections of times before through ritual remembrance.

The Study of Religion captured an intellectual epoch. "Now, after the lapse of twenty years, the book is without peer in its special sphere," wrote one reader in 1921.[48] Neither Jastrow nor the scientific study of religion survived the twentieth century with such consistent acclaim. "*The Study of Religion* is a veritable masterpiece, which deserves to be much better known than it is," remarked Walter Capps.[49] When the American Academy of Religion inaugurated the Classics in Religious Studies reprint series through Scholars Press, the first selection was *The Study of Religion*. In their introduction to the work, William Clebsch and Charles Long attributed the book's disappearance to an alternative ascendance:

> Many who lived after World War I tried to forget or repudiate what was accepted before it. In one such change of mind, the Christian exclusivism and the negativism toward all religion that had forestalled until the nineteenth century the comparative study of religions once again took hold, the former fostered by Karl Barth . . . and his disciples, the latter by Sigmund Freud . . . and his. On Barth's reading all religions but Christianity, and on Freud's all religions without exception, were a snare and a delusion. Why study them at all?[50]

In his defining survey of comparative religion, Eric Sharpe described the situation in the years following World War I similarly: "Eventually, comparative religion was to suffer something of an eclipse, despite its promising beginnings, under the pressures of conservatism and orthodoxy."[51] These pressures might be pursued elsewhere in greater historical detail. For now, let us summarize the shift, noting that in this postwar moment the confessional gained ascendance while the scientific became associated with either a German empiricism that led to fascism or a primitive slumming that contributed to moral indignity. From this perspective, we needed Christianity in America, or we needed therapy. Everything else meant madness.

If Jastrow could comment upon his eclipse, he would not mind it—personal acclaim means nothing to the true scientist—but he would elaborate upon its reasons, speaking on subjects he often cited in his own writings on the study of religion. First, he would identify resources—financial and administrative—that are necessary to the fostering of an independent study of religion. In the absence of universities supplying those funds, religious agencies would fill the gap, and the theological inclinations of the donors would determine the results of the studies. Second, he would discuss the failure of the United States to involve itself responsibly with Europe before, during, and after World War I. His popular writings reflected how concerned he was with America's retreat from Europe following that war's conclusion. For Jastrow and his other academic developers, Europe modeled intellectual practice, and the United States was too young in its educational structures to function altogether independently of those models. The scholarly turn inward during the interwar period encouraged an already swelling anti-liberalism while also inhibiting the development of the human sciences. In this account, the American study of religion flailed like an orphaned toddler until after World War II, when it matured with the arrival of Joachim Wach in 1944 and Mircea Eliade in 1957.

Finally, Jastrow would ask to be read, and read again. Those of us seeking shelter in the study of religion may be frustrated by his universalizing chatter, or by the naïveté of his secular scientism. But the bulk of his labor was directed not to the prescriptive subject, but to the gathering of the data of religion: "In the first place, as already indicated, the fundamental principle of this method is the careful and impartial accumulation of facts, and what is more, the facts of religion everywhere."[52] More to the point, he would say that his methodology left much interpretive elbow room for the dissenting voice. Contribute to the body of religious facts, he would command; offer interpretations that show your strategic and documentary steps. Read voluminously. Read, respect, and reexamine historiography. Write for multiple audiences. These are the practices of the religionist, of the scholar, of the intellectual. How is this not a study of religion, commonly understood? Jastrow would say that to see only his evolutionary schema and not his beloved sources was to see the forest and miss the trees. And those sources for his histories are ours, too. Scholars of religion may narrate them however they like. The process of selection, classification, and analysis should not silence anyone; it should only encourage new interpretations, contradictions, and dignified disagreements in the pages of journals.

Even today, with our tender regard for real religious subjects and their inviolable complexity, we remain unresolved on the point. If Jastrow was tainted by Orientalist schematics and United Nations dreams, we are so worried about harming our subjects that we smother them in simplified notions of cultural storytelling. Clebsch and Long summarized the difference when they concluded, about *The Study of Religion,* "The book is not hermeneutically oriented to the modern sense of intellectual crises, of cultural discontinuities, of personal ambiguities."[53] The personal, the recessively peculiar, and the messiness of cataloguing held little interest for Jastrow or his society brethren. Jastrow didn't worry about whether he did his subjects harm, since his form of liberalism led him to believe that whatever the violence of classification was, it was a far cry from the potential cruelties of prejudice and ignorance. Yet such classifications left fingerprints, and serious material effects, as Uday Singh Mehta argues in his study of liberalism and empire.[54] But the compensations to come—our protection of not only the idea of the holy, but also the incommensurable sovereignty of its holy purveyors—may have compromised our ability to do any self-respecting study of religion at all. "The cause of religion has nothing to fear from any investigations when carried on in an earnest and sincere spirit, and least of all from investigations which reveal the steadily upward tendency of religious thought, commensurate always with the general advance of mankind," Jastrow wrote.[55] As religious studies continues to seek its critical stride, perhaps instead of asking whether "religion" is a real object of inquiry, scholars might better ask to what end they should pursue any inquiry at all. If not Jastrow's liberalism, if not his sympathies, then which ones, how deployed, and why?

NOTES

1. See Timothy Fitzgerald, *Discourse on Civility and Barbarity: A Critical History of Religion and Related Categories* (New York: Oxford University Press, 2007); Russell T. McCutcheon, *Manufacturing Religion: The Discourse on Sui Generis Religion and the Politics of Nostalgia* (New York: Oxford University Press, 2003); and Matt Waggoner, "Religion's Death Drive and the Future of Religious Studies," *Method and Theory in the Study of Religion* 21, no. 2 (2009): 213–29.

2. Within departments and programs of religion and religious studies, the easiest way to discern this discord would be to observe debates over required theory courses at the undergraduate or graduate level. The role of method and theory in curricula for the study of reli-

gion is by no means consistent or unquestioned from department to department, with some programs never requiring students in Islamic Studies to study the meaning of "religion" with those from the History of Christianity. This is despite the fact that it is this very category—and its histories of method and theory—which explain why the scholars gathered within those institutional locations are under the rubric of "religion" rather than employed under the auspices of anthropology, history, literature, or area studies programs. William E. Arnal, "Black Holes, Theory and the Study of Religion," *Studies in Religion/Sciences Religieuses* 30, no. 2 (June 2001): 209–14; Darlene M. Juschka, "The Construction of Pedagogical Spaces: Religious Studies in the University," *Studies in Religion/Sciences Religieuses* 28, no. 1 (March 1999): 85–97; and Eve Paquette, "Religion as the Academic's Enemy: A Case Study of an Ineffective Discursive Strategy," *Studies in Religion/Sciences Religieuses* 35, nos. 3–4 (September 2006): 431–46.

3. Russell T. McCutcheon, "Words, Words, Words," *Journal of the American Academy of Religion* 75, no. 4 (December 2007): 952–87.

4. Morris Jastrow, *The Study of Religion* (London: Walter Scott, 1901), 394.

5. Walter H. Capps, *Religious Studies: The Making of a Discipline* (Minneapolis, Minn.: Fortress, 1995), 124.

6. Leigh Eric Schmidt, *Restless Souls: The Making of American Spirituality* (San Francisco: HarperSanFrancisco, 2005), 107–108.

7. Jastrow, *Study of Religion*, 373.

8. Eric J. Sharpe, *Comparative Religion: A History*, 2nd ed. (London: Open Court, 1986), 138.

9. Morris Jastrow Jr., "Cornelis Petrus Tiele," *The Independent*, February 27, 1902, 512. See also Morris Jastrow, "Cornelis Petrus Tiele: In Commemoration of His Seventieth Birthday," in *The Open Court: A Monthly Magazine Devoted to the Science of Religion, the Religion of Science, and the Extension of the Religious Parliament Idea* 14 (1900): 728–33.

10. Kurt Rudolph, *Historical Fundamentals and The Study of Religions: Haskell Lectures Delivered at the University of Chicago* (New York: Macmillan, 1985).

11. Hans G. Kippenberg, *Discovering Religious History in the Modern Age* (Princeton: Princeton University Press, 2002), 49.

12. Jastrow, *Study of Religion*, 165.

13. Arie L. Molendijk, *The Emergence of the Science of Religion in the Netherlands* (Leiden: Brill, 2005), 87.

14. Sharpe, *Comparative Religion*, 121.

15. Peter van der Veer, "The Imperial Encounter with Asian Religions," *Radical History Review*, no. 99 (fall 2007): 257.

16. Arie L. Molendijk, "Transforming Theology: The Institutionalization of the Science of Religion in the Netherlands," in *Religion in the Making: The Emergence of the Sciences of Religion*, ed. Arie L. Molendijk and Peter Pels (Leiden: Brill, 1998), 77.

17. Harold S. Wechsler, "Pulpit or Professoriate: The Case of Morris Jastrow Jr.," *American Jewish History* 74, no. 4 (June 1985): 338–55.

18. Joseph Jastrow, *The Psychology of Conviction: A Study of Beliefs and Attitudes* (Boston: Houghton Mifflin, 1918).

19. See Joseph Jastrow, *Keeping Mentally Fit: A Guide to Everyday Psychology* (Garden City, N.Y.: Garden City, 1928).

20. Quoted in Andrew R. Heinze, *Jews and the American Soul: Human Nature in the Twentieth Century* (Princeton: Princeton University Press, 2004), 111.

21. Jastrow, *Study of Religion*, 19, 20.

22. Ibid., 356.

23. Morris Jastrow, "Recent Movements in the Historical Study of Religions in America," *The Biblical World* 1, no. 1 (January 1893): 24.

24. See Albert Tobias Clay and James A Montgomery, *Bibliography of Morris Jastrow, Jr., Ph.D., Professor of Semitic Languages in the University of Pennsylvania* (Philadelphia: privately printed, 1910). For other biographical information about Jastrow, see the Jastrow Alumni Records file in the University of Pennsylvania Archives.

25. Morris Jastrow Jr., "The Liver as the Seal of the Soul," in *Studies in the History of Religions,* ed. David Gordon Lyon and George Foot Moore (New York: Macmillan, 1912), 157, 164.

26. Morris Jastrow Jr., "The Historical Study of Religions in Universities and Colleges," *Journal of the American Oriental Society* 20 (1899): 320.

27. Bonnie G. Smith, *The Gender of History: Men, Women, and Historical Practice* (Cambridge, Mass.: Harvard University Press, 1998), 7.

28. Jastrow Alumni Records file, University of Pennsylvania Archives.

29. Michel de Certeau, *The Writing of History* (New York: Columbia University Press, 1988), 30.

30. Smith, *Gender of History,* 103

31. Ibid., 104.

32. Ibid., 110, 111.

33. Jastrow, "The Historical Study of Religions," 320.

34. George A. Barton, "The Contributions of Morris Jastrow, Jr. to the History of Religion," *Journal of the American Oriental Society* 41 (1921): 332.

35. "In Memoriam: Dr. Morris Jastrow," *The Nation* 113, no. 2927 (August 10, 1921): 151.

36. This discourse has been given little sustained scholarly study. Only Eric J. Sharpe's 1978 essay, "Universal Religion for Universal Man" (in *The Charles Strong Lectures, 1972–1984,* ed. Robert B. Crotty [Leiden: Brill, 1987], 157–71), attempts to historicize "universal religion," focusing particularly on the Hindu responses to Western discussions of universal religion. See also Tomoko Masuzawa, *The Invention of World Religions, or, How European Universalism Was Preserved in the Language of Pluralism* (Chicago: University of Chicago Press, 2005), 107–20.

37. Thomas Wentworth Higginson, "Johnson's *Oriental Religions,*" *The Index* 3 (November 9, 1872): 361, quoted in Carl T. Jackson, *Oriental Religions in American Thought* (Westport, Conn.: Greenwood, 1981), 133.

38. Samuel Johnson, *Oriental Religions and Their Relation to Universal Religion—India* (Boston: James R. Osgood, 1872), 2. Johnson published a second volume, on China, in 1877. His volume on Persia was published posthumously in 1884.

39. For critical appraisals of Johnson, see Carl T. Jackson, "The Orient in Post-Bellum American Thought: Three Pioneer Popularizers," *American Quarterly* 22, no. 1 (spring 1970): 68–72.

40. Johnson, *Oriental Religions,* 27.

41. Masuzawa, *Invention of World Religions,* 118.

42. *Bethlehem Globe,* November 20, 1902, in the Jastrow Alumni Records file in the University of Pennsylvania Archives.

43. Jastrow, "The Historical Study of Religions," 318.

44. Jastrow, *Study of Religion,* 88, 85.

45. Ibid, 158, 180.

46. Molendijk, *Emergence of the Science of Religion,* 102.

47. Jastrow, *Study of Religion,* 103.

48. Barton, "Contributions of Morris Jastrow, Jr.," 328.

49. Capps, *Religious Studies,* 122.

50. William A. Clebsch and Charles H. Long, introduction to *The Study of Religion,* by Morris Jastrow, Jr. (1901; Chico, Calif.: Scholars Press and the American Academy of Religion, 1981), 13.

51. Sharpe, *Comparative Religion,* 138.

52. Jastrow, *Study of Religion,* 19.

53. Clebsch and Long, introduction to Jastrow, *The Study of Religion* (1981 edition), 14.

54. Uday Singh Mehta, *Liberalism and Empire: A Study in Nineteenth-Century British Liberal Thought* (Chicago: University of Chicago Press, 1999).

55. Jastrow, "Recent Movements in the Historical Study of Religions in America," 31–32.

TWELVE

Jewish Liberalism through Comparative Lenses

Reform Judaism and Its Liberal Christian Counterparts

YAAKOV ARIEL

In the opening years of the twenty-first century, the Episcopal Church in the United States of America faced one of its worst crises. A number of leaders and parishes threatened to secede unless the ordination of a gay bishop by the diocese of New Hampshire was censured and revoked.[1] The Episcopal Church eventually underwent a minor schism, when a few dozen conservative parishes in the United States seceded and created their own, more conservative, Episcopal union. By contrast, over the past two decades, the Reform movement in contemporary Judaism has ordained dozens of gay and lesbian rabbis and voted almost unanimously in 2000 to allow rabbis to perform same-sex unions, but without undergoing any split like that experienced by the Episcopal Church.[2] Reform Judaism also did not face any crises when it decided, in the 1980s, to ordain gay and lesbian rabbis or when, as early as the 1970s, it accepted gay synagogues into the Union of American Hebrew Congregations (renamed, in 2003, the Union for Reform Judaism). There were minor disagreements when the Central Conference of Reform Rabbis decided to allow gay rabbis to perform ceremonies for gay couples, but the very few rabbis who objected to gay unions in 2000 did not lead a movement of protest, much less secession, similar to that of their conservative Episcopal counterparts.

In spite of taking a consistently progressive path, the Reform movement has avoided more than strife and splits. Since the 1970s, liberal Christian groups in America have lost membership and influence. No such demographic downturn has taken place in the Jewish Reform movement, which, during the same period, advocated similar policies but has nonetheless gained in members and prestige, becoming the largest and most influential movement within American Judaism.

A comparison of the effects of social and cultural developments on Reform Judaism and on liberal Christianity, and of the manner in which Reform Jews and liberal Christians have reacted to those developments, can offer a better understanding of where Reform Judaism stands within the larger spectrum of religious views and practices in America. It can give us a better perspective on Reform Judaism and its relation to contemporary cultural and political choices. It can also tell us something about the nature of the Jewish liberal mainstream and some of its anomalies. Likewise, such a comparative outlook can yield new and unexpected understandings of liberal Christianity and its characteristics. No less important, such an examination can provide new insights into the relationship between liberal Christians and Jews. That gay Jewish services started in the early 1970s in an Episcopal church tells us, for example, something about liberal Judaism's sources of inspiration, in spite of the fact that eventually Reform Judaism adapted to gay liberation more smoothly and comprehensively than many Protestant groups.

A LONG AND COMPLICATED RELATIONSHIP

Since its inception in early nineteenth-century Germany and mid-nineteenth-century America, Reform Judaism has been inspired by liberal Protestantism.[3] The interaction with liberal Christianity has affected Reform Jewish thought, congregational life, and liturgical practices. To Jewish antagonists from the Orthodox camp, it seemed at times that the essence of Reform Judaism was the Protestantization of Judaism. However, this is not to say that the relationship between Reform Jews and liberal Protestants was one of mutual admiration. For Jews, liberal Protestantism offered both a model and a challenge, and an ambivalent relationship developed between the two groups, which included cooperation and rivalry.[4] Since the nineteenth century, Reform Jews defined their theological, liturgical, and cultural positions in relation to both more traditionalist Jews and liberal Christians. Many of the polemics produced by the Reform movement during the first generations were intended to confront claims made by Christian liberals about the originality and authenticity of the Christian and Jewish messages. Reform Jews adopted lifestyles similar to those of their liberal middle-class Protestant neighbors, while keeping their own distinctive identity. They sought to gain the Protestants' respect, while competing with the latter to present a better model of progressive rational monotheistic faith.

Reform Judaism shared a great deal with its Protestant counterparts. Like liberal Christians, nineteenth-century Reform Jews saw themselves as rational, enlightened, "modern" people and defined their faith in terms that meshed well with the premises of the European Enlightenment. Reform Jews, who were usually commercial and professional urban elites, embraced the idea of progress and developed a liberal messianic understanding of world history compatible with that of postmillennial, progressive Protestant eschatology.[5] The academically educated Reform rabbinical elite set out to update Jewish practices and thought to bring them up to par with the spirit of the age. Both liberal Christians and Reform Jews considered it necessary to adapt to changing cultural norms and progressive thinking in order to keep their traditions alive and relevant. Both liberal Christians and Reform Jews saw themselves as committed to embracing scientific discoveries, meaning theories produced by the academic community. This embrace ultimately included acceptance of the higher criticism of the Bible, the philological, archeological, and literary analysis of sacred scriptures.

Those similarities notwithstanding, Reform Jewish thinkers were not always enchanted by how liberal Christians utilized scientific tools to interpret Jewish sacred texts. Reform leaders complained that liberal Christian thinkers were unwilling to treat Judaism with the respect that sophisticated and enlightened theologians should demonstrate. Protestant scholars, they charged, did not apply the same rigorous academic standards to the study of the New Testament and early Christianity that they brought to bear, with great zeal, when they studied the Hebrew Bible.[6] Likewise, to the horror of Jews, Protestant scholars of the ancient Near East produced studies that at times shattered the primacy and authenticity of the theological, ethical, and juridical messages of the Hebrew Bible.[7] Moreover, relying on seemingly objective scientific discoveries offered by the fledgling academic discipline of the history of religions, liberal Protestants insisted that theirs was the more advanced faith on the religious evolutionary ladder. Judaism, according to this theory, was merely a stepping-stone on the road toward a superior faith.[8] Protestant thinkers and scholars, Jewish leaders complained, had little doubt as to the authenticity and originality of their own faith and were unwilling to grant Judaism any credit for the emergence of Christian teachings.[9]

Reform Jewish scholars, such as Abraham Geiger in Germany and Kaufmann Kohler in the United States, set out to defend Judaism against what they considered to be ostensibly objective, but in fact biased, scholarship. Providing their own, alternative version of the history of the emergence of the two faiths, Jewish thinkers returned the Protestant compliments. Christianity's Trinitarian and Christological dogmas were an intellectually and spiritually downgraded form of Judaism. Reform leaders and scholars insisted that Judaism, not Christianity, was the more advanced monotheistic faith and the most compatible with both the idea of progress and the universal messianic times that were gradually unfolding by means of human reforms and technological improvements. A series of Reform leaders and scholars in Germany, Britain, and the United States pursued research on Second Temple Judaism and the rise of Christianity with the aim of pressing Christian thinkers to reconsider their theories and alter their views. Not surprisingly, these Jewish Reform scholars reached the conclusion that Christianity owed its Jewish elder sister a huge debt.[10] There were, however, realms in which Reform leaders considered Christianity to have exceeded Judaism and where they believed that Judaism should learn from its younger sister. These included religious art, architecture, and music, areas in which, for various historical reasons, the Reformers claimed, Judaism lagged behind.

The relationship between liberal Protestants and Jews in America, however, was not limited to theological and scholarly arguments. Reform Jews cooperated with liberal Christians over civic improvement and progressive social policies. There was, however, an anomaly in the position of Reform Jews on social issues. The Reform constituency of German-speaking Jews immigrated to America at about the same time that German Christians did. Most Protestant and Catholic German immigrants formed conservative enclaves within American Christianity and culture, with German Christian congregations serving, as a rule, as conservative currents within their respective traditions.[11] Galvanized by a progressive Reform leadership, most Jewish immigrants from Germany chose a different path. Even while retaining a partial use of the German language and some degree of German identity, Reform Jews became much closer—socially, culturally, and religiously—to American Christian progressives, most of whom were Anglo-Saxon in their background.[12] The Jewish anomaly can be partially explained by the middle-class, urban character that Reform congregations had attained by the turn of the twentieth century. Much of the difference was also due to the fact that Jews saw America as a land that could offer so much more than Europe and looked upon progressive policies as a means of ensuring their own well-being, a notion not necessarily shared by other German immigrants. The prestigious position of the intellectually inclined rabbinical elite also played a role, as the transformation of Judaism into a highly progressive religious community was largely their doing.[13]

Such rabbis felt particularly close to the Unitarians, an influential group in American life, though this relationship was also highly ambivalent. While Reform leaders associated and cooperated with Unitarian ministers, feeling that they had a great deal in common with them, they were also apprehensive. Some Jews joined the Unitarian ranks, and Reform leaders sensed danger and competition, not merely friendship and shared values.[14] Jenkin Lloyd Jones (1843–1918), a noted modernist Unitarian, and Emil G. Hirsch (1852–1923), a leader of Reform Judaism, became friends, met regularly, cooperated over social reform and the organizing of interfaith meetings, and, at times, preached from the same pulpits.[15] Hirsch, who also taught at the University of Chicago Divinity School, a liberal, modernist, Protestant (officially Baptist) institution, pursued his research on Jewish-Christian relations along Jewish triumphalistic and apologetic lines. Jewish Reform leaders also interacted with members of other modernist Protestant groups, including Episcopalians, Presbyterians, Methodists, Congregationalists, Quakers, and American Baptists. But there were differences between the mainstream Protestant groups and Reform Judaism. From the 1880s, when a group of traditionalist congregations seceded from the Union of American Hebrew Congregations, Reform Judaism enjoyed relatively great cohesion, with little opposition in its ranks to theologically or culturally progressive stands. This was hardly the case among liberal Protestants, whose groups were more heterogeneous. Many liberal Protestants struggled within their own denominations, well into the late twentieth century, competing with more conservative elements over the character of their groups.[16] But this advantage did not always pacify the anxieties of Reform leaders, who felt threatened by the more radical modernist groups. The Ethical Culture movement, in particular, acted as a thorn in the side of Reform Judaism. The fact that this movement was founded by Felix Adler, son of a Reform rabbi and designated for the rabbinate himself in his early years, added insult to injury.[17] In that, however, Reform Jews were not completely alone. Modernist Protestants, too, had to contend with more radical options, including Theosophy, New Thought, and the Society of Ethical Culture, and their relationships with these groups were rather mixed.[18]

Reform Jews often found themselves, alongside other progressives, at the forefront of social and civic initiatives to create urban environments congenial to middle-class citizens of varied ethnic and confessional backgrounds.[19] Reform Jews were not socialists. There were Jewish socialists in America in the late nineteenth century and the early and middle decades of the twentieth century, but they were far removed from the Reform milieu. Such "radicals" tended to come from the circles of East European Jewish immigrants, and they were not very interested in religious life or affiliation.[20] Reform Judaism represented more veteran, well-rooted, middle-class Jews, who were comfortable, on the whole, with the American political and economic order—who, in fact, thrived within that order. The attitude of Reform Jews toward social issues could be described as humanitarian philanthropy with some reformist tendencies. Affluent Reform members were willing to contribute money generously for the sake of educational progress, medical services, welfare agencies, and cultural refinement. In that they differed only marginally from their wealthy Protestant neighbors, often surpassing the latter in their philanthropic zeal.[21] Jews showed at times a sensitivity to racial inequality and ethnic suffering that emerged, perhaps, from their own experience as a vulnerable minority.[22] Inspired by their rabbi, Emil G. Hirsch, Chicago's Jewish social elite were active in assisting the disadvantaged.[23] In addition to supporting art, education, medicine, and welfare in Chicago itself, members of the community, notably Julius Rosenwald, gave large sums to such projects as the building of educational institutions intended to benefit African Americans in the southern United States. More radical Jewish Reform leaders, such as Judah Magness, cooperated with progressive elements in the Christian Protestant community, adapting ideas and policies taken from the Protestant Social Gospel movement to the Jewish scene.[24] Such exchanges point to the influence of the Protestant movement for social responsibility on a series of Jewish activists, who applied its teachings to the Jewish communal scene.[25]

INTERFAITH DIALOGUE AND (LIBERAL) PROTESTANT-JEWISH RECONCILIATION

The complicated interaction between liberal Christians and Jews continued throughout the twentieth century. Beginning in the late nineteenth century, liberal Jews and liberal Protestants pursued, often intermittently, a movement of interfaith dialogue, which did not result in any official changes to doctrines or policies. A number of liberal Jewish thinkers used the opportunity afforded by the World Parliament of Religions, in 1893, to deliver a series of lectures on Judaism and its historical mission. In the 1920s, liberal Protestants, Catholics, and Jews established a committee to fight racial and ethnic defamation and discrimination in American public life. This group served as a forerunner to a more permanent organization for the promotion of interfaith relations in America.[26] It was within this early atmosphere of Jewish-Christian cooperation over civic and social matters that the first liberal Protestant theologians in America granted legitimacy to an independent Jewish existence alongside the Christian church. Reinhold Niebuhr, who served as a pastor in Detroit in the 1920s, was strongly impressed by Jewish social consciousness and reached the conclusion that Jews were not in need of the Christian message, their own tradition offering them sufficient spiritual and moral guidance. Liberal Protestants were not all cut from the same cloth, and Niebuhr was a very different liberal than the Protestant modernists of the earlier generation. A neo-orthodox theologian whose views were shaped by, among other realities, the world wars and the rise of anti-democratic regimes in Europe and elsewhere, Niebuhr defined himself as a Christian realist and was concerned with social justice. He pioneered a new relationship between liberal Christians and Jews. The Jewish position also underwent a transformation. Following World War I, Reform rabbis such as Solomon Freehof and Stephen Wise developed a more appreciative attitude toward Christianity and expressed their wish to engage in interfaith dialogue as equals, giving up on former triumphalistic notions. Niebuhr's pioneering position found more willing ears following World War II, when liberal Protestants and Jews in America were granting each other a growing degree of legitimacy and joined ranks, alongside liberal Catholics, over mutual social concerns such as civil rights.[27] By that time, liberal Protestant involvement included, first and foremost, mainstream ecumenists, who were giving up on missions in favor of dialogue and reconciliation.[28]

A further breakthrough in the relationship between liberal Christians and liberal Jews took place between 1960 and 1970, during and following the Roman Catholic ecumenical council Vatican II. The council, which met intermittently between 1961 and 1965, produced a declaration, *Nostra Aetate,* which asserted that Christians owed Jews a historical debt. It also absolved contemporary Jews of corporal guilt for the execution of Jesus. Convinced of the need to amend Christian-Jewish relations in the generation after the Holocaust, liberal Protestants followed the Catholic example. Mainstream and liberal Protestant bodies issued declarations exonerating the Jews from accusations of deicide, often more emphatically than Vatican II. Most mainstream Protestant church bodies and theologians came to recognize the legitimacy of the existence of a Jewish faith alongside Christianity.[29]

Reform Jews filled an important role in advancing the new trends, although Conservative Judaism and the fledgling Reconstructionist and Renewal movements also took part in the dialogue. Not unexpectedly, Reform Jews dialogued with, and hosted in their temples, middle-class liberal Christians. It was left to the Renewal and Reconstructionist Jews to engage in dialogue and exchange of ideas with members of new religious movements. Discussions and cooperation with conservative Christians would become, rather ironically, the realm of representatives of the more traditional segments of Judaism. The growing rapprochement between the two traditions and the willingness of mainstream Western churches to look upon Judaism as a sister tradition has eased many of the tensions between liberal Protestants and liberal Jews, but some issues remain.

From the 1960s through the 1980s, most liberal Jews in America developed a protective attitude toward the state of Israel, and a number of Jewish activists expressed frustration over liberal Protestants' unwillingness to share the Jewish point of view. While Reform Judaism shares a great deal socially, culturally, and ideologically with liberal Christianity, and while liberal Christian churches have come to accept Judaism as a legitimate and viable religious tradition, it would be a mistake to assume that the relationship between liberal Christians and liberal Jews has become a long honeymoon. Since 1967, and especially during the 1970s and much of the 1980s, Reform Jewish leaders have been at odds with their liberal Christian comrades over the latter's often unfavorable opinions of Israel. During these years, American Jewry, including its more politically progressive elements, has been protective of the state of Israel and its policies. In spite of the rapprochement between the two faiths and the commitment of a number of liberal theologians and activists to mending the relationship between Christianity and Judaism, a growing number of liberal Protestant activists have become critical of Israel and its policies. Many of them have expressed sympathy with the Palestinians and their plight. In the first decade of this century, the liberal Presbyterian Church USA decided to withdraw its investments in companies that sell equipment that, in Presbyterian eyes, Israel has been using for the wrong purposes.[30] But by that time, tensions between politically progressive American Jews and their Christian counterparts had generally eased up. By the 1990s, criticism of Israeli policies became standard among Reform leaders and some of their congregants, and while the Reform movement at large has remained attached to Israel, the protective attitude has mostly disappeared. Voices that blame Protestants for siding with the Palestinians do not come, as a rule, from the Reform camp.

REFORM JEWS AND THE NON-LIBERAL PROTESTANTS

The growing rapprochement between liberal Jews and liberal Protestants becomes more evident when one compares this relationship to those that existed between Reform Jews and conservative Christians and Jews. Reform Jews have related to conservative Protestants very differently than to liberal ones. They have not looked upon them as role models, and they have considered them more a nuisance than a challenge. There have been huge cultural and ideological differences between Reform Jews and conservative Christians. Conservative Protestants have continued to insist that their faith is the only valid one and have refused to enter into interfaith dialogue, which assumes recognition of other faiths. Believing that all human beings need to accept Jesus as a personal savior in order to be "saved" and enjoy eternal life, they have continued to make extensive efforts to evangelize Jews, and they have criticized liberal Jews who in their eyes maintain a misguided understanding of the Jewish role in God's plans for humanity. Reform Jews, for their part, have often looked upon conservative Christians as enemies of an enlightened, open, and egalitarian society. Such suspicions have colored the relationship between Reform Jews and conservative Christians into the twenty-first century, pointing to the character of Reform Judaism as a movement situated on the liberal side of the American religious map. Like liberal Protestant groups of the last generation, Reform Judaism has been active, as a movement, in promoting civil liberties in

America, sponsoring a Commission on Social Action and the Religious Action Center in Washington, D.C., to advocate its progressive causes. "To be a Reform Jew," the movement declares, "is to hear the voice of the prophets in our head; to be engaged in the ongoing work of *tikkun olam:* to strive to improve the world in which we live."[31] These social, cultural, and political positions put Reform Judaism in the same boat with the liberal elements in American Christianity, which would not endear them to conservative Christians.

In recent years, liberal Jews have been unable to avoid the company of conservative Christians, who have become ubiquitous in American public life. Since the 1970s, the American religious tide has reversed, and conservatives have gained numbers and influence surpassing those of more liberal groups.[32] Students of American religious life claim that authoritative religious teachings have become more appealing than the openness and autonomy that liberal messages convey.[33] In the last decades, the more conservative religious groups have been on the rise, and their influence on American social and political agendas has increased considerably. For the past thirty years evangelical Christians and conservative Jews have cooperated over civic issues as well as over support for the state of Israel. A number of Orthodox rabbis, including Yechiel Eckstein, Yechiel Pupko, and Daniel Lapin, have attempted to build bridges between the Jewish community and conservative evangelical Christianity.[34] In part, such alliances have improved the relationship between the Jewish minority and one of the now more influential groups in contemporary American politics. Many Orthodox Jewish leaders also appreciate conservative policies. They oppose abortion and pornography and have no problem with prayer in schools as long as the government supports their independent religious school systems. However, the foremost motivation for conservative Jewish leaders to promote a closer relationship with conservative Christians is the realization that many in the evangelical community support the state of Israel, at times enthusiastically.[35] Such Christians, conservative Jewish leaders conclude, are friends of the Jews.

Reform Jewish leaders, on the other hand, have been less inclined to build a warm friendship with conservative evangelicals. Rabbi Eric Yoffie, who as leader of the Union of Reform Judaism was the leader of the largest Jewish movement in America, tried to walk a fine line, weighing his liberal leanings against his sense that a constructive relationship with major Christian groups was in the interest of American and world Jewry. Yoffie accepted, for example, an invitation by the late evangelist Jerry Falwell to speak at Liberty University, which Falwell established.[36] At other times, Yoffie has been less than enthusiastic about evangelical political and social positions and has pointed to the distance between liberal Jewish views and those of politically non-progressive evangelical Christians. Yoffie and many of his fellow Reform leaders do not share the opinions of the Orthodox rabbis who have advocated an evangelical-Jewish alliance. During the last three decades, an increasing number of Reform leaders have felt that their commitment to an open society and progressive politics takes precedence over the need to create alliances in order to protect Israel. Liberal Jews have also not always appreciated conservative positions on the Middle East. Since the 1990s, there has been a growing understanding between liberal Christians and progressive Jews on the Palestinian-Israeli conflict, as well as a mutual lack of agreement with more conservative Jews or Christians on that subject. Liberal Jews, including some Reform activists, have come to regard the conservative Christian, pro-Israeli stand as counterproductive to the building of a better relationship between Jews and Arabs in the Middle East. Both as Jews and as supporters of progressive policies and a reconciliatory stand on the prospect of peace in the Middle East, Reform leaders have chosen to look upon conservative Christians as less than friends.

The choice Reform Jewish leaders needed to make between a protective attitude toward Israel and a more critical attitude, based on universal principles, points to a major difference between them and their liberal Protestant counterparts. There is a tribal element in Reform identity, evidenced in the theology and liturgy of the group, as well as in some Jewish cultural components. Such tribal features are for the most part missing in Protestant liberal groups. Episcopalians see themselves only marginally as English, and there is hardly anything Scottish about the Presbyterian Church. Moreover, Protestant denominations do not worry themselves constantly about the well-being of Protestants around the globe. And yet Reform Judaism is much closer in its cultural and intellectual atmosphere to middle-class white Anglo-Protestantism than to "ethnic" Protestantisms of any kind. Reform Jews are in conversation with their Jewish brethren who are moderately more conservative than they, but not with those who are further to the right. Culturally and ideologically, many Reform Jews feel they have more in common with their Christian liberal counterparts in America than with, for example, Orthodox Jewish settlers in the West Bank or Hasidic Jews in Brooklyn. This feeling prevails in spite of recent trends in the Reform movement to search, in a progressive egalitarian manner, for spiritual roots in historical Hasidism.

A LIBERAL ALLIANCE?

It has seemed, at times, that Reform Jews, Unitarian Universalists, Zen Buddhists, liberal Quakers, liberal Episcopalians, liberal Presbyterians, and liberal members of other denominations have more in common with each other culturally, and at times even theologically, than they have with their conservative counterparts within their respective traditions.[37] Many Reform Jews feel more comfortable socially, culturally, and ideologically when associating with liberal Christians than with ultra-Orthodox Jews. Unitarians and liberal Episcopalians have, on some levels, more in common with Reform Jews than with those members of their tradition who seceded and organized alternative church bodies, not to mention with members of veteran conservative denominations such as the Southern Baptist Convention.

The Reform movement is not the only group of Jews sharing common ground with liberal Christianity. Since the 1960s, new progressive Jewish groups have entered the scene, at times being more open to alternative cultural developments than Reform congregations. In the 1960s and 1970s, this included a positive attitude toward the counterculture, which took a while for the better-established and more mainstream Reform movement to catch up with. The 1960s through the 1980s saw the rise of the Renewal movement, the Havura movement, the development of the Reconstructionist movement into a fully independent denomination within contemporary Judaism, and the rise of Humanistic Judaism. While these fledgling groups have remained small, they have joined the liberal wing of Judaism, at times voicing opinions that place them to the left of Reform Judaism. Likewise, the opposition of such left-wing Jews to many American policies in the last decades has been, at times, more vocal and decisive.

While Reform Jews and liberal Protestants have often disagreed over U.S. foreign policy relating to Israel, the two groups have found themselves struggling with similar challenges in American culture and public life. Both had to adjust to almost unparalleled changes, and even outright revolutions, in sexual morality and the relationships between the genders. They also had to contend with a reversal of fortunes: the decline of liberal religion in America and the rise to prominence of the religious right. Since the 1970s, most liberal religious groups have lost membership and standing in American society. In the last generation, liberal Jews and liberal Christians found themselves in a minority progressive alliance over social and moral issues in American public policy.

Many of those issues have related to sexuality and gender, topics that at the turn of the twenty-first century have become the litmus tests that define the character of groups on the American religious and cultural maps. Many other components—doctrinal platforms, theological constructions, scriptural exegeses, denominational liturgies, and leadership roles—have followed attitudes in the realms of gender and sexuality.

Like their liberal Christian counterparts, Reform Jews in the last decades have changed their opinions on many aspects of gender equality and the legitimate range of human sexuality, except that in Reform Judaism these changes have been more consistent and consensual.[38] As compared to most mainstream Christians, Reform Jews have shown themselves to be more uniformly, albeit cautiously, open to the revolution in gender roles and sexual morality that has taken place in American culture in the later decades of the twentieth century. An example is the gradual yet peaceful evolution of Reform attitudes toward gays and lesbians. The women's division of the movement was the first segment of Reform Judaism to come out, as early as 1965, in favor of gay rights and against the mistreatment of gay people.[39] In 1977, the general assembly of the Union of American Hebrew Congregations voted to support a human rights bill for gays and lesbians. In 1990, Hebrew Union College officially changed its guidelines to admit openly gay students. In 2000, the Central Conference of American rabbis asserted that "the relationship of a Jewish, same gender couple is worthy of affirmation through appropriate Jewish ritual."[40] Few religious groups have embraced the new progressive standards in the realm of sexual orientation as homogeneously as the Reform movement. (Notably, Reform stances on issues of gender and sexuality have been more unanimous than Reform opinions on Israel.) Even those Christian groups that are in principle on the liberal side of the religious map did not implement similar changes without serious internal struggles and, at times, secessions.

There are a number of possible explanations for the Reform movement's relatively smooth adaptation to changes in the realm of gender and sexuality. Its liberal theology offered a theoretical framework that encouraged the adoption of the cultural and ideological changes that the progressive, educated segments of society advocated. But theological principles offer only a limited explanation. The liberal adaptive impulse proved to be a mechanism of survival. Many of the current members of Reform congregations, like those of liberal Christian ones, would not have found their homes in those communities had they felt that their life choices and personalities were not respected there.

The relative smoothness with which the Reform movement implemented changes in the realm of gender and sexuality also resulted from the fact that demands for those reforms came from the rank and file of the movement. There was a difference in that respect between the theological and liturgical changes that Reform Jews initiated in the nineteenth century and those they have adopted in the later part of the twentieth century. Acting often within systems that respected structure and hierarchy, many nineteenth-century Jewish reformers led changes from above. A group of rabbi-patriarchs initiated many of the changes, while arguing between themselves as to the extent of the reforms they should implement. They utilized traditional communal and theological structures to implement modernist interpretations of the faith. In the late twentieth century, the paradigm reversed. Changes often came from below and made their way gradually to wider acceptance and official sanction in the movement at large. Groups such as Reform women, who were the first to voice opposition to discrimination against gay people, signaled demand for change. Such grass-roots laypersons lobbied extensively to achieve their goals. In addition to the democratic process that accompanied the changes at the end of the twentieth century, another key difference from earlier reforms is that the emphasis this time has been not merely on *tikkun olam,* the gradual building of the messianic age, but on a commitment to the equality of all humans, regardless of gender, sexual orientation, or ethnic background. Likewise, Reform Jews have come to place a greater emphasis on the dignity and autonomy of individual members.[41] These new outlooks, perhaps unintentionally, helped boost the Reform ranks.

The difference between the reactions of Reform Jews and liberal Protestants to the implementation of progressive agendas also points to a difference in the denominational structures of liberal Protestantism and Reform Judaism. A number of American mainline churches, mostly liberal in character, nevertheless contain conservative wings. These churches are also marked by significant differences in the attitudes of members in different parts of the nation. United Methodists in Illinois and in South Carolina are virtually two different communities of faith.

Whatever weight is given to the various explanations for this difference, it is evident that in comparison to their Christian counterparts, Reform Jews have altered policy over matters of sexuality and gender gradually and peacefully, and these changes have had little negative effect on the movement's membership patterns. Like many liberal Christians and other liberal Jews, Reform

Judaism has sanctioned reconstructed sexual norms and gender roles but has not fully deconstructed the older standards. Very few religious groups in America have advocated a total deconstruction of traditional norms, even at the height of the sexual revolution.[42] The new norm has become monogamous, stable relationships between two mature adults, albeit not necessarily between a man and a woman, and not necessarily consummated only after official matrimonial ceremonies. Like liberal Christians, Reform Jews have reread their sacred scriptures in order to build new understandings of God's messages to the faithful in the realms of gender and sexuality and have constructed new theologies that are more egalitarian and less homophobic.[43] Reinterpreting sacred texts signaled Reform Jews' willingness to bring about changes while demonstrating commitment to and continuity with the traditional teachings of Judaism.

Contrary to the usual predictions of sociologists of religion, progressive policies have helped boost Reform membership and morale. From the perspective of liberal communities in the last generation, the rise in Reform membership has been against the general tide and therefore unexpected. In spite of particularly low birth rates and the unavoidable aging of the American liberal Jewish population, the Reform movement has managed to enlarge its ranks both in absolute numbers and in relative size.[44] Alongside, but on a larger scale than, the younger Reconstructionist movement, Renewal congregations, and independent Havurot, Reform congregations attracted feminists, openly gay men and women, religiously mixed couples (both heterosexual and same-sex), and Jews by Choice—converts to Judaism, spouses of Jewish congregants, and persons exploring the Jewish option without converting. From the 1920s to the 1970s, the Conservative movement was the largest group in American Judaism, with its congregations serving as the standard choice for run-of-the-mill American Jews of Eastern European origins. Now Reform congregations have become the default affiliation for most middle-class, professional Jews holding moderately liberal, inclusive, and egalitarian views.[45]

While the movement does not grow by natural means, and loses a certain percentage of its children to other religious groups or to non-affiliation, the percentage of members and semi-members of Reform congregations who were not raised Jewish has sky-rocketed. At the turn of the twenty-first century, the liberal wings of Judaism have become a viable option for middle-class American seekers of spirituality and community. The ethnic amalgam of Reform members and their children has changed dramatically. While, merely a half century ago, Reform congregations were composed of people who could be easily recognized as ethnically and culturally Jewish, this is not the case any more. Many of the participants in services in Reform synagogues come from ethnic, geographical, or racial backgrounds that are far removed from the traditional ethnic stereotypes of Jews. In many congregations, the percentage of Jews by Choice is growing; such participants even, at times, make up the majority. The Reform movement, like its younger and smaller counterpart, the Reconstructionist movement, officially accepted changes in Jewish demography and identity when it decided that children of Jewish fathers whose mothers had not converted would be regarded as Jews. Most Reform congregations have been hospitable to mixed couples, accepting as members in good standing families composed of Jews married to non-Jews and their children, and often treating the non-Jewish spouses as members for all practical intents and purposes.[46] A look at many mainstream and liberal churches in America also reveals a multiethnicity that would not have been evident on such a large scale a generation ago. Like Reform congregations, these churches too have a high percentage of first-generation members, who have come from all sorts of ethnic, geographical, and religious backgrounds but have chosen to join congregations different from the ones in which they were brought up, having been attracted to the open and inclusive atmosphere of the liberal communities. Membership in liberal Jewish communities, like membership in Protestant churches, has become, at the turn of the twenty-first century, a matter of choice, based on individual preferences and not on an inherited sense of obligation.

Not relying on tribal identities and loyalties, Reform Jews in the last decades have tended, somewhat paradoxically, to feel a commitment not only to progressive policies but also to the incorporation into religious services of a greater range of traditional rituals, in the interest of cultivating Jewish spirituality. A similar tendency has been evident, at times, in liberal Protestant groups in the last generation. In the last decades, for example, some Episcopalians have adopted Pentecostal practices, such as speaking in tongues, which until a generation ago were identified with right-wing conservative evangelical groups.[47] Likewise, a number of American Christian congregations have taken a renewed interest in what they have come to regard as authentic Christian rites borrowed from Greek Orthodoxy or Roman Catholicism. Paradoxically, these liturgically traditionalist congregations tend to be on the progressive side of contemporary social and cultural choices. It should come as no surprise, therefore, that Reform Judaism has given voice in its newly printed *sidurim* and *machzorim* (prayer books for year-round use and for the high holidays) to the wisdom of the mystical Hasidic master Rabbi Nahman of Braslav, at the same time that it has amended the language of prayer to fit in with its egalitarian understanding of gender in relation both to congregants and to God.[48]

CONCLUSION

Throughout its history, the Reform movement has shared a great deal with its liberal Protestant counterparts. Both Reform Jews and Protestant modernists have adhered to the same ideologies, first and foremost among them the need to adjust their theologies and liturgies to the changing norms of an enlightened society and the scientific findings of the age. Both liberal Jews and Christians have been committed to *tikkun olam,* or social justice, the need for righteous humans to work toward the reformation of society without waiting for the messianic times and divine intervention.[49] Such notions have remained central to the liberals in both traditions and have informed many of their political opinions and social stands. At times, Reform Jews have found themselves disagreeing with their liberal Protestant comrades in arms over specific policies concerning Jews and Israel. Committed to universal values of social and political justice, Reform Jews have also contended with their identity as Jews, trying to walk a fine line between, on the one hand, their loyalty to Jewish causes and their wish to preserve Judaism and Jewry and, on the other hand, their commitment to universal progressive values. When Reform Jews responded to the demands of the women's and gay liberation movements, they were certain that they were remaining loyal both to the spirit of their tradition and to social justice and humanitarian principles. They have endured fewer dilemmas and internal struggles over these issues than over their positions on Middle East politics; indeed, on these issues Reform Jews have been freer than most Protestant groups to amend their policies.

In the last analysis, therefore, examining Reform Judaism through comparative lenses reveals substantial similarities between Reform Judaism and liberal Christianity. It also points to some long-existing differences between the way some Jews relate to society and culture and the way non-Jews in similar socioeconomic positions do. The values and choices of Reform Judaism as a community are reminiscent of those of the more progressive religious groups in America, some of which are situated beyond the boundaries of Christianity, such as Unitarian Universalism and Zen Buddhism. At the same time, Reform

Jewish implementations of progressive agendas have often been moderate, a fact that, combined with the membership's general willingness to incorporate such changes, has resulted in fewer controversies and caused less of a breach with the movement's traditional characteristics.

NOTES

1. On the Episcopal Church and the ordination of a homosexual bishop, see John Shelby Spong, "A Bishop Speaks: Homosexual History," http://www.beliefnet.com/story/130./story_13022_3.html; Elizabeth Adams, *Going to Heaven: The Life and Election of Bishop Gene Robinson* (Brooklyn, N.Y.: Soft Skull Press, 2006); and Mary Jane Rubenstein, "An Anglican Crisis of Comparison: Intersections of Race, Gender, and Religious Authority, with Particular Reference to the Church of Nigeria," *Journal of the American Academy of Religion* 72, no. 2 (June 2004): 341–65.

2. In 2001, a group of lesbian rabbis and scholars published an anthology on the experiences of lesbian rabbis in the last generation. While the book highlights the novelty of these experiences and the challenges embodied in them, it also describes the rabbis' struggles as ultimately successful. Rebecca T. Alpert, Sue Levi Elwell, and Shirley Idelson, *Lesbian Rabbis: The First Generation* (Piscataway, N.J.: Rutgers University Press, 2001).

3. On the history of the Reform movement in Judaism, see Michael A. Meyer, *Response to Modernity: A History of the Reform Movement in Judaism* (New York: Oxford University Press, 1988).

4. See Egal Feldman, *Dual Destinies: The Jewish Encounter with Protestant America* (Urbana: University of Illinois Press, 1990).

5. William R. Hutchison, *The Modernist Impulse in American Protestantism* (New York: Oxford University Press, 1976).

6. See Yaakov Ariel, "Christianity through Reform Eyes: Kaufmann Kohler's Scholarship on Christianity," *American Jewish History* 89, no. 2 (June 2001): 181–91.

7. Yaacov Shavit and Mordechai Eran, *The War of Tables: The Defence of the Bible in the 19th Century* (Tel Aviv: Am Oved, 2003). The book deals mostly with the Jewish neo-Orthodox reaction to Protestant research.

8. For example, Eric J. Sharpe, *Comparative Religion: A History,* 2nd ed. (Chicago: Open Court, 1986); and Daniel L. Pals, *Seven Theories of Religion* (New York: Oxford University Press, 1996).

9. See Friedrich Schleiermacher, *On Religion* (London: Kegan, Paul, Trench, Trubney, 1893), lecture 5, 210–56.

10. Significantly, these scholars included a number of outstanding leaders of the Reform movement in America at the turn of the twentieth century, who were engaged in writing books with that message: Isaac M. Wise, Emil G. Hirsch, and Kaufmann Kohler. See George L. Berlin, *Nineteenth-Century American Jewish Writings on Christianity and Jesus* (Albany: State University of New York Press, 1989); and Susannah Heschel, *Abraham Geiger and the Jewish Jesus* (Chicago: University of Chicago Press, 1998).

11. Martin E. Marty, *Pilgrims in Their Own Land* (Boston: Little, Brown, 1984). On German Catholics in America, see Jay Dolan, *The American Catholic Experience* (New York: Doubleday, 1985), 96–155. The literature on German Protestants deals often with very different de-

nominations and regions. See, for example, Carol K. Coburn's study of Lutherans in the rural Midwest, *Life at Four Corners: Religion, Gender, and Education in a German-Lutheran Community, 1868–1945* (Lawrence: University Press of Kansas, 1992).

12. See Naomi W. Cohen, *Encounter with Emancipation: The German Jews in the United States, 1830–1914* (Philadelphia: Jewish Publication Society, 1984); Avraham Barkai, *Branching Out: German-Jewish Immigration to the United States, 1820–1914* (New York: Holmes and Meier, 1994); and Alan Silverstein, *Alternatives to Assimilation: The Response of Reform Judaism to American Culture, 1840–1930* (Hanover, N.H.: University Press of New England for Brandeis University Press, 1994).

13. Yaakov Ariel, "Miss Daisy's Planet: The Strange World of Reform Judaism in America, 1870–1930," in *Platforms and Prayer Books: Theological and Liturgical Perspectives on Reform Judaism*, ed. Dana Evan Kaplan (Oxford: Rowman & Littlefield, 2002), 49–60.

14. Benny Kraut, "The Ambivalent Relations of Reform Judaism with Unitarianism in the Last Third of the Nineteenth Century," *Journal of Ecumenical Studies* 23 (1986): 58–68.

15. For records of such interactions, see Sinai Congregation Records, manuscript collection no. 50, boxes 2–4, American Jewish Archives, Cincinnati, Ohio.

16. Bradley J. Longfield, *The Presbyterian Controversy: Fundamentalists, Modernists and Moderates* (New York: Oxford University Press, 1993); and Martin E. Marty, *The Noise of Conflict, 1919–1941*, vol. 2 of *Modern American Religion* (Chicago: University of Chicago Press, 1997).

17. Benny Kraut, *From Reform Judaism to Ethical Culture: The Religious Evolution of Felix Adler* (Cincinnati, Ohio: Hebrew Union College, 1979).

18. See Leigh E. Schmidt, "Introduction: The Parameters and Problematics of American Religious Liberalism," in this volume.

19. John Henry Hepp, *The Middle-Class City: Transforming Space and Time in Philadelphia, 1876–1926* (Philadelphia: University of Pennsylvania Press, 2003).

20. See Emma Goldman, *Living My Life* (1931; New York: Penguin Group, 2006).

21. Leon Harris, *Merchant Princes: An Intimate History of Jewish Families Who Built Great Department Stores* (1979; New York: Kodansha International, 1994).

22. Peter M. Ascoli, *Julius Rosenwald: The Man Who Built Sears, Roebuck and Advanced the Cause of Black Education in the American South* (Bloomington: Indiana University Press, 2006); and Henry Morgenthau, *Ambassador Morgenthau's Story* (Detroit, Mich.: Wayne State University Press, 2003).

23. David Einhorn Hirsch, *Rabbi Emil G. Hirsch: The Reform Advocate* (Northbrook, Ill.: Whitehall, 1968).

24. Arthur A. Goren, ed., *Dissenter in Zion: From the Writings of Judah L. Magness* (Cambridge, Mass.: Harvard University Press, 1982).

25. Arthur A. Goren, *New York Jews and the Quest for Community: The Kehillah Experiment* (New York: Columbia University Press, 1979).

26. On the development of the interfaith movement in the United States, see Yaakov Ariel, "The Interfaith Movement in America," in *The Cambridge Companion to American Judaism*, ed. Dana Kaplan (New York: Cambridge University Press, 2005), 327–44.

27. On the religious atmosphere in the postwar era, see Will Herberg, *Protestant, Catholic, Jew* (New York: Bantam, 1960); and Martin E. Marty, *Under God Indivisible, 1941–1960*, vol. 3 of *Modern American Religion* (Chicago: University of Chicago Press, 1996).

28. See David A. Hollinger's afterword, "Religious Liberalism and Ecumenical Self-Interrogation," in this volume.

29. Yaakov Ariel, "American Judaism and Interfaith Dialogue," in *The Cambridge Companion to American Judaism,* ed. Dana Evan Kaplan (New York: Cambridge University Press, 2005), 327–44.

30. For the complicated relationship of liberal Presbyterians to Jews, Judaism, and Israel, see Rev. Jon M. Walton, "Everlasting Covenant: Presbyterian and Jews at the Crossroads," a sermon preached at First Presbyterian Church, New York City, September 26, 2004, available on the website of Presbyterians Concerned for Jewish, Christian, and Muslim Relations, http://www.pcjcr.org/waltonsermon.htm.

31. Marla Feldman, "Why Advocacy Is Central to Reform Judaism," Union for Reform Judaism, http://urj.org/socialaction/judaism/advocacy. The quoted sentence appears frequently on the URJ's website and also on the website of the Religious Action Center of Reform Judaism, http://rac.org.

32. There are a number of theories explaining the rise of conservative evangelicalism; one of the more interesting is put forward by the sociologist Christian Smith in his *American Evangelicalism: Embattled and Thriving* (Chicago: University of Chicago Press, 1998).

33. See David W. Lotz, Donald W. Shiver Jr., and John F. Wilson, eds., *Altered Landscapes: Christianity in America, 1935–1985* (Grand Rapids, Mich.: William B. Eerdmans, 1989).

34. See Jeffrey Ballabon, "Jews and Christians in America," *National Review Online,* June 7, 2002, http://old.nationalreview.com/comment/comment-ballabon060702.asp; and David Klinghoffer, "Testing Christian Patience," *National Review Online,* June 20, 2002, http://old.nationalreview.com/comment/comment-klinghoffer062002.asp.

35. See Zev Chafets, "The Rabbi Who Loved Evangelicals (and Vice Versa)," *New York Times,* July 24, 2005, http://www.nytimes.com/2005/07/24/magazine/24RABBI.

36. See Eric Yoffie, "Rev. Falwell's Influence Will Be Felt for Years, Even Generations, to Come," press release, Union for Reform Judaism, May 15, 2007, http://urj.org/about/union/pr/2007/falwell.

37. For example, Martin E. Marty, *The One and the Many: America's Struggle for the Common Good* (Cambridge, Mass.: Harvard University Press, 1997); and William R. Hutchison, *Religious Pluralism in America* (New Haven: Yale University Press, 2003).

38. On Reform Jewish understanding of gender and sexuality, see, for example, Walter Jacob and Moshe Zemer, eds., *Gender Issues in Jewish Law: Essays and Responsa* (New York: Berghahn, 2001); and Sylvia Barack Fishman, *A Breath of Life: Feminism in the American Jewish Community* (Hanover, N.H.: University Press of New England for Brandeis University Press, 1995), especially 41–42, 130–31, 148–50, 205–207.

39. "Resolution of the Women of Reform Judaism National Federation of Temple Sisterhood: Homosexuality," 25th Biennial Assembly of Women of Reform Judaism, available on the website of the Institute for Judaism and Sexual Orientation at Hebrew Union College–Jewish Institute of Religion, http://www.huc.edu/ijso/PoliciesResponsa/.

40. "Resolution on Same Gender Officiation," adopted at the 111th convention of the Central Conference of American Rabbis, March 2000, http://data.ccarnet.org/cgi-bin/resodisp.pl?file=gender&year=2000.

41. On liberal theology in the later decades of the twentieth century, see Peter Gomes, *The Scandalous Gospel of Jesus: What's So Good about the Good News?* (New York: HarperOne, 2007).

42. James D. Chancellor, "The Children of God," in *Introduction to New and Alternative Religions in America,* ed. Eugene V. Gallagher and W. Michael Ashcraft, vol. 2 (Westport: Greenwood, 2006), 135–55.

43. For example, Rosemary Radford Ruther and Rosemary Skinner Keller, eds., *In Our Own Voices* (San Francisco: HarperSanFrancisco, 1995); and Frederick Greenspan, "Homosexuality and the Bible," *CCAR Journal: The Reform Jewish Quarterly,* fall 2002, 38–48.

44. On the demographics of American Jewry, see Sidney Goldstein, "Profiles of American Jewry: Insights from the 1990 National Jewish Population Survey," *American Jewish Year Book* 92 (1992): 77–173. On demographies in relation to denominationalism, see Bernard Lazerwitz, J. Alan Winter, Arnold Dashefsky, and Ephraim Tabory, *Jewish Choices: American Jewish Denominationalism* (Albany: State University of New York Press, 1998); and United Jewish Communities in cooperation with the Mandell L. Berman Institute–North American Jewish Data Bank, "The National Jewish Population Survey, 2000–01: Strength, Challenge and Diversity in the American Jewish Population," September 2003 and updated January 2004, http://www.ujc.org//local_includes/downloads/4606.pdf.

45. Neil Gillman, *Conservative Judaism: The New Century* (West Orange, N.J.: Behrman House, 1993).

46. Rahel Musleah, "Jewish Jeopardy," *Reform Judaism* 30, no. 1 (fall 2001): 18–24.

47. Randall Balmer has visited such a community: *Mine Eyes Have Seen the Glory: A Journey into the Evangelical Subculture in America,* 3rd ed. (New York: Oxford, 2000), 109–28.

48. See, for example, Elyse D. Frishman, ed., *Mishkan T'filah: A Reform Siddur* (New York: Central Conference of American Rabbis, 2007).

49. Catherine Wessinger, "Millennialism with and without the Mayhem," in *Millennium, Messiahs, and Mayhem,* ed. Thomas Robbins and Susan J. Palmer (New York: Routledge, 1997), 47–59.

PART THREE

Pragmatism, Secularism, and Internationalism

THIRTEEN

Each Attitude a Syllable

The Linguistic Turn in William James's Varieties of Religious Experience

LINDSAY V. RECKSON

> Often, though, the differences between liberalism and secularism are those of inflection.
>
> —*William E. Connolly*

LISTENING TO WILLIAM JAMES

When William James began the Gifford Lectures in Natural Religion before a larger than expected and by all accounts sympathetic audience at Edinburgh, in May 1901, he did so with a bit of anxiety (or at least, performed anxiety) around the very act of speaking: "To us Americans," he intoned, "the experience of receiving instruction from the living voice, as well as from the books, of European scholars, is very familiar. . . . It seems the natural thing for us to listen whilst the Europeans talk. The contrary habit, of talking whilst the Europeans listen, we have not yet acquired; and in him who first makes the adventure it begets a certain sense of apology due for being so presumptuous."[1] Like his brother Henry James, William knew how to work a room of Europeans; but this was not simply a show of cultural modesty or a tribute to his philosophical progenitors. De-naturalizing the scene of the lecture, James began *Varieties of Religious Experience* by carving out a novel rhetorical moment, transforming the unfamiliar territory of the European lectern into a veritable transatlantic verbal "adventure." Five and a half years later, he would begin the Lowell Lectures on Pragmatism—this time to an American audience—with a similar, self-deprecatory nod to the conventions of the lecture form: "Whatever universe a professor believes in must at any rate be a universe that lends itself to lengthy discourse. A universe definable in two sentences is something for which the professorial intellect has no use" (*Pragmatism,* 487).

To take note of such disarmingly humorous moments is to recognize in James's lectures a sustained, playful awareness of the relation between philosophical content and its delivery; it is also to proffer the rather presumptuous suggestion that attending to these idiosyncratic moments may yield significant information about the practice of religious liberalism. As my epigraph signals, this essay turns to a more ephemeral instantiation of the loose network of ideas and cultural phenomena that characterized liberalism's flourishing at the turn of the century; working to catch a certain inflection at work in James's lectures, I argue that *Varieties of Religious Experience* set the tone for a pragmatic approach to religion that increasingly characterized liberal belief. Such an argument depends on the possibility that liberalism might be described not just as a historical development but also as a linguistic practice. Over the course of twenty lectures, James did not simply ventriloquize a variety of religious sentiments—he also performed religion as a practice of linguistic uncertainty. Having no use for "a universe definable in two sentences," James insisted on the extended task of articulating experience, while offering an antinomian wink at the traditional standards governing that task. And James's speech—with its starts and stops, anxious tremors and sure resonances—has much to tell us about how we might begin to speak now about the varieties of American religious liberalism.[2]

Listening to James, then, we might recognize that what he called the "adventure" of speaking was just that: an adventurous romp through the inflections of religious liberalism. This despite James's acknowledgment that he drew much of his material from the "extremer examples" of religious experience, collating "radical expressions" and "extravagances of the subject" in hopes that they might "[yield] the profounder information" (*Varieties,* 436). James's selections perhaps indicate his playful experimentation with the nascent disciplinary and experiential boundaries of "religion" *tout court.*[3] Indeed the most explicit articulation of liberalism in *Varieties* rests precisely—if reductively—on a change of tone to suit the prevailing winds of optimism: "The advance of liberalism, so-called, in Christianity, during the past fifty years, may fairly be called a victory of healthy-mindedness within the church over the morbidness with which the old hell-fire theology was more harmoniously related" (*Varieties,* 88).[4] Such a description makes clear the stakes of reading James's liberalism more as a linguistic method than as a matter of content; even from within a decidedly facile account of liberalism, the almost tic-like acknowledgments of verbal maneuvering ("so-called" and "may fairly be called") signal James's more radical attention to the constructions of cultural discourse as well as to the ways in which language, and particularly religious language, actively shapes experience.

Against the shorthand of dogma, James's conversational gestures—preserved without revision in his published works—register the need for a lengthier discourse, and one not fully confined to the time of the lecture or the space of the text. As we will see, if James's beginnings dwell self-consciously on the work of speaking and listening, his endings indicate that such work is both interminable and insufficient; every effort is necessarily partial, yet crucial to a larger collective project of transcription and translation. Privileging risk over comfort, such an approach makes room for false steps and false starts, linguistic or otherwise. Scholars of James's pragmatism have been continually rankled, for example, by what they read as an oscillation in *Varieties* between positive statements of religious truth and more pragmatic articulations of religion's use-value; the effort to pin down James on these points runs up against his resistance to concluding, his penchant for delay and detour. If James's text, as Gerald Myers has argued, "sometimes appears to accept the separation of paths between believers and non-believers, and at other times insists upon having the last word," it remains steadfastly wary of authority of all sorts, including its own.[5]

TRANSLATING EXPERIENCE

By the time he delivered the eighteenth lecture of *Varieties of Religious Experience,* James was ready to concede that his audience might be onto him: "I imagine that many of you at this point begin to indulge in guesses at the goal to which I am tending." Having presumably reduced religion to "an affair of faith," loosening it from its theological moorings over the course of his seventeen previous lectures, James confesses that, as his listeners may have guessed, his task in lecture eighteen, "Philosophy," is partly to highlight the belatedness of any attempt to codify the divine in philosophical terms:

> To a certain extent I have to admit that you guess rightly. I do believe that feeling is the deeper source of religion, and that philosophic and theological formulas are secondary products, like translations of a text into another tongue. But all such statements are misleading from their brevity, and it will take the whole hour for me to explain to you exactly what I mean. (*Varieties,* 387)

Slowing down and stretching out the task of explanation, James playfully evokes both the predictability of his lectures' repetitive formulations and the rather benign, almost subconscious tendency of listeners to anticipate speech. Acknowledging the subtle pleasure of guessing "rightly," and thereby linking the work of listening with the stakes of "religious philosophy" that he will treat in the coming lecture, James implicitly undermines the possibility of advance knowledge. When he describes the speculative quality of philosophy only a few paragraphs later, he notes, "These speculations must, it seems to me, be classed as over-beliefs, buildings-out performed by the intellect into directions of which feeling originally supplied the hint" (*Varieties,* 388). By drawing his listeners' attention to their own customary speculations—the habitual reliance on hints of feeling that allow us, for example, to anticipate the progress of a lecture—James links the work of philosophy to the cognitive functions of everyday life, even as he artfully exposes the misleading ease of reaching even the most foregone conclusions. Allowing generous intellectual space for the habit of anticipation—and the deeper necessity of prospective thought—James nevertheless insists on the "whole hour," literally coming to terms with the slow, meandering work of translating religious experience.

Reading James's lectures in this way highlights the tension between what has been read as their pragmatic expediency—insofar as they anticipate "a method of settling metaphysical disputes that otherwise might be interminable" (*Pragmatism,* 506)—and James's commitment to the interminable project of registering and explaining experience. In *Varieties,* this tension has everything to do with the function of language, its ability to serve the dual project of denotation and deferral. Indicating how words serve the subjective aims of philosophy, James notes for example that reason "finds arguments for our conviction, for indeed it *has* to find them. It amplifies and defines our faith, and dignifies it and lends it words and plausibility. It hardly ever engenders it; it cannot now secure it" (*Varieties,* 392). If reason amplifies faith through language, and thereby lends plausibility to religious or philosophical prediction, it is importantly neither a first cause nor a guarantee. It is instead a kind of grammar, which James indicates in a footnote to this passage, where he cites Harold Fielding's 1902 tract, *The Heart of Man:*

> "Creeds," says the author, "are the grammar of religion, they are to religion what grammar is to speech. Words are the expression of our wants; grammar is the theory formed afterwards. Speech never proceeded from grammar, but the reverse. As speech progresses and changes from unknown causes, grammar must follow" (p. 313). The whole book, which keeps unusually close to concrete facts, is little more than an amplification of this text. (*Varieties,* 392n1)

Distinguished from grammatical "creeds," religion becomes—for Fielding and, I would argue, for James—the progression of words before their breakdown into parts of speech, before any attempt to diagram the sentence. Before and, indeed, *after* any attempt to diagram the sentence, for if grammar offers a way to anticipate the patterns of speech, it cannot account ahead of time for the variations in speech to which grammar's explanatory mechanism must necessarily adapt.[6] Drawing on Fielding to make the analogy between creed and grammar, religion and speech (and more implicitly, between the progress of speech and the amplification of "the whole book"), James lets the course of his own speech remain uncharted, performing the linguistic uncertainty by which he will offer a provisional approximation of religious experience. George Santayana noted this proclivity for unmoored speech when he later memorialized James:

> While he shone in expression and would have wished his style to be noble if it could also be strong, he preferred in the end to be spontaneous, and to leave it at that; he tolerated slang in himself rather than primness. The rough, homely, picturesque phrase, whatever was graphic and racy, recommended itself to him; and his conversation outdid his writing in this respect. He believed in improvisation, even in thought; his lectures not minutely prepared. . . . One moment should respect the insight of another, without trying to establish too regimental a uniformity.[7]

And yet minute distinctions were sometimes crucial to James's project, often resting (if precariously) on specific verbal formulations. Thus, however intricately bound up in one another they might be, Fielding asserted that "religion" was separate from "creed," a differentiation that echoes in James's insistence, throughout *Varieties,* on the distinction between religion and the "over-beliefs" that almost always attend it, the theoretical or theological doctrines that help to parse and codify the "varieties" of religious experience. After giving full rein to those varieties in his lectures—often preserving the "grammar" of first-person testimony—in his concluding lecture James determines to move from "preliminaries" to a "final summing up" of what religion might look like apart from creed:

> I am expressly trying to reduce religion to its lowest admissible terms, to that minimum, free from individual excrescences, which all religions contain as their nucleus, and on which it may be hoped that all religious persons may agree . . . and on it and round it the ruddier additional beliefs on which the different individuals make their venture might be grafted, and flourish as richly as you please. I shall add my own over-belief . . . and you will, I hope, also add your over-beliefs, and we shall soon be in the varied world of concrete religious constructions once more. (*Varieties,* 450–51)

In seeking the "lowest admissible terms," words that might precipitate out of "concrete religious constructions," James acknowledges himself to be in dangerous territory: "I am well aware that after all the palpitating documents which I have quoted, and all the perspectives of emotion-inspiring institution and belief that my previous lectures have opened, the dry analysis to which I now advance may appear to many of you like an anticlimax, a tapering-off and flattening out of the subject, instead of a crescendo of interest and result" (*Varieties,* 450). Invested as James is in the performance of delay, the attempt here to come to "terms" treads a careful line, offering to draw some conclusions without allowing the text its climax or crescendo, which—as we will see—must be continually postponed. After the "palpitating documents" both included and produced by *Varieties,* James looks for a steadier, more vital rhythm. Sensitive to what is at stake—for both believers and secularists alike—in reducing religion to its lowest common verbal denominator, James "expressly" looks for terms broad and benign enough to forge a general agreement.

Given recent reconsiderations of pragmatism as an approach to language, this search for the "lowest admissible terms" in James's concluding lecture to *Varieties* has given some scholars pause in attempting to sketch out a pragmatic approach to religion. When such attempts are made—and attempts have been made, increasingly since the onset of what has been called "the revival of pragmatism"—scholars have understandably turned to the more suggestive characterization of belief in James's *The Will to Believe* and John Dewey's *A Common Faith.* Robert Westbrook and Sandra Rosenthal, for example, have highlighted Dewey's distinction between theistic "religion" and the naturalized "religious" aspects of experience—a very different distinction than the one James makes between "religion" and "over-beliefs"—as an important demonstration of pragmatism's democratic or liberal amenability to faith.[8] Similarly, Gerald Myers concludes in his influential study that "James's philosophy of religion is distinctive not in its pragmatism, but rather in its special interpretation of the range of religious experiences presented in *Varieties*."[9] When scholars have sought to synthesize James's exertions on behalf of religious experience with the pragmatic philosophy that he articulated several years later, "pragmatism" becomes the name not of a philosophical effort but of a utilitarian compromise between the natural and the supernatural, a meeting of psychological and spiritual explanations for religious phenomena.[10] While these various contributions have furthered our understanding of the highly charged relation between religion and pragmatism (and between religion and philosophical discourse more generally), none has examined the extent to which James's linguistic experimentation—his attention to the syntax of experience and the grammar of belief—offers a form of religion that is neither stripped of its (always tentative) metaphysical claims, nor at odds with the humanistic commitments of James's pragmatism.

Drawing on the work of scholars who have examined pragmatism's deep investment in the trajectories of language, and looking closely at texts that have proved problematic or have been overlooked by scholars of pragmatism and religion (namely "The Pragmatic Method" [1898], the "Conclusion" to *Varieties* [1902], and the last lecture of *Pragmatism*, "Pragmatism and Religion" [1907]), this essay offers a reading of James on religion that will begin to bridge the gap between literary or philosophical approaches to pragmatism and efforts to read James's religious texts as instructive cultural artifacts. Without minimizing the importance of these different interpretive "grammars," James's own attempts to stretch the boundaries of intellectual context point to the need to read across such boundaries, to examine the pragmatic aspects of James's religious language, and to begin to register the impact of pragmatic language on religion itself. Importantly, such work is never merely linguistic; rather, it depends on the precarious role that language plays in mediating relations, in translating—however imperfectly—the "individual excrescences" that James classed as over-beliefs, and that we might recognize in historical perspective as characterizing a burgeoning field of religious diversity at the turn of the century. As James recognized in a footnote to his first lecture, "Religious language clothes itself in such poor symbols as our life affords" (*Varieties*, 19n1);

acknowledging the poverty of the religious idiom, James nevertheless understood that the vestments of faith come with stringent dialects, demanding an endless project of translation.[11]

DISPLACEMENTS AND SUBSTITUTIONS

As Giles Gunn has pointed out, religion's role in the revival of pragmatism has been marginal at best, and largely due to the influence of the philosopher Richard Rorty, who continually linked "the development of pragmatism" to "[secular] liberalism's project of disenchanting the world religiously."[12] Inheriting his grandfather Walter Rauschenbusch's emphasis on the social efficacy of creed, Rorty nevertheless worked to divest liberalism and pragmatism of their religious counterparts, describing religion as "a conversation-stopper" in public discourse.[13] Rorty's phrase is meant to be suggestive; like James, Rorty understood intimately that the production of truth is a linguistic process, and one in which new vocabularies are constantly being forged.[14] Indeed, Rorty began his seminal text *Contingency, Irony, and Solidarity* (1989) with a turn of phrase that James himself frequently employed: "I begin, in this first chapter, with the philosophy of language because I want to *spell out* the consequences of my claims that only sentences can be true, and that human beings make truths by making languages in which to phrase sentences."[15] As we will see, "spelling out" became a crucial metaphor for James in the articulation of religious truth; no "conversation-stopper," James's philosophy of religion depended on a poetics of deferral, an ongoing process of sentence making.[16]

Toward the end of his career, Rorty modified his strictly secular approach to the pragmatic production of truth, offering a version of pragmatism as "romantic polytheism." To make this argument, he cited a passage from the final lecture of *Varieties of Religious Experience:*

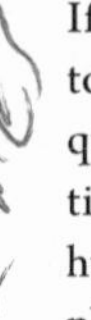

> If an Emerson were forced to be a Wesley, or a Moody forced to be a Whitman, the total human consciousness of the divine would suffer. The divine can mean no single quality, it must mean a group of qualities, by being champions of which in alternation, different men may all find worthy missions. Each attitude being a syllable in human nature's total message, it takes the whole of us to spell the meaning out completely.[17]

Rorty's reading of this passage bears consideration both for what it enacts and for what it potentially eclipses; he writes, "James's loose use of the term 'the divine' makes it pretty much equivalent to 'the ideal.' In this passage he is doing for theology what Mill had done for politics when he cited von Humboldt's claim that 'human development in its richest diversity' is the aim of social institutions." James's insistence on the heterogeneity of individual experience is a move from theological dogmatism to what Rorty calls "romantic polytheism," a move he links to Mill's articulation of political liberalism. Several paragraphs later, Rorty offers a more secularly inflected analogy for the Jamesian "divine": "Polytheism, in the sense I have defined it, is pretty much coextensive with romantic utilitarianism."[18] Uncomfortable as he is with James's "total human consciousness of the divine," Rorty moves subtly from James to Mill, from "divine" to "ideal," and from "polytheism" to "utilitarianism," forcing the very substitution of "qualities" that James cautions against in the above passage. For Rorty, they are "pretty much equivalent," or "pretty much coextensive." Given James's resistance to this interchangeability, it is no surprise that Rorty turns to Dewey's tepid tolerance for theism (and not to James's "brave and exuberant" belief) as the model for religion's place in neopragmatism.[19]

What allows (or perhaps necessitates) this bait and switch is what Rorty calls James's "loose" terminology, the kind of linguistic inconsistency that Rorty critiques elsewhere when he suggests that *Varieties* offers two possible understandings of religious truth: one purely pragmatic, the other with a positive intellectual content.[20] This latter reading is based on what Rorty notes as James's occasional slips into metaphysical pronouncements, most noticeably his appeal to "*a wider self through which saving experiences come,*" where he exchanges an emphasis on utilitarian belief for positivist doctrine, and thereby—at least implicitly—moves from tolerance to imposition (*Varieties,* 460, emphasis in original). Rorty suggests that these conflicting tendencies offer an interpretive conundrum: to read *Varieties* as a pragmatic text (where religious truth is solely what works in the world) is to wonder "why we need bother with all those virtuosi" when we have a more streamlined version of this pronouncement in "The Will to Believe"; to read it for its "Bergsonian metaphysics" is to acknowledge that "James is *betraying* his own pragmatism."[21] Settling on this latter conclusion, Rorty suggests we read *Varieties* more as an intellectual portrait than as a philosophically pragmatic tract: another substitution.

But Rorty's use of "betraying" here offers its own interpretive conundrum: either Rorty's terminology is itself "loose," or, having read Richard Poirier's meticulous reading of the word "betray," Rorty is offering a kind of ironic critique, setting up a choice that is really no choice at all. In Poirier's *Poetry and Pragmatism,* "betray"—as it is used by Emerson, but easily with broader application—signals "a telling instance of that linguistic play or punning which everywhere . . . precipitates mutations and superfluities of meaning, of saying by unsaying."[22] Betrayal and superfluity are corollary linguistic efforts, both crucial to James's project in *Varieties,* which uses the uncertain trajectories of language to temper the necessity of metaphysical decision-making. If James is "betraying his own pragmatism," he is both revealing and compromising his metaphysical commitments, and in so doing, he performs what Poirier describes as that most pragmatic of speech acts: the recognition, in language, of something "wider" than the linguistic structures available to it. By neglecting the complexity of James's "loose" or "vague" language, Rorty (perhaps despite himself) points us to the possibility that "all those virtuosi"—those superfluous religious testimonies filling the pages of *Varieties*—are just so many crucial "syllables" in the pragmatic spelling out of religious experience.

In Rorty's analysis, "the substitution of poetry for religion" characterizes pragmatism's turn to polytheism, and in this substitution, one cannot help but wonder whether or not he implicitly erases Wesley and Moody from the Jamesian equation. If so, one wonders additionally why Rorty would choose a passage from *Varieties* that works so tenaciously against any such erasure; James explicitly rejects the substitution of priest for philosopher, and of poet for priest, even as he refuses to reify those positions (and as Michael Robertson argues in this volume, Whitman's saint-like status in James's era upends any such rigid distinction). Gunn offers a similar critique of Rorty's romantic polytheism when he notes, "If Rorty were not so attached to a Romantic aesthetic that views art . . . as a substitute for religion, he might see more clearly the virtues of a pragmatic aesthetic that views art, as in Henry James, Kenneth Burke, and, most recently, Richard Poirier, as a complement to, sometimes even a corollary of, religion." Gunn goes on to describe Poirier's invaluable "reinstatement of the vague" (after James), the "saving uncertainty" that language offers in its constant conversion of fixed meaning into fluid significance, its inability to demarcate without marking its effort as only a starting point for new discovery.[23]

In drawing on Poirier in his response to Rorty, however, Gunn shows a similar tendency to substitute poetry for religion; interested as Poirier is in the creative, salvific quality of language's skeptical manipulations, his text does not treat the implications of such a reading for pragmatism's encounter with religious experience.[24] Even allowing that James defined religion pragmatically, or "arbitrarily," as "*the feelings, acts, and experiences of individual men in their solitude, so far as they apprehend themselves to stand in relation to whatever they may consider the divine*"—and furthermore that James insisted the "divine" be considered "very broadly, as denoting any object that is god*like,* whether it be a concrete deity or not" (*Varieties,* 36–38, emphasis in original)—Poirier treats pragmatism as "essentially a poetic theory"; neither *Varieties of Religious Experience* nor the "Pragmatism and Religion" chapter of *Pragmatism* appear in his study.[25] And even as Poirier points to the way that Emerson and James worked to reshape the "conceptual terminologies" of philosophy, religion, and even poetry itself, he does not examine pragmatism's turn to the transitive as offering a fertile hermeneutic for rethinking the place of religion in pragmatic language and thought, which is what I hope to do here. Poirier's readings will be crucial to any attempt to address the religious aspects of pragmatic language, but valuable as they are, they are only (and would likely only profess to be) a starting point.

SPELLING IT OUT

More recently than Poirier, and with more attention to the decidedly "ministerial" inflection of some of its most poetic voices, Joan Richardson has offered a natural history of pragmatism, a study of the linguistic processes of repetition and amplification that mark the pragmatic method of engaging with texts and the natural world they inhabit. Beginning her chapter on William James with an epigraph from Nietzsche's *Twilight of the Idols* ("I fear we are not getting rid of God because we still believe in grammar"),[26] Richardson charts James's conversion of a religiously inflected faith in the over-soul to an empirical revelation of the relation between the human and the larger, invisible order of its environment. As Richardson illustrates, James preserved and naturalized religious feeling as the aesthetic response to this relation, a response encoded in the affective work of language. She examines James's performance, in *Varieties,* of language as a material fact upon which we must continually focus our ever-shifting attention; the preservation of the spoken syntax and references to the duration of speech produce the sensation of voiced words as objects of thought, even as James discusses the very operation of consciousness by which we register and respond to the immaterial.

In this linguistic demonstration of the "reality of the unseen," the cloaked narrative of James's "vastation" in lectures six and seven of *Varieties* ("The Sick Soul") becomes central to Richardson's argument, as she reads its hypertextual incorporation of Emerson's famous "transparent eye-ball" passage as well as a parallel section from Bunyan's *Pilgrim's Progress.* Arguing that this kind of textual encoding draws on James's abiding interest in the insights of the natural sciences, Richardson notes, "Newton, Davy, Faraday, Lyell live in the imaginings these sentences imitate for the writer and stimulate for the reader or listener. The imitation is in the performance of reception . . . it is religious experience, and it gives pleasure."[27] Here, James's ongoing textual adaptation marks the pitch of the aesthetic, the homeostatic equilibrium that all organisms seek in a changing environment, the elusive project of continual adjustment of which religious feeling is both an impetus and an effect.

That language is the medium of this aesthetic adjustment for pragmatism is perhaps Richardson's key claim, and building off of this insight, we might look again at James's insistence in the concluding lecture of *Varieties,* "The divine can mean no single quality, it must mean a group of qualities. . . . Each attitude being a syllable in human nature's total message, it takes the whole of us to spell the meaning out completely." Here, the divine is necessarily dynamic, inextricably tied to the syntax of an ever-unfolding sentence, and composed of infinitely idiosyncratic "grammars"; to listen to James at this moment is to hear pluralism manifested quite literally at the sentence level. Stretching through time and across the bounds of individual belief, the "total message" is only *potentially* linked to complete meaning; James's interest lies in the process of spelling it out, linking the literal work of making and using language to the ongoing effort of making and using religious truth. In the process, he undermines a presumably straightforward linguistic project that would "spell the meaning out completely" and thereby provide a measure of comforting certainty. Evoking as it does the earliest steps in the development of language skills, "spelling out" becomes James's metaphor for the always preliminary, hypothetical, and laborious production of religious truth, a collective labor in which communication and contact are urgent imperatives. This focus on the construction of belief at the level of syntax finds its macro equivalent in James's repeated evocation, in *Varieties,* of what is possible in the time of the lecture or in the space of the printed book, spans of linguistic effort that James is deeply invested in marking as "unsatisfactory in their brevity," or nowhere close to spelling out the total message. James closes his supplementary postscript to *Varieties* by repeating this phrase: "But all these statements are unsatisfactory from their brevity, and I can only say that I hope to return to the same questions in another book," indicating that even the lectures' transcription into a nearly five-hundred-page text could not offer a definitive end to the conversation (*Varieties*, 469).

Importantly, it is the very "unsatisfactory" force of explanation that is linked to religious hope, in *Varieties* and elsewhere: a version of what Poirier notes when he asserts "that by a conscious effort at linguistic skepticism it is possible to reveal, in the words and phrases we use, linguistic resources that point to something beyond skepticism." While Poirier names this "beyond" as the "possibilities of personal and cultural renewal,"[28] James might have also called it (and here is my own substitution) religion, and it is worth examining why scholars of James's pragmatic language have hitherto left the ongoing question of religious belief relatively untouched. Where they have addressed it, as we have seen, it tends to be subsumed under the aegis of poetry or the aesthetic writ large. Richardson argues, for example, that James's interest in language acquisition and other mechanisms of cognitive reception allowed him, over time, to convert his religious conception of the "more" of experience into an understanding of the "vague" as the linguistic corollary to mental processes. In Richardson's reading, religion offered James "what he would eventually come to realize, purely, as an aesthetic solution—in his case, at this point, an atavistic reflex reaction offering him redemption, temporary balance, made possible by the language of his culture." It is this recognition that allowed James to develop his pragmatic philosophy, "where in place of any lingering idea of God the Creator or any lesser *deus ex machina,* he substituted the machinery of the mind."[29] While elsewhere in Richardson's study religion remains an important element of the aesthetic, here the aesthetic seems to take the place of rote religious practice, which becomes a rather stale literary construction in the face of the more challenging frameworks of natural science and psychology.

Without forcing too neat a distinction between "aesthetic" and "religious" experience, or ascribing a stable intellectual content to either, one might still examine how James's language lingers over problems specific to religious belief—lingers even over the idea of God—from his 1898 essay "The Pragmatic Method," to the pages of *Pragmatism,* arguably his most abiding philosophical statement. To approach James's religious discourse in this way is to highlight the extent to which religion—defined in and through language—retains the openness and creative receptivity of the pragmatic aesthetic, without being stripped of its status as a "*real hypothesis,*" as James described it in his concluding lecture to *Varieties* (462, emphasis in original). This is necessarily a larger project than this particular text can cover, but we might begin by looking closely at a few key moments from *Varieties,* "The Pragmatic Method," and *Pragmatism,* to highlight how intricately James's religious formulations are bound up in the precarious project of using words.

Positing God as "a very considerable over-belief" in the conclusion to *Varieties,* James refuses to spell out the specifics of this nevertheless real "claim," which is not simply an effect of language ("It is only transcendentalist metaphysicians who think that . . . by simply calling [Nature] the expression of absolute spirit, you make it more divine just as it stands") (*Varieties,* 463). Rather it is bound up in language production itself, as James notes when he appeals to prayer as "a sense that *something is transacting,*" tabling the question of any objective truth in the transaction: "This act is prayer, by which term I understand no vain exercise of words, no mere repetition of certain sacred formulae, but the very movement itself of the soul, putting itself in a personal relation of contact with the mysterious power of which it feels the presence—it may be even before it has a name by which to call it" (*Varieties,* 416). From "spelling it out," James moves even further back in the production of language to the moment before the pronunciation of syllables, the exercise of prayer being a kind of groping for linguistic expression before any knowledge of—or determination by—the grammatical forms of over-belief.

This kind of prelinguistic groping also finds expression, pointedly, in the last words of *Varieties* as it was delivered in lecture form; citing one of his more vocal opponents, W. K. Clifford (whose staunch naturalism James addressed more directly in "The Will to Believe"), James writes, "I *can,* of course, put myself into the sectarian scientist's attitude, and imagine vividly that the world of sensations and of scientific laws and objects may be all. But whenever I do this, I hear that inward monitor of which W. K. Clifford once wrote, whispering the word 'bosh!'" (*Varieties,* 463, emphasis in original). Playfully adopting what is perhaps the "lowest admissible term" of scientific skepticism to express instead a kind of intuitive religiosity (or even the hearing of voices), James lets the word "bosh" link these categorically opposed "tempers"—as he would later describe them in *Pragmatism*—to highlight the extent to which both are bound up in grammatical conventions. He also performs the stubborn effectiveness of language itself, using a word that literally means nonsense to create not only a very clear sense of resistance to one particular philosophical vocabulary, but also—at the end of *Varieties*—to hold out for a syntax that might, eventually, spell out its meaning. Both skeptically monitoring overreaching truth claims and providing a space for hypothetical religious truth, "bosh" is perhaps an absurdly sensible expression of the relation James is forging between religion and its poetic possibilities.

Indeed, James repeatedly found "bosh" to be a serendipitous expression for what we might call a liberal skepticism qua skepticism. In his 1909 essay "The Confidences of a 'Psychical Researcher,'" James conceded that even for a "liberal heart," the investigation of psychical phenomena provided overwhelming evidence of imposture; nevertheless, he refused to reject the possibility of a more generous interpretation:

> The "bosh" end of the scale gets heavily loaded, it is true, but your genuine inquirer still is loathe [*sic*] to give up. He lets the data collect, and bides his time. He believes that "bosh" is no more an ultimate element in Nature, or a really explanatory category in human life than "dirt" is in chemistry. Every kind of "bosh" has its own factors and laws; and patient study only will bring them definitely to light. . . . To settle dogmatically on this bosh-view would save labor, but it would go against too many intellectual prepossessions to be adopted save as a last resort of despair.[30]

If James here expresses a scientifically inflected willingness to bide his time—to sit with an inconclusive data set—he also achieves a verbal bait-and-switch, reclaiming the "bosh" of dogmatic skepticism as itself an object of skeptical observation.

We can contrast this "bosh" to the more rigid theological language that James critiques in "The Pragmatic Method," originally delivered as a speech to the University of California's Philosophical Union in August 1898: a text that, as David Hollinger points out, is "almost entirely about God," and—perhaps not so coincidentally—has been almost entirely ignored by scholars of pragmatism.[31] Here, James scorns the verbal maneuvering of "systematic theologians": "Their orthodox deduction of God's attributes is nothing but a shuffling and matching of pedantic dictionary-adjectives, aloof from morals, aloof from human needs, something that might be worked out from the mere word 'God' by a logical machine of wood and brass as well as by a man of flesh and blood."[32] Throughout "The Pragmatic Method," James's concern is with a kind of religious terminology that might be pragmatically attuned to human needs, with what might constitute dynamic linguistic belief in the place of theological deduction.

After asking his listeners to think ahead to the last moment of the world, and demonstrating that the language of materialism vs. theism would have no traction in a "finished" universe, James then asks us to "revert" back to these questions, placing ourselves "*this time* in the real world we live in, the world that has a future, that is *yet uncompleted whilst we speak.* In this unfinished world the alternative of 'materialism or theism?' is intensely practical; and it is worth while for us to *spend some minutes of our hour* in seeing how truly this is the case." Linking the time of the speech to the significance that ongoing temporal experience lends to linguistic distinctions (as we have seen him do in *Varieties*), James retains the verbal formulation as such, working through what it might mean to believe in "a world with a God in it to say the last word." Repeated verbatim in the conclusions to *Varieties,* the "last word" here can only be the promise of more words: "Where He is, tragedy is only provisional and partial, and shipwreck and dissolution not the absolutely final things."[33] Here, the word "God" offers no *deus ex machina* guarantee of narrative closure or ultimate knowledge; instead, it signals the hope inherent in the very provisional and necessarily partial nature of our efforts (linguistic, critical, or otherwise).

Similarly, James anticipates his later work in *Pragmatism* (1907), *A Pluralistic Universe* (1909), and *The Meaning of Truth* (1909) when he exposes the verbal circumlocutions plaguing the metaphysical dispute between monism and pluralism: "Is it not first of all clear that when we take such an adjective as 'One' absolutely and abstractly, its meaning is so vague and empty that it makes no difference whether we affirm or deny it?" With painstaking attention to the possible meanings of the word "one," James demonstrates that "this absolutely total connection either means nothing, is the mere word 'one' spelt long, or else it means the sum of all the partial connections that can possibly be conceived."[34] Prefiguring his description of the collectively formulated message-in-progress—"each attitude a syllable"—James rejects the merely verbal for the ongoing work of producing meaning, a work bound up in the heterogeneous, cooperative effort to communicate, and intimately connected to the provisional, poetic language of religious hope.

DILATORY AND DUMB

By way of demonstrating that these issues do not drop out of James's later works, I want to turn now to another text that has received insignificant critical attention, despite its being a part of what is likely the most widely read of James's philosophical tracts. The last lecture of James's *Pragmatism,* "Pragmatism and Religion," has been examined largely for the contrast it offers to James's assertion, in "The Pragmatic Method" and later in *Varieties,* that "where He is, tragedy is only provisional and partial, and shipwreck and dissolution not the absolutely final things." The end of *Pragmatism* sounds decidedly different, however concerned it remains with last words:

> May not the notion of a world already saved *in toto* anyhow, be too saccharine to stand? May not religious optimism be too idyllic? Must *all* be saved? Is *no* price to be paid in the work of salvation? Is the last word sweet? Is all "yes, yes" in the universe? Does n't the fact of "no" stand at the very core of life? Doesn't the very "seriousness" that we attribute to life mean that ineluctable noes and losses form a part of it, that there are genuine sacrifices somewhere, and that something permanently drastic and bitter always remains at the bottom of its cup? (*Pragmatism,* 617, emphasis in original)

In its insistence on the moral efficacy of tragedy, this passage is an early instantiation of Cornel West's prophetic pragmatism, which sees in philosophy an opportunity for cultural criticism, and which enlists the religious thought of James, Reinhold Niebuhr, and W. E. B. Du Bois, among others, to critique the "optimistic theodicy" of pragmatism in the Emersonian strain.[35] Against the world "already saved *in toto,*" James writes, "I am willing that there should be real losses and real losers, and no total preservation of all that is. I can believe in the ideal as an ultimate, not as an origin, and as an extract, not the whole" (*Pragmatism,* 617). But I would argue that the more tragic tenor of this passage is still invested—like *Varieties* and earlier texts—in the space that language offers for the deferred possibility of salvation, itself a linguistic production of meaning: "Each attitude being a syllable in human nature's total message, it takes the whole of us to spell the meaning out completely." If as West points out, James "temporalizes knowledge," on a different scale he also temporalizes language, linking religious truth to the "last word" that we are ever in the process—and only ever in the process—of formulating.[36] Pragmatism, for James, must "postpone dogmatic answer," settling for a sentence in progress and made up of syllables that we can only begin to translate (*Pragmatism,* 619).

The text that receives very little scholarly attention in *Pragmatism* is Whitman's "To You," which appeared in the 1891–92 version of *Leaves of Grass,* and which James reads almost in full at the beginning of "Pragmatism and Religion."[37] While Rorty ends his call for romantic polytheism with a turn to Whitman's *Democratic Vistas* and an invocation of "the United States of America . . . as a symbol of openness to the possibility of as yet undreamt of . . . forms of human happiness," James needs Whitman's longer, more poetic line in his appeal to linguistic uncertainty as the meeting point of pragmatism and religion. While in *Varieties* James cited Whitman, in less than complimentary terms, as an example of willfully blind optimism—one particularly venerated soldier in liberalism's "victory of healthy-mindedness"—his turn to Whitman in the final lecture of *Pragmatism* operates quite differently. Here James evokes a more tentative, more intimate version of the possibility that language carries, and of the delay encoded in possibility itself:

> O I have been dilatory and dumb,
> I should have made my way to you long ago,
> I should have blabbed nothing but you, I should have
> chanted nothing but you. (*Pragmatism,* 606)

Evoking his own dilatory speech, and linking Whitman's vague apostrophe to the "you" that he has been addressing throughout his lectures, James subtly confesses to the sense of having missed something, to finding himself somehow "tangent to the wider life of things" (*Pragmatism,* 619). It is this sense, for James, that signals "a genuine pragmatist . . . willing to live on a scheme of uncertified possibilities which he trusts; willing to pay with his own person, if need be, for the realization of the ideals which he frames" (*Pragmatism,* 618). If James is "spelling it out" here, at the end of *Pragmatism,* he is doing so in the cadence of Whitman's refrain, itself a kind of chant or prayer, that form of speech which James called, in *Varieties,* "religion in act" (416). He is offering a pragmatic articulation of religious hope, without claiming to have the last word.

NOTES

My deepest thanks to Ross Posnock, Michael Robertson, Leigh Schmidt, Tom Ferraro, and my courageous writing group for their generous feedback on drafts of this essay. Discussions at the Cultures of Religious Liberalism conferences in Princeton and New Haven were essential to the development of my thinking, and I thank the participants for sustained and sustaining conversation.

The epigraph is from William E. Connolly, *Why I Am Not a Secularist* (Minneapolis: University of Minnesota Press, 2000), 10.

1. William James, *Varieties of Religious Experience* (1902), in *Writings, 1902–1910,* ed. Bruce Kuklick (New York: Library of America, 1987), 11. This volume also contains *Pragmatism: A New Name for Some Old Ways of Thinking* (1907), as well as other works. Further citations are given in the text, with page numbers preceded by *Varieties* or *Pragmatism* as appropriate. On James's Edinburgh audience, see Robert D. Richardson, *William James in the Maelstrom of American Modernism* (New York: Houghton Mifflin, 2006), 403.

2. To give just one example, in his 2002 lecture "The Specific Regime of Enunciation of Religious Talk," philosopher Bruno Latour began his talk in the spirit of Jamesian articulation: "I have no authority whatsoever to talk to you about religion and experience because I an neither a predicator, nor a theologian, nor a philosopher of religion—nor even an especially pious person. . . . It is from this very impossibility of speaking to my friends and to my

own kin about a religion that matters to me, that I want to start tonight: I want to begin this essay by this hesitation, this weakness, this stuttering, this speech impairment. Religion, in my tradition, in my corner of the world, has become impossible to enunciate." Like James, Latour preserved the form of the address in his published essay. Bruno Latour, "'Thou Shall Not Freeze-Frame,' or, How Not to Misunderstand the Science and Religion Debate," in *Science, Religion, and the Human Experience,* ed. James Procter (New York: Oxford University Press, 2005), 27.

3. On James's ecumenicalism, see Richard Gale, "The Ecumenicalism of William James," in *William James and "The Varieties of Religious Experience": A Centenary Celebration,* ed. Jeremy Carrette (New York: Routledge, 2005), 147–56. Francesca Bordogna has offered the compelling argument that such playful transgression of boundaries was an "essential strategy" in James's larger intellectual project. Francesca Bordogna, *William James at the Boundaries: Philosophy, Science, and the Geography of Knowledge* (Chicago: University of Chicago Press, 2008), 7.

4. Situating liberalism rather conservatively "within the church," James's description here sounds remarkably similar to what Leigh Schmidt describes in his introduction to this volume as "the drumbeat of neo-orthodox critique—one in which liberal faith had often been reduced to little more than a religion of gush, cheerfulness, and sentimentality." Elsewhere in *Varieties,* James links liberalism to a more far-flung emphasis on the validity of individual experience: "From Catholicism to Lutheranism; from that to Wesleyanism; and from this, outside of technical Christianity altogether, to pure 'liberalism' or transcendental idealism, whether or not of the mind-cure type, taking in the medieval mystics, the quietists, the pietists, and quakers by the way, we can trace the stages of progress towards the idea of an immediate spiritual help, experienced by the individual in his forlornness and standing in no essential need of doctrinal apparatus or propitiatory machinery" (196).

5. Gerald E. Myers, *William James: His Life and Thought* (New Haven: Yale University Press, 1986), 457.

6. Directly after the portion of text that James quotes, Fielding writes, "But if not? If grammarians are hide-bound, are we to refuse to talk? In this latter case, if the reason were mine, I think reason would say 'Bother these theologians, their dogmas and creeds, their theories and grammars, what do they matter? The instinct of prayer remains, of confession, of sacrifice.'" Harold Fielding, *The Hearts of Men,* 3rd ed. (London: Hurst and Blackett, 1904), 303.

7. George Santayana, "William James," in *William James Remembered,* ed. Linda Simon (Lincoln: University of Nebraska Press, 1996), 93.

8. Robert Westbrook, "An Uncommon Faith: Pragmatism and Religious Experience," and Sandra B. Rosenthal, "Spirituality and the Spirit of American Pragmatism: Beyond the Theism/Atheism Split," both in *Pragmatism and Religion: Classical Sources and Original Essays,* ed. Stuart Rosenbaum (Chicago: University of Illinois Press, 2003), 190–205, 229–42. See also Robert B. Westbrook, "Pragmatism and Democracy: Reconstructing the Logic of John Dewey's Faith," in *The Revival of Pragmatism: New Essays on Social Thought, Law, and Culture,* ed. Morris Dickstein (Durham: Duke University Press, 1998), 128–40.

9. Myers, *William James: His Life and Thought,* 469.

10. See, for example, Ann Taves, *Fits, Trances and Visions: Experiencing Religion and Explaining Experience from Wesley to James* (Princeton: Princeton University Press, 1999); and Ann Taves, "The Fragmentation of Consciousness and *The Varieties of Religious Experience*: William James's Contribution to a Theory of Religion," in *William James and a Science of Reli-*

gions: Reexperiencing "The Varieties of Religious Experience," ed. Wayne Proudfoot (New York: Columbia University Press, 2004), 48–72.

11. James Kloppenberg has suggested that James's gestures toward the inadequacy of language help explain his varying importance to philosophers and historians: "Whereas philosophers who have made the linguistic turn might scoff at James's insistence on the inadequacies of language to capture and pin down the magic of experience, historians have good reasons to pay attention." In contrast, I read such gestures in line with Richard Poirier's description of pragmatic speech acts, which continually recognize (through language) that which exceeds the linguistic structures available to describe it. Hence James's insistence on the ever-unfolding syntax of experience in contrast to the fixed grammars of belief, a contrast which might be analogously seen in the distinction between the syntax of scholarship—an ever-unfinished, collaborative effort—and the belated disciplinary grammars of history and philosophy, for example. James T. Kloppenberg, "Pragmatism: An Old Name for Some New Ways of Thinking?" in Dickstein, *The Revival of Pragmatism,* 99.

12. Giles Gunn, "Religion and the Recent Revival of Pragmatism," in Dickstein, *The Revival of Pragmatism,* 404. It might be noted that Rorty's view stands in direct contrast to this volume's understanding of the relationship between religious and political or secular modes of liberalism, which, as Leigh Schmidt notes in his introduction, are "taken to be dynamic and mutually constitutive" and in "continual interplay."

13. Richard Rorty, "Religion as Conversation-Stopper" (1994), in *Philosophy and Social Hope* (London: Penguin, 1999), 171. On the relationship between Walter Rauschenbusch's Social Gospel Protestantism and Richard Rorty's pragmatism, see Casey Nelson Blake, "Private Life and Public Commitment: From Walter Rauschenbusch to Richard Rorty," in *A Pragmatist's Progress? Richard Rorty and American Intellectual History,* ed. John Pettegrew (Rowman & Littlefield, 2000), 85–101.

14. Richard Poirier offers an important critique of Rorty's insistence on the possibility of "new" vocabularies, noting that "language can and must, if it is to remain a medium of communication, pay due respect to already constituted versions of reality even as it sets out to dislodge them; it accommodates itself to 'previous truths' and to the 'heirlooms' of language, as James called them." Richard Poirier, "Why Do Pragmatists Want to Be Like Poets?" in Dickstein, *The Revival of Pragmatism,* 350.

15. Richard Rorty, *Contingency, Irony, and Solidarity* (Cambridge: Cambridge University Press, 1989), 9 (emphasis added).

16. As William Gavin notes of *Varieties,* "The text is never finished; closure is always deferred. The text for James is doomed to eternal incompleteness, first, in the sense that any theory, as directional, is incomplete; second, the text as such is vague in the sense that it is James's own form of rebellion, of living 'heroically' as it were." William Joseph Gavin, *William James and the Reinstatement of the Vague* (Philadelphia: Temple University Press, 1992), 10.

17. James, *Varieties,* 437, quoted in Richard Rorty, "Pragmatism as Romantic Polytheism," in Dickstein, *The Revival of Pragmatism,* 23.

18. Rorty, "Pragmatism as Romantic Polytheism," 23–24.

19. Ibid., 29.

20. Richard Rorty, "Some Inconsistencies in James's *Varieties,"* in Proudfoot, *William James and a Science of Religions,* 86–97.

21. Rorty, "Some Inconsistencies," 96 (emphasis added). On the "why bother?" question—or why James's pluralistic commitment to variety constituted a "serious theoretical

intervention"—see Carrie Tirado Bramen, *The Uses of Variety: Modern Americanism and the Quest for National Distinctiveness* (Cambridge, Mass.: Harvard University Press, 2000), 30.

22. Richard Poirier, *Poetry and Pragmatism* (Cambridge, Mass.: Harvard University Press, 1992), 38.

23. Gunn, "Religion and the Recent Revival of Pragmatism," 411, 413.

24. For example, of Emerson's "soul," Poirier notes, "he could as readily have called it 'desire,'" without accounting for what is at stake in this transposition. Poirier, *Poetry and Pragmatism,* 25.

25. Poirier, *Poetry and Pragmatism,* 135.

26. Joan Richardson, *A Natural History of Pragmatism: The Fact of Feeling from Jonathan Edwards to Gertrude Stein* (New York: Oxford University Press, 2007), 98.

27. Ibid., 112.

28. Poirier, *Poetry and Pragmatism,* 11.

29. Richardson, *Natural History,* 99–100.

30. William James, "The Confidences of a 'Psychical Researcher' (1909)," in *Essays in Psychical Research,* ed. Fredson Bowers (Cambridge, Mass.: Harvard University Press, 1986), 368–69.

31. William James, "The Pragmatic Method" (1898), *Journal of Philosophy, Psychology and Scientific Methods* 1, no. 25 (December 1904): 673–87; and David Hollinger, "'Damned for God's Glory': William James and the Scientific Vindication of Protestant Culture," in Proudfoot, *William James and a Science of Religions,* 22.

32. James, "The Pragmatic Method," 681.

33. Ibid., 677 (emphasis added), 679.

34. Ibid., 684–85.

35. Cornel West, *The American Evasion of Philosophy: A Genealogy of Pragmatism* (Madison: University of Wisconsin Press, 1989), 226.

36. Ibid., 67.

37. Richard Poirier, Joan Richardson, and Ross Posnock, among others, have noted James's debt to Whitman without citing this particular text. See Poirier, *Poetry and Pragmatism;* Richardson, *Natural History;* and Ross Posnock, *The Trial of Curiosity: Henry James, William James, and the Challenge of Modernity* (New York: Oxford University Press, 1991).

FOURTEEN

Protestant Pragmatism in China, 1919–1927

GRETCHEN BOGER

The teachings of Jesus can be best brought to our people by appealing to our mind and intellect in addition to our heart. Their usefulness and reasonableness should be demonstrated along with their power.

—*Chengting T. Wang, 1921*

The missionary press itself reveals a profound ferment, a passion to justify faith by works.

—*Lewis S. Gannett, 1926*

In May 1919 John Dewey arrived in China for what he imagined would be a brief visit. Chinese scholars eagerly anticipating the arrival of the great pragmatist philosopher met him at the docks. Dewey intended to stay for two months and wound up staying over two years, during which time attendance at his lectures regularly was in the thousands. Some enthusiasts followed him from city to city; others read the translated texts of his talks published in hundreds of daily newspapers and literary journals. His lectures on educational philosophy, democracy, and the experiential approach to the acquisition of knowledge all were of keen interest to Chinese intellectuals engaged in a cultural reform effort known alternately as the Chinese Renaissance, the New Thought Movement, or the New Culture Movement.[1] The initiative had begun several years earlier among scholars at Peking University who believed that overhauling Chinese society's cultural foundations might be the means to erecting a vital modern state. Though the ideas it encompassed were diverse, the movement put its greatest emphasis on rational inquiry as the means of liberating the Chinese people, struggling under unstable rule since the 1911 overthrow of the Ch'ing (Qing) dynasty.[2] New Culture founding member Chen Tu-Hsiu (Chen Duxiu) declared science and democracy the keystones of reform and saw them as related: people who were educated to use the scientific method in the pursuit of knowledge would be freed from submission to tradition and empowered to develop and sustain democratic institutions. Scientific inquiry, applied to human relationships as well as to the physical world, thus assumed a central role in the movement. One manifesto declared, "We believe that politics, ethics, science, the arts, religion, and education all should meet practical needs in the achievement of progress for present and future social life. . . . We believe that it is requisite for the progress of our present society to uphold natural science and pragmatic philosophy and to abolish superstition and fantasy."[3] This was not the pursuit of knowledge for knowledge's sake: it was aimed always at invigorating a fractured, weakly governed, economically distressed Chinese state.[4]

Despite the manifesto's mention of religion among potentially useful fields of knowledge, movement intellectuals in general were suspicious of religious faith as a hindrance to progress. Even as they embraced Dewey, as well as Darwin, Spencer, and Huxley, movement leaders largely rejected Western spiritual traditions. As one scholar puts it, "For many Chinese Nationalists the acquisition of Western science and technology did not mean the embrace of facets of Western culture deemed morally bankrupt or unscientific."[5] In 1920 the Young China Association, founded to increase national unity through scientific inquiry, questioned whether religion was of any use in the modern age. Devoting both a lecture series and multiple issues of its journal to the question, the association answered resoundingly in the negative. Religion was "superstitious," a vestige of a prescientific era incompatible with the rational methods that would govern the modern age.[6] Other movement leaders sounded similar judgments.

Though it began as an elite endeavor, the New Culture Movement gained momentum with the eruption of a student strike on May 4, 1919—just days after Dewey's arrival—that brought it into contact with the nascent nationalist sentiment of a wider public. The demonstration began in Peking in response to news from the peace talks at Versailles that the Allied Powers had secretly agreed to grant Japan control of former German concessions in Shantung

(Shandong) Province in northeast China, rather than return them to Chinese sovereignty. Furious at their country's betrayal by its wartime allies, three thousand university students turned out in the streets of Peking to declare themselves opposed to further Western influence in China. Strikes spread to cities nationwide in the next couple of months, as students and then workers and businessmen protested both the terms of the peace treaty and the arrest of hundreds of fellow strikers in Peking. Though the initial spate of political activity subsided in late summer, after the Chinese delegation at Versailles agreed not to sign the treaty, the experience ignited what came to be known as the May Fourth Movement. Drawing on the cultural renaissance already in progress, the May Fourth Movement increased popular participation in the Chinese nationalist project, gave it a more overtly political cast, and advanced a distinctly anti-Western strain in the campaign—even as nationalists continued to celebrate scientific and philosophic trends that had originated in the West. China might adopt Western ideas and make them indigenous, but popular sentiment increasingly dictated that it must reject Western control of its territory, institutions, and people.

The New Culture Movement's emphasis on pragmatism and its skepticism about religion, coupled with growing anti-Western sentiment, had significant implications for the eight thousand Protestant missionaries in China. At the start of the 1920s American foreign missions were at their historic peak, as measured by the number of volunteers serving in the field. A major enterprise of most mainline denominations, the modern mission movement boasted infrastructure, funding, and enthusiasm at home sufficient to support thousands of long-term evangelists throughout Asia. In China they taught in schools and universities, worked in hospitals, and served remote villages in the interior, building on a century's worth of precedent. In the decade following Dewey's visit to China, however, a series of nationwide political protests, beginning with the May Fourth demonstrations and ending with full-scale civil war in 1927, would not only disrupt the Western mission enterprise but would challenge the missionaries' understandings of their work and faith itself. Chinese nationalists, including Chinese Christian nationalists, increasingly compelled Western evangelists in the 1920s to engage the cultural and political currents most critical to local audiences. In the face of new and rapidly accumulating pressures on them, missionaries of all stripes found themselves struggling to articulate and adopt perspectives that would appeal to their audiences. Among these efforts were the attempts of a considerable contingent to develop a pragmatic approach to Christianity, one shaped by the New Culture Movement's emphasis on rationalism, experiential knowledge, and practically applicable truths. At the same time, this emphasis on a pragmatic faith influenced many missionaries' own belief and practice, as demonstrated most clearly in their foray into international politics in 1925 to campaign against the so-called "unequal treaties" between China and the Western powers.

The emphasis on practical application that emerged in Christianity in the mission field was not the simple continuation of prewar Western Social Gospel tendencies—though medical and educational work did play a huge role in China missions. American Social Gospelers had boldly claimed that one could discern what Jesus would do under any circumstances.[7] The emphasis on an ethical, applied Christianity in 1920s China was less ebulliently confident. The prospect for mission in the face of an increasingly hostile nationalist movement appeared much less certain than had human progress in the West before World War I. Responding to a society in turmoil, evangelists made adjustments to their practice that were at once more urgent and more tailored to the local setting. Whatever the religious predilections they brought to the field, their practice was shaped by the specifics of the Chinese context. The pragmatic message they developed in Asia was the peculiar product of Western Christians' interactions with, and responses to, the exigencies of an alien society in revolution.

The story of American Protestant modernism as it developed in the late nineteenth and early twentieth centuries is one that usually has been told as a geographically delimited narrative. For the most part it locates debates over Higher Criticism versus Fundamentalism, premillennialism versus postmillennialism, and faith versus works in American seminaries, pulpits, and religious journals. Missionaries appear in these accounts simply as further examples of domestic trends, mirroring the larger story. If they struggled to define their message in the 1920s, their struggle reflected uncertainties in the American church. If their debates were particularly rancorous, they demonstrated what one scholar has called the "missions intensifier" effect, in which evangelistic service abroad focused and invigorated diffuse dialogues already underway on the home front.[8]

What is obscured in narratives that look to the United States and Europe as the source of all developments in Protestantism in the early twentieth century is the degree to which missionaries, as transnational actors refashioning the faith in unfamiliar cultural contexts, operated as key agents in the promotion of an evolving, newly flexible Christianity. If mission work acted as a lens intensifying the heat of certain debates, it also acted as a prism, refracting American religious conversations and bending them in new directions. Growing interest in an ethically based, socially oriented theology in the years between the world wars owed much to the experience of Protestant missionaries in the culturally productive, interstitial space of the Chinese mission field.

The potential impact of the Chinese nationalist struggle on Christian evangelism still eluded most Protestant missionaries in the early 1920s. John Leighton Stuart, American Presbyterian missionary and president of Yenching University, observed with some surprise that "many missionaries seem strangely indifferent to, almost unconscious of, an outburst of mental activity so charged with new potentialities and so self-revealing" as the May Fourth Movement.[9] The community instead remained riven by internal debates that had grown increasingly acrimonious in recent years. American Fundamentalist theologian William Henry Griffith Thomas reported of his 1921 trip to China, "Before leaving America I was advised by one who knows the Chinese situation not to introduce controversial topics in any of my addresses but to leave these to be mentioned by missionaries. . . . I soon found to be true, what I had learned long before I left America, that missionaries were already divided into two camps."[10] Preeminent American preacher Harry Emerson Fosdick, also touring Asia in 1921, marveled after eight days spent speaking to a conference of missionaries in Kuling, "It was like walking a tightrope. . . . The tension was terrific," and vowed never to speak before so divided an audience again.[11] Perhaps owing to generational differences between older missionaries and college-educated recruits who had come of age since 1900, a deepening fissure seemed to be dividing evangelists committed to literal interpretations of scripture and to formal conversion as the critical component of mission work and evangelists who were open to a wider range of Biblical interpretations and who stressed the importance of missionaries' service through educational, medical, and agricultural work. In 1919 it indeed appeared as if a "missions intensifier" was at work, magnifying the Fundamentalist-modernist controversies experienced in the United States. Distrust accompanied disagreement, such that first-year missionary Rachel Brooks judged, "The words I have heard most frequently among missionaries are the words 'protect' and 'careful.' . . . But this use of 'protect' and 'careful' is not the speech of freedom, it is the speech of fear."[12] The missionaries whom Brooks encountered seemed to be guarding their faith from attack rather than sharing it joyfully—and the attackers they most feared were their fellow evangelists.

Missionaries were not the only Christians in China, however: by the 1920s Chinese Christians were developing leadership and self-direction sufficient to provide a counterbalance to the Westerners. Indeed, indigenous Christian leaders were growing increasingly frustrated with the tenor of religious conversations dominated by the missionaries. Though they were aware of the Westerners' disputes, working closely with missionaries as most of them did, they tended to find the issues at stake irrelevant to what they saw as the pressing needs of the local church and Chinese society. Tzu Ch'en Chao, a prominent Christian voice in the press and a professor of sociology at Soochow University, particularly lamented the intrusion of doctrinal bickering on the National Christian Conference in Shanghai in 1922. To the dismay of the Chinese delegates who had earmarked the bulk of the conference for questions of social service, Dixon Edward Hoste of the conservative China Inland Mission brought proceedings to a halt by insisting that the assembly hammer out a statement of belief to which all delegates would pledge their loyalty.[13] The achievement of such a statement was for many Westerners in attendance the most critical result of the conference, allowing them to leave momentarily reassured that the missionary community would hang together. But for Chao and other Chinese delegates, it missed the mark. Bemoaning the denominationalism, doctrinal rigidity, and general chariness of the Westerners present, Chao lamented, "So charged were the delegates with electric readiness to fight against whatever was unsuitable to them that one did not dare touch the live wire of suspicion, distrust, spiritual disunion and keen apprehension."[14] Though more than half the delegates to the conference were Chinese, a national Christian convention in the early 1920s still suffered the impress of Western infighting that bore little relation to the cultural currents with which Chinese leaders were engaging.

For their part, indigenous Christian leaders were more concerned with how to make Christianity fit local sensibilities in an age of political and cultural revolution. Despite the anti-religious tenor of much May Fourth nationalism, a number of prominent Chinese Christians nevertheless sought a place as legitimate contributors to the cultural renaissance. Asserting their loyalty to the nation, they insisted that they, too, were working to promote reform in China—within a Christian framework. "The Christian people of China are certainly as patriotic—if not more so—than the leaders of the Renaissance movement," wrote Hsü Pao Ch'ien, a Y.M.C.A. worker. "We, as Christians, feel that we have a very important part to play in the salvation of the nation."[15] To give their effort some heft, a group of Chinese Christians based in Peking formed a promotional organization they called the Christian Apologetic Group (Cheng Tao Tuan), later renamed the Life Fellowship. They described it as "an organization of Christians who wish to do their share in meeting the religious needs of the Chinese in response to the Renaissance Movement. Its aim is to witness to the real power and strength of the truth of Christianity."[16] Wrote Hsü, who was a founding member,

> Leaders of the new popular movement say that the conflict between religion and science is an everlasting and therefore irreconcilable one, that religion is a retarding force in human progress, and that Christianity, being the most influential, is therefore the worst enemy to civilization. Whether these charges are the result of misunderstanding and prejudice, or not, it is up to us Christians to make our case.[17]

The Christian Apologetic Group proposed to make that case through a journal, *The Life (Sheng Ming),* as well as in lectures, pamphlets, and conferences.

In its efforts to legitimize Christians as participants in nationalist reform, *The Life* elicited reflections on faith from other New Culture leaders, many of whom emphasized that to be credible in the new China, religion had to have practical applications. Toong Sheng Chang, editor of the *China Times,* wrote that if religion were necessary at all, Christianity would be the best available choice. Though Buddhism had what he judged to be higher ideals, Christianity was more accessible to the masses and "has quite a few things which can help to correct the habits of the Chinese people. Therefore, from the point of view of practical use alone, I regard Christianity as comparatively more suitable than other religions."[18] Illustrious New Culture leader Hu Shih similarly endorsed the ethical components of Christianity as worthy of adoption. Hu argued that the Chinese people as a whole were little interested in theology and that even Chinese Christians paid little attention to this aspect of their own religion. Jesus, whom Hu considered a social revolutionary, was responsible for moral teachings; the theology was the product of later accretions by his disciples and latter-day clerics. Thus Christians could discard all but the applied ethical content of Christianity without being guilty of infidelity to the core of the faith.[19] Where New Culture thinkers gave any credence to Christianity, they valued it most for the immediate pragmatic effects it might have on its followers' daily lives.

Like Hu, Christian leader T. C. Chao thought that earthbound approaches to Christianity were inherent in scripture but had been obscured over time.

In his book *Life of Jesus,* he downplayed the miraculous elements of the Gospels and concentrated on Jesus' power as an unparalleled example of virtue. While American Bruce Barton extrapolated from the Gospels to depict Jesus as a modern ad man and corporate executive in his popular 1925 book, *The Man Nobody Knows,* Chao interpreted him as the ideal Chinese eldest son, staying at home well into adulthood and beginning his ministry only after his siblings were old enough to care for his aging mother in his place.[20] According to Chao, Jesus' death was significant not as a predestined act of divine atonement but because it represented the sacrifice of a perfectly virtuous man for his ideals, a concept he claimed was in keeping with the Analects of Confucius and which Westerners were unable to understand in its exquisite significance. The Chinese church, by contrast, "understands that her divine mission is to right human relationships through the power of the living Lord." Chao rejected eschatological schemes, arguing that they played no part in Jesus' ministry, and faulted Western disciples for failing to focus on the need to bring about the Kingdom of God on earth.[21] As Sumiko Yamamoto has emphasized, Chao's interpretation of the Gospels in many respects was in keeping with trends in liberal theology in the West—indeed, he had spent time studying in both the United States and Great Britain—but it was also shaped by the peculiar dynamics of Chinese society. She notes that Chao "follows an essential characteristic of Chinese culture that tends to put more stress on 'this world' than 'the other world' hereafter." In drawing on classical tradition to situate Christ as the ideal eldest son and in emphasizing the ethical content of Christ's message and ministry, Chao sought to move Christianity in a direction that he believed would speak to fellow Chinese.[22]

Chinese Christian leaders encouraged Western missionaries to follow them in this direction. In fall 1922 the Christian Apologetic Group proposed publishing periodic English-language editions of *The Life,* suggesting that this would be a way of alerting Western missionaries to the currents in Chinese Christian thought. They hoped *The Life* might come to complement the *Chinese Recorder,* the English-language missionary journal of record in China, known for its attention to substantive ideas.[23] Chao and others also contributed regularly to the *Recorder* in an effort to reach the missionary audience nationwide.

Though few missionaries responded to the events of May Fourth, a cascade of events in 1922 brought greater outside pressures to bear on them, making it a watershed year for Christianity in China.[24] In March, Chinese students launched a formal Anti-Christian Student Movement in anticipation of a meeting of the World Christian Student Federation in Peking. The Christian students' meeting appeared especially provocative in the wake of the recent Washington Naval Conference, at which the United States and Western European powers had declined to relinquish extraterritorial privileges in China. Western powers had enjoyed such privileges since the 1840s: American and European nationals were not subject to Chinese law in either civil or criminal cases, Western powers might use military forces to protect their nationals at will, and—of particular importance to missionaries—the Chinese state could not restrict Westerners' advocacy of Christianity. The "unequal treaties" granting these extraterritorial privileges were a particular irritant to Chinese nationalists, who sought their abolition.[25] Though the Washington political summit and the world Christian student meeting had no formal relation to each other, to Chinese youth it seemed as though the West was compounding its rejection of China's full political sovereignty with a symbolic reassertion of its religious intrusion on Chinese soil. The student effort soon spawned a broader Great Anti-Religious Federation that involved a range of youth, scholars, leftist politicians, and others sympathetic to the nationalist cause. Federation members took the establishment of the National Christian Council in May as further evidence that the Christian community in China was making a concerted effort to institutionalize and expand its presence. The core leadership published prodigious propaganda opposing this and other Christian activity for several feverish months before slackening its pace. Though the group's long-term power was uncertain, its emergence prompted concern in the Christian press, both Chinese and English, as Christians asked how they best could meet the challenges posed by an organized, educated opposition.[26]

Although the institution of a formal anti-Christian movement was perhaps the loudest wake-up call to Christian missionaries, other events in 1922 helped pit Western evangelists and Chinese nationalists more squarely against each other. A nascent Chinese communist movement had gained stronger hold with the establishment of the Chinese Communist Party a year earlier. With backing from the Soviet Union, the Kuomintang (Guomindang) Party and the CCP now discussed terms for a united front, providing an alternative ideological framework for Chinese nationalism and changing the cast of anti-Christian sentiment.[27] Where New Culture opponents of Christianity formerly objected to its unscientific, "superstitious" nature, popular rhetoric as the decade advanced grew increasingly anti-imperialist, equating Christianity indiscriminately with all Western imperialist endeavor in Asia. Imperialist charges against Christian missions had a long history in China, but they gained fresh momentum in the 1920s with the introduction of a Marxist framework for their renewed articulation. Missionaries had to find a way to counter this newly focused hostility to all things Western and to religion in particular.[28]

Finally, several major studies of mission work appeared in 1922 that garnered attention not only among missionaries but among Chinese observers, too, with critical repercussions. That year saw the completion of an encyclopedic study of Protestant missions almost a decade in the making, *The Christian Occupation of China*. Though its primary purpose was simply to present tabulated data about mission organizations operating in the country, and though such limited recommendations as it made emphasized the sympathetic study of Chinese religions, the title alone touched a nerve in the newly electric national atmosphere.[29] A second American study, a thorough survey of the work of mission schools by the Foreign Missions Conference of North America, also prompted local reaction. The very comprehensiveness of the report focused public attention on the fact that the best schools in the country were run by foreign religious groups, an embarrassing state of affairs for Chinese nationalists in the midst of a movement that affirmed education as the key to a modern state. Though its authors had no such intentions, the report helped advance a budding campaign to wrest Chinese education from foreign control. This effort bore fruit in 1924 when the Ministry of Education endorsed educational reforms with direct impact on the vast mission school apparatus. The reforms required that all educational institutions register with the government in order to receive accreditation, without which their graduates would be ineligible for the coveted civil service jobs that many Chinese students still made their goal. In order to register, schools had to be governed by a native Chinese principal or president and have a majority Chinese governing board, and—even more critically for mission schools—they could not make religious instruction mandatory. The reforms thrust on the missionaries a new debate about strategy and purpose, forcing them to ask whether they still could fulfill Christ's Great Commission to "go ye therefore and teach all nations" in schools where students could choose whether or not to attend instruction in the holy Word.[30]

As missionaries became aware of the external pressures on their work, they turned from a preoccupation with questions of creedal orthodoxy to asking how Chinese events were shaping the possibilities for evangelism. The answers were not clear, and the confusion was unsettling. "Everywhere we who are foreign Christian workers are thinking and re-thinking our duty, and deeply troubled, are trying to find our new place in the changed conditions of work on the mission field," wrote Jane Shaw Ward, a member of the Y.W.C.A. National Committee, in 1924.[31] Missionaries like Ward began to realize that they were out of step, not connecting with audiences effectively. Educational missionaries in particular encountered student resistance to their religious teaching, one noting that "there are often enough critical questions in one hour in a class room or a few minutes in a conference to arouse dogmatism or antagonism from even a liberal thinker with deep religious convictions."[32] Often those returning from furloughs in the United States were especially struck by the new confusion. Pearl Buck's sister, Grace Sydenstricker, noted "the lack of organized scheme in the work we are doing" and asked, "Why is it that one still hears the question among educated Chinese—'What have the missionaries come to do?'"[33]

Greater attention to Chinese initiatives eventually led many of the missionaries toward the pragmatic thrust in the cultural renaissance. Edward Perry recommended that Christian evangelists "realize, in this our own time, a more fundamental and pertinent nexus in our thinking. Is it not possible for us all to get together on a basis of experimental reality in the things of God as taught by Jesus Christ?"[34] The call for Christian evangelism based on "experimental reality" echoed the positivism resounding throughout the May Fourth Movement. Christians needed to test their message against the demands of the moment, rather than discussing belief in the abstract. Y.W.C.A. secretary Eleanor MacNeil reported that Chinese students seemed to understand Christianity best when it was expressed in behavioral terms rather than as an article of faith. In conducting a survey of Chinese girls about their religious experiences in mission schools, she found that the students objected to instructors asking them to join the church without providing any sense of the practical effects of such a step. "They also say that the questions asked are all concerned with belief, not life. 'Do you believe?' . . . Some girls have said that they would prefer to stand up in front of people and say 'I take Jesus for my Savior and Guide, and will follow Him all my life.'"[35] For MacNeil's Chinese respondents, trying to follow Christ's example was more important than professing a more abstract "belief" in him once and for all.

Increasingly, missionaries with an eye toward changes in Chinese society urged their fellow spiritual workers to meet the Chinese on their own terms. Methodist James Maxon Yard argued for an overhaul of the Chinese seminary curriculum to make it relevant for a pastorate that would serve primarily agricultural communities. He cited the course "Modernist Attacks on the Bible," offered at one seminary, as an example of misguided efforts by missionaries too absorbed with their own debates to recognize that the question of modernism versus Fundamentalism was irrelevant to the Chinese people. Instead, he argued, "The whole course should naturally be related to the inspiring intellectual movements of modern China." Chinese initiative, not Western precepts, ought to guide the way.[36] Pearl Buck meanwhile tried to impress on new missionary recruits training at the Nanking Language School her sense that the right approach to evangelism was to commit to an active search for truth in company with the Chinese. The Christian evangelist began from the hope that he or she might eventually come to proper expression of Christianity's merits through existential effort. Professions of one-time conversion and absolute belief were ill-founded, as were efforts to obtain them from others:

> Now if we mean by that phrase, "possessed by Christ" that we are endeavoring to become so imbued with the ideals of Christ that we make them our own in a practical working out, so that when we express ourselves we express Him, that is what we all want, of course. But too many people use the words as a sort of evangelical slang or slogan. They expect that by singing, "I surrender all," with considerable sentimental fervor and a good deal of emotion, the trick is turned.

Buck suggested that a steady search for enlightenment, conducted with humility, was the only meaningful approach to faith. Christians were foolish if they insisted they possessed truth for all time; they arrived at truth only through systematic search and testing.[37]

John Leighton Stuart, who was in close touch with student intellectuals as the administrator of a mission college, believed that embracing the New Culture Movement would help the Christians in their cause: "It may well be that one of the happy results of scientific study will be to lead [the Chinese] to seek and reach the only adequate explanation," he wrote, with confidence in the ultimate logic of Christianity. "With their strong pragmatic bent and the dangers threatening them at present we have superlative opportunity to stress such distinctively Christian teachings as that regarding service, love, international brotherhood . . ." Pragmatic Christianity did not mean simply providing social service in a Social Gospel tradition. Though good works were important, they had their limits. Stuart spoke of Buddhist priests who had

> expressed wonder that Christians attached so much importance to philanthropies and organized activities of all kinds instead of the thing in which that religion was so supremely rich, its spiritual teaching. Ethical idealism and spiritual vitality rather than philosophical or theological formulation of our faith and its embodiment in visible organizations, would seem to be our proper emphasis.[38]

His insistence on "ethical idealism and spiritual vitality" was something more complicated than either a total devotion to things of the spirit or simple social activism. He believed wholeheartedly that missionaries' faith ought to result in service, but he feared that for Westerners, such service too often resulted in a focus on the busywork of mastering the local environment and achieving concrete results. Christians ought instead to focus on conveying through their service the remarkable, indeed unmatched, ethical content of Christianity as the expression of divine truth.

In 1925 Chinese politics again propelled mission dialogue in new directions, this time encouraging missionaries to demonstrate the practical effects of Christian belief through direct political involvement. At the end of May another student demonstration acted as a catalyst for nationwide protest when a Japanese factory foreman in Shanghai shot and killed a Chinese laborer who was sabotaging factory machinery in the course of a strike. Student demonstrators attended the laborer's funeral and distributed protest literature in the streets before leading a restive crowd to a police station in the International Settlement. There a British police officer eventually ordered constables to fire into the unarmed assembly, killing eleven demonstrators and wounding about fifty others. The incident reignited rage against the foreign presence in China, bringing to a head tensions over foreign concessions in Chinese port cities, the punitive tariff structures imposed on China by Western powers, and the extraterritorial legal protections granted foreigners under the unequal treaties. In the wake of the May 30 Incident, strikes and demonstrations again erupted all over China, this time led primarily by workers rather than students, though the latter participated. The violence was greater than it had been in 1919, with scores killed in clashes around the country, and the anti-foreign sentiment was more intense. The Western and Japanese powers declared martial law in their concessions and summoned gunboats for protection of their interests. May 30 had become the newest flashpoint for a nationalist movement that was turning ever more overtly political and stridently anti-Western.[39]

Unlike the student demonstrations six years earlier, the May 30 Incident prompted a rapid response from the missionary community in China, newly sensitive to the impact of Chinese nationalism on its work. Editors announced on the first page of the July edition of the *Chinese Recorder* that they had eliminated two regular sections of the paper so as to attempt to give a detailed account of the events, "as the future of all missionary effort is involved."[40] Missionaries recognized that the crisis, which was garnering worldwide news coverage, threatened to turn the Chinese public against them perhaps as violently as during the Boxer Rebellion of 1900. Mission educators now encountered hostile pupils who not only posed challenging questions but often renounced their Christian conversions altogether. In one blow the May 30 Incident crippled missionaries' efforts to show that Western Christians wanted to build a religious brotherhood across racial lines. Not only students but some adult Chinese church members began to fall away. "We wish to point out an open secret that the very foundation of the Christian faith of many people has been shaken by the present situation," wrote the National Christian Council's executive committee in an official statement on the incident. "Men and women are asking if Christianity is a practical and all-adequate religion, and if the Christian way of life is a practical and all-adequate way of life."[41] As *Recorder* editor Frank Rawlinson saw it, "The present is one of the times when 'Christian' civilization is on the dissecting table of public opinion."[42]

In an effort to distinguish between themselves and those who had committed the killings, missionaries across China issued formal statements of regret at the incident, but they soon realized that this gesture would not be enough. Again Chinese Christians were key in pushing missionaries forward, urging them to make a more definitive response. Now was the time for Western Christians to demonstrate the power of faith in action, they argued. The Chinese faculty and administrators at Soochow University collectively issued a statement in which they thanked missionaries for their expressions of concern but suggested, "Time and time again we have heard such expressions of high sounding principles but we have now come to the point where we find ourselves unable to have faith in words which are not validated by corresponding deeds." A teacher at Hangchow Christian College urged foreign missionaries to read English-language accounts of the tragedy critically and to speak with Chinese co-workers about the incident, but most importantly to "influence their government to abandon its imperialistic policies and actions."[43] As Chinese Christians had long been suggesting, the proof of Christianity was in the actions it engendered—never more so than in a moment of international crisis.

Much of the mission community now seemed to agree that political engagement was rightfully within the scope of its call.[44] In the months that followed, foreign evangelists in favor of disavowing the unequal treaties sought to use their leverage as unique transnational actors to influence politics. Making much of their position as Western residents of China benefiting from extraterritorial privilege, they claimed moral authority by calling for its abolition even though that would mean relinquishing personal military protection in times of civil unrest and would make them subject to Chinese judicature. Fieldworkers for the American Church in China published an open letter to their administrative board in New York explaining,

> In preaching a Gospel of the triumph of love over force, of right over might, we are increasingly convinced that our case is immeasurably weakened by our connection with rights and privileges gained and maintained through the use of foreign military force. We therefore, wish to free ourselves from such rights and privileges, and to this end express our desire to waive the special privileges of extraterritoriality. We are willing to be governed by Chinese laws, and in case of danger to our person or property, we desire no other protection than afforded by the Chinese authorities.[45]

They were not alone in such sentiments. Dozens of missionary societies, particularly those dominated by Americans, issued statements along these lines.[46] So did individuals: Maxwell Chaplin, serving in remote North Anwhei (Anhui), wrote to the Presbyterian mission board to renounce any extraterritorial privilege exercised on his behalf and to request that if anything were to happen to him the board not demand indemnities in exchange.

Missionaries went further in lobbying their governments for formal abolition. The China National Committee of the Y.W.C.A cabled the Y.W.C.A. in New York its unanimous appeal that the organization lobby for an adjustment of treaties with China to abolish extraterritoriality.[47] The American Board missionaries in China issued a declaration pledging to campaign for abrogation of the treaties; all signatories committed to sending a copy "without delay either to my local consulate, to my legation in Peking, or to some official in my home government, also to my foreign mission board, at the same time seeking to promote united action by my mission on the field."[48] In October representatives of thirty-seven mission organizations meeting in New York called for the abolition of extraterritoriality in China and for new treaties that would include no special legal protections for missionaries. The Peking Missionary Association meanwhile proposed "an International Conference looking towards the revision of existing treaties between China and other nations, in which treaties we as missionaries are specifically involved." Though the international conferences that materialized did not include missionary delegates, some Christians in China met with government officials to express their views in advance. In October Silas Strawn, the American representative to a new treaty powers' commission on extraterritoriality, met in Shanghai with missionaries and commercial groups about their position on the issue of extraterritoriality. Before traveling to a similar meeting in Peking, he invited missionaries throughout China to submit position statements to him for review.[49]

Not all missionaries supported treaty abrogation: some fieldworkers in turbulent interior regions appealed for a realistic assessment of the current situation rather than unthinking embrace of the loftiest ethical ideals. Yet even those who affirmed the benefits of Western military protection in helping Christian work continue amidst violence could see the harm in clinging to this privilege. In a piece for the *Recorder* recounting the ways in which he had benefited from extraterritorial privileges, American Baptist missionary Archibald Adams nevertheless admitted, "This bothersome question keeps asserting itself. Really to help this people spiritually in their sore distress must not one share their burdens?"[50]

Though the Western powers did not concede to abrogation of extraterritorial privileges in China until 1943—doing so then as a goodwill gesture toward their ally in the Pacific war—the experience of campaigning for abolition was nevertheless important for the missionaries' own outlook. In choosing to take a public stand on the issue, many missionaries were confirmed in the belief that Chinese nationalism was the inescapable context for their work and that Christian faith required that they respond.[51] In the context of revolutionary China, they had come to see overt participation in the political process as a logical extension of the effort to demonstrate Christianity's practical value. Lobbying their home governments to abolish unequal treaty rights was part of their call to demonstrate the radical equality of life in Christ to Chinese audiences. *Atlantic* editor Lewis Gannett, touring China, was struck by the change:

> The red-hot days of 1925, following the foreign shootings of May and June, taught the missionaries things about themselves that they had never known, forced movements that had been long in germination to bloom early. New buds appeared upon the branches which the gardeners at home had never suspected were there. Every anti-foreign outbreak seems to work changes in the missionary garden.[52]

As late as 1907, the mission community had decreed political involvement in Chinese affairs inappropriate for foreign evangelists. That position had softened somewhat when Christian convert Sun Yat-sen assumed control of the new republic in 1911, prompting some missionaries to praise the new regime.[53] Yet Protestant missionaries had never before weighed in collectively on Chinese politics as they did in 1925. Their public position statements no doubt reflected a certain instinct for self-preservation as they hedged against anti-foreign backlash. More critically, however, their lobbying revealed the degree to which they had come to see themselves as legitimate actors in the transformation of Chinese society on terms dictated by their host country's politics.

Rather than order their activities according to their own lights, they proposed to hold Christianity to the test of experience as China thrust it on them to demonstrate the worth of their faith amid social revolution.

Eventually that revolution would overwhelm their efforts, as the outbreak of civil war in late 1926 forced the vast majority of missionaries to evacuate their stations.[54] Though many declared their intention to endure the war in the company of their Chinese neighbors, the Western consulates eventually ordered them out and asserted extraterritorial privilege in sending boats to retrieve them, as at Nanking, where communists assassinated the missionary vice president of Nanking University before targeting the rest of the mission population. Pearl Buck later commented regretfully on having felt compelled to flee Nanking under American protection after her family spent a harrowing day hiding from soldiers. "I was glad not to die," she wrote, "but I wished that I had not needed to justify, against my will, what still I knew to be wrong."[55]

The idea that accepting military protection was a moral wrong and that their place as Christians was with their Chinese brethren was just one sign of a growing gap in perspective between many missionaries and their sponsors at home. "The centralisation of control at home, away from the scene of actual operations, has resulted in a lack of contact with the facts and circumstances, the ever-changing problems and difficulties, in the 'things as they are,'" wrote English missionary Percy J. Smith in 1924.[56] The civil war exacerbated the split. Returning missionaries who spoke to American audiences about the fact that Chinese social convulsions made evangelism more complicated did not come bearing a message that the administrators soliciting funds wanted to hear. Some American mission boards tried to control the news from China reaching the United States in the late 1920s. Administrators for both the Methodist Episcopal and Presbyterian U.S.A. boards censored letters that missionaries sent home for public dissemination. The Presbyterians also stopped all money for furloughs as civil war broke out, afraid to let the fieldworkers speak for themselves at home lest their perspective on Chinese political affairs exacerbate tensions in a denomination already facing theological schism.[57]

At mid-decade *Chinese Recorder* editor Frank Rawlinson already was struck by the distance between active missionaries and Christians at home. In 1925 he attended the ecumenical North American foreign mission conference in Washington, D.C., where he thought that missionaries' energy and innovation contrasted starkly with the plodding ways of stateside administrators. "The program worked almost as stiffly as a slot machine. Hymns, prayers, speeches tramped after each other with a sort of thumping orderliness," he reported. "Do Western Christians as represented in this Convention sense fully the awakening that has come to the Orient? And I am compelled to say that I fear they do not." Rawlinson instead praised a speech by Eli Stanley Jones, preeminent Methodist missionary to India, who spoke enthusiastically about reshaping the Christian message for Indian audiences. In Jones, Rawlinson recognized a kindred spirit, adapting his faith to meet local peoples on their own terms.[58]

Evangelists who had been changed by their experiences abroad were conscious that they bore "a message for Jerusalem and Corinth alike"—that is, not only for the far edges of the Christian community in Asia but also for its center in North America and Europe.[59] Despite temporary wartime censorship, missionaries in general were in constant communication with churches, family, and members of the American public through letters, articles in the religious and popular press, and personal appearances on furlough. Those who returned permanently to the United States—as they did in increasing numbers during the 1930s—continued to preach, teach, and write vigorously because of their practice doing so overseas and the perspective it afforded them, often finding themselves in forms of reverse mission to their compatriots for the rest of their lives. In the early twentieth century, their accounts were still for many Americans the most immediate window onto distant cultures.[60]

The challenge was to make their perspective fully understandable to those who had not shared their experiences and who often misinterpreted what they heard and saw. To some observers, for example, it appeared that theology had disappeared entirely from mission work in China in the 1920s, missionaries shedding the spiritual component of religion in favor of a stripped-down ethic of service. In the early 1930s Henrietta Otis Shaw, an American visitor to China, observed of some of the missionaries she met that

> years of working among people of a different culture have not left [them] intellectually unchanged. Some of these have quietly shifted the emphasis of their spiritual lives from St. John to St. James; they no longer accept literally the dogma that belief in certain arbitrary facts is essential for salvation, but considering that good works are a sound basis for religion they carry on and say nothing.[61]

Shaw believed that much of the work done by these missionaries could be done by secular service agencies rather than the church, if only such agencies existed. In the same vein a reporter for *Good Housekeeping* praised a medical missionary he had encountered as the embodiment of modern missions: "He wasn't bothering about souls—he was bothering about sores." Lewis Gannett, a non-believer, was hopeful that changes in the China mission field signaled missionaries' transition to a form of secular cultural ambassadorship. He predicted, "The permanent service of the missionaries will, I believe, be less in the religious field than as a bridge between two civilizations that had lost contact with each other."[62]

Such observers painted perhaps too simplistic a picture of the transformations occurring among American missionaries. Even as some missionaries imagined a new role for Western Christians in China as spiritual servants, come to learn and aid as much as to teach and save, they did not imagine themselves as mere cultural interpreters between two peoples. Nor did their dedication to good works bespeak, for most, a total abandonment of their belief in salvation through grace. Instead, they struggled to walk a fine line. If the intricacies of theology were not the most persuasive aspects of Christianity for Chinese audiences, it did not mean that missionaries abandoned all belief in their creeds. In the pages of the *Recorder* and in their writings and speeches for those at home, they continued to assert that their actions sprang from conviction of Christ's saving grace, the component of their faith not found in any secular ethical system.

Presbyterian Maxwell Chaplin, protesting extraterritoriality and working to expand social services at his post in the interior, found himself at the same time ever more sure of the need for Christ. Even while arguing that "Christianity meets us where we are and we must learn to see God in the common things," he was learning lessons in faith from his rural neighbors. In a letter home about how working in China had changed him he wrote,

> I find myself coming to a deeper appreciation of the things in Christianity which are not emphasized by the Modernists and which the Conservatives are shouting for, but I have come to it by such a different path than they travel. . . . The practical problem has solved many theological questions for me as to what is necessary for salvation. Salvation is a personal experience of getting set free from the power of habits, fears, evil desires, and an entering into a new life of victory and love and service.[63]

The Chinese nationalist movement, in both its cultural and political iterations, propelled many missionaries in the 1920s toward a more pragmatic stance, in which they presented Christianity as a system of beliefs whose truth might be discovered in the application of its precepts. At the same time, most denied that good works and sympathetic political stands were the sum total of their religion. It was a delicate balance to strike, and not all missionaries resolved the tensions between faith and works, conviction and adaptation, in the same way. Some abandoned the effort entirely. Yet a significant portion continued to look for ways to be at once faithful and flexible and to share with their fellow Christians back home their sense that such a balance was necessary.

NOTES

The first epigraph is from Chengting T. Wang, "Making Christianity Indigenous in China," *Chinese Recorder* (hereafter *CR*), May 1921, 327. The second is from Lewis S. Gannett, "I Never Liked Missionaries . . . ," *Nation*, July 28, 1926, 80.

1. Barry Keenan, *The Dewey Experiment in China: Educational Reform and Political Power in the Early Republic* (Cambridge, Mass.: Council on East Asian Studies, Harvard University, 1977), 22, 30–31, 35, 37, 44; and John Dewey and Alice Chipman Dewey, *Letters from China and Japan* (New York: E. P. Dutton, 1920).

2. In this article I include the modern pinyin spelling of Chinese names in parentheses but otherwise use the Wade-Giles spellings used by my early twentieth-century historical actors.

3. As translated in Tse-tsung Chow, *The May Fourth Movement: Intellectual Revolution in Modern China* (Cambridge, Mass.: Harvard University Press, 1960), quoted in Jonathan D. Spence, *The Gate of Heavenly Peace: The Chinese and Their Revolution, 1895–1980* (1981; New York: Penguin, 1982), 160.

4. Kae-Che Yip, "The Anti-Christian Movement in China, 1922–1927: With Special Reference to the Experience of Protestant Missions" (Ph.D. diss., Columbia University, 1970), 43–46, 50–51; Spence, *Gate of Heavenly Peace*, 143–44; H. C. Hu, "The New Thought Movement," *CR*, August 1923, 447–55; Vera Schwarcz, *The Chinese Enlightenment: Intellectuals and the Legacy of the May Fourth Movement of 1919* (Berkeley: University of California Press, 1986), 5–7; Kenneth Scott Latourette, *A History of Christian Missions in China* (1929; New York: Macmillan, 1932), 691–94; and Lian Xi, *The Conversion of Missionaries: Liberalism in American Protestant Missions in China, 1907–1932* (University Park: Pennsylvania State University Press, 1997), 151–53.

5. Kae-Che Yip, "China and Christianity: Perspectives on Missions, Nationalism, and the State in the Republican Period, 1912–1949," in *Missions, Nationalism, and the End of Empire*, ed. Brian Stanley (Grand Rapids, Mich.: William B. Eerdmans, 2003), 133.

6. Jessie G. Lutz, "Chinese Nationalism and the Anti-Christian Campaigns of the 1920s," *Modern Asian Studies* 10, no. 3 (July 1976): 397–98.

7. For the origins of the actual catchphrase "What would Jesus do?" see Charles M. Sheldon, *In His Steps: What Would Jesus Do?* 100th anniversary edition, with a foreword by Garrett W. Sheldon (1897; Nashville, Tenn.: Broadman & Holman, 1995). On Social Gospel Christianity in the late nineteenth and early twentieth centuries, see Walter Rauschenbusch, *A Theology for the Social Gospel* (New York: Macmillan, 1917); Paul A. Carter, *The Decline and Revival of the Social Gospel: Social and Political Liberalism in American Protestant Churches, 1920–1940* (Ithaca, N.Y.: Cornell University Press, 1954); Robert T. Handy, ed. *The Social Gospel in America, 1870–1920* (Oxford: Oxford University Press, 1966); Susan Curtis, *A Consuming Faith: The Social Gospel and Modern American Culture* (Baltimore: Johns Hopkins University Press, 1991); and Sydney E. Ahlstrom, *A Religious History of the American People*, 2nd ed. (New Haven: Yale University Press, 2004), 785–807.

8. The term "missions intensifier" is Joel Carpenter's, and is quoted in Daniel H. Bays and Grant Wacker, "The Many Faces of the Missionary Enterprise at Home," introduction to *The Foreign Missionary Enterprise at Home: Explorations in North American Cultural History*, ed. Daniel H. Bays and Grant Wacker (Tuscaloosa: University of Alabama Press, 2003), 4.

9. J[ohn] L[eighton] Stuart, "The Christian Dynamic for China," *CR*, February 1923, 72.

10. W[illiam] H[enry] Griffith Thomas, "Modernism in China," *Princeton Theological Review* 19, no. 4 (October 1921): 630–31.

11. Quoted in Robert Moats Miller, *Harry Emerson Fosdick: Preacher, Pastor, Prophet* (Oxford: Oxford University Press, 1985), 108–109.

12. Rachel Brooks, "Impressions of a Junior Missionary," *CR*, August 1921, 555.

13. "The Outstanding Christian Problem," editorial, *CR*, November 1921, 734–35.

14. T[zu] C[h'en] Chao, quoted in "My Impression of the National Christian Conference," *CR*, June 1922, 416.

15. Pao Ch'ien Hsü, "The Christian Renaissance," *CR*, July 1920, 460.

16. *Sheng Ming (The Life)*, special edition conference number, [March 1922], [i]. All quotations from *The Life*, whose title was always printed in both Chinese and English, are from English-language editions. These editions have no publication dates, and pagination begins again at 1 with each article. The copies I accessed are found on Harvard-Yenching Microfilm FC390, Harvard University.

17. Hsü, "Christian Renaissance," 460–61.

18. Toong Sheng Chang in "The Attitude of the Modern Chinese Intellectuals toward Christianity: A Symposium," *The Life*, [March 1922], 2.

19. Suh Hu [Hu Shih] in "Attitude of the Modern Chinese Intellectuals," 6–7. Within five years, Hu evidently had concluded that modern Christianity had taken the wrong turn. Referring to Sinclair Lewis's morally corrupt fictional evangelists, he wrote, "Christianity itself is fighting its last battle. . . . The religion of Elmer Gantry and Sharon Falconer must sooner or later make all thinking people feel ashamed to call themselves 'Christians.'" Hu Shih, "China and Christianity," *Forum*, July 1927, 2.

20. Daniel H. Bays, "Chao, T(zu) C(h'en) (Zhao Zichen)," in *Biographical Dictionary of Christian Missions*, ed. Gerald H. Anderson (Grand Rapids, Mich.: William B. Eerdmans, 1999), 125–26; and Sumiko Yamamoto, *History of Protestantism in China: The Indigenization of Christianity* (Tokyo: Toho Gakkai [Institute of Eastern Culture], 2000), 259.

21. Yamamoto, *Protestantism in China*, 244–45, 249–50, 260; and T. C. Chao, "The Relation of the Chinese Church to the Church Universal," speech delivered at the first annual meeting of the National Christian Council, *CR*, June 1923, 352.

22. Yamamoto, *Protestantism in China*, 247–48, 257.

23. "Shall the Life Journal Have an English Supplement?" *The Life*, [summer 1922], 5–9. In 1921 some 39 percent of active Protestant missionaries subscribed to the *Chinese Recorder*, representing every missionary organization with at least ten members in the field. Paying readers presumably shared the paper within mission compounds, schools, and hospitals. Many missionaries on furlough also took the paper, as did a contingent of Chinese Christians. The *Recorder* was published in Shanghai and included material from writers of all denominational and ideological backgrounds, though Frank Rawlinson, the journal's editor in the 1920s, had himself traveled the road from fervent Southern Baptist to heterodox Marxist sympathizer.

24. Daniel H. Bays similarly judges that the impact of the May Fourth Movement on the church first started to become clear to the Protestant missionary community at large in 1922. Daniel H. Bays, "Foreign Mission and Indigenous Protestant Leaders in China, 1920–1955:

Identity and Loyalty in an Age of Powerful Nationalism," in Stanley, *Missions, Nationalism, and the End of Empire,* 151.

25. Wesley R. Fishel, *The End of Extraterritoriality in China* (Berkeley: University of California Press, 1952), 5–14, 102.

26. "The Non-Christian Students Federation," *The Life,* [March 1922], 7; Lutz, "Chinese Nationalism and the Anti-Christian Campaigns," 399–402; Yip, "Anti-Christian Movement," 92–96; C. S. Chang, "The Anti-Religion Movement," *CR,* August 1923, 459–67; and T. L. Shen, "A Study of the Anti-Christian Movement," *CR,* April 1925, 230.

27. Spence, *Gate of Heavenly Peace,* 204; and Yip, "Anti-Christian Movement," 88–89.

28. On continuities and junctures in a tradition of Chinese opposition to Christianity, see Paul A. Cohen, "The Anti-Christian Tradition in China," *Journal of Asian Studies* 20, no. 2 (February 1961): 169–80.

29. Yip, "Anti-Christian Movement," 91; and Milton Stauffer, ed., *The Christian Occupation of China: A General Survey of the Numerical Strength and Geographical Distribution of the Christian Forces in China Made by the Special Committee on Survey and Occupation, China Continuation Committee, 1918–1921* (Shanghai: China Continuation Committee, 1922), 31.

30. China Educational Commission, *Christian Education in China* (New York: Committee of Reference and Counsel of the Foreign Missions Conference of North America, 1922); Latourette, *History of Christian Missions in China,* 814–15; Gordon Poteat, "Shall We Surrender the Christian Characters of Our Schools?" letter to the editor, *CR,* May 1925, 332–35; and "Proposed New Educational Regulations," *CR,* January 1926, 68.

31. Jane Shaw Ward, "One Definition of Indigenous," *CR,* September 1924, 575, 578.

32. P[aul] D. Twinem, "The Student Mind," *CR,* May 1923, 265.

33. Grace C. Sydenstricker, "What Have the Missionaries Really Come to Do?" letter to the editor, *CR,* November 1923, 693.

34. Edward W. Perry, letter to the editor, *CR,* July 1921, 508.

35. Eleanor MacNeill, "What the Average Student Thinks about Christianity," *CR,* May 1925, 306.

36. James Maxon Yard, "Our Theological Seminaries and the Rural Pastors," *CR,* December 1924, 784.

37. Pearl S. Buck, "The Conflict of Viewpoints," *CR,* September 1923, 538–39.

38. Stuart, "Christian Dynamic for China," 72, 76–77.

39. Spence, *Gate of Heavenly Peace,* 221–22; Latourette, *History of Christian Missions in China,* 698; Paul A. Varg, *Missionaries, Chinese, and Diplomats: The American Protestant Missionary Movement in China, 1890–1952* (Princeton: Princeton University Press, 1958), 186–87; and Schwarcz, *Chinese Enlightenment,* 148–49.

40. "A Match and an Explosion," editorial, *CR,* July 1925, 413.

41. "Message of the National Christian Council to the Christians in China," *CR,* August 1925, 523.

42. F[rank] Rawlinson, "The Golden Rule," *CR,* October 1925, 653.

43. "A Broadcast Letter and a Personal Reply," *CR,* August 1925, 514; and Siao Bing-Shih, "From a Chinese Teacher," *CR,* July 1925, 476.

44. For historians' assessment that a majority of missionaries probably supported the abolition of extraterritoriality, see Latourette, *History of Christian Missions in China,* 811; Peter Conn, *Pearl S. Buck: A Cultural Biography* (Cambridge: Cambridge University Press, 1996), 86; and Wayne Flynt and Gerald W. Berkley, *Taking Christianity to China: Alabama Missionaries in the Middle Kingdom, 1850–1950* (Tuscaloosa: University of Alabama Press, 1997), 304–305. Although Paul Varg has argued that the missionary community was less re-

sounding in its disavowal of treaty rights than traditionally believed, even he suggests that opposition to abrogation developed only after Westerners were targeted in the civil war of 1926–27, and that even then, American missionaries continued to petition the State Department for revision or abolition of the treaties. Before 1926, he allows, sentiment and activity in opposition to the treaties was widespread. Paul A. Varg, "The Missionary Response to the Nationalist Revolution," in *The Missionary Enterprise in China and America,* ed. John Fairbank (Cambridge, Mass.: Harvard University Press, 1974), 311; and Varg, *Missionaries, Chinese, and Diplomats,* 196–97n5.

45. Robert E. Wood, Edmund L. Souder, Emily L. Ridgely, et al., "The Christian Way Out," *CR,* December 1925, 812.

46. See, for a further sample, *China Christian Year Book, 1926* (Shanghai: Christian Literature Society, 1926), 483–534; A. L. Warnshuis, "Christian Mission and Treaties with China," *CR,* November 1925, 705–15; and "Important Actions on China Situation," *CR,* December 1925, 834–38.

47. "Western Christians Think Hard," *CR,* November 1925, 766.

48. "American Board Missionaries in China," *CR,* December 1925, 838.

49. "The Diplomats and Missionary Viewpoint," *CR,* December 1925, 841–42; Russell D. Buhite, "Nelson Johnson and American Policy toward China, 1925–1928," *Pacific Historical Review* 35, no. 4 (November 1966): 455–57; and Fishel, *End of Extraterritoriality,* 105, 109–110.

50. Archibald G. Adams, "Extraterritoriality and the Missionary in an Interior City," *CR,* January 1926, 54.

51. Fishel, *End of Extraterritoriality,* 1–2.

52. Gannett, "I Never Liked Missionaries," 79.

53. Flynt and Berkley, *Taking Christianity to China,* 301–303.

54. By summer 1927, only some 500 of more than 8,000 Western mission workers remained in the interior, with another 2,500 living as refugees behind military lines in coastal international settlements. Latourette, *History of Christian Missions in China,* 820.

55. Pearl S. Buck, *My Several Worlds: A Personal Record* (New York: John Day, 1954), 216.

56. Percy J. Smith, "Does the Church Need to Reform Its Methods?" *CR,* July 1924, 432.

57. Shirley Stone Garrett, "Why They Stayed: American Church Politics and Chinese Nationalism in the Twenties," in Fairbank, *Missionary Enterprise in China and America,* 290, 299–300, 309.

58. F[rank] Rawlinson, "The Christian Renews His Mind," *CR,* April 1925, 241–43.

59. W[illiam] W[ashington] Pinson, *Missions in a Changing World* (Nashville, Tenn.: Cokesbury, 1928), 42.

60. On this point see Bays and Wacker, "Many Faces of the Missionary Enterprise at Home"; John K. Fairbank, "Assignment for the '70s," *American Historical Review* 74, no. 3 (February 1969): 861–79; Dana L. Robert, "From Missions to Mission to Beyond Missions: The Historiography of American Protestant Foreign Missions since World War II," in *New Directions in American Religious History,* ed. Harry S. Stout and D. G. Hart (Oxford: Oxford University Press, 1977), 362–93; and Lian, *Conversion of Missionaries.*

61. Henrietta Otis Shaw, "These Missionaries," *Forum,* March 1932, 169–70.

62. Frazier Hunt, "The Model Missionary," *Good Housekeeping,* December 1921, 91; and Gannett, "I Never Liked Missionaries," 81.

63. George Stewart, ed., *The Letters of Maxwell Chaplin* (New York: Association, 1928), 204, 183–84.

FIFTEEN

Demarcating Democracy

Liberal Catholics, Protestants, and the Discourse of Secularism

K. HEALAN GASTON

Fears that Catholicism would undermine the cultural foundations of American democracy abounded in the World War II era. As the historian John T. McGreevy explains in *Catholicism and American Freedom* (2003), many liberal Protestants, Jews, humanists, and naturalists believed that democracy required a thoroughly anti-authoritarian culture, and they suspected Catholicism of being fundamentally authoritarian in character. This political critique of Catholicism peaked in 1949 with the publication of the muckraking journalist Paul Blanshard's infamous bestseller *American Freedom and Catholic Power,* which called for an organized "resistance movement" to combat the "antidemocratic social policies of the hierarchy." Prominent non-Catholic liberals hailed Blanshard's "exemplary scholarship, good judgment, and tact" and sang the book's praises in the mainstream press. McGreevy argues that postwar American liberalism took shape in opposition not only to racism and totalitarianism but also to Catholicism, which non-Catholic liberals regarded as a politically authoritarian other to America's free society and institutions.[1]

Although hardly the first scholar to recount these cultural battles, McGreevy has introduced them to non-specialist audiences, thereby making Blanshard and what John Courtney Murray termed "the New Nativism" central to our understanding of twentieth-century American liberalism.[2] Curiously, however, McGreevy's account omits Catholic participants, focusing exclusively on the contributions of Catholicism's fiercest critics—primarily naturalists in the universities and on the Supreme Court, along with a few Protestant progressives. These non-Catholic liberals articulated a potent discourse of authoritarianism that cast doubt upon the ability of Catholics to defend democracy.[3] But the dearth of Catholic voices in McGreevy's treatment raises the question of how Catholics themselves described the cultural requirements of democracy.

In this chapter, I suggest that historians ought to view the discourse of authoritarianism identified by McGreevy as interwoven with a countervailing discourse of secularism. Each of these discourses involved the construction of a negative other—a frightening image of a group whose core beliefs negated social order itself.[4] My research indicates that even the most liberal Catholics joined their more conservative coreligionists in employing the discourse of secularism both to combat charges of authoritarianism and to call into question the ability of non-Catholic liberals to adequately defend democracy. Using the writings of four prominent liberal Catholics—John A. Ryan, Carlton J. H. Hayes, John Courtney Murray, and John Cogley—I offer a new perspective on the struggle over the meaning of democracy between Catholic critics of liberal "secularism" and liberal critics of Catholic "authoritarianism" during the middle decades of the twentieth century. This chapter demonstrates that the discourses of authoritarianism and secularism functioned as two sides of a larger postwar debate about the cultural foundations of democracy.[5] It also shows that by the early years of the Cold War, the discourse of secularism to which Catholics so powerfully contributed had begun to drive a wedge through the liberal Protestant camp.

JOHN A. RYAN: LIBERAL CATHOLIC IDENTITY AND DEMOCRATIC ORTHODOXY

John A. Ryan (1865–1945) personified liberal Catholicism for countless interwar Catholics, including Father Charles E. Coughlin, who dubbed him the "Right Reverend New Dealer." Indeed, Ryan did much to make Catholics a cornerstone of Roosevelt's New Deal coalition, to the chagrin of Coughlin and other critics. Growing up on a farm in Minnesota, Ryan had witnessed firsthand the rise and fall of the Populist movement before joining the priesthood in 1898 and becoming a leading voice of American Catholicism during World War I. Ryan's unflagging commitment to social justice and many contributions to Catholic social thought soon became legendary. In his joint capacities as a professor of political science and moral theology at the Catholic University of America and the head of the Social Action Department of the National Catholic Welfare Conference (NCWC), Ryan championed a living wage and industrial democracy between the wars.[6]

Yet Ryan cautioned in 1930 that being a liberal in economic matters did not necessarily require one to be a liberal in other realms, including "politics, governmental policy, religion, education, science, philosophy, ethical theory and practice, and social conventions." An individual, said Ryan, "can logically and consistently be a liberal in some of these departments and a conservative or authoritarian in others." Most pertinently, one could be "a liberal in politics and economics and at the same time an authoritarian in religion."[7] This was precisely where he and other liberal Catholics stood. On key questions of political theory, economically progressive Catholics such as Ryan sounded very little like liberals of other religious backgrounds—and quite a bit like the conservatives of recent decades.

In numerous publications between the wars, Ryan crafted a theory of democracy that diverged markedly from the prevailing liberal views of the time. His contributions on the question of church-state relations display the imprint of the "Catholic Revival," a post–World War I wave of Catholic Americanism in which Catholic thinkers applied Thomistic principles to all areas of modern life. Ryan contributed mightily to this project, joining other neo-Scholastics in arguing that the core principles of democracy originated in Catholic sources, especially the writings of the late medieval cardinal Robert Bellarmine. According to Zachary R. Calo, Ryan introduced his reading of Bellarmine in a 1918 article in the *Catholic World*. Calo explains that Ryan rejected views of democracy as "the by-product of a social contract or the exaltation of the people as the supreme political authority," instead defining it as "the mechanism by which the people participated in the transference of justly derived political authority from God to a ruler." In sum, Ryan identified a conception of popular sovereignty rooted in the natural law as the key feature of democracy.[8]

A 1939 speech at the University of Virginia entitled "Religion, the Indispensable Basis of Democracy" demonstrates how Ryan applied this theory to the struggle between democracy and totalitarianism in the late 1930s. In it, Ryan insisted that "only those who profess religion . . . have a logical ground for maintaining individual rights and rejecting all forms of the totalitarian state." By "religion," he meant "at least, the acceptance of God as Creator and Ruler of the Universe." Ryan insisted that moral authority in a democracy came "immediately from the people" but "ultimately from the Creator." This view, which he attributed not only to Bellarmine but also to Thomas Jefferson, belied Rousseau's claim that "the people were the ultimate as well as the immediate source of authority."[9]

Building on this assumption, Ryan enumerated the beliefs he thought a person needed to embrace in order to defend the natural rights at the heart of democracy:

> Unless man accepts God as Creator and Ruler of the Universe he cannot believe in natural rights. Unless he believes that man was created in the image and likeness of God; unless he believes that man possesses a spiritual and immortal soul; unless he believes that man is a human *person,* endowed with worth and intrinsic sacredness, he cannot logically talk about human rights. In Kant's fine phrase, 'man is an end in himself,' therefore, a man may not be treated as a mere means to any other man, to any group of men, or to any organization, even to the organization called the State.

In short, Ryan's theory held that the preservation of democratic rights required a substantive, theological conception of "the human person as intrinsically sacred." Although Ryan granted that "a small minority of highly-educated and high-minded men may be satisfied with the sense of obligation which they derive from consideration of natural reason, independently of God," he asserted that "the vast majority of persons demand a personal God as the source and guarantor of their ethical convictions."[10]

Many non-Catholic liberals—be they Protestants, Jews, or secularists—would have rejected specific elements in Ryan's litany of necessary beliefs. In fact, Ryan's enumeration of the beliefs he considered central to any solid defense of human rights constituted an explicitly religious test of democratic orthodoxy. As such, it implicitly challenged the religious and political authenticity of liberal Protestants and Jews, humanists, naturalists, and secularists of all persuasions—the very people who tended to label Catholicism authoritarian.

CARLTON J. H. HAYES: NATIONALISM AND THE LIMITS OF INTERFAITH TOLERANCE

Like Ryan, the historian and diplomat Carlton J. H. Hayes (1882–1964) participated in the Catholic Revival and articulated a distinctly Catholic form of liberalism. Born a Baptist, Hayes converted to Catholicism in 1904 while a senior at Columbia, where he subsequently earned a Ph.D. in 1909 and joined the faculty. A path-breaking historian of modern Europe, Hayes specialized in the history of nationalism, contributing much to the "New History" that emerged at Columbia during the interwar years. In 1920, when Hayes married a cradle Catholic, Catholicism became a focal point of his scholarship.[11] Soon thereafter, he began to offer strong claims about the Catholic roots of democracy. "Study any institution or ideal which has commonly been regarded as an aspect of true Americanism," Hayes declared in 1924, "and you will discover that no matter who is immediately responsible for its erection and formulation, its embryo and antetype are to be found in Catholic theory or practice." Hayes argued that Catholicism represented the matrix within which all of Western civilization had emerged, and therefore its sway extended far beyond "its formal adherents" to "all human beings within its orbit of influence." Thus the achievements of America's Protestant colonists and citizens, as well as those of Catholic Americans, could be credited to a medieval Catholic heritage that formed the patrimony of the West. Catholicism appeared in Hayes's writings as "an idea, a type of culture, a habit," one that dovetailed seamlessly with the culture of democracy.[12]

Hayes's most distinctive contribution to the Catholic Revival was his identification of modern nationalism as what we would call today a "political religion"—a thin and bellicose substitute for the lost unity of medieval Christendom.[13] According to Hayes, nationalism had waxed as the fortunes of Western Christianity had waned; lacking recourse to God, individuals increasingly focused their energies on the state as an object of worship. But this new global faith, the inevitable product of secularization, represented a potent force for division rather than unification. Hayes described nationalism as "a reaction against historic Christianity, against the universal mission of Christ," with its emphasis on human brotherhood.[14] He attributed its rise in large part to the rampant denominationalism of Protestantism. In 1926, for instance, Hayes described American nationalism as a product of

> the very fact that American Protestantism is divided into numerous sects and denominations. No Protestant sect is strong enough—and certainly the Catholic Church (even if it were so minded) is not strong enough—to establish itself as the official church of the United States. Hence, there can be in a common Christianity, no oneness of faith and worship for the whole American people. Consequently, the spiritual unity, which almost everyone deems desirable, must be sought in nationalism.

Especially culpable, Hayes charged, were Protestant "modernists" who seemed "to thicken Americanism in measure as they dilute Christianity."[15] Hayes's anxieties about the anarchic tendencies of Protestantism matched in intensity his longing for a more genuine spiritual unity.

To be sure, Hayes went far beyond other Catholic historians of his time in questioning the stock Catholic account of the Reformation period, as well as the usual Protestant line.[16] Still, in his presidential address to the American Catholic Historical Association in 1931, Hayes took aim at the Reformers' assumption that "authority resided in the infallibility of every individual" rather than in "an infallible institution or church." Here, he stressed, lay the source of Protestantism's potent secularizing tendencies. However, Hayes speculated that, had the Reformers "grasped the full significance of their theory of authority," which functionally "allowed as many interpretations of the Christian religion as there were individual Christians," they would have beaten a hasty retreat. It was no wonder, then, that Protestant-Catholic tensions had begun to ease. Yet Hayes suggested that contemporary Protestantism lacked the theological substance needed to sustain its distinctiveness:

> How can one wax eloquent about the superiority of Protestantism over Catholicism when one recognizes that the former was derived from the latter and disbelieves in both? How can one center one's whole attention on religious phenomena when one is far more interested in natural science or in social conditions? How can the Protestant attack when he begins to admire his foe? Or how can the Catholic attack, when the object of attack quickly shifts?[17]

Hayes regarded the vast majority of modern-day Protestants as de facto secularists—fellow travelers with Enlightenment liberalism—and he did not hesitate to say so.

Hayes pursued this challenge to contemporary Protestants in the context of the American interfaith movement. As the dominant Catholic voice in the National Conference of Christians and Jews (NCCJ) after 1934, he articulated an expressly anti-secularist conception of American religious pluralism and linked it to the defense of democracy against totalitarianism. Hayes targeted, in particular, the ideal of tolerance, which he took to be a mere cloak for the forced unity of secular nationalism. Against those who viewed a secular public sphere as the precondition for religious diversity, Hayes identified secularism as the major impetus toward cultural conformity in the modern world, and he worked to reshape the interfaith movement into an alliance of religious believers against the secular threat. For example, at an interfaith conference of 1935, Hayes turned his satirical wit on the language of religious harmony:

> The most obvious short cut to a solution of our difficulties would be through unity. We would simply unite and agree upon one and the same set of beliefs. For example, if all of you were Catholics, sincere, practicing Catholics, and if you could get the en-

> tire population of the United States to be the same, you would not have to worry so much about human relations. . . . Or, again, what a help it would be . . . if all Christians, Catholics and Protestants alike, should return to Judaism. Better still, let Jews repudiate Judaism just at the moment when we Christians repudiate Christianity and all of us join in an antireligious front under the banners of a communist or a Fascist dictatorship! . . . No half-way measures should be tolerated. The choice which should be left to dissenters would be conversion or death.

Identifying secularism as the most likely source of this homogenizing ambition in the modern world, Hayes sharply rejected the suggestion of many NCCJ members that the group should cooperate, or even engage in dialogue, with "the anti-religious."[18] In 1938, Hayes extended this analysis to the global situation, arguing that totalitarianism represented the logical endpoint of the long ascent of secular nationalism. By undermining "the supernatural and absolute bases of our traditional morality," he explained, nationalism led to "an utter denial of any moral law superior to the might of dictators."[19]

JOHN COURTNEY MURRAY: A COMMON CAUSE AGAINST A COMMON ENEMY

The Jesuit theologian John Courtney Murray (1904–67) became the leading Catholic commentator on church-state relations during the late 1940s and 1950s. Murray was a long-time member of the faculty at Woodstock College who had received his doctorate from the Pontifical Gregorian University in Rome in 1937. He became the editor of *Theological Studies* in 1942 and quickly built up the journal's reputation, in no small part by publishing his own brilliant and densely reasoned analyses of contemporary debates on intercreedal cooperation and church-state relations. Animated by the spirit of the Catholic Revival and armed with arguments fashioned by the likes of Ryan and Hayes, Murray crafted a new solution to the long-standing problem of religious liberty by reformulating American liberalism in Catholic terms. His 1960 book *We Hold These Truths* marked the culmination of efforts by many generations of liberal Catholics to articulate a distinctively Catholic reading of American democracy grounded in the natural law.[20]

Even more than Ryan or Hayes, Murray made the discourse of secularism a defining feature of his thought.[21] One of his earliest essays appeared in *Man and Modern Secularism* (1940), a conference volume describing the modern era as the scene of a titanic battle between Christians and secularists. Murray filled out that analysis in his second major statement on religious liberty, a

1945 article proposing that Protestants and Catholics form an alliance against their common enemy, secularism. Murray doubted that the two Christian communions would ever resolve their theological disputes, but he nevertheless hoped that they could "abolish mutual distrust" and achieve "social unity, civic amity, harmony of action and mutual confidence in a common pursuit of the common good." Should they fail to do so, Murray ominously predicted, "the secularists and totalitarians will move in and solve the problem in their own way—the secularists, by evacuating the concept of religious liberty of all ethical content; and the totalitarians, by forcibly destroying the concept itself, whatever its content." Surely, Murray wrote, Catholics and Protestants could join hands against both "the totalitarian authoritarianism that denies the natural rights of conscience" and "the secularist liberalism that denies the natural obligations of conscience." He hoped that, as Catholics and Protestants backed away from the poles of authoritarianism and secularism and toward one another, they would meet on the common ground of the natural law, which he considered the only reliable foundation for democracy.[22]

Murray suggested that Catholic acceptance of this proposed alliance would "assure Protestants that we are more decisively dissociated from totalitarian views of conscience and society than they are perhaps inclined at the moment to think that we are." Conversely, he asserted, its acceptance by Protestants "would do much to assure me that they are more decisively dissociated from secularist views of conscience and society than I am inclined at the moment to think they are." In essence, Murray constructed a religious loyalty test of true Americanism, using the discourse of secularism to question the religious authenticity of theological liberals and others who favored strict church-state separation. On Murray's terms, Protestants could prove their loyalty to an authentic American liberalism only by condemning its degenerate French cousin: "secularist Liberalism, with its twin theories of the absolute autonomy of conscience and of the juridical omnipotence of the State."[23]

Working to shepherd Protestants and Catholics into a common fold, Murray repeatedly confronted Protestants with their latent "secularism" in the 1940s. "It has been hammered into us of late, by events more powerfully than by words," he wrote in a 1946 review, "that genuine freedom is a function of religion, that society will remain free only when it is structured according to the demands of the religious conscience, and that a secularized society is the matrix in which are inevitably formed all kinds of dynamisms that are hostile to human freedom." Murray insisted that M. Searle Bates, the Protestant author of the book under review—*Religious Liberty* (1945), a massive volume commissioned by the Federal Council of Churches—dimly recognized that "'freedom of religion' as conceived in the thought-world of secularist Liberalism" had been "a contributing factor in the secularization of society." Yet he contended that Bates's book was simply "too Protestant to deal vigorously with this fact."[24] Meanwhile, Murray sought to establish that the Church's unqualified condemnations of liberalism in the nineteenth century applied only to its secular French variant, not to the religion-friendly American model. All true liberals, he asserted, could surely agree on the disastrous effects of nineteenth-century liberalism's "militant secularism," its "systematic denial of the relevance of religion to social life." Characterizing "those who deny the sovereignty of God over human society" as "the most dangerous enemies of human liberty," Murray insisted that the Church's campaign against secularism should be "the cause of all men of good will."[25]

Postwar efforts to strengthen the separation of church and state alarmed Murray. In the spring of 1948, he responded to a manifesto by the newly founded group Protestants and Other Americans United for Separation of Church and State (POAU) by facetiously calling for the creation of "another organization with a still lengthier but more meaningful title, 'Catholics and Protestants and Jews and Other Americans United for Cooperative Relations between Church and State in View of the Peril of Secularism, Especially in Education.'" Demanding that Protestants "give up the scare techniques, the appeal to fear," Murray urged them to recognize that democracy stood in grave peril from "the secularism that bears within itself the seeds of future tyrannies." He insinuated that the threat posed by Catholic authoritarianism paled in comparison with the danger posed by secularism.[26]

In a nation teetering on the brink of a global struggle against "godless communism," Murray could draw on a deep wellspring of popular fears regarding secularism. The language of the *Everson* and *McCollum* decisions of 1947 and 1948, which interpreted the First Amendment's religious clauses as requiring a high wall between church and state, ratcheted up these fears dramatically.[27] In the wake of the decisions, Murray rallied a group of Catholic and non-Catholic leaders against secularism in Wilmington, Delaware. Describing *McCollum* as "a legal victory for secularism" and "a radical departure from our Federal constitutional tradition," Murray urged all members of America's Judeo-Christian faiths to unite behind a "common cause—the defense of the 'established habits' of our people, which are religious habits, and habits of cooperation between church and state within the wise constitutional guarantees of personal liberties." They should, he insisted, "make common cause against a common enemy—secularism, which strikes not only at our respective religions, but at our common American freedom."[28]

In his Wilmington speech, Murray simultaneously challenged the religious authenticity of the *McCollum* decision's Protestant supporters and dismissed them as a fringe group of nativist bigots. He described *McCollum* as the work of "a few, a very few, radical Protestants" who, "to the distress of their more temperate fellow Protestants," had entered into "a dubiously holy alliance with a strange assortment of Masons and secularist educators in order to launch a campaign of political action, along religious lines, against the Catholic Church." In point of fact, POAU's successful challenge to federal aid for religious groups had enjoyed considerable Protestant support. Murray, however, reduced the supporters to a small cadre of fellow travelers with secularism, dedicated anti-Catholics who indiscriminately befriended all "who consider the Catholic Church as 'the enemy'" and thereby imperiled both true religion and democracy. In his portrayal, the real winners in the *McCollum* case were "the secularists . . . whether they call themselves atheists, agnostics, humanists or what you will." By contrast, Murray contended, the "sober judgment" of "the thoughtful, religious men—Catholic, Protestant and Jewish . . . looks upon the decision as a defeat."[29]

Murray concluded his Wilmington speech by directly addressing Protestant fears of secularization:

> You boast of your primary contribution to the formation of American culture as a religious culture; then you cannot shrink from primary responsibility for the defense of this heritage. If the myth of democracy as a religion is triumphant, and achieves its "establishment" as our national religion, the triumph will be over you. Your God will have been supplanted by an idol.

As "the largest religious force and the most powerful in the country," Murray argued, Protestantism bore a heavy "obligation of leadership" in the cultural struggle against secularism.[30] A few years later, Murray would coin the term "the New Nativism" to describe Blanshard's position in *Communism, Democracy, and Catholic Power* (1951). Scoring the book's use of "'American' and 'un-American'" to denote "ultimate categories of value," Murray accused Blanshard of having rendered Catholicism incompatible with democracy by idiosyncratically rooting the latter in "a naturalist or secularist philosophy."[31] Yet Murray's rhetoric in the Wilmington speech worked in much the same manner, identifying a Christian or Judeo-Christian faith as the foundation of American political institutions.

JOHN COGLEY: CATHOLIC ANTI-COMMUNISM AND DEMOCRACY AS A METHOD

Among mid-twentieth-century liberal Catholics, John Cogley (1916–76) hewed the most closely to mainstream conceptions of liberalism. An editor of *Commonweal* during the tumultuous 1950s, Cogley's radical past gave him an expansive perspective on the relationship between Catholicism and American liberalism, one that prefigured sensibilities that would become widespread after Vatican II. A member of the Catholic Worker movement in 1930s Chicago, Cogley served in the military during World War II and then attended Loyola University through the GI Bill. After graduating, he joined the staff of *Commonweal* and, later, became project director of the Fund for the Republic. During the 1960 presidential campaign, he helped to prepare John F. Kennedy Jr. for the tough questions that followed his famous Houston speech endorsing church-state separation. Cogley's writings expanded the theological and political boundaries of liberal Catholicism for a generation of progressive "Commonweal Catholics."[32]

Cogley's liberalism found particularly dramatic (and controversial) expression in his outspoken denunciations of Catholic anti-communism and the actions of Senator Joseph McCarthy. In his debut *Commonweal* editorial, published in October of 1949, Cogley described anti-communism as a colossal waste of time and resources. He suggested that "the sheer energy being expended in the realm of thought and spirit for an *anti,* largely rhetorical enterprise" should instead be channeled into a "genuinely Christian social reconstruction."[33] Nine months later, in an editorial on "The Failure of Anti-Communism," Cogley observed that "throughout my entire adult life Catholicism in this country has been obsessed with the question of Communism." Since roughly the mid-1930s, Cogley declared, "opposition to Communism" had been the milieu in which "we Catholics lived and moved and had our being." Anti-communism, he continued ruefully, had "colored almost everything we said and did," becoming "the one unfailing constant, the touchstone by which we made our judgments and determined to a great extent the political line we followed."[34] During the 1950s, Cogley penned editorial after editorial questioning the wisdom of McCarthy's approach and encouraging his coreligionists to do the same.

Yet, even as Cogley highlighted the perils of Catholic anti-communism, he joined his fellow editors in renouncing the secular philosophy they saw behind the conception of democracy held by many non-Catholic liberals. "As long as pure economics or pure politics provide the meeting-ground for Catholics and liberals," *Commonweal*'s editors wrote in June of 1950, liberalism and Catholicism could not conflict. But when liberalism reached beyond the realm of practical economic and political issues and into the realm of ultimate truths, it became "a rival religion." The editors argued that "dynamic secularism" served many liberals as an "ultimate reality" that made "demands in all areas of living," playing a role in their lives "equivalent to [that which] religion plays in the life of a Catholic." To the extent that dynamic secularism defined the character of American liberalism, the editors asserted, a clash between Catholics and liberals was unavoidable.[35]

Echoing this sentiment in a review of Blanshard's 1951 book, Cogley wrote that "Paul the Apostle of Secularism" had "exalted what he chooses to call Democracy but is properly known as dynamic Secularism, to the status of a pseudo-religion." By defining "American democracy as the political incarnation of his secularist philosophy," Cogley continued, Blanshard could summarily dismiss "Catholic teaching on Natural Law, objective morality, Revelation, asceticism, etc." as "patently 'un-American.'" Cogley charged that Blanshard "demands from us, in the name of 'democracy' and under the threat of our being anathematized as bad Americans, that we accept the fool-proof position of the secularist." He felt sure that Blanshard's book would "stimulate the growing anti-Catholicism in this country, despite its author's pious insistence that he would not welcome anything of the sort."[36]

Did American liberalism represent a rival religion, or had it simply been evacuated of all moral content—"deeply infected with the germ of positivism," as *Commonweal*'s editors put it? Although the editors found liberalism in either form incompatible with true Americanism, they could not quite decide how to characterize the standoff between liberalism and Catholicism.[37] Open conflict on that question erupted in the spring of 1954, after Cogley penned an editorial endorsing a view of democracy articulated by Horace B. Donegan, the Episcopal bishop of New York. According to Donegan, the oft-heard defense of McCarthy on the grounds that his "aims are good, though his methods are bad," failed to acknowledge that democracy is "a method" rather than "a content." Democracy, Donegan stressed, did not require "a uniform set of social and political opinions." Cogley agreed that there was no such thing as "'Americanism' in the sense that there are such things as Nazism, Communism, fascism, etc." A term such as "un-American" could apply only to "method and procedure," Cogley continued, because "there is no body of political dogma or any full-fledged philosophy of life to which all Americans are bound."[38]

Cogley sharply separated the realm of philosophical and theological convictions from that of politics, seeking thereby to protect Catholics against liberal charges of disloyalty to America:

> We are not obliged to profess belief in, say, the rationalist view of the universe in order to qualify as citizens. We do not require immigrants to subscribe to capitalist economics, progressive educational theories or even basic Judaeo-Christian religious beliefs before they are permitted to become citizens of the United States. Up to now, by and large, we have escaped the political ideologue's equating the acceptance of his own convictions with the essence of good citizenship. We have been a live-and-let-live people.

Cogley decried the "growing rumblings of attempts to 'ideologize' democracy" that he saw in both McCarthyism and the liberalism of those who "identif[ied] their own dreary secularism with American democracy," after Blanshard's fashion. "The only real test of a good American," Cogley wrote sharply, "is whether he subscribes to the 'method' of government which is democracy. His philosophical and religious views, even his political philosophy, can not be called into question as long as democracy escapes the burden of a political orthodoxy—or 'content.'"[39]

In these reflections on the nature of democracy, Cogley had gone too far for the editors of the Jesuit weekly *America*. They responded swiftly, challenging his assumption "that to attach any content to what we call democracy is to make it an 'ideology.'" According to *America*'s editors, Cogley's view mirrored "the thinking of certain positivistic jurists and political theorists," and thus contradicted "both the Christian and the Anglo-American traditions." All democratic societies, they explained, "guarantee fundamental human rights, usually in carefully defined Bills of Rights," and "profess certain ethical purposes, such as, in the Preamble to our Constitution, the promotion of 'justice,' the 'general welfare' and 'liberty.'" Whereas "majoritarian democracy, understood as mere method, can readily lead to tyranny," *America*'s editors emphasized, genuine democracy "acknowledges as its standard of right and wrong a 'higher law' which is the only safe repository of freedom and justice."[40]

In his response, Cogley accused *America*'s editors of portraying democracy as the *source* of this higher law, a charge that added little clarity to the debate.[41] But the exchange highlighted the distance between the two journals on questions of political strategy. For Cogley and *Commonweal,* the notion of democracy as a method promised to end the conflict between Catholics and secularists by enabling them to bracket competing truth claims and simply agree to disagree. By contrast, the editors of *America* sought to vanquish "dynamic secularism" in a different manner, by once again placing religious commitments at the heart of American liberalism.

The lay editors of *Commonweal* clearly worried about the theologically grounded defense of democracy championed by *America.* Indeed, they openly lamented the fact that "certain Catholics, in their fury against secularism, viciously turn on persons who honestly, however tragically, purvey that secularism in the belief that they are serving their fellow man." As with the case of communism, however, *Commonweal* condemned both sides in the mainstream debate. Its editors portrayed secularists as the victims of false consciousness and the source of modern ills, while finding Catholic anti-secularism misguided in its means but not its ends.[42] Cogley agreed with *America* about the foundational status of basic religious truths in a democratic context but simply considered it unwise to claim that democracy required any philosophical system for its maintenance, be it the natural law or naturalism.

In this regard, Cogley followed the lead of Protestant and Jewish adherents to neo-orthodoxy, a theological movement for which he expressed considerable appreciation in the 1950s. In its various guises, neo-orthodoxy sought to reorient contemporary thinking toward a more a pessimistic account of human nature derived from Christian teachings on original sin. Cogley, stunned by the ability of Protestants to overlook Blanshard's dabbling in "the boldest kind of Caesarism," lauded the Jewish neo-orthodox thinker Will Herberg for unmasking "Blanshard's 'statist-secularist idolatry'" and for recognizing that Blanshard was "totalitarianizing 'democracy'" in addition to criticizing the Church.[43] Elsewhere, Cogley praised the Protestant theologian Reinhold Niebuhr, a pioneer of neo-orthodoxy who shared Cogley's misgivings about secularism. Lauding neo-orthodoxy's influence on American Protestantism, Cogley hoped that Protestant liberals would condemn more systematically the adoption of liberalism as a secular religion and stick to "a limited goal and a limited scope—the political order." As he quipped, "I'll take my religion straight, thank you."[44]

LIBERAL PROTESTANT RESPONSES TO THE DISCOURSE OF SECULARISM

A growing number of Protestants agreed with Murray about the dangers posed by secularism during the late 1940s. Just days before his Wilmington speech, Murray joined Niebuhr in addressing a group of religious leaders in New York City. Some Protestant participants in that meeting subsequently released a statement in *Christianity and Crisis* condemning the *Everson* and *McCollum* decisions. Declaring that the Court had improperly "extended the meaning of the constitutional prohibition of an establishment of religion so that any action by the state that is intended to benefit all bodies without discrimination is forbidden," they warned that the Court's "hardening of the idea of 'separation'" promised to "greatly accelerate the trend toward the secularization of our culture" and undermine "the religious foundations of our national life." In an accompanying editorial, John C. Bennett argued that Protestants had become "so preoccupied with the Roman Catholic problem" that they had unthinkingly taken church-state separation to a dangerous extreme. Bennett and his counterparts joined Murray in a different reading of the First Amendment: "Cooperation, entered into freely by the state and church and involving no special privilege to any church and no threat to the religious liberty of any citizen, should be permitted." These Protestant thinkers believed, in Bennett's words, that the Supreme Court had illegitimately moved "from the idea that the State should be neutral as between the churches or religious faiths to the idea that the State should be neutral as between all positive forms of religion on the one side and an aggressive secularism on the other." Bennett argued that the Court's position "tends in practice to give an advantage to aggressive secularism," by which he meant "the tendency to make the institutions and assumptions of American democracy into a religious faith or into a substitute for religious faith."[45]

The *Christianity and Crisis* statement appeared amid an upwelling of concern about secularism, including statements by the American Catholic bishops in 1947 and 1948.[46] During the next several years, liberal Protestants published a spate of books on secularism: Richard J. Spann's *The Christian Faith and Secularism* (1948), Albert T. Mollegen's *Christianity and the Crisis of Secularism* (1951), Georgia E. Harkness's *The Modern Rival of the Christian Faith: An Analysis of Secularism* (1952), and, as the wave of McCarthyism crested, Edwin E. Aubrey's *Secularism a Myth: An Examination of the Current Attack on Secularism* (1954). Of these, Aubrey's book mounted the most direct challenge to the assumptions underlying the discourse of secularism, providing a lightning rod for differences of opinion within the liberal Protestant camp. An examination of its content and reviewers' responses provides a valuable window onto liberal Protestant thinking on secularism in 1950s America.

Aubrey, a native of Glasgow, Scotland, who came to the United States in 1913, received his Ph.D. from the University of Chicago in 1926 and joined the Chicago faculty in 1929. In 1944, he took up the presidency of Crozer Theological Seminary, an independent but historically Baptist divinity school that had close ties to Chicago and counted Martin Luther King Jr. among its students between 1948 and 1951. Aubrey left Crozer in 1949 for the University of Pennsylvania, where he remained until his death in 1956. Like other modernists at Chicago and elsewhere, Aubrey was friendly to the social sciences and hoped to integrate developments in secular knowledge with the ethical insights of Christ.[47]

In the preface to *Secularism a Myth,* Aubrey observed that "secularism" had recently become "a rallying cry for religious forces, much as paganism was in the early Christian church, or 'the infidel' in the Middle Ages, or popery in seventeenth-century Protestantism." It provided a "convenient slogan" to "arouse the loyalty of a group against a common enemy" by "differentiating the in-group from the out-group." Like most analogous terms of demarcation, Aubrey continued, "secularism" was remarkably protean, referring variously to

> scientific humanism, naturalism and materialism; agnosticism and positivism; intellectualism, rationalism, existentialism and philosophy; nationalism, totalitarianism, democratic faith and communism; utopian idealism, optimism and the idea of progress; moralism and amoralism, ethical relativism and nihilism; the industrial revolution and its divorce from nature; modern education in separation from religion; historical method when applied to the biblical revelation; [and] mass atheism and the depersonalization of man.

At base, Aubrey specified, "secularism" denoted "the whole tendency of contemporary culture to ignore the doctrines of Christian theology in its attempts to solve the problems of life and thought." In this sense, the term functioned as "the modern substitute for the older theological phrase 'the world.'" But Aubrey thought the ascription of a vast range of additional characteristics to "secularism" had undercut the term's constructive capacity by divorcing it from "any specific reality" and thereby rendering it "an imaginary entity." Likening "secularism" to the constellation of epithets, including "ecclesiasticism, dogmatism, absolutism, pessimism, credulity, conservatism, cynicism and moral indifferentism," that were directed at various theologies, he urged his readers to resist using the term to foster "a spurious sense of crusading unity."[48]

Behind the growing use of the discourse of secularism in Protestant ecumenical pronouncements, Aubrey detected the deleterious influence of neo-orthodoxy on liberal Protestant thinking about the relationship between the church and the world. He judiciously directed the brunt of his criticism of neo-orthodoxy toward European theorists and portrayed the movement's leading American interpreters as moderating forces in ecumenical discussion. But despite this self-protective strategy, the overall thrust of Aubrey's critique pointed directly at the categorical assumptions underlying the neo-orthodox paradigm, which posited a sharper distinction between the church and the world than had earlier forms of liberalism. Portraying contemporary Protestant theology as long on transcendence and short on immanence, Aubrey called upon Protestants "to recover the truth of the immanence of God as a balance for the transcendentalism of neo-orthodoxy."[49]

Aubrey did acknowledge the attempts of neo-orthodox thinkers to render their invocations of secularism more nuanced. On the whole, however, the neo-orthodox "determination not to succumb to contemporary culture" struck him as a mere rationalization for an "imperious attitude toward society" that mistook "ecclesiastical pride" for "loyalty to God" and turned "fear of social impotence" into "strident defiance." Aubrey even proposed that anti-secularism represented "a pathological phase of ecclesiastical psychology": "In times of stress the church tends to set itself over against the world or human society and to make sharp differentiations in order to save itself from engulfment in that world." Aubrey found deeply disturbing this "tendency of the church to attack when it might be learning, and to treat with contempt many contemporary forces that might be its allies in the struggle for righteousness." Urging "acceptance of the so-called secular society as an opportunity for growth," he cautioned Christians against "a rejection of the very body of experience in relation to which our faith will find its relevance."[50]

Stressing that "people may co-operate even when they hold different theoretical positions," Aubrey counseled churchmen to focus on their real enemies—human sins such as greed and hypocrisy—rather than constructing a mythological common enemy out of "secular movements as such." He insisted that "the church has no corner on goodness and secular movements on badness; correct theology is no guarantee of ethical sensitivity, and an inadequate theory may be found in a very effective worker for spiritual values." Aubrey also noted that "many valuable allies of the Christian church are being alienated by the current attacks on secularism in general. They properly resent the imputation that, because they do not share a particular theological viewpoint, they are a menace to society." Calling for a critical strategy "at once humbler and bolder, less plaintive and more responsible" than the current attack on secularism, Aubrey advised the church to cease its "ill-defined and ill-considered attacks" on potential allies and stop "asserting a kind of independence of society which it does not in fact possess."[51]

It would be deceptively easy to see little more than anti-Catholicism in Aubrey's unwillingness to follow the lead of Niebuhr and the other signers of the *Christianity and Crisis* statement. However, the existence of competing discourses of authoritarianism and secularism in mid-twentieth-century America suggests a more complex account of the anxieties that many non-Catholic liberals felt about the prospect of an all-out war on secularism. Anti-Catholicism certainly played a role in shaping the views of many, and perhaps most, liberal Protestants. Yet so too did genuine convictions about the proper relationship between church and state, as well as a sense of the potential for constructive cooperation with social scientists, social workers, and members of other secular professions. After all, as McGreevy demonstrates, figures such as Niebuhr also expressed concerns about Catholic authoritarianism, even as they decried the rising influence of secularism.[52]

In the end, the two groups of liberal Protestants I have chronicled here split most clearly over a strategic issue concerning the church's relation to the world. Both sought to make religion relevant again in the modern world. But Niebuhr and his neo-orthodox compatriots understood relevance as a matter of foundational criticism, believing that the churches should take aim at the core tenets of modern life. Their clarion call for the church to adopt a stance of "prophetic witness" assumed a significant degree of dynamic tension between the church and the world. By contrast, those of Aubrey's ilk believed they could best attain relevance by continuing to engage with the most promising tendencies in the secular realm, encouraging their growth toward a fully Christian expression. In Aubrey's words, a truly humble believer would recognize that "there have been spiritual values in secular movements which Christianity cannot claim to have originated and which should, in plain justice, be acknowledged."[53] Here, however, Aubrey ran afoul of one of the most potent forms of jeremiad on display in the Cold War years—the discourse of secularism, shared by leading liberal Catholics and neo-orthodox Protestants alike.

NOTES

1. John T. McGreevy, *Catholicism and American Freedom: A History* (New York: Norton, 2003), 166–67. Blanshard's book is *American Freedom and Catholic Power* (Boston: Beacon, 1949). See also Philip Hamburger, *Separation of Church and State* (Cambridge, Mass.: Harvard University Press, 2002).

2. John Courtney Murray, "Paul Blanshard and the New Nativism," *Month* 5 (April 1951): 214–25.

3. McGreevy, *Catholicism and American Freedom*, 166–88. See also John T. McGreevy, "Thinking on One's Own: Catholicism in the American Intellectual Imagination, 1928–1960," *Journal of American History* 84, no. 1 (June 1997): 97–131.

4. I use the phrase "discourse of secularism," rather than referring to "anti-secularism," in order to avoid reifying the category of secularism itself. My approach mirrors that of McGreevy, who focuses on the discourse of authoritarianism mobilized by non-Catholic liberals rather than referring to their "anti-Catholicism."

5. On the broad contours of this debate, see Edward A. Purcell Jr., *The Crisis of Democratic Theory: Scientific Naturalism and the Problem of Value* (Lexington: University Press of Kentucky, 1973); Philip Gleason, "Controversy: Backlash against the Catholic Revival," in *Contending with Modernity: Catholic Higher Education in the Twentieth Century* (New York: Oxford University Press, 1995), 261–82; Fred W. Beuttler, "Organizing an American Conscience: The Conference on Science, Philosophy and Religion, 1940–1968" (Ph.D. diss., University of Chicago, 1995); David Hollinger, "Science as a Weapon in *Kulturkämpfe* in the United States during and after World War II," in *Science, Jews, and Secular Culture: Studies in Mid-Twentieth-Century American Intellectual History* (Princeton: Princeton University Press, 1996), 155–74; James Gilbert, *Redeeming Culture: American Religion in an Age of Science* (Chicago: University of Chicago Press, 1997); and Jan C. C. Rupp, "The Cultural Foundations of Democracy: The Struggle between a Religious and a Secular Intellectual Reform Movement in the American Age of Conformity," in *Religious and Secular Reform in America: Ideas, Beliefs, and Social Change*, ed. David K. Adams and Cornelis A. van Minnen (New York: New York University Press, 1999), 231–47. Crucial sources on Catholics and liberalism include R. Bruce Douglass and David Hollenbach, eds., *Catholicism and Liberalism: Contributions to American Public Philosophy* (New York: Cambridge University Press, 1994); and Jay P. Corrin, *Catholic Intellectuals and the Challenge of Democracy* (Notre Dame, Ind.: University of Notre Dame Press, 2002).

6. For more on Ryan's life, see Francis L. Broderick, *Right Reverend New Dealer: John A. Ryan* (New York: Macmillan, 1963); David J. O'Brien, *American Catholics and Social Reform: The New Deal Years* (New York: Oxford University Press, 1968); Robert G. Kennedy, ed., *Religion and Public Life: The Legacy of Monsignor John A. Ryan* (Lanham, Md.: University Press of America, 2001); and Zachary R. Calo, "'The Indispensable Basis of Democracy': American Catholicism, the Church-State Debate, and the Soul of American Liberalism, 1920–1929," *Virginia Law Review* 91, no. 4 (June 2005): 1037–73.

7. John A. Ryan, "Catholicism and Liberalism," *Nation* 131, no. 3396 (August 6, 1930): 150, 152. Ryan stressed that he had "never experienced any temptation to become a liberal in the sense of rejecting any part of the authority claimed and exercised by my church" (152).

8. Calo, "'The Indispensable Basis of Democracy,'" 1058. Ryan's article is "Catholic Doctrine on the Right of Self Government," *Catholic World* 108, no. 645 (December 1918): 314–30.

For more on the Catholic Revival, see William M. Halsey, *The Survival of American Innocence: Catholicism in an Era of Disillusionment, 1920–1940* (Notre Dame, Ind.: Notre Dame University Press, 1980); and Philip Gleason, "How Catholic Is the Declaration of Independence?" *Commonweal* 123, no. 5 (March 8, 1996): 11–14.

9. John A. Ryan, "The Indispensable Basis of Democracy," *Vital Speeches of the Day* 5, no. 21 (August 15, 1939): 670, 667, 669. Calo borrows the title of Ryan's article but offers no analysis of the article's content.

10. Ibid., 670, 669.

11. Patrick Allitt, *Catholic Converts: British and American Intellectuals Turn to Rome* (Ithaca, N.Y.: Cornell University Press, 1997), 240–41; and Patrick Allitt, "Carlton Hayes and His Critics," *U.S. Catholic Historian* 15, no. 3 (summer 1997): 23–37.

12. Carlton J. H. Hayes, "Obligations to America. I. Catholic America," *Commonweal* 1, no. 8 (December 31, 1924): 200–201.

13. For more on "political religions," see Emilio Gentile, *Politics as Religion* (Princeton: Princeton University Press, 2001).

14. Carlton J. H. Hayes, *Essays on Nationalism* (New York: Macmillan, 1926), 124.

15. Carlton J. H. Hayes, "Nationalism as a Religion. V. A Tribal Creed," *Commonweal* 3, no. 10 (January 13, 1926): 262–63.

16. Allitt, "Carlton Hayes and His Critics," 27.

17. Carlton J. H. Hayes, "Significance of the Reformation in the Light of Contemporary Scholarship," *Catholic Historical Review* 17, no. 4 (January 1932): 401, 398.

18. "Comments by Carlton J. H. Hayes," in *The American Way: A Study of Human Relations among Protestants, Catholics, and Jews,* by Newton Diehl Baker, Carlton J. H. Hayes, and Roger Williams Straus (New York: Willett, Clark, 1936), 148, 152.

19. Carlton J. H. Hayes, "Dangers and Safeguards of Democracy: The Challenge of Totalitarianism," *Public Opinion Quarterly* 2, no. 1 (January 1938): 22–23.

20. John Courtney Murray, *We Hold These Truths: Catholic Reflections on the American Proposition* (New York: Sheed and Ward, 1960). In addition to the sources listed below, helpful texts on Murray's thought and career include Thomas T. Love, *John Courtney Murray: Contemporary Church-State Theory* (Garden City, N.Y.: Doubleday, 1965); Donald E. Pelotte, *John Courtney Murray: Theologian in Conflict* (Ramsey, N.J.: Paulist Press, 1976); Thomas P. Ferguson, *Catholic and American: The Political Theology of John Courtney Murray* (Kansas City: Sheed and Ward, 1983); Robert W. McElroy, *The Search for an American Public Theology: The Contribution of John Courtney Murray* (Mahwah, N.J.: Paulist Press, 1989); Patrick Allitt, "The Significance of John Courtney Murray," in *Church Polity and American Politics: Issues in Contemporary American Catholicism,* ed. Mary C. Segers (New York: Garland, 1990), 51–65; and Robert P. Hunt and Kenneth L. Grasso, eds., *John Courtney Murray and the American Civil Conversation* (Grand Rapids, Mich.: William B. Eerdmans, 1992).

21. Despite recent efforts to place Murray in a Cold War context, relatively little attention has been paid to his use of the term "secularism." See, e.g., Thomas W. O'Brien, *John Courtney Murray in a Cold War Context* (Lanham, Md.: University Press of America, 2004), xvi; and Donald J. D'Elia and Stephen M. Krason, eds., *We Hold These Truths and More: Further Catholic Reflections on the American Proposition* (Steubenville, Ohio: Franciscan University Press, 1993).

22. John Courtney Murray, "Freedom of Religion: I. The Ethical Problem," *Theological Studies* 6, no. 2 (June 1945): 240–41, 286.

23. Ibid., 286.

24. John Courtney Murray, "Religious Liberty: An Inquiry," *Theological Studies* 7, no. 1 (March 1946): 154.

25. John Courtney Murray, "How Liberal Is Liberalism?" *America* 75, no. 1 (April 6, 1946): 6–7.

26. John Courtney Murray, "Religious Liberty: The Concern of All," *America* 48, no. 19 (February 7, 1948): 513–16.

27. James E. Zucker, "Better a Catholic than a Communist: Reexamining *McCollum v. Board of Education* and *Zorach v. Clausen*," *Virginia Law Review* 93, no. 8 (December 2007): 2069–2118.

28. John Courtney Murray, "A Common Enemy, a Common Cause" (1948), published in *First Things* 26, no. 1 (October 1992): 34, 32, 37.

29. Ibid., 34–35.

30. Ibid., 37.

31. Murray, "Paul Blanshard and the New Nativism," 216.

32. John Cogley, *A Canterbury Tale: Experiences and Reflections, 1916–1976* (New York: Seabury, 1976). Cogley reflects on the meaning of "Commonweal Catholic" on pages 51–53 of these memoirs.

33. John Cogley, "The Best Defense," *Commonweal* 51, no. 2 (October 21, 1949): 28.

34. John Cogley, "The Failure of Anti-Communism," *Commonweal* 52, no. 15 (July 21, 1950): 357.

35. "Clearing the Air," editorial, *Commonweal* 52, no. 10 (June 16, 1950): 238. Cogley was listed as "feature editor" at this point.

36. John Cogley, "The Unspoken Ism," *Commonweal* 54, no. 6 (May 18, 1951): 144–46.

37. "Catholics can never accept a wholly pragmatic approach to the practical issues of the day," the editors insisted, because "Catholicism upholds the claims of an immutable natural law . . . and an objective code of morals." "Clearing the Air," 238.

38. John Cogley, "Question of Method," *Commonweal* 59, no. 23 (March 12, 1954): 570.

39. Ibid..

40. "Democracy as Procedure and Substance," editorial, *America* 90, no. 25 (March 20, 1954): 646.

41. John Cogley, "Democracy's 'Content,'" *America* 91, no. 1 (April 3, 1954): 28. Cogley cited a supportive passage by William E. McManus of the National Catholic Welfare Conference's Department of Education: "Unlike a totalitarian state, the government in a democracy has of itself nothing to teach. It does not attempt to impose itself upon the citizens."

42. "Clearing the Air," 238.

43. Cogley, "Question of Method," 570.

44. John Cogley, "Liberalism as Virtue," *Commonweal* 67, no. 6 (November 8, 1957): 147.

45. "Statement on Church and State" (June 17, 1948), *Christianity and Crisis* 8, no. 12 (July 5, 1948): 90; John C. Bennett, "Implications of the New Conception of 'Separation,'" ibid., 89. The signers of the *Christianity and Crisis* statement were James C. Baker, Eugene E. Barnett, John C. Bennett, John Crosby Brown, Robert L. Calhoun, Angus Dun, Harry Emerson Fosdick, Charles W. Gilkey, Douglas Horton, Walter M. Horton, Lynn Harold Hough, Umphrey Lee, Henry Smith Leiper, Francis J. McConnell, Benjamin E. Mays, Francis P. Miller, H. Richard Niebuhr, Reinhold Niebuhr, Justin Wroe Nixon, Edward L. Parsons, Andrew H. Phelps, Liston Pope, Francis B. Sayre, William Scarlett, H. Shelton Smith, Henry P. Van Dusen, and Charles T. White.

46. The 1947 statement, written in the wake of *Everson*, declared belief in God to be the

only possible source of personal morality and political rights: "Secularism, or the practical exclusion of God from human thinking and living, is at the root of the world's travail today." "Catholic Bishops' Statement on Secularism," *New York Times,* November 16, 1947, 54. The following year, after the *McCollum* decision, the National Catholic Welfare Conference declared that secularism had recently "scored unprecedented victories in its opposition to governmental encouragement of religious and moral training, even where no preferential treatment of one religion over another is involved." "Catholic Bishops Hit Supreme Court," *New York Times,* November 21, 1948, 1, 63.

47. "Dr. Edwin Aubrey, a Theologian, 60," *New York Times,* September 12, 1956, 37; and Gary J. Dorrien, *The Making of American Liberal Theology,* vol. 3, *Crisis, Irony, and Postmodernity, 1950–2005* (Louisville, Ky.: Westminster John Knox, 2006), 145. For Aubrey's views of science and naturalism, see Edwin E. Aubrey, "Naturalism and Religious Thought," *Journal of Philosophy* 48, no. 3 (February 1, 1931): 57–66.

48. Edwin E. Aubrey, *Secularism a Myth: An Examination of the Current Attack on Secularism* (New York: Harper & Brothers, 1954), 11, 25, 12, 26.

49. Ibid., 182. Long associated with the Theological Discussion Group, which counted among its members the American theologians most strongly influenced by the neo-orthodox turn in Protestant theology—namely, Reinhold and H. Richard Niebuhr, Paul Tillich, and John C. Bennett—Aubrey needed to frame his critique carefully. In a 1936 review, another Theological Discussion Group member, Henry P. Van Dusen of Union Theological Seminary, had taken Aubrey to task for categorizing Niebuhr with Barth and Brunner ("in the chapter on the dialectical theology!"). Henry P. Van Dusen, review of *Present Theological Tendencies,* by Edwin E. Aubrey, *Journal of Religion* 16, no. 3 (July 1936): 350–52.

50. Aubrey, *Secularism a Myth,* 27, 30, 105. Having served as the president of the University of Chicago Settlement during World War II, Aubrey worried in particular about "alienat[ing] the scientific worker or the social reformer who is a believer or open-minded agnostic by insisting that he is a menace along with the atheist or the morally indifferent person" (121). As Aubrey's statement suggests, he too placed forthright atheists beyond the pale. Yet he refused to apply the term "atheist" to humanists, agnostics, and other heterodox thinkers, reserving it for the most hardened opponents of moral idealism. For instance, he counseled Christians to learn from the historical accounts of ethics offered by the likes of Durkheim, Westermarck, and Dewey, "lest we lose contact with the values for which nonecclesiastical movements are struggling" (134).

51. Ibid., 136, 13, 12.

52. McGreevy, *Catholicism and American Freedom,* 167, 205–206.

53. Aubrey, *Secularism a Myth,* 12–13.

SIXTEEN

Religious Liberalism and the Liberal Geopolitics of Religion

TRACY FESSENDEN

This essay was originally titled "Liberalism and Ambivalence." The ambivalence was my own, and in the company of the vibrant scholars and champions of religious liberalism collected here it made itself felt as a kind of embarrassment, a desire to trot out my own religious-liberal bona fides before proceeding further. I believe in gay marriage as a religious as well as a civil right. I believe that Jesus would have shielded George Tiller, the slain abortion provider, with his body, and I found solace during the Bush administration in the hour a week I got to pretend, with other viewers of *The West Wing,* that my president was really a Jesuit-educated Democrat played by Martin Sheen. My nostalgia for the Berrigan-brothers Catholicism of my childhood, where the long-haired seminarian strumming guitar on the altar was as likely to play from the Leonard Cohen songbook as from *Glory & Praise,* is as real and abiding as any of an earlier generation's for the Latin Mass. I may not map perfectly onto the vivid historical schema given in Leigh Schmidt's *Restless Souls,* but my undergraduates don't need convincing: the words "religious liberal" regularly show up in their official and unofficial evaluations of my classes, the conjunction variously framed in curiosity, relief, or alarm.

So my students are often unsure what to make of my strong reservations about what might be called a liberal geopolitics of religion, the ways in which the project of bringing religions into line with a liberal, democratic world order has emerged as an insistent feature of United States policy. An example would be the George W. Bush–era strategy of Muslim World Outreach, a $1.3-billion program of enlisting both state and non-state actors (the latter including "Islamic radio, Islamic TV, Islamic schools, mosques, and monuments") to promote the "values of religious tolerance" in the so-called Muslim world.[1] Another is the International Religious Freedom Act (IRFA), a complex regulatory machinery signed into law by Bill Clinton that empowers the U.S. government to monitor and to punish violations of religious freedom in every other country of the world.[2] In a new set of recommendations to the Obama administration, the former director of the State Department's Office of International Religious Freedom urged that IRFA be integrated more fully into international security policy and retooled in the image of Muslim World Outreach, its new focus less on targeting specific abuses than on "facilitating the political and cultural institutions necessary to religious freedom." This would be a way for the U.S. to "tackle religious politics abroad," he suggested, by drawing "lessons from its domestic success."[3] "America . . . is the spiritual home of modern choice-based religion and pluralism," notes *The Economist* in an essay commending this course. "It is also the world's most powerful country. . . . Why has a country so rooted in pluralism made so little of religious freedom" in its statecraft?[4]

I'm not the first to note the irony in the fact that the U.S. mandate to "tackle religious politics abroad" is grounded in appeals to its vaunted tradition of *non*-interference in the religious lives of its citizens, or that the goal of advancing a more liberal Islam, conceived now as a state function, has been integrated into the agendas of conservative Christian groups.[5] Of more concern to me are the normative assumptions such projects carry and enforce: their articulation of some religions and relations to religion, but not others, as normal and salutary, some as compatible with democracy and some as ominously incompatible. The imperative of rendering some forms of religious subjectivity, association, and practice out of bounds within a liberal democratic world order will thus on occasion justify the violence such regulation claims to deter: a military and strategic analysis provided by the American Enterprise Institute (AEI) in the run-up to the war in Iraq, for example, framed the preemptive strike on Iraq as a step toward fulfilling "the Bush Doctrine's promise to liberalize the Islamic world."[6]

I leave it to others to debate the merits of the United States' efforts to realize its policy objectives through the cultivation of particular religious subjectivities as normative. What I wish to do here is to consider the possible relationships between such projects and the category of religious liberalism.[7] This is to subject religious liberalism to the kinds of questions I'm admittedly more used to putting to religious conservatism. When I teach R. Marie Griffith's *God's Daughters: Evangelical Women and the Power of Submission,* for example, I try to open a broader discussion of power than the one the book's subtitle usually prompts. *God's Daughters* has sparked rich debate on the degree to which their participation in the activities of the conservative Christian group Women's Aglow empowers or disempowers evangelical women within their families and faith communities. I encourage my students also to consider how the practices and articulations of Women's Aglow members situate them within larger operations of power, among them the forms of juridical and state power that nurture the particular configurations—of families, religions, and states—that their prayers and advocacy inscribe as desirable, holy, and good. (To give a sense of what these are, Women's Aglow identifies as its three divine "mandates" 1) "to promote gender reconciliation between male and female in the Body of Christ as God designed"; 2) "to minister to the Muslim people, while bringing awareness of the basic theological differences between Islam and Christianity," elsewhere phrased as a call to "unravel the garment of Islam" or to "unveil . . . the system [of Islam]"; and 3) "to stand in loving support for Israel and the Jewish people."[8]) To invoke Foucault's notion of governmentality, or the means by which a particular form of governance produces the subjects best suited to fulfilling its ends, How might the practices of Women's Aglow go to the making of subjects for whom the desiderata of Aglow are self-evidently good, the means to their end legitimate? My question for American religious liberalism, then—a formation from which I cannot (nor would I wish wholly to) exempt or extricate myself—is, what is its relationship to the operations of power that would cultivate those forms of religious life that abet or at least do not obstruct what the AEI policy paper I cited earlier calls the global "expansion of the American perimeter"—a "liberal, democratic . . . world environment where the American system can survive and flourish"?[9]

Let me be clear that in questioning religious liberalism I have no wish to mount an assault either from the right or from further left. Perhaps the force of liberalism is such that to engage it at all is to feel compelled to stake one's place on the left-right spectrum that liberalism appears to organize, as though this were the only legitimate terrain of critique. To note this, though, is also to confront both the capaciousness and the slipperiness of "liberal" as a descriptor. If you search for the word "liberal" in the online archives of the American Enterprise Institute or *The Economist,* for example, you'll see approving and derogatory uses about equally divided. In the first category you'll find terms like "American-led liberal international order," "liberal international order of nation-states," and "liberal foundations of global free-trade"; in the second, "liberal judges," "liberal bias," "liberal journalists," "liberal pack-mentality," and "liberal solipsism of righteous Democrats." In these contexts, "liberal" is a good thing to be if you're a democracy but a bad thing to be if you're a democrat, salutary in international settings and suspect in domestic ones. The international settings in which "good" liberalism is to be found are nevertheless those where American values hold sway, or are given the best odds of succeeding.

However differently *The Nation* or *Mother Jones* might weight the liberal spectrum, the classical, free-market liberalism favored on the right and the just-society liberalism associated with the left do share a set of foundational, normative commitments. Foremost among them are a commitment to the autonomy of the individual and a commitment to what might be thought of as the autonomy of liberalism itself. In the first case, liberalism posits individual freedom as innate to personhood. Locke famously assumed humans to be "naturally in . . . a *State of perfect Freedom* to order their actions . . . without asking leave, or depending on the Will of any Man," as well as in a "*State* . . . of *Equality,* wherein all the Power and Jurisdiction is reciprocal, no one having more than another."[10] In the second case, liberalism as the basis for democratic governance must be what John Rawls called "freestanding." As Rawls put it in *Political Liberalism,* the goal is a not a "comprehensive doctrine" of human flourishing to compete with other comprehensive doctrines, but instead a neutral framework for "reasoned, informed, and willing political agreement" among citizens regardless of the comprehensive doctrines to which they may or may not adhere.[11] The principle of liberalism's autonomy provides the framework both for multiculturalism, with its promise of overlapping consensus among differing comprehensive doctrines, and for the rule of law, for which the rival claims of any comprehensive doctrine must stand aside.

Two features of liberalism in its broadest theoretical foundations, then, are that it places freedom, conceptualized in individual terms, above other human goods, and that it is something importantly *other* than religion. Not only is liberalism other than religion in the sense that it stands apart from any comprehensive doctrine, but running through liberal theory is the suspicion that religion itself represents a constraint on freedom that cannot always be justified by recourse to liberal principles. For Mill, the "*a priori* assumption . . . in favour of freedom" puts "the burthen of proof . . . [on those] who contend for any restriction or prohibition."[12] Religious authority, like democratic governance, can only be justified on the grounds that it is freely chosen, and that it nurtures rather than constrains the freedom and equality of its followers. (Here we begin to see the complex historical articulations between liberalism and Protestantism, particularly in America.[13])

Leigh Schmidt's genealogy of American religious liberalism documents myriad ways in which liberal assumptions found vibrant expression in loosely religious idioms, bent to the convictions and whims of the heterodox.[14] Whitman's point in *Democratic Vistas* that "only in the perfect uncontamination and solitariness of individuality may the spirituality of religion positively come forth at all" sits comfortably alongside Mill's near-contemporaneous insistence in *On Liberty* that "the cultivation of individuality" alone among "any condition of human affairs" "brings human beings . . . nearer to the best thing they can be."[15] Liberalism's vision of the self as free in relation to the comprehensive doctrines from which it may choose its conceptions of flourishing finds resonance in William James's definition of spirituality as "susceptibility to ideals" but "with a certain freedom to indulge in imagination about them. A certain amount of 'otherworldly' fancy. Otherwise you have mere morality." As liberalism seeks to nurture a variety of comprehensive doctrines without identifying itself with any one, so religious liberalism in Schmidt's account is marked by a "cosmopolitan spirit that emphasize[s] the appreciation of religious variety," its "ecumenical pursuit of unity amid diversity" both accommodating and provisionalizing particular traditions and creeds.[16] It is egalitarian in its agenda and global in its reach, identifying as what is most authentic, desirable, and praiseworthy in religion a state of personal spiritual freedom available to anyone—whether "in occident [or] orient," as the Rev. Robert Alfred Vaughan put it in 1856, "whether Romanist or Protestant, Jew, Turk, or Infidel." From this newly globalized conception of personal spiritual freedom, Schmidt argues, religious liberalism derives its ethical commitment to progressive, justice-producing reforms.

We could continue to mark points of convergence between liberal theory and religious liberalism as Schmidt portrays it. To do so, however, is to risk naturalizing a relation between liberalism and religion that is this easy, this untroubled, when in political practice the encounter between them is often a great deal more fraught. Perhaps one function of religious liberalism in its canonical versions is to smooth over these more conflictual relationships, to render them ideally unproblematic, such that what problems do arise in the confrontation of liberalism with religion can be ascribed to the latter rather than to the former. I want then to focus for the remainder of this essay on five nodes or points of conjuncture between religion and liberalism that suggest a less settled relationship between them.

1. Insofar as religion and liberalism are seen as potentially compatible but intrinsically separate from one another, the conjunction of religion and liberalism might instead direct attention to religious sources of liberalism that typically go unacknowledged. The publication in 2009 of Rawls's undergraduate thesis at Princeton, a rich exercise in theological ethics he titled "A Brief Inquiry into the Meaning of Sin and Faith," has now attracted a flurry of interest, but one wonders why it remained so long overlooked, or why the theological undercurrents in his mature work have only recently come in for discussion.

2. The conjunction of liberalism and religion (with its etymological resonance in *religare,* to tie or bind) also condenses a key question in liberal political theory, which is the extent to which selves can even be constituted as such apart from their attachments, including attachments they do not or cannot freely choose.

3. The joining of the two terms in "religious liberalism" suggests a mode of production: How does liberalism, by recognizing some forms of religion and relations to religion, but not others, as compatible with its norms, go to the making of religion in liberal societies?

4. The conjunction of religion and liberalism also brings to mind what Mahmood Mamdani has called the "culturalization" of conflict in liberalism, the transposition of debate over what is liberal or non-liberal from the market and the state to "culture," which tends to shake out as another name for religion.[17] To the degree that liberalism, as Stanley Hauerwas suggests, "is assumed to be irreversibly institutionalized economically as market capitalism and politically as democracy,"[18] religion (a.k.a. "culture") remains the site where liberalism still has work to do.

5. Finally, "religious liberalism" suggests that liberalism operates as a party to differences with or among religions and not merely as a tool for managing them. This is not to say that liberalism is itself a religion, but that its own thick normativities, like those of any religion, are culturally and historically situated and so something less than transparent or freestanding.

To pursue the question of American religious liberalism in relation to a liberal geopolitics of religion, let me move backward through this list, and begin with some ways in which liberalism operates as a party to religious debate even as it purportedly remains strongly autonomous from religion.[19]

The principle of liberalism's autonomy from culture means that liberal commitments will typically be seen to operate as remedies or terms of analysis for, not aspects of, the conflicts on which they are brought to bear. Recent liberal engagement with issues of gender justice within a non-liberal or insufficiently liberal religious culture, for example, will often start by describing a conflict internal to that culture, momentarily reframe the tension as one between liberalism and its other, and then pursue the encounter as a challenge for *liberalism,* a kind of procedural problem to be solved by getting liberal commitments in their proper axiological order. In her consideration of religion and women's human rights, for example, Martha Nussbaum begins by recounting cases in which women are subject to violence or denied equality in global religious contexts. Her examples include the corporal punishment of women in Iran who reject the hijab, the objections by conservative Hindu male members of the Indian parliament to legislation that extends to women the right to divorce and remarry, and Chinese policies that appeal to Confucian norms to justify economic harms to women. Each of these instances of injury to women arises within a very different cultural system, but taken severally they pose what Nussbaum calls a "liberal dilemma." This is a dilemma *for* liberals—what to do?—and also a dilemma within liberalism, namely, a tension between the liberal commitment to diversity, including religious diversity, and the liberal commitment to equality and the rule of law, both of which, as noted earlier, flow from the principle of liberalism's alleged autonomy from culture.[20]

Externalizing religious conflict in this way—rewriting the confrontation of opposing desires, obligations, and appeals to authority within a particular religious culture as a tension within *liberalism*—misses ameliorative possibilities that may inhere in the terms of the conflict itself. Framing the problem as one of liberal vs. non-liberal cultures, meanwhile (Nussbaum does both), insulates liberal principles from negotiation or debate to the degree that they are seen as solutions for rather than strands within the underlying conflict. (This may also be the case when liberal principles really *are* external to a particular debate; as Peter van der Veer suggests, the liberal tendency to address the question of headscarves in French schools as an issue above all of *equality*—Are Muslim girls disadvantaged by the headscarf? Are crosses and yarmulkes likewise prohibited by the ban on religious attire?—is likely "to result in a strategic essentialism on the part of Muslim girls who want to assert their difference."

Thus liberalism becomes a part of the conflict it seeks to manage.[21]) In either case, putting liberalism beyond or above religious difference allows liberalism to disown the regulative force of its own interventions on religion to the degree that these are seen to flow from commitments that are themselves religiously neutral. As Rawls put it, "The question of equal liberty of conscience is settled."[22]

But "liberty of conscience" suggests a certain relationship to religion, one in which the individual stands back to assess, compare, evaluate, and make choices. Any other relation to religion suggests coercion or false consciousness, an overvaluation of received authority, a lack of critical distance. This is also a normative relation to culture within liberalism—as Wendy Brown parses it, you either *have* a culture (in which you reflect critically on its ideals, do not blindly follow custom, etc.) or else your culture *has you*.[23] To move up then to the fourth item on my list, the culturalization of conflict in liberalism: a well-known example is Susan Moller Okin's essay "Is Multiculturalism Bad for Women?" and the many responses it generated, which focus almost entirely on the dangers to women of accommodating minority religions within liberal polities, even though "culture" remains the operative rubric throughout. "Most if not all [cultures] have patriarchal pasts," Okin writes, "but some—western liberal culture in particular—have departed from them far further than others. . . . In the case of a more patriarchal minority culture in the context of a less patriarchal majority culture, no argument can be made on the basis of self-respect or freedom that the female members of the [more patriarchal] culture have a clear interest in its preservation. Indeed, they *may* be much better off if the culture into which they were born were . . . to become extinct (so that its members would become integrated into the less sexist surrounding culture)." This indeed is the position of some women who have found themselves unable to inhabit liberal majority and religious minority cultures simultaneously, among them several whose passionate denunciations of Islam have earned them international platforms; for Okin their view is one that brooks, as she says, "no argument."[24]

In this respect Okin's account of the optimal relation of women to culture—stepping back from, appraising, and reconfiguring or discarding to the degree that culture does not accord with liberal norms—is also a normative account of the liberal state's relation to religion. Writing in support of Okin's proposal, Katha Pollitt relates a friend's shifting allegiance in the French controversy over headscarves: "A gentle, tolerant, worldly-wise leftist, she sided with the girls against the government: why shouldn't they be able to dress as they wished, to follow their culture? Then she came across a television debate in which a Muslim girl said she wanted the ban to stay because without it, her family would force her to wear a scarf. That changed my friend's view of the matter: the left, and feminist, position, she now thought, was to support this girl and the ones like her in their struggle to be independent modern women—not the parents, the neighbors, the community and religious 'leaders.' I think my friend was right."[25] The point to be made about this position—agree or disagree—is that the liberal state is seen properly to trump the claims of religion and tradition, even when the state does precisely the opposite of multiplying choice in religious observance and practice.

In this sense, the liberal production of religion—item three on my list of conjunctures—proceeds as the production of a distinction between "good" and "bad" religion, or between more and less autonomous relations to religious authority. Tisa Wenger has shown how state and juridical formulations of religion and religious freedom in the early twentieth-century United States both extended legitimacy to Pueblo Indian ritual practice and retracted it, organizing ceremonial participation along "religious" lines of individual conscience and choice while severing this religion from community obligation and tribal governance.[26] Saba Mahmood calls attention to a more recent example of the liberal production of religion in a 2003 report by the National Security Division of the Rand Corporation titled *Civil and Democratic Islam: Partners, Resources, Strategies.* In its program of cultivating an Islam in which a "Western vision of civilization, political order, and society" could be made to prevail, the report rejected as a potential partner those whom it identified as Muslim "traditionalists," that is, those whose habits of deference to communal authority are "causally linked with backwardness and underdevelopment, which in turn are the breeding ground for social and political problems of all sorts." This problematic relation to religious authority, according to the report, could be see in Muslim traditionalists' 1) reluctance to regard the Quran as a historical document; 2) unwillingness to realize that Mohammad was a product of his time who offers little help to the solving of contemporary problems; and 3) failure to denounce the Quran for its contradictions.[27]

Note that a policy recommendation about Islam is also a normative definition of religion to which only a minority of religious practitioners anywhere probably adhere. The report does note that the Bible, specifically the Old Testament, "is not different from the Quran in endorsing conduct and containing a number of rules and values that are literally unthinkable . . . in today's society. This does not pose a problem because few people would today insist that we should all be living in the exact literal manner of the Biblical patriarchs. Instead, we allow our vision of Judaism's and Christianity's true message to dominate over the literal text, which we regard as history and legend."[28] Now, the Rand Corporation is clearly wrong to suggest that all but a few who read them regard the sacred texts of Judaism and Christianity as "history and legend," best apprehended through the tools of historical and literary analysis. But I do. My better students do. My guess is that you do, too.

One answer, then, to the question with which I began, the question of the relationship between religious liberals and the liberal geopolitics of religion advocated in the Rand report is that we are its advertisers, its enablers, its apprentices, its dealers, its models for export. We are what the liberal geopolitics of religion wants more of, our concern for the flourishing of embattled forms of religious possibility counterbalanced, when necessary, by the stronger claims for personal autonomy that sound from elsewhere on the liberal spectrum, or from elsewhere in our own hearts. This would also be a "no" answer to Mark Lilla's question of whether liberal religion can ever do more in the end than sanctify the purposes of the implicitly liberal state.[29] I'd like, however, to retrieve a different possibility.

In the conjunctions considered so far, liberalism *works on* religion, even as it claims to float free of it. I'd like to think about how the exchange might work both ways. I'm up to item two on my list, which is the question for liberal theory of whether a self conceived of as autonomous in relation to various attachments, obligations, and so on is really a self at all. Might it not instead be the case, as Mahmood puts it, that religious and cultural norms and the varying modes of their articulation "are not simply a social imposition on the subject" but go to "the very substance of her intimate, valorized interiority"?[30] Leigh Schmidt recognizes as a feature of religious liberalism the spiritual disposition toward "searching and questing": an "adventuresome embrace of the seeker's endless curiosity . . . paired with a nostalgic longing for the finder's clarity."[31] This is perhaps not so far from what Michael Warner sees as the propensity of the "liberal framework for the construction of religion" to generate "a melancholic desire for strong attachments, no matter what they are."[32]

In either case, the figure of religious liberalism's "seeker" would seem to comport with liberal formulations of good religion as an abstracted category of beliefs and practices from which the individual stands back to assess, compare, evaluate, embrace or discard, and generally mix and match. It would also seem, however, that even the most deracinated seeker is after something that feels like roots, some connection or attachment without which she would not be authentically herself. It's worth noting too that in Schmidt's canon of religious liberalism's patron saints—among them Albert Schweitzer, Mohandas Gandhi, Dorothy Day, Martin Luther King Jr., Abraham Joshua Heschel, and Howard Thurman—are some who in fact hewed pretty closely to particular religious traditions, traditions whose ways of thinking about diversity and flourishing do not rely on a conception of the self as an autonomous chooser and do not frame heteronomous sources of authority as unjust constraints.

To raise the possibility that non-autonomous relations to norms may go to the "valorized interiority" at the heart of liberalism is also to get to the top of my list and the question of liberalism's religious sources. To limit consideration here, very briefly, to Rawls, the full title of Rawls's Princeton thesis is "A Brief Inquiry into the Meaning of Sin and Faith: An Interpretation Based on the Concept of Community"; it was recently republished, together with several commentaries and a later piece by Rawls himself on his move away from Christian conviction after serving in World War II. Faith, according to the undergraduate Rawls, is the "inner state of a person who is properly integrated and related to community" with others and with God, a relation that sin severs and grace restores; thus "there can be no separation between religion and ethics, since the problems they deal with are in the same nexus of relations."[33] The young Rawls boldly concludes that the mistake of philosophers is to proceed without a comprehensive account of human nature of the kind he sets forth; the mature Rawls, of course, would go on to proceed without a comprehensive account and to insist on the necessity of so proceeding. In their commentary, Joshua Cohen and Thomas Nagel elaborate several points of contact between the mature Rawls's conceptions of political liberalism and the unflinchingly theological ethics of the younger Rawls. The interesting question then becomes, did Rawls bury the theological foundations of his developing thought, or did he abandon them? If the former, we might seek to excavate the possible religious sources of his theory of justice; if the latter, we might debate whether his account of the inviolability of personhood at the heart of just communities is sufficiently grounded in a priori assumptions about freedom. Doing either requires, again, that the conversation between religion and liberalism be a two-way exchange.

Martha Nussbaum defends her use of violent examples drawn exclusively from beyond the "modern liberal regime" of the West to illustrate the problems religion might make for women's human rights. "My international examples manifest, I believe, what parts of most religious traditions . . . will try to do when they are not so shaped by liberal traditions [as they are in North America and Europe]. I believe, therefore, that a focus on current international issues is valuable to give us a vivid sense of the reality of our topic. Without this focus, we might fail to acknowledge that religions (like many non-religious political actors) can propose atrocities; we might therefore fail to ask what liberals who care about religion should say when they do."[34] But what should liberals who care about religion say when the "non-religious political actors" who propose or wage atrocities include "modern liberal regimes"? Imagined as a two-way conversation, a conjuncture of reciprocally unsettling terms, "religious liberalism" implies that religion and liberalism might have something to do with one other beyond submitting the former to the relentlessly global trajectory of the latter. Liberals who care about religion have liberal principles to which to appeal in order to regulate the legitimate scope of religious authority. Perhaps the same liberals who care about religion can find in religion a productive terrain from which to question liberalism's ostensibly impervious grounding, its manifestly imperious reach.

NOTES

1. David Kaplan, "Hearts, Minds, and Dollars: In an Unseen Front in the War on Terrorism, America Is Spending Millions . . . to Change the Very Face of Islam," *U.S. News and World Report,* April 5, 2005, http://www.usnews.com/usnews/news/articles/050425/25roots.htm (accessed January 11, 2010). I learned of this program from Saba Mahmood, "Secularism, Hermeneutics, and Empire: The Politics of Islamic Reformation," *Public Culture* 18, no. 2 (spring 2006): 323–47.

2. The full text of the International Religious Freedom Act of 1998 is available at http://www.state.gov/documents/organization/2297.pdf (accessed January 11, 2010).

3. Thomas Farr, "Diplomacy in an Age of Faith: Religious Freedom and National Security," *Foreign Affairs* 87, no. 2 (March–April 2008): 123. Among Farr's recommendations are that a "privately funded Islamic Institute of American Studies on U.S. soil" be established to "bring the best jurists and religious leaders from across the Muslim world to study U.S. history, society, politics, and—most important—religion" (124).

4. "The Lesson from America," *The Economist,* online edition, November 1, 2007, http://www.economist.com/node/10015163 (accessed September 9, 2011).

5. See, e.g., Mahmood, "Secularism, Hermeneutics, and Empire"; Winnifred Fallers Sullivan, "Exporting Religious Freedom," *Commonweal* 126, no. 4 (February 26, 1999): 10–11; and Elizabeth A. Povinelli, "Beyond Good and Evil, Whither Liberal Sacrificial Love?" *Public Culture* 21, no. 1 (winter 2009): 77–100.

6. Thomas Donnelly, "The Underpinnings of the Bush Doctrine," American Enterprise Institute for Public Policy Research, National Security Outlook, February 1, 2003, http://www.aei.org/outlook/15845 (accessed January 11, 2010). The historical trajectories of liberalization also encompass the violence by which liberal societies have sometimes literally cast purportedly undemocratic peoples out of bounds, the struggles waged by those dispossessed by liberal regimes to gain legal and political recognition within or outside of them, and the violence of imposing, resisting, or acceding to the governance of liberal colonial powers. See, e.g., Tisa Wenger, *We Have a Religion: The 1920s Pueblo Indian Dance Controversy and American Religious Freedom* (Chapel Hill: University of North Carolina Press, 2009); Saba Mahmood, "Questioning Liberalism, Too," *Boston Review* 28, no. 2 (April–May 2003), http://www.bostonreview.net/BR28.2/mahmood.html (accessed January 11, 2010); Wendy Brown, "Tolerance as Governmentality: Faltering Universalism, State Legitimacy, and State Violence," in *Regulating Aversion: Tolerance in the Age of Identity and Empire* (Princeton: Princeton University Press, 2006), 78–106; and Courtney Bender and Pamela Klassen, eds., *After Pluralism: Reimagining Religious Engagement* (New York: Columbia University Press, 2010).

7. Leigh Schmidt's call for "more empirical research and fewer foregone conclusions" in the matter of American religious liberalism's relation to "America's varied empires—colonial, commercial, educational, and missionary" would seem to narrow the scope of permissible inquiry here to the collection of data, lest the project become dangerously partisan. A richer grounding for the same inquiry comes, however, in Schmidt's question of "what kind of catchment remains" if we attempt to "break the all too prevalent equation of American religious liberalism with American liberal Protestantism without slighting the latter's cultural force." To pursue the possible links between "America's varied empires" and American religious liberalism is, in part, to ask what makes the latter (no longer simply Protestant, but) *American.* For a case for the strong relationship between the administration of empire and the consolidation of national culture, see Gauri Viswanathan, *Masks of Conquest: Literary Study and British Rule in India* (New York: Columbia University Press, 1989).

8. Aglow International, "Aglow's Mandates," http://www.aglow.org/Default.aspx?id=140 (accessed January 11, 2010). See also "Why Aglow and Islam? Unveiling the System . . . Loving the People," "Why Israel?" and "Why Aglow and Israel?" all available for download at http://www.aglow.org/resourceshandouts.aspx (accessed January 11, 2010). R. Marie Griffith's book is *God's Daughters: Evangelical Women and the Power of Submission* (Berkeley: University of California Press, 1997).

9. Donnelly, "Underpinnings of the Bush Doctrine."

10. John Locke, *Two Treatises of Government,* ed. Peter Laslett (Cambridge: Cambridge University Press, 1988), 269.

11. John Rawls, *Political Liberalism* (New York: Columbia University Press, 1993), 154–55, 9.

12. John Stuart Mill, *The Subjection of Women,* ed. Edward Alexander (New Brunswick, N.J.: Transaction, 2001), 2.

13. See, e.g., Talal Asad, Wendy Brown, Judith Butler, and Saba Mahmood, *Is Critique*

Secular? Blasphemy, Injury, and Free Speech (Berkeley: University of California Press, 2009); Jared Hickman, "The Theology of Democracy," *New England Quarterly* 81, no. 2 (June 2008): 177–217; Elizabeth Fenton, "Birth of a Protestant Nation: Catholic Canadians, Religious Pluralism, and National Unity in the Early U.S. Republic," *Early American Literature* 41, no. 1 (March 2006): 29–57; and Michael Warner, "Is Liberalism a Religion?" in *Religion: Beyond a Concept*, ed. Hent de Vries (New York: Fordham University Press, 2007), 610–17. In the present volume, Leigh Schmidt makes a case for broadening the conversation about American religious liberalism "beyond the familiar interpretive tropes of the modernist impulse and the social gospel—indeed, in many instances, beyond Protestantism itself," while David Hollinger argues for the continued centrality of "ecumenical Protestantism" to the story, suggesting in the latter's "omnivorous" "embrac[e of] the diversity of the world beyond white Protestantism" the trajectory by which American religious liberalism ceases to be identical with this self-transcending Protestantism at its heart.

14. The quotations from Whitman, James, and Vaughan that follow appear in Leigh Schmidt's "The Aspiring Side of Religion: Nineteenth-Century Religious Liberalism and the Birth of Contemporary American Spirituality," *Spiritus: A Journal of Christian Spirituality* 7, no. 1 (spring 2007): 89–92, and are from Walt Whitman, *Poetry and Prose* (New York: Library of America, 1996), 989; William James, *The Letters of William James*, ed. Henry James, 2 vols. (Boston: Atlantic Monthly Press, 1920), 2:212, 214; and Robert Alfred Vaughan, *Hours with the Mystics: A Contribution to the History of Religious Opinion*, 2 vols. (London: Slark, 1888), 1:54.

15. John Stuart Mill, *On Liberty*, in *Basic Writings* (New York: Modern Library, 2002), 63.

16. Schmidt, "Aspiring Side of Religion," 91.

17. Mahmood Mamdani, *Good Muslim/Bad Muslim: America, the Cold War, and the Roots of Terror* (New York: Pantheon, 2004), 18; and Wendy Brown, *Regulating Aversion*, 150.

18. Stanley Hauerwas, "Preaching as Though We Had Enemies," *First Things*, no. 53 (May 1995), http://www.firstthings.com/article/2008/09/003-preaching-as-though-we-had-enemies—9 (accessed September 9, 2011). I am grateful to Michael Warner for this reference. My thanks also to Arie L. Molendijk for pointing out in his comments on this essay that the formula of a "transposition of debate" over what counts as liberal from the state and the market to religion may miss the ways that religion is liberalized through the "internal appropriation of 'liberal' principles" and not simply as a cultural manifestation of political and economic developments. To press this observation, indeed, is to trouble the assumption that the liberalization of religion, pursued as a goal of U.S. policy, inevitably accompanies and advances the spread of economic and political liberalism.

19. My thinking here and in the paragraph that follows about the managerial and "curatorial" functions of liberalism is indebted to Benjamin Berger, "The Cultural Limits of Legal Tolerance," in Bender and Klassen, *After Pluralism*, 98–123.

20. Martha C. Nussbaum, *Sex and Social Justice* (New York: Oxford University Press, 1999), 81–119.

21. Peter van der Veer, "Pim Fortuyn, Theo van Gogh, and the Politics of Tolerance in the Netherlands," in *Political Theologies: Public Religions in a Post-secular World*, ed. Hent de Vries (New York: Fordham University Press, 2006), 538.

22. John Rawls, *A Theory of Justice* (Cambridge, Mass.: Harvard University Press, 1971), 206, quoted in Nussbaum, *Sex and Social Justice*, 84.

23. Wendy Brown, "Subjects of Tolerance: Why We Are Civilized and They Are the Barbarians," in *Regulating Aversion*, 149–75.

24. Susan Moller Okin, "Is Multiculturalism Bad for Women?" *Boston Review* 22, no. 5 (October–November 1997), http://www.bostonreview.net/BR22.5/okin.html (accessed January 11, 2010). Ates Altınordu notes the irony in the fact that American Enterprise Institute Fellow Ayaan Hirsi Ali, the Somali-born feminist and former member of the Dutch Parliament whose best-selling memoirs *Infidel* and *The Caged Virgin* narrate her self-liberation from Islam, together with her counterparts in Europe who have likewise abandoned and bitterly denounced the Muslim faith in which they were raised, "are welcomed passionately [in the West] as authentic 'liberal' *Muslim* voices" (my emphasis). Ates Altınordu, "Varieties of Anti-religious Imagination," *The Immanent Frame*, Social Science Research Council, http://blogs.ssrc.org/tif/2008/04/30/varieties-of-anti-religious-imagination/ (accessed January 11, 2010).

25. Katha Pollitt, "Whose Culture?" *Boston Review* 22, no. 5 (September–October 1997), http://www.bostonreview.net/BR22.5/pollitt.html (accessed January 11, 2010).

26. Wenger, *We Have a Religion.*

27. Saba Mahmood, "Secularism, Hermeneutics, and Empire," 329, 333 (quoting Cheryl Benard, *Civil and Democratic Islam: Partners, Resources, Strategies* [Pittsburgh, Penn.: Rand Corporation, 2003], 4, 34), 334.

28. Bernard, *Civil and Democratic Islam,* 37, quoted in Mahmood, "Secularism, Hermeneutics, and Empire," 336.

29. See David Hollinger's review of Lilla's *The Stillborn God* in the *London Review of Books,* January 24, 2008, 15–18.

30. Saba Mahmood, *Politics of Piety: The Islamic Revival and the Feminist Subject* (Princeton: Princeton University Press, 2005), 23.

31. Schmidt, "Aspiring Side of Religion," 91.

32. Warner, "Is Liberalism a Religion?" 617.

33. Rawls, *A Brief Inquiry into the Meaning of Sin and Faith, with "On My Religion,"* by John Rawls, ed. Thomas Nagel (Cambridge, Mass.: Harvard University Press, 2009), 113, 114.

34. Nussbaum, *Sex and Social Justice,* 84–85.

Afterword and Commentary

Religious Liberalism and Ecumenical Self-Interrogation

DAVID A. HOLLINGER

The inability of the provincial American Christian to deal with the cosmopolitan confrontations of modern, urban life was a theme of *The Secular City*, a runaway bestseller of 1965 written by the liberal theologian Harvey Cox. This manifesto for a politically engaged religion was organized around human responsibility for the destiny of a world wrongly assumed by so many Christian believers to be in God's hands, as if popular songs about God ("He's got the whole world in his hands") were to be taken seriously. Cox celebrated "secularization" as a liberation from "all supernatural myths and sacred symbols." Convinced of the virtues of "heterogeneity" and "the color and character lent by diversity," Cox pressed the case for "pluralism and tolerance" throughout the world, but especially in the United States, where the recent "emancipation of Catholics, Jews, and others" from "an enforced Protestant cultural religion" bode well for further diversification. "Secularization" took place "only when the cosmopolitan confrontations of city living exposed the relativity of the myths and traditions" once thought to be "unquestionable." While insisting that God was present throughout secular domains as well as within what traditionalists called "religion," Cox concluded iconoclastically that the very name of God was so misleading that it might be well to stop even mentioning God until our worldly experience gives us a new vocabulary. "Like Moses," he wrote in the book's concluding sentence, let us be "confident that we will be granted a new name by events of the future," but for now "we must simply take up the work of liberating the captives."[1]

Cox's book can now be seen as an artifact of a remarkable but insufficiently recognized historical episode in the history of American Protestantism. In the middle decades of the twentieth century, ecumenical leaders vigorously interrogated themselves about their own traditions. The rise of evangelicalism dominates most scholarly and popular accounts of American Protestantism. It is well known that the National Association of Evangelicals, Fuller Theological Seminary, and *Christianity Today*—three formidable institutions created between 1942 and 1956—defined evangelicalism against the socially and politically prominent liberals. But too often lost from view has been the voluntary renunciation by ecumenical intellectuals of many of the same ideas being consolidated in evangelical circles, including the notion that the United States was a Christian nation. While the evangelicals were trying to build confidence in themselves and to hold firm to what they saw as the faith of their fathers, ecumenical leaders were excoriating themselves for their own provinciality and conservatism. William Stringfellow's boldly titled *My People Is the Enemy* got the message across very directly. Wilfred Cantwell Smith, Martin Marty, and dozens of other writers filled the pages of *Christian Century* with efforts to move the Presbyterians, the Methodists, the Episcopalians, the Congregationalists, the Northern Baptists, and other groups associated with the old "Protestant Establishment" yet farther from orthodoxy and into greater engagement with a diverse and contingent world.[2]

Hence Cox's themes can flag for us several issues that invite attention in the wake of the persistently engaging and informative essays collected in this volume. One issue is the place, in the story of American religious liberalism, of the ecumenical Protestant leadership represented by the Federal and National Councils of Churches, the *Christian Century,* and faculties at the greatest of the seminaries, especially Union, Chicago, Yale, Princeton, Boston, and Harvard. If a great virtue of this book is the broad construction it has offered of "religious liberalism," consciously transcending the Buckham-Hutchison-Dorrien historiographical tradition and the larger hegemonic claims of the institutionalized Protestant establishment itself, one topic that has been addressed only indirectly and episodically is where even a historiographically downgraded Protestant establishment fits into the now enlarged history of religious liberalism. To be sure, the chapters by Sally Promey, Matt Hedstrom, and Yaakov Ariel give us some access to this question, but one of the things I want to do in this afterword is to confront that question more directly.

A second and closely related issue that Cox can flag for us is the relation of religious liberalism to the non-religious (or, since agreeing upon a valid analytic language here is a real challenge, the relation of religious liberalism to the secular, or the post-religious, or the post-Christian, or the post-Protestant). Several of our essays do address this relationship. We see it in Robert Ingersoll's engagement with Whitman as invoked by Michael Robertson, in Charles Fort's religion-transcending inquiries as explained by Jeffrey Kripal, in John Rawls's transition from an Episcopalian to a secular theory of justice as mentioned by Tracy Fessenden, and we see the absolute rejection of any such relationship in the Catholic intellectuals analyzed by Healan Gaston. Josef Sorett's study of Alain Locke can also be considered in this light. I will be suggesting that when we bring the ecumenical establishment back into the picture, we can attend even more productively to this relationship between religious liberalism and the secular. There are strong hints of this relationship, of course, in Promey's account of the abstract art engagements of the 1950s, and in Hedstrom's observations about the directions taken by the religious book club.

A third issue to which Cox's diversity-affirming outlook can introduce us is the function of alterity in making religion liberal and in promoting varieties of pluralism. Several of these pieces remind us of the importance of this function. Christopher White's account of the appeal of Middle Eastern holy men to Juliet Thompson and Mark Tobey is one example; Kathi Kern's discussion of Clara Colby's interest in Rabindranath Tagore is another. The ecumenical leadership was preoccupied with a radically diverse global population once served by Protestant missions but suddenly achieving independence from Western political as well as religious tutelage. I will argue that another benefit of bringing the ecumenical establishment back into the picture is that it greatly illuminates the function of alterity in religious liberalism. Although the presence within the United States of Catholics, Jews, and non-whites had generated a number of ecumenical initiatives, it was diversity beyond American borders as experienced by missionaries that had first and most powerfully propelled ecumenism itself, and shaped the basic ideas about both religious and ethnoracial diversity that the ecumenists would then advance domestically as well as globally.

A fourth issue Cox can flag for us is the location and character of the boundary of the religious as a category of analysis, and, consequently, just what epistemic attitude we as scholars should adopt toward that boundary. Here, the essay by Kathryn Lofton on Morris Jastrow is exactly on point. Carrie Bramen's interpretation of Stowe's representation of religious faith in the form of the mundane and the banal is also pertinent here, because Bramen presents us with a methodologically ambitious explanation for the dynamics of religious community-maintenance.

I want to begin with this last issue, the epistemic setting in which we study religious liberalism. Bramen's bold defense of what in a context other than her own might well be called "sentimental trash" can be construed as an application of Jastrow's combination of "science and sympathy" as vindicated by Lofton. Bramen invites us to look with scientific detachment on the ways in which the saccharine niceness of the late Victorian Jesus actually consolidated the community of faith about which Stowe cared. Bramen also invites us to achieve empathic identification with Stowe as a historical actor highly sensitive to the needs of her community and resourceful in addressing those needs with the skills of her writer's craft. This willingness to depict Stowe's religious and social situation as radically different from our own enables Bramen to recognize the historical particularity of Stowe's religious liberalism rather than trying to make it more palatable to our tastes by downplaying its historically salient features. The sympathetic study of religion, Jastrow well understood, did not mean making over historical figures in the image of our own ideas. Nor did it mean translating the phenomena of religious liberalism into either secular therapy or theological orthodoxy, as the intellectuals of the generation after Jastrow too often did, as Lofton correctly alleges.

Lofton is no doubt right to warn us that Jastrow's work was sometimes weakened by the credibility he gave to a universal religion incorporating the elements of the various religious traditions. I agree; that Kumbaya type of stuff is hard to take. And Lofton is even more right, I believe, to defend Jastrow's *wissenschaftliche* element, which can be mobilized against what Lofton rightly describes as today's tendency to smother religiously inclined historical actors with respectful but non-analytical storytelling. That Jastrowian *Wissenschaft* can also be mobilized against what Lofton rightly calls "our protection of not only the idea of the holy, but also the incommensurable sovereignty of its holy purveyors."

This last complaint of Lofton's leads me to call attention to a minor controversy swirling around the recent assertions of Brad Gregory, Richard Bushman, and others to the effect that we must not exclude supernatural causation when we write history, and that to refuse to do so is to partake of an indefensible secular bias.[3] This renewed effort to get the field of religious history to treat God as a historical actor, recognized as an epistemically respectable part of historical explanation, along with social structure, ideologies, the economy, state power, and the agency of individuals and groups, strikes me as a serious threat to the flourishing of the field. I feel this as one who has spent a lot of time trying to get my colleagues in what is sometimes called mainstream American history, as opposed to "church history" or "religious history," to take religion seriously, to get it included in textbooks and syllabi and anthologies and conference programs and the like. But I find that the single most formidable obstacle to this greater appreciation for the history of religion in the United States is the assumption that if you study it, you have to be a partisan of supernaturalist ideas. I have argued in symposium after symposium that religion is too important to be left in the hands of those who believe in it, but then this new initiative by Gregory, Bushman, et al. undercuts my efforts and resoundingly confirms the suspicions of my secular colleagues.

Those suspicions have been overcome in many instances, of course, but before I leave this topic I want to observe that the field of American religious history continues to be affected to some extent by the Barth-Freud syndrome to which Lofton referred. This syndrome in recent years has expressed itself by the mainstream profession's quite generous acceptance of the work of Mark Noll, George Marsden, and others who not only focus their work on evangelicals but who espouse evangelical beliefs themselves, while neither Martin Marty nor the late William Hutchison, no matter how many books they wrote and how good they were, ever gained the same degree of acceptance by the bulk of my colleagues in the Organization of American Historians. Religion was easier to handle if it was orthodox religion, so perceived, while the liberal topics pursued by the openly liberal Protestant Marty and the fellow traveler Hutchison never got the same measure of acceptance. I do not believe this differential treatment can be explained by the relative quality of the scholarship at issue, which is good in all of the cases I have mentioned. I believe it is another example of the Barth-Freud syndrome, according to which religion is religion only if it's a bit wacky. Folks who profess a sensible faith, consistent perhaps even with some Freudian insights into what human beings are and why they do what they do, can't really be seriously religious, so this line of thought goes.

One consequence of the continued operation of this syndrome is that the history of religious liberalism is often left entirely out of the story. One convenient example is Mark Noll's recent book, *God and Race in American Politics.*[4] Noll blandly credits *Christianity Today* with an editorial of 1957 supporting the Supreme Court in *Brown v. Board of Education,* but never mentions *Christian Century,* which of course published King's "Letter from Birmingham Jail." Noll never cites the work of Mark Toulouse and others that establishes beyond doubt the huge gap between *Christianity Today* (which published J. Edgar Hoover's attacks on civil rights workers for communist connections) and *Christian Century* throughout the period.[5] Noll's treatment of this topic misleads because it leaves the liberal Protestants entirely out of the story, and invites the reader to believe that among whites it was evangelical rather than ecumenical Protestants who mobilized against Jim Crow. Noll never even mentions the Federal Council of Churches or the National Council of Churches, nor does he mention George E. Haynes, the black executive cited by Josef Sorett, who worked indefatigably on racial issues for both councils. Noll provides fleeting references to the influence of Edgar Sheffield Brightman and A. J. Muste on Martin Luther King, Jr., individually, but from Noll's account one would have no idea of the sustained support the liberal Protestant establishment gave to Channing Tobias, Benjamin Mays, and other black clergy from the late 1930s onward.[6] The almost total erasure of ecumenical Protestants from an account of the civil rights era plays into the prejudice of which I have been complaining: religion is orthodox or it can be left out of any historical discussion of religion.

These complaints about Noll provide a convenient bridge from epistemic and methodological concerns to the issue of the Protestant establishment's role in the story of religious liberalism. Here I want to emphasize the utility of the concept of "ecumenical," which helps distinguish the liberal seminaries and councils and magazines from other twentieth-century varieties of liberal religion that have flourished outside the so-called mainline denominations and their transdenominational enterprises. Although "liberal" and "ecumenical" are often used interchangeably, I prefer the term "ecumenical" because it seems to me more specific and less confusing for the period since about 1910, when ecumenism became so prominent a concern of the intellectual and institutional leaders of the mainstream denominations and their cooperative enterprises.

The ethnodemographic and religious transformation of American life since the 1960s has so diminished the once-hegemonic status of ecumenical Protestantism that the latter's earlier authority and influence is hard for many people to imagine. Surely, the doings of all those white Presbyterians and Baptists and Methodists and Congregationalists and Episcopalians could not have mattered that much. Most of my colleagues in "mainstream American history" seem confident that they did not matter at all. But they did matter.

The population of the United States remained, after all, overwhelmingly white and Protestant during the mid-century decades. Membership in the major, classical denominations was at an all-time high. Persons at least nominally affiliated with these denominations were in comfortable control of all branches of the federal government and most of the business world, as well as the nation's chief cultural and educational institutions. The public face of Protestantism, moreover, remained in the control of the politically and theologically liberal ecumenists of the National Council of Churches until the 1970s. Only well after the 1960s did the evangelicals gain the public standing they enjoy today. The evangelicals gained that public standing, moreover, partly because they continued to espouse a number of diversity-denying ideas and programs that remained popular with the white public even as these ideas and programs were being renounced by self-interrogating ecumenist intellectuals.[7]

Among the popular diversity-denying ideas and programs renounced by many ecumenical leaders was the crucial claim that Christians, and especially Protestants, had a proprietary relation to the American nation. Marty asked that the inauguration of a Catholic as president in 1961 be treated as "the end of Protestantism as a national religion and its advent as the distinctive faith of a creative minority." At issue was not only the acceptance at long last of Catholics into full partnership as Americans; Marty also explicitly recognized "Jewish and secular" voices as part of the diversity of American life. Marty speculated that this withdrawal from the traditional idea of a Christian nation—an idea which had been endorsed even by ecumenical leaders until only a few years before—might even enable Protestants to find in their new modesty a measure of self-respect amid the "orgies of public scourging and self-examination" that had recently taken "the Protestant principle of self-criticism" to "almost masochistic extremes."[8]

Yet the orgies were far from over. Stringfellow's 1964 volume, *My People Is the Enemy,* was written by an Episcopal layman who had by then spent seven years living amid poverty in Harlem while serving as a lawyer to indigent black people. This book lacerated American churches for not responding more aggressively to the evils of racism and for not accepting black people more fully. A second illustrative volume of 1964, Ralph E. Dodge's *The Unpopular Missionary,* was written by a senior Methodist missionary to Angola. This book pushed with novel passion and urgency the long-standing complaint of liberal missionary theorists that missions had been too closely connected to colonialism. By failing to turn more control and resources over to the indigenous churches of Africa, India, and other mission fields, Ralph E. Dodge warned, American and European missionary projects were doomed to go the way of colonial governments: out for good, and for the same reasons. The basic problem, Dodge explained, was that the missionary project was still too slow and tepid in accepting indigenous peoples as "*human beings*" and as "full brothers in Jesus Christ" on their own terms—not as copies of Christians in Memphis and Minneapolis. The church "must reject categorically all attitudes and practices of racial superiority."[9]

Other voices pushed self-critique in directions that distinguished the ecumenical discourse yet more starkly from evangelical discourse, and that embraced the diversity of the world beyond white Protestantism even more omnivorously. *Honest to God* was written in England by an Anglican bishop, John A. T. Robinson, but gained enormous notoriety in the United States from the moment of its publication in 1963. Robinson attacked as hopelessly anachronistic the ideas about God and Jesus that were common among Christians, mocking the supernaturalism that "suggests that Jesus was really God almighty walking about on earth, dressed up as a man . . . taking part in a charade."[10] Although much of Robinson's message was already incorporated into the discourse of liberal seminaries as a result of the calls for "demythologized" and "religionless" Christianity made somewhat cryptically by German theologians Rudolph Bultman and Dietrich Bonhoeffer, Robinson's breakaway bestseller popularized as never before the strivings of a theological elite to update Christian teachings in relation to contemporary culture and modern notions of cognitive plausibility. For a prominent cleric to characterize as downright dishonest the sincere god-talk to which the average churchgoer was accustomed served to expose as never before the gap between the people in the pew, on the one hand, and the increasingly cosmopolitan Protestant leadership on the other.

Robinson and his champions were quick to insist that the Christian faith was just as true as it ever was, once properly understood. But by taking to a new extreme ecumenical Protestantism's impulse to engage with the world rather than to withdraw from it, Robinson dramatically legitimized the diverse world of contemporary culture as an arena for sympathetic engagement, no longer a domain to be held at a biblically warranted distance. Robinson, like Cox, blurred the line between what most people thought Christianity was and the rest of modern life.

Might the blurring of that line lead outside the faith, to a post-Protestant or post-Christian orientation, influenced by the Protestant tradition but defined by elements of the secular world? In the civil rights era vehicles other than the church presented themselves as more rapid and maneuverable means of advancing causes to which the ecumenical leadership was committed. To be sure, the National Council of Churches had been among the sponsors of "Freedom Summer" in 1964, and there had been a small but steady stream of Northern liberal clerics and laypersons in Martin Luther King Jr.'s demonstrations, but if one were looking in 1965 for ways to "liberate the captives," as Cox had called upon Christians to do, and if one were now authorized to apply oneself to this task without any god-talk, one could quickly find secular organizations like the Congress of Racial Equality and the Student Nonviolent Coordinating Committee that were trying to do just that. These secular liberators were not encumbered, moreover, as were the National Council of Churches and its denominational affiliates, by a reluctant rank and file who paid the bills and who sometimes listened to the complaints of increasingly vocal evangelicals to the effect that the ecumenical elite was selling out true religion for social activism.

I have been trying to show that when we bring ecumenical Protestantism into our story of religious liberalism, we soon push up against what ecumenism's evangelical critics saw as a slippery slope to secularism. This leads to my third issue, the relation of religious liberalism to the irreligious or the post-religious or the post-Protestant. A major function of ecumenical Protestantism's rigorous self-interrogation was to enable many persons of Protestant origin to feel comfortable moving outside of the Protestant community of faith and to enable many others to invest most of their energies in secular projects even if they continued a nominal affiliation with a church, to define their lives less religiously than before.

The Methodist youth magazine *motive* illustrates this function. Through the 1940s and 1950s the editors of this magazine sympathetically engaged with modern arts, especially, but also modern literary and philosophical currents, consciously pushing the borders of ecumenical Protestant sensibility in directions very much like those Sally Promey has discussed. The magazine, which always refused to capitalize its name and was resolutely lower-cased right to the end, was often described as too radical. *Time* magazine in the mid-1960s enjoyed referring to it as the only miniskirted member of the family of religious periodicals. G. Bromley Oxnam, the great Methodist bishop who also served as the head of the National Council of Churches and the World Council of Churches, famously defended *motive* in a contentious meeting of the national United Methodist board at which he showed up with a stack of recent issues and declared himself in agreement with everything printed in their pages. But the editors of *motive* were moving too fast even for the liberal Methodists, who soon withdrew their sponsorship of it, after which the magazine folded, by way of detonating a suicide bomb. Its final two issues, in the spring of 1972, were devoted to gay and lesbian sexuality. Indeed, in histories of same-sex liberation, these two issues, appearing only three years after Stonewall, are celebrated as landmarks in the attack on homophobia. Douglas Sloan and others who have studied the trajectory of *motive* find that *motive* was a space which nurtured people who were trying to get to someplace else, and they did. Charlotte Bunch, one of those who executed *motive*'s spectacular demise, has described her migration out of the faith in a moving memoir in Sara Evans's revealing collection, *Journeys That Opened Up the World*.[11]

Among the things that happened in the late 1960s and early 1970s is that a number of modern causes with which the ecumenical Protestant leadership had allied itself, even while continuing to proclaim that only Christianity ultimately had the right answer for the world, proved so attractive in their own right, and so well equipped with energies and constituencies not authorized by the faith, that those causes themselves took over the lives of many descendants of the Protestant establishment. One important historic function of ecumenical Protestantism was to enable some people to cease to be Protestants, even to cease to be importantly religious at all. This is problematic only for those who look at history as Christian survivalists, evaluating events in large part by the extent to which they promote or retard the fortunes of the Christian project. If one looks at history emancipated from Christian survivalism, then the morphing of ecumenical Protestantism into any number of secular causes is no longer a cause for alarm. One might say that some of the values for which the Christian project had been a vehicle moved from one set of earthen vessels to other sets of earthen vessels.

This is not to imply that the only action was exit from the faith. On the contrary, even Cox remained a churchman, although I want to mention parenthetically that Dorrien's magisterial volume on liberal Protestant theology between 1950 and 2005 does not include Cox.[12] I asked Dorrien about this recently and he explained that it was all very simple: Cox had gone in the direction of liberation theology, and thus was not really a liberal. Religious liberalism does not include Harvey Cox? Technically, perhaps not. But I believe that attention to Cox, perhaps the greatest of all of ecumenical Protestantism's prophets of a post-Protestant world, reminds us how our understanding of religious liberalism in the United States is enriched when we keep the ecumenical intellectuals of the mid-century decades within our focus.

My fourth issue is the role of contacts with alterity in making religion liberal and in promoting varieties of pluralism. Here, the chapters by Christopher White and Kathi Kern are highly relevant. Beyond what they have to say, a great value of bringing mainstream, ecumenical Protestants into the picture is the opportunity it provides to focus on the missionary movement. Missions were central to American interaction with the world beyond the North Atlantic West from the late nineteenth century until World War II. It was largely though contact with missionaries, especially by way of their writings and reports, that the bulk of Americans formed impressions of non-European peoples. The lectures delivered by missionaries home on furlough were widely attended events in local communities as well as at regional and national meetings of denominations and cross-denominational organizations.

Our historians of ecumenism agree that the conditions of the mission field generated cooperation among the various denominations and missionary boards. Convincing the indigenous peoples of India and China, and so forth, that it was really important to be Dutch Reformed instead of German Reformed, or Missouri Synod Lutheran instead of Wisconsin Synod, or Southern Presbyterian rather than Northern Presbyterian, proved difficult. As early as the great Edinburgh missionary meeting of 1910 this ecumenism was formidable, and the later missionary conferences at Jerusalem in 1928 and Madras in 1938 are constantly cited by historians of ecumenism as landmarks.

But there is much more to it. From the 1920s right on through the 1960s missionaries, former missionaries, the children of missionaries, and those closely connected with the mission endeavor through institutional roles or personal ties were again and again among the most liberal voices, both theologically and politically. To be sure, John Birch was a missionary. Nelson Bell, the father-in-law of Billy Graham, and indeed the whole Bell family, was deeply embedded in the missionary project yet was vehemently anti-liberal. Bell persecuted Princeton Theological Seminary president John Mackey for his early advocacy of the diplomatic recognition of the People's Republic of China.[13] But in denomination after denomination it was the most missionary-intensive groups that found fault with sectarian theology and ritual practices, supported the independence of the Indians and other colonial peoples, came to the defense of the Japanese Americans when they were interned in 1942, criticized American imperialism, and offered support to the black civil rights movement in the Jim Crow south. Missionary influence saturated the major "study conferences" of the Federal Council of Churches in 1942 and 1945, which are best remembered for the depth and range of their condemnation of colonialism abroad and racism at home. Repeatedly, missionary-connected Protestants took the lead in pressing their own churches to welcome black people and other non-whites fully into the Body of Christ. It was the missionary movement that inspired the most forceful of the pre-1960s anti-imperialist, anti-racist writings, exemplified by Buell Gallagher's 1946 *Color and Conscience* and Edwin Soper's 1947 *Racism: A World Issue,* to come out of ecumenical Protestantism.[14]

I want to conclude by returning to the issue of boundaries. I believe the boundaries of religious history could be expanded yet further, even beyond the varieties of liberalism that Leigh Schmidt has outlined for us so well, and that the essays collected here have addressed so effectively. If the field of religious history were to be understood not so much as the history of various religions (however broadly defined, including Walt Whitman and the Bahá'ís and the types of spiritual seeking that take place outside any ecclesiastical framework), but rather as the history of engagements with religious issues, we would open up for inclusion in our courses and our anthologies and our textbooks and our monographic literature David Hume and Thomas Paine and Robert Ingersoll and John Dewey and Bertrand Russell and, yes, even Sam Harris. When the freethinkers and agnostics and atheists are included, we expand what we professionally denote as religious history to embrace religious engagements rather than religion. This expansion, which some people have already enacted, but not many, promises to direct more attention to the ways in which various religious communities sustain themselves, transform themselves, or decline, in relation to intellectual critique as well as in response to social conditions.

We do see some of what I have in mind in studies of the Darwinian controversy, where the ideas of Huxley and Tyndal and Clifford are at least cited, but even there the critics of Christian belief are rarely addressed except in passing. A case in point is the way in which James's great essay, "The Will to Believe," is repeatedly interpreted, with the impression left that James dispatched Clifford handily, when this is anything but true. I find that when I have students actually read Clifford's "Ethics of Belief" alongside "The Will to Believe," they get an altogether different impression of James and of the character of this pivotal episode in the history of American religious liberalism.

I hope it is not unfair to observe that the field of religious history is too often a shelter for religion, as Kathryn Lofton implied in her chapter, rather than a professional space for its critical study. It interests me that the field of history of science, which for many years was a shelter for science, became, in the wake of Thomas Kuhn, a much more widely ranging field, in which the actual dynamics of scientific practice and the critiques of that practice as a historically particular phenomenon flourished, and in which the long-guarded boundaries between science and the rest of learning gradually diminished. I think a similar expansion awaits religious history, so that it becomes not so much the history of religions, but the history of engagements with religious issues.

NOTES

1. Harvey Cox, *The Secular City: Secularization and Urbanization in Theological Perspective* (New York: Macmillan, 1965), 1–3, 85, 99, 268.

2. William Stringfellow, *My People Is the Enemy: An Autobiographical Polemic* (New York: Holt, Rinehart, and Winston, 1964); Wilfred Cantwell Smith, "Christianity's Third Great Challenge," *Christian Century*, April 27, 1960, 505; and Martin Marty, "Protestantism Enters Third Phase," *Christian Century*, January 18, 1961, 74.

3. "Historians and Belief," *Fides et Historia* 43, no. 2 (summer–fall 2011): 34–37.

4. Mark Noll, *God and Race in American Politics: A Short History* (Princeton: Princeton University Press, 2008), 156.

5. Mark G. Toulouse, "*Christianity Today* and American Public Life: A Case Study," *Journal of Church and State* 35, no. 2 (spring 1993): 241–84; and Mark G. Toulouse, "*The Christian Century* and American Public Life: The Crucial Years, 1956–1968," in *New Dimensions in American Religious History: Essays in Honor of Martin E. Marty*, ed. Jay P. Dolan and James P. Wind (Grand Rapids, Mich.: W. B. Eerdmans, 1993), 44–82.

6. Noll, *God and Race*, 108–109.

7. This paragraph and several following draw upon my article "After Cloven Tongues of Fire: Ecumenical Protestantism and the Modern American Encounter with Diversity," *Journal of American History* 98, no. 1 (June 2011), 21–48.

8. Marty, "Protestantism Enters Third Phase," 72–75.

9. Ralph E. Dodge, *The Unpopular Missionary* (Westwood, N.J.: F. H. Revell, 1964), 30, 164.

10. John A. T. Robinson, *Honest to God* (London: SCM Press, 1963), 66.

11. "Charlotte Bunch," in *Journeys That Opened Up the World: Women, Student Christian Movements, and Social Justice, 1955–1975,* ed. Sara M. Evans (New Brunswick, N.J.: Rutgers University Press, 2003), 139; and Douglas Sloan, *Faith and Knowledge: Mainline Protestantism and American Higher Education* (Louisville, Ky.: Westminster John Knox, 1994), 83.

12. Gary Dorrien, *The Making of American Liberal Theology,* vol. 3, *Crisis, Irony, and Postmodernity, 1950–2005* (Louisville, Ky.: Westminster John Knox, 2006).

13. William Inboden, *Religion and American Foreign Policy, 1945–1960: The Soul of Containment* (New York: Cambridge University Press, 2008), 74–75.

14. For a fuller account of the "study conferences" of the 1940s and of the careers of Gallagher and Soper, see David A. Hollinger, "The Realist-Pacifist Summit Meeting of March 1942 and the Political Reorientation of Ecumenical Protestantism in the United States," *Church History* 79, no. 3 (September 2010): 654–77.

CONTRIBUTORS

Yaakov Ariel is a graduate of the Hebrew University of Jerusalem and the University of Chicago. He focuses his research on Protestant-Jewish relations and on the Jewish reaction to modernity and postmodernity. He teaches in the Department of Religious Studies at the University of North Carolina at Chapel Hill.

Gretchen Boger received her Ph.D. in American History from Princeton in 2008 and is currently Visiting Assistant Professor of History at Colorado College. Her book project examines American missionaries between the world wars as transnational cultural brokers, looking in particular at how missionary encounters with nationalist movements in China and India helped shape Protestantism in the 1920s and 1930s.

Carrie Tirado Bramen is Associate Professor of English and Executive Director of the Humanities Institute at the University at Buffalo. She is author of *The Uses of Variety: Modern Americanism and the Quest for National Distinctiveness* (Harvard University Press, 2000), which was co-winner of the Thomas J. Wilson Prize, awarded by the Board of Syndics at Harvard University Press for the best first book. She has published articles on a range of topics from the nineteenth-century urban picturesque to the experimental fiction of Gayle Jones. Her current book project is a history of American niceness.

Tracy Fessenden is Associate Professor of Religious Studies at Arizona State University and author of *Culture and Redemption: Religion, the Secular, and American Literature* (Princeton University Press, 2007). Her current research focuses on metanarrative in American religion, questions of secularism and gender, and the place of New Orleans in the national imaginary.

K. Healan Gaston received her Ph.D. in U.S. History from the University of California, Berkeley in 2008 and currently teaches at Harvard Divinity School. She is at work on a book that chronicles the rise and fall of the "Judeo-Christian" formulations of democracy and national identity that were ubiquitous in American public discourse through the better part of the twentieth century.

Matthew S. Hedstrom is Assistant Professor of American Studies and Religious Studies at the University of Virginia. He is author of *The Rise of Liberal Religion: Book Culture and American Spirituality in the Twentieth Century* (Oxford University Press, forthcoming). He is beginning work on a new book project on race and the search for religious authenticity from the Civil War to the 1960s. He received his Ph.D. in American Studies from the University of Texas at Austin, and he has held postdoctoral fellowships at Valparaiso University and Princeton University.

David A. Hollinger is past president of the Organization of American Historians, the Preston Hotchkis Professor of History at Berkeley, and an elected Fellow of the American Academy of Arts and Sciences. His books include *Science, Jews, and Secular Culture* (Princeton University Press, 1996) and *Cosmopolitanism and Solidarity* (University of Wisconsin Press, 2006). Currently, he is studying the impact of the Protestant foreign missionary project on the life of the United States in the middle decades of the twentieth century.

Kathi Kern is Associate Professor of History at the University of Kentucky. She is the author of *Mrs. Stanton's Bible* (Cornell University Press, 2001). Her current book project focuses on the ways in which American suffragists explored world religions and the impact of those explorations on women's views on gender, sexuality, and emancipation in the United States.

Jeffrey J. Kripal holds the J. Newton Rayzor Chair in Philosophy and Religious Thought at Rice University. His recent books include *Mutants and Mystics: Science Fiction, Superhero Comics, and the Paranormal* (University of Chicago Press, 2011); *Authors of the Impossible: The Paranormal and the Sacred* (University of Chicago Press, 2010); and *Esalen: America and the Religion of No Religion* (University of Chicago Press, 2007). His areas of interest include the comparative erotics of mystical literature and the history of Western esotericism from ancient Gnosticism to the New Age.

Kathryn Lofton is Assistant Professor of American Studies and Religious Studies at Yale University. Prior to her arrival at Yale in 2009, she taught at Reed College in Portland, Oregon, and at Indiana University Bloomington. Her first book is *Oprah: The Gospel of an Icon* (University of California Press, 2011).

Emily R. Mace received her Ph.D. from the Department of Religion at Princeton University in 2010 and currently teaches at Brevard College. Her first book project is entitled *Cosmopolitan Communions: Practices of Religious Liberalism in America, 1875–1930.*

Sally M. Promey is Professor of American Studies and Professor of Religion and Visual Culture at Yale University, where she is also Deputy Director of the Institute of Sacred Music. She holds a secondary appointment in the Department of Religious Studies and an affiliation with the Department of the History of Art. She directs the Initiative for the Study of Material and Visual Cultures of Religion and convenes the Sensory Cultures of Religion Research Group. Current book projects include volumes on the public display of religion, sensory cultures of American Christianities, and relations between religion and art in constructions of Western modernities.

Lindsay V. Reckson is a postdoctoral fellow in English at the University of Texas at Austin. She received her Ph.D. in English from Princeton University in 2011, where she was a graduate fellow at the Center for the Study of Religion. Her current book project examines ecstatic experience and performance in American literary realism.

Nathan Rees received his Ph.D. in 2010 from the Department of Art History and Archaeology at the University of Maryland, College Park, where he held the George Levitine Fellowship. His first book project is titled *Synthesizing Transcendental Painting: Race, Religion, and Aesthetics in the Art of Emil Bisttram, Raymond Jonson, and Agnes Pelton.*

Michael Robertson is Professor of English at The College of New Jersey. He is the recipient of two NEH Fellowships and author of two award-winning books, the most recent of which is *Worshipping Walt: The Whitman Disciples* (Princeton University Press, 2008). His current project, *The Last Utopians,* is a study of religious liberalism and utopian socialism in the United States and the United Kingdom during the late nineteenth and early twentieth centuries.

Leigh E. Schmidt is the Edward C. Mallinckrodt University Professor in the Humanities at Washington University in St. Louis. He is author of several books, including *Hearing Things: Religion, Illusion, and the American Enlightenment* (Harvard University Press, 2000); *Restless Souls: The Making of American Spirituality* (HarperSanFrancisco, 2005), which will soon appear in an updated edition from the University of California Press; and *Consumer Rites: The Buying and Selling of American Holidays* (Princeton University Press, 1995). His most recent book is *Heaven's Bride: The Unprintable Life of Ida C. Craddock, American Mystic, Scholar, Sexologist, Martyr, and Madwoman* (Basic Books, 2010).

Josef Sorett is Assistant Professor at Columbia University, with appointments in the Department of Religion and the Institute for Research in African-American Studies. He has published a range of essays that explore the intersections of religion, race, and the arts and popular culture. His first book, *That Spirit Is Black: A Religious History of Racial Aesthetics,* is slated for publication by Oxford University Press in 2013.

Christopher G. White is Assistant Professor of Religion in America at Vassar College. He received his Ph.D. in Religious Studies from Harvard University, where he studied religion and culture in nineteenth- and twentieth-century America. He is particularly interested in religion and science, spirituality and "unchurched" religion, religion and popular culture, new religious movements, and American religious encounters abroad. His first book is *Unsettled Minds: Psychology and the American Search for Spiritual Assurance* (University of California Press, 2009).

INDEX

Note: Page numbers in *italics* indicate photographs and illustrations.